A STONE OF HOPE

DAVID L. CHAPPELL

A Stone of Hope

PROPHETIC RELIGION AND

THE DEATH OF JIM CROW

The University of North Carolina Press   Chapel Hill & London

Designed by C. H. Westmoreland
Set in Janson by Tseng Information Systems, Inc.
Manufactured in the United States of America

Portions of Chapters 1, 5, 6, and 8 appeared in articles or essays in the following publications, respectively: *The Role of Ideas in the Civil Rights South*, ed. Ted Ownby (Jackson: University Press of Mississippi, 2002); *African American Review*, Winter 2002; *Journal of American Studies* 32 (August 1998); and *Georgia Historical Quarterly* 82 (Spring 1998). Those materials are used here by permission of the publishers.

The paper in this book meets the guidelines for permanence and durability of the Committee on Production Guidelines for Book Longevity of the Council on Library Resources.

Frontispiece: Detail of photograph of Fred Shuttlesworth
(© Danny Lyon/Magnum Photos)

Library of Congress Cataloging-in-Publication Data
Chappell, David L.
A stone of hope: prophetic religion and the death of
Jim Crow / David L. Chappell.
p. cm.
Includes bibliographical references and index.
ISBN 0-8078-2819-x (cloth: alk. paper)
1. African Americans—Civil rights—History—20th century. 2. African Americans—Segregation—History—20th century. 3. Civil rights movements—United States—History—20th century. 4. Civil rights workers—Religious life—United States—History—20th century. 5. Civil rights—United States—Religious aspects—Christianity—History—20th century. 6. Christianity and politics—United States—History—20th century. 7. Church and social problems—United States—History—20th century. 8. United States—Race relations. 9. United States—Church history—20th century. I. Title.
E185.61 .C5435 2003
323.1196'073—dc22
2003017334

08 07 06 05 04   5 4 3 2 1

To my father,

Vere Claiborne Chappell

History says, *don't hope*

On this side of the grave.

But then, once in a lifetime

The longed-for tidal wave

Of justice can rise up,

And hope and history rhyme.

—SEAMUS HEANEY,

The Cure at Troy

Hope is definitely not the same thing as optimism. It is not the conviction that something will turn out well, but the certainty that something makes sense, no matter how it turns out.

—VACLAV HAVEL,

Disturbing the Peace

Contents

Introduction 1

1 Hungry Liberals: Their Sense That Something Was Missing 9

2 Recovering Optimists 26

3 The Prophetic Ideas That Made Civil Rights *Move* 44

4 Prophetic Christian Realism and the 1960s Generation 67

5 The Civil Rights Movement as a Religious Revival 87

6 Broken Churches, Broken Race: White Southern Religious
  Leadership and the Decline of White Supremacy 105

7 Pulpit versus Pew 131

8 Segregationist Thought in Crisis: What the Movement Was
  Up Against 153

Conclusions: Gamaliel, Caesar, and Us 179

Appendix: A Philosophical Note on Historical Explanation 191

Notes 195

Archival and Manuscript Sources 293

Bibliographical Essay 297

Acknowledgments 327

Index 331

Illustrations

John Dewey 16

Arthur Schlesinger Jr. 29

Gunnar Myrdal with his family 40

Martin Luther King Jr. 49

Bayard Rustin 61

Modjeska Simkins 64

James Lawson 70

Fannie Lou Hamer 74

John Lewis 77

Bob Moses 79

Fred Shuttlesworth 89

Religious forms of protest 93

Andrew Young with Fannie Lou Hamer
and Martin Luther King Jr. 99

Strom Thurmond 106

The Rev. W. A. Criswell 115

L. Nelson Bell 118

Roy Harris 129

The Rev. Billy Graham 142

James F. "Jimmy" Byrnes 157

John Temple Graves 159

Charles J. Bloch 166

James J. Kilpatrick 169

A STONE OF HOPE

Introduction

In his famous "I Have a Dream" speech at the Lincoln Memorial, Washington, D.C., in 1963, Martin Luther King Jr. said that he was going back to the South with faith that his people could hew "a stone of hope" from "a mountain of despair." That image captures the philosophy of the civil rights movement. The faith that drove black southern protesters to their extraordinary victories in the mid-1960s, this book argues, grew out of a realistic understanding of the typically dim prospects for social justice in this world. Despair was the mountain. Hope was by comparison small, hard to come by. "Freedom isn't free," one of the movement's songs observed: "You gotta pay a price, you gotta sacrifice, for your liberty." In another one of his 1963 speeches King said that the jailed black children of Birmingham were "carving a tunnel of hope through the mountain of despair."

King's public career had begun in 1955, in a period defined by Joseph McCarthy and Joseph Stalin; by the homogeneity of Levittown and the Man in the Gray Flannel Suit; by a popular president, Dwight D. Eisenhower, who opposed federal action to promote equality; and by equally popular racial demagogues in the southern states. The Democratic Party, in its 1948 platform, and the U.S. Supreme Court, in its 1954 *Brown v. Board of Education* decision, appeared to repudiate their long-standing support of white supremacy. But neither could do much to change the discriminatory laws and customs in the South. The Democrats retreated from their bold statement, and the Court seemed to consign victims of discrimination to an endless, costly series of individual lawsuits. Many black southerners—including King, for a time—concluded that the rosy promises of change were as false as innumerable promises in the past. Hopes of racial justice seemed as distant as ever.

Yet over the twelve-odd years of King's career, a mass movement rose up in the South and brought city governments, bus companies, and chambers of commerce to their knees. The movement created disorder so severe as to force a reluctant federal government to intervene—on the side of black southerners, which was more surprising then than it seems in hindsight today. The civil rights movement—aided by Democratic-Republican competition for the votes of recent black migrants to the North and by U.S.-Soviet competition for allies among newly independent African and Asian nations—destroyed Jim Crow, the vast system of legal segregation and disfranchisement named after a nineteenth-century minstrel character. In addition to provoking Congress to turn against its powerful southern bloc in the sweeping Civil Rights and Voting Rights Acts of 1964 and 1965, the movement forced a change in the Constitution. The Twenty-fourth Amendment and new interpretations of the Fifteenth guaranteed black Americans the vote. The movement shut down a political culture of racist demagoguery and one-party rule in the southern states, a culture long underwritten by the threat of mob violence.

The movement did all this with remarkably few casualties. Ugly as white southern resistance was, Maya Lin's memorial to martyrs of the civil rights movement has only 40 names engraved on it. The apartheid regime in South Africa beat that figure in a single day, at Sharpeville in 1960, when it killed 67 people and wounded 200 more. In a freedom struggle closer to our own time, Chinese authorities killed some 2,600 in the immediate aftermath of Tiananmen Square. America's own war to destroy slavery, with 600,000 deaths, makes the destruction of segregation a century later appear astonishingly nonviolent. Its destruction appears a feat of moral and political alchemy, well represented by King's stone of hope from a mountain of despair.

How did it happen? The civil rights struggle did not consist entirely of politics and grassroots organizing, as books and documentaries on the subject have so far implied. It also involved a change in American culture, a change in what Americans thought and felt when they talked about things like freedom, equality, race, and rights. It involved a change in Americans' expectations about these things, what they considered realistic as opposed to idealistic.

This book tries to account—and claims only to begin the accounting—for the cultural changes behind the civil rights movement by answering four questions: Why did the dominant voice in American political culture, liberalism, fail to achieve anything substantial for black rights at the height of liberal power in the 1930s? Where did black southerners find a philosophical inspiration to rebel, given the failure of liberalism as they knew it? How did black southerners sustain the confidence, solidarity, and discipline of their rebellion through years of drudgery, setbacks, and risk? Finally, why were the enemies of the civil rights movement, for one fleeting but decisive moment, so weak?

Chapters 1 through 4 reconsider the intellectual roots of the civil rights movement. The black southern movement's political successes depended on an alliance with northern liberals. Yet the liberals' animating faith was radically different from that of the southern movement. Liberals believed in the power of human reason to overcome "prejudice" and other vestiges of a superstitious, unenlightened past. Liberals believed, with Gunnar Myrdal, the Swedish social scientist whose famous 1944 report on American racism they embraced, that "progress" was under way: further education, along with economic development, would lead white southerners to abandon their irrational traditions. Therefore liberals, though sincere in their devotion to black rights, did not see any reason to do anything drastic to promote them. Indeed, they thought that pushing too hard for black rights would provoke a violent reaction in the backward white South.

Liberals' most sensitive and articulate spokesmen, such as John Dewey and Lionel Trilling, were acutely aware of the cultural weakness of their faith in reason. Especially after seeing how difficult it was for the West's liberal democracies to fight the Nazis, liberals envied and feared conservatives' power to draw on irrational wellsprings of myth and tradition. Yet in the South of the 1950s, it was liberals' new black allies, rather than their white supremacist enemies, who drew most effectively on such irrational wellsprings.

The black movement's nonviolent soldiers were driven not by modern liberal faith in human reason, but by older, seemingly more durable prejudices and superstitions that were rooted in Christian and Jewish myth. Specifically, they drew from a prophetic tradition that runs from David and Isaiah in the Old Testament through Augustine and Martin Luther to Reinhold Niebuhr in the twentieth century. (That tradition also traveled down a different path, via the seventh-century prophet Muhammad, to the mind of the mature Malcolm X and some of his followers, though that path is not examined in this book. The prophetic tradition was not confined to Christianity or even to religion: strictly Christian thinkers like Karl Barth and Reinhold Niebuhr were quick to admit that an atheist might take a prophetic stance more readily and faithfully than a typical twentieth-century Christian.) The thinkers who were active in the black movement — at least the ones for whom I was able to track down an extensive intellectual record — believed that the natural tendency of this world and of human institutions (including churches) is toward corruption. Like the Hebrew Prophets, these thinkers believed that they could not expect that world and those institutions to improve. Nor could they be passive bystanders. They had to stand apart from society and insult it with skepticism about its pretensions to justice and truth. They had to instigate catastrophic changes in the minds of whoever would listen, and they accepted that only a few outcasts might listen. They had to try to force an unwilling world to abandon sin—in this case, "the sin of segregation." The world to them would never know automatic or natural "progress." It would use education only to rationalize its iniquity.

Like all nonmythical figures, the thinkers of the civil rights movement were inconsistent. They understandably strayed from the Prophets' lonely, undiplomatic, often downright antisocial path. At times they spoke the language of liberal Christianity and secular liberalism, which had in common a very unprophetic faith in human autonomy and self-improvement. They were political strategists, who recognized that the human hopes they needed to cultivate were entwined with consumerist striving for a piece of American prosperity, which was spreading like mad in the post–World War II boom. They were also human: they could forgive consumerist striving in the poor sinners around them and in themselves. The paper trail of more serious moral failings than consumerism on the part of Martin Luther King is now too conspicuous to be ignored. American law dictates a presumption of innocence for the less famous leaders whose trails have not been uncovered. But common sense, not to mention their own prophetic view of human nature, dictates the opposite. The thinkers in the civil rights movement could not live up to their own austere moral vision, could not entirely separate themselves from the world or from the worldview they condemned. That said, they departed from modern liberal faith in the future—from the Humanism that had been rising in Western culture, with occasional setbacks, since the Renaissance—far more than historians have recognized. They strayed far more than the allegedly "chastened" liberals of the post–World War II generation, who read Reinhold Niebuhr and claimed to embrace his pessimism about human nature. (In Chapter 1 I argue that liberals only applied that newfound pessimism to foreign affairs, leaving their optimism about life inside the United States, even for the poor and for racial minorities, intact.) The alliance between black Christian civil rights groups and American liberals was more an alliance of convenience than one of deep ideological affinity. Viewed in this light, the alliance's unraveling after the 1960s may not seem as baffling and bewildering as it ordinarily does.

The movement's few prophetic spokesmen and spokeswomen aside, how can we account for the masses of poor, disfranchised protesters? How did they have the guts and the discipline to stand against the dogs and firehoses when there was no reason to think they would win on this earth? Chapter 5 considers these questions. There is much testimony about conversion experiences during the mass meetings and demonstrations, which no historian or social scientist has put at the center of the story before.

The conviction that God was on their side comes through in many statements by black movement participants during the 1950s and 1960s. This conviction often came to participants in ritualistic expressions of religious ecstasy. Experiencing and witnessing such expressions gave participants confidence, not simply in the righteousness of their protest, but also in the effectiveness of that protest in this world. Historians have not scrupulously separated the two kinds of confidence, perhaps because they have not entirely forgone their own liberal faith in human progress. To know that one is morally right is easy and common; to believe one is going to defeat one's enemies requires rather extraordinary faith. Being right about the latter matter requires something even more extraordinary than faith.

Perhaps the hardest and greatest hope of the civil rights protesters was hewn from that impassible, snow-capped range of bigotry, hypocrisy, and social conservatism, the southern white church. That is the subject of Chapters 6 and 7. Though the white churches of the South drew indignant criticism from black and northern white ministers for their failure to fall into line behind the black protesters—criticism that historians have echoed—what was surprising was that those churches did not lend much support to the other side. White southern churches, though they were then celebrating the centennial of the Civil War, did not follow the example of their antebellum ancestors. A hundred years earlier, ministers and theologians had led the pro-slavery cause with brilliance and vigor. (It is hard to account for the suicidal devotion of nonslaveowning white southern families—three-fourths of the South's white population—to the slave system without the faith they learned to have in the moral superiority of slavery. Their ministers and theologians taught them to see slavery as a benevolent bulwark against the North's anarchical and irresponsible "freedom," which let workers go homeless and starve.)[1] More recently, southern white churches had worked aggressively and creatively to instill industrial discipline (sobriety, obedience to authority, and individualist disdain for labor unions) during the great social struggle over industrialization of the Carolina Piedmont.[2] And, not so long after the civil rights battles, southern churches mobilized masses in the antiabortion movement and other political feuds over "family values."

But unlike white southern social conservatives before and after them, the segregationists in the 1950s–60s tended to identify their own white southern churches as their enemy. Most readers today are surprised to learn that the southern Baptists and southern Presbyterians went on record in favor of desegregation in the mid-1950s by a majority vote of representatives of their member churches. In the Southern Baptist Convention (SBC), the vote was roughly 9,000 to 50 in favor of desegregation; in the General Assembly of the southern Presbyterians, it was 239 to 169.[3] These figures are more striking in light of the near-unanimity of elected officials against desegregation.

It is important to remember that the southern Baptists and southern Presbyterians in the 1950s–60s were still maintaining the separate denominations their forebears had created when they broke from their northern counterparts over slavery: segregationists could not blame the desegregationism of their denominational assemblies on Yankee control. White churches at the local level were less unified than the regionwide denominational bodies. The vocal opposition of lay segregationists and, in rare instances, politicized clergy, made the issue so controversial that most ministers seem to have tried to avoid it. The most important consequence of this was that segregationist propaganda often condemned the southern white clergy en bloc for its failure to stand up for the white South's cause. Segregationists condemned their churches, that is, for exactly the same sin as Martin Luther King condemned them in his 1963 "Letter from the Birmingham Jail": for neutrality in a moral crisis.

Scholars who notice the apolitical stance of the southern churches generally see it as de facto support of segregation. So it was for many years. But by the mid-1950s, segregationists needed more than de facto support. They needed somebody with more cultural authority than an opportunistic politician to embrace their cause. They needed legitimacy. They needed the cultural depth and tradition their church represented. They thought that the church had the ability to instill discipline and to demand sacrifice. They wanted that discipline and sacrifice to galvanize the white South for an honorable show of force worthy of Robert E. Lee and Stonewall Jackson. But they did not get what they wanted. Instead, they enviously watched as prominent black southern protesters got political support from *their* churches—which was almost as rare and surprising as their getting support from the federal government.

White supremacists in the South failed to get their churches to give their cause active support. That was their Achilles' heel. Again, this was more significant at the time—at the height of the Billy Graham revival, in the heart of the Bible Belt—than it appears in hindsight today. Compared to the thorough, confident support that slaveowners received from their leading theologians and other cultural authorities a century earlier, the segregationists look disorganized and superficial.

The segregationists had other cultural strengths—ones that historians have not taken seriously. They had brilliant rhetoricians and constitutional scholars on their side who defended the "southern way of life" with much more confidence and coherence than their religious leaders. Most scholars have dismissed the segregationists as simpleminded racists and opportunistic demagogues. There were plenty of both in the white South. But as I argue in Chapter 8, serious intellectuals—particularly editors and lawyers —also attempted, with sophistication and moral sincerity, to dignify and reinforce segregation. Their failure to persuade their enemies (presumably most people who read this book) should not distract attention from a concern that plagued them more than their enemies: how to control their allies. How they dealt with that concern is a key to understanding how black protesters beat them. Segregationists outspent, outvoted, and outgunned the black protesters. But the black protesters found the segregationists' weak points.

The irrational prejudice, economic exploitation, and political opportunism that most historians see at the root of the system do not explain the problem that absorbed most white southern propagandists' energy: how to maintain respectability while drumming up sufficient popular militancy. The white South's most influential editors supported segregation, but they were as serious as northern liberals were about repudiating bigotry, backwardness, and ignorance. They believed that segregation was the best way to maintain peace—to avoid an irrational emotional backlash. Yet they needed to stir their followers to face the alarming new threat of mass organization in the black South—and to face what they saw as northern politicians' growing temptation to appease that mass organization. They needed to inspire sacrifice and risk. They fretted over the difficulty of inspiring the white southern masses, whom they saw as complacent and apathetic. How could they motivate those masses to put up a good fight without going the demagogic route of relying on impractical and uncontrollable emotions like racism? The segregationist intellectuals were racists themselves, to the extent that the record can reveal such things. But they had little confidence in racism's power to hold the white South together through a long battle.

Segregationist intellectuals put most of their hopes in constitutional arguments about state rights. Most historians refuse to admit that these arguments were constitutionally sound, however unsavory their political effects may have been. Fortunately for the civil rights movement, legal arguments did not decide the political dispute. Segregationist intellectuals tried to keep the white South under control. They were haunted by a sense of their own ineffectiveness. They saw the franker racists of the white South coming up with more exciting, more inspiring battle cries. The trouble was that the effective battle cries pushed white southerners away from what even the poorest ones seemed to want: respectability. Those battle cries would thus fail to unify and sustain the population throughout the struggle.

The segregationists' tone was often defeatist: segregationism had the wry honor of sounding like a lost cause before the battle even began. Segregationist violence in this light appears to have been more an expression of desperation than determination. The forty martyrs of the movement should be seen in that perspective, as well as in the perspective of moral outrage. The outrage is—thankfully—still fresh; it is a salutary outrage, which may be all this nation has to counter the still-powerful temptations of racial profiling. But a ray of hope should illuminate the outrage, or a stone of hope should balance the outrage: The peculiar racial institution of the twentieth-century South was destroyed by means considerably short of civil war. That makes its destruction in many ways a more rather than a less impressive achievement than the destruction of slavery.

The civil rights movement succeeded for many reasons. This book isolates and magnifies one reason that has received insufficient attention: black southern activists got strength from old-time religion, and white supremacists failed, at the same moment, to muster the cultural strength that conservatives traditionally get from religion. Who succeeded in the great cultural battle over race and rights in the 1950s and early 1960s? Those who could use religion to inspire solidarity and self-sacrificial devotion to their cause. Who did not have such religious power? Two groups: those who failed — the segregationists — and those who succeeded only by attaching themselves to the religious protesters — the liberals.

Black southern activists did not win all of their goals, especially in the economic realm: they did not achieve equality. But, grounded as they were in a long tradition of disappointed prophecy, they could not have expected to gain anything like heaven on earth. Measured by historical standards of realism, their achievement was extraordinary — arguably the most successful social movement in American history, one that has been an inspiration from Soweto to Prague to Tiananmen Square. The cultural and religious perspectives that follow do not provide the whole story of this extraordinary movement, but they outline the extent and depth of its imprint on the national psyche. They tell us not only what happened during the civil rights struggle, but also what the struggle meant to its participants on both sides.

1

Hungry Liberals

THEIR SENSE THAT SOMETHING

WAS MISSING

The destruction of Jim Crow was one of the crowning achievements of the period when liberals dominated American politics, from 1933 to 1969. Yet the overall liberal commitment to Jim Crow's destruction is easy to exaggerate when looking backward through the lens of the 1960s. There were no significant gains in civil rights in the first part of the period, the 1930s, when liberals' power was greater and more secure than ever before or since. A few New Deal liberals believed that it was morally necessary—and that it was politically possible—to do something about racial prejudice in the 1930s. To say that such antiracist liberals were few is not to denigrate their integrity or courage. Rather the opposite. The few included First Lady Eleanor Roosevelt and Interior Secretary Harold Ickes, abetted by New Deal supporters and officials like Will Alexander, Mary McLeod Bethune, Virginia and Clifford Durr, Clark Foreman, George Mitchell, Rexford Tugwell, Senator Robert Wagner, Palmer Weber, and Aubrey Williams.[1] Black leaders often considered the minor but unprecedented gestures of these few to be heroic. Their gestures probably had something to do with black voters' swing from overwhelmingly Republican before 1932 to overwhelmingly Democratic since 1934.[2] Still, liberals could not—at least they did not—alleviate discrimination for most African Americans during the New Deal.

Secretary Ickes—former head of the Chicago branch of the National Association for the Advancement of Colored People (NAACP)—sketched out the position of Negro sympathizers in the New Deal in his diary.[3] When Senator Josiah Bailey of North Carolina accused Ickes of "trying to break down the segregation laws" in a speech in 1937, Ickes wrote to Bailey that opposition to segregation "had never been my position." He explained, "As a matter of fact, I think it is up to the states to work out their own social problems if possible, and while I have always been interested in seeing that the Negro has a square deal, I have never dissipated my strength against the particular stone wall of segregation." Like most liberals, Ickes had more faith in the gradual processes of education and economic development than in political action. He believed that the stone wall of segregation would "crumble when the Negro has brought himself to a higher educational and economic status. After all, we can't force people on each other who do not like each other, even when no question of color is involved." Like Bailey, Ickes took it for granted that public association of New Deal officials with desegregationism would be "prejudicial"—would injure Roosevelt's standing with his key constituency, the enfranchised white South. Ickes also assumed the futility of any attack on segregation.[4]

The few liberals who joined Ickes in taking up the cause of "seeing that the Negro has a square deal" in the 1930s strove to connect that cause with the general liberal program—an abstractly plausible connection, in the sense that freedom and equality were liberal goals.[5] More important to liberals with a practical eye, including Mrs. Roosevelt, the connection had some political plausibility: abolishing the poll tax, she believed, would create a massive pro–New Deal constituency. Millions of poor white as well as black southerners would get the vote. The new voters' presumable loyalty to FDR might be enough to compensate the Democrats for the inevitable reaction: retaliation from the white supremacist oligarchs of the South, who were so strong in the Democratic Party—and often so supportive of the New Deal—that the president had to be very careful not to offend them.[6]

Unfortunately, however, the antiracist link with liberalism did not have enough political plausibility: for the time being, the oligarchs had the poll tax and were strong enough to prevent its abolition in most states. Nor could New Dealers be certain, even if they could abolish the poll tax, that the new voters would be loyal to them: the black break with the Party of Lincoln was too recent to look reliable, and poor white southerners were, rightly or wrongly, assumed to be more devoted to racial restrictions than rich ones. As journalist Marquis Childs wrote in 1942, "The issue of the poll tax, which keeps from one third to one half of all the eligible white voters away from the polls in the South, has been talked about by the younger New Dealers, but no direct attack has ever been made on it."[7] Those who did attack the poll tax, including the NAACP and the Southern Conference for Human Welfare, got little support from New Dealers in Washington.

Despite most New Dealers' failure to support anti–poll tax legislation, or even (for northerners) apple-pie proposals like federal antilynching legislation, NAACP leaders sought to connect black hopes to liberalism. Thus

NAACP leaders did their bit to redefine liberalism in the 1930s, or at least to increase liberals' emphasis on substantive equality.[8] Liberals, especially Democratic ones, were slow to respond, though they responded more than those who were known as conservatives, and they were more politically viable than the communists, socialists, and Christian radicals who embraced the antiracist cause with greater abandon. In their prime, New Deal liberals had more urgent and realistic things to strive for than racial equality.

It is hard to sort out whether liberals cared a great deal about racism, but lacked the power to challenge it, or simply cared too little about racism, until black voters and protesters forced their hand three decades later, in the 1960s. It is clear, however, that to do something about Jim Crow, liberals needed something more forceful—either stronger conviction or greater power—than they had in the 1930s. A sense of needing more, of lacking what they needed to realize their own goals, pervaded liberal thought. Liberals expressed that sense frequently in the 1930s and 1940s. Though not always connected in their minds with racial equality, this sense of incompleteness provides a window into liberalism's fundamental limitations. Through it, one can begin to see the path to the civil rights movement's eventual success in overcoming those limitations.

Liberal insiders at the 1948 Democratic National Convention remembered the post–New Deal shift in favor of civil rights as a dramatic break with the past. According to Chester Bowles:

> The national strength of the Democratic party had for a century and a half been based on a coalition between Northern liberals and city organization leaders on the one hand and Southern Populists on the other. . . . It was leaders such as James Byrnes of South Carolina and Sam Rayburn of Texas who had guided through Congress Roosevelt's proposals for Social Security, subsidized agriculture, TVA and work relief for the unemployed.
>
> The political price that Roosevelt and the Northern liberals had been forced to pay for Southern support for the New Deal was a heavy one: a political moratorium on the issue of civil rights.[9]

Yet in some ways New Dealers appeared less useful to devotees of civil rights after the war than before. We now know that, twenty years after the end of World War II, liberals finally won enough votes in Congress to pass serious civil rights laws. But over most of those twenty years, liberals in the Democratic Party still depended on the support of southern members of Congress, who in turn depended on racist laws. As black people migrated to northern cities, where they could vote, many northern liberals grew bold in speaking out against southern politicians. But at the same time, liberals felt a new sense of powerlessness in domestic affairs.

Congress drove home liberals' sense of powerlessness by overriding President Harry Truman's veto of the Taft-Hartley Act of 1947. Northern Democrats depended on unions the way southern Democrats depended on the poll tax. But enough reactionaries had been elected in 1946 to reverse the pro-labor trend of the New Deal. Senator Robert Wagner, who epitomized the new liberalism of the New Deal days, viewed the reversal from the hospital: the override of the Taft-Hartley veto was "one of the bitterest disappointments I have ever experienced. For I was forced to see the work of a lifetime destroyed, while I lay on my back in bed."[10] Though liberalism after World War II was more strongly identified with black civil rights than before the war, liberals lacked the popular mandate they had had, or believed they had had, in the age of Roosevelt. To judge them by their own words, liberals were in deep trouble after World War II. One of their most vigorous minds, historian Richard Hofstadter, observed in 1948 that liberals were in a "rudderless and demoralized state." They were anxious and defensive, filled with self-doubt, and fighting among themselves.[11]

Postwar liberals feared that Franklin Roosevelt's personality, rather than their own ideology, was what had attracted vast majorities to the New Deal. This fear was reinforced by their great loss in popularity after FDR's death. For this and other reasons, liberals trimmed their sails.[12] The depression was one of the many great things the war killed, but in doing so it killed a lot of liberal hope. Absence of economic crisis made serious reform hard to sell, and FDR's successor, Harry Truman, was at once less committed to reform and a lousier salesman than FDR. The depression did not return, as so many experts believed it would. Instead, liberals had to convince voters of the urgency of reform through the greatest boom ever in American history, which was rather like urging medicine upon a healthy and increasingly spoiled child. Liberals on the whole abandoned the large-scale planning by which they had tried to alter the basic structural inequities of capitalism in the 1930s. Instead, they tried to ensure greater individual rights[13] and the continuation of economic growth.[14] Their domestic concerns were often set aside in foreign policy disputes.

THE QUEST FOR SECULAR FAITH

To understand postwar liberals' lack of confidence, one must look at the historical roots of their sense of alienation from the masses. They feared that they could not communicate with the public they so earnestly wanted to help. Liberals had long suspected that their program would have a troubled relationship with democracy. The roots of this suspicion were visible in liberals' frequent exasperation with the popularity—the democratic power— of irrational, that is to say illiberal, appeals. Liberals' enemies always felt free to whip up popular nostalgia for tradition, respect for authority, and religious enthusiasm. Liberals thought that their enemies fought unfairly, but they could not deny the advantages of illiberal appeals in a democracy.

Even in their confident days, the most sensitive and articulate liberals sensed that something was missing from their method and program. They always understood their method and program to be based on faith that human reason could solve the "problems" of human society.[15] Yet the deepest believers in reason perceived that reason was not enough. The pragmatist philosopher who gave American liberalism its distinctive cast in the Progressive Era, William James, memorably expressed the need for an irrational crusade to inspire the sacrifices that reason could not inspire in his famous essay "The Moral Equivalent of War" (1910). James hated war and hoped that it could be abolished, but he wrote that those who campaigned against "war's irrationality and horror" missed the point. Modern man still had "all the innate pugnacity and all the love of glory of his ancestors." War was thrilling in a way that meeting human needs was not. That was why people loved it. Armies bred pride in collective effort. Groups that pursued such nonmilitary goals as "pacific cosmopolitan industrialism," on the other hand, bred only "shame at the idea of belonging to *such* a collectivity." James supported efforts to outlaw war, and he believed in "the gradual advent of some sort of socialistic equilibrium." But he worried about inspiring people to get there. In a utopian program of good wages and short hours, "Where is the sharpness and precipitousness, the contempt for life, whether one's own, or another's? Where is the savage 'yes' and 'no,' the unconditional duty? Where is the conscription? Where is the blood-tax? Where is anything that one feels honored by belonging to?"[16]

James, the scientific thinker who had suffered a nervous breakdown, was echoing the patron saint of modern English-speaking liberalism, John Stuart Mill, who had suffered a similar breakdown in the early nineteenth century. Mill's famous breakdown came with the revelation that, if all his desires for social reform came true, he would still be unhappy. Reforms could satisfy the calculations of his father's great utilitarian system, but the human soul craved something deeper. Thus began Mill's search into the irrational urges and unscientific flights of Romanticism for the missing elements of liberalism.[17] Liberals have not always had time to continue that search, but they have never satisfied the hunger that led to it.[18]

John Dewey, who played the role of patron philosopher of American liberals more often than anybody after James's death in 1910, was more cautious and more persistent than James or Mill in exploring what liberalism lacked. At the beginning of American liberals' political ascendancy in 1929, Dewey noted that "liberals are notoriously hard to organize." Reason was just not as good a basis for solidarity as the conservatives' basis, tradition. Liberals "must depend upon ideas rather than upon established habits of belief; and when persons begin to think upon social matters they begin to vary." Conservatives, by contrast, had "a natural bond of cohesion. . . . They hold together not so much by ideas as by habit, tradition, fear of the unknown and a desire to hold on to what they already have." Though Dewey eschewed dogmatic systems that claimed to have all the answers, he recognized the pragmatic necessity to develop a coherent set of goals around which liberals—and, he hoped, new converts—might rally. "The history of liberal political movements in this country is one of temporary enthusiasms and then steady decline. If liberals are 'tired,' it is chiefly because they have not had the support and invigoration that comes from working shoulder to shoulder in a unified movement."[19] The injustices of the 1920s (especially the Sacco-Vanzetti case) and the stock market crash finally convinced Dewey that neither of the major parties could be trusted to come up with any attractive course. But the vacuum was not easily filled. "It would be difficult," he wrote in 1930, "to find in history an epoch as lacking in solid and assured objects of belief and approved ends of action as is the present. . . . The lack of secure objects of allegiance, without which individuals are lost, is especially striking in the case of the liberal."[20]

Some observers—notably H. Richard Niebuhr and Robert and Helen Lynd—saw Christianity as equally factious and demoralized,[21] but Dewey became possessed by a sense that religion had what liberalism lacked. He came to believe that liberals could appropriate the inspiration they needed from religion, if only they changed their way of thinking about religion. Toward the end of his 1929 book, *The Quest for Certainty*, Dewey tried to dissociate "religious" belief, which might be beneficial to liberals, from existing "religion," which was the most damaging excrescence of civilization's misguided "quest for certainty." He developed this effort to rescue useful "religious" qualities from "the historic religions" more fully in 1934 in *A Common Faith*. He admired what he called the "truly religious" habits in human experience. But unfortunately mankind, in its prescientific ignorance, had allowed these admirable, socially indispensable habits to get tied up with "religion," with irrational superstitions, enforced by intimidation and propaganda. The "religious" impulses of generosity and self-sacrifice, of humility and communal solidarity, he insisted, could be severed from the corruptions of every known religion—from closed-minded bigotry and dogma, from the tendency to persecute outsiders.[22]

Dewey was generally deaf to and suspicious of religious feeling as it actually existed (this is the starkest contrast between Dewey and James), yet he thought that some kind of "piety" might be philosophically justifiable.[23] Some postreligious "faith" might foster a socially useful "sense of dependence" and ward off pride. Such "faith" might nourish "a sense of common participation in the inevitable uncertainties of existence . . . coeval with a sense of common effort and shared destiny."[24] In this Dewey echoed, among others, Auguste Comte and Emile Durkheim, who strained to find some way to replace religion—which, Durkheim observed, was losing its credibility whether we liked it or not—as a tool for the moral instruction of children.[25]

Dewey was more concerned than Durkheim with the specific problem of political morality. He felt an urgent need to transform public institutions (schools and other instruments of a potentially democratic state). These institutions often inculcated a salutary moral sense in children, but they could be reformed to do more: to express the people's moral sense and enforce it against the competing sense of the privileged few. Dewey believed that the people's moral sense was being drowned out by those with undemocratic privileges, particularly industrial corporations, which he thought were the principal cause of a crisis in democracy in the late 1920s and 1930s.[26] As the crisis deepened, Dewey expanded his quest for a viable public morality by criticizing the all-encompassing faiths that sustained communism and fascism. He also criticized the faith that bolstered capitalism, a faith that was just as dogmatic as communism and fascism, but worse in a way: it opened the way for the extremist alternatives because it was so unsatisfying.[27] The mid-twentieth-century rise of new nationalist movements, which "pretend to represent the order, discipline, and spiritual authority that will counteract social disintegration," was, to Dewey, "a tragic comment upon the unpreparedness of the older liberalism to deal with the new problem which [liberalism's] very success precipitated." Liberals needed to compete with the modern secular faiths that inspired the murderous and suicidal devotion of the masses in Europe and Russia.[28]

Dewey's *Liberalism and Social Action* (1935), which his disciple Sidney Hook hoped would be to the twentieth century what the Communist Manifesto had been to the nineteenth, expanded on Dewey's diagnosis of liberals' great failing. Liberals, with their spirit of open debate and reasoned compromise, with their "watered down" dialectic, failed to command the enthusiasm of the public. They could not dispel the dishonest propaganda with which the state and corporations maintained an unjust order.[29] This preoccupied Dewey because he was a democrat as much as he was a liberal. He wanted majority rule, that is, as much as he wanted liberty. He acknowledged and wrestled with the tension between those two commitments better than his fellow liberals. But reconciling majority rule with liberty was not easy, and Dewey may have failed to inspire the faithful following that Marx and Engels had because he was more honest than they in acknowledging how difficult it was to reconcile the basic elements of his faith. Where they blithely claimed to reconcile French Romantic dreams of socialist bliss with the skeptical economic theory of British Utilitarianism, he saw that devotion to human freedom and reason was sometimes incompatible with mass popularity.

John Dewey, patron philosopher of independent liberals, believed
solidarity and sacrifice were necessary to achieve freedom and
equality. But liberals' devotion to reason left them incapable of
inspiring such solidarity and sacrifice. To inspire what reason could
not inspire, Dewey tried to prove that modern man could invent a
new "faith"—even a "God"—compatible with materialistic science.
(Special Collections Research Center, Morris Library, Southern
Illinois University, Carbondale)

Dewey's task, then, was to establish a new social organization with some new "central spiritual authority" that could "nurture and direct the inner as well as the outer life of individuals." This new authority had to be created in a scientific spirit, not a dogmatic or nationalistic one. Liberal education would have to renew "the springs of purpose and desire." To do this, education would have to be transformed—an admittedly difficult thing to accomplish before the economic and political institutions that controlled educational budgets were themselves transformed. The transformation of education would be especially difficult, since Dewey admitted that actually existing liberalism was as much an impediment to the establishment of a rational and egalitarian order as actually existing religion was. Liberalism had been a "fighting" creed in its youth, in the late eighteenth and early nineteenth centuries. It had rallied the emerging capitalist middle class and some others when it sought only to destroy monarchical and feudal impediments to middle-class rule. But liberalism was "well-nigh impotent" when "it came to the problem of organizing new social forces" to extend and protect the liberty it had established. Instead, liberalism had hardened into a defense of the status quo. Despite its rigidity and decadence, however, liberalism still had "precious" values at its core. There was no alternative source of humane values. All liberals had to do, besides generate a quasi-religious enthusiasm for liberty, was to recognize two things: that "material insecurity" had become the prime threat to liberty, and that "unchecked power" in the "private" realm of corporations destroyed liberty as much as unchecked power in politics.[30]

In his effort to come up with inspiring ideals to rally the liberals, Dewey tried to rescue some of the socially useful aspects of religion from faith in "the supernatural." Despite his flexible metaphysics, Dewey could not countenance belief in anything supernatural. He was a scientific naturalist. On the other hand, he had seen the power of irrational faith work in the real world. Faith drove people to great sacrifice and effort. The willingness to lose oneself in a cause, to sacrifice self-interest and bind together with others, was something that he and other liberals hungered for. Dewey wanted conviction, but all he could honestly believe in was uncertainty. "Conviction in the moral sense signifies being conquered, vanquished in our active nature by an ideal end; it signifies acknowledgment of its rightful claim over our desires and purposes." The source of conviction could not be knowledge. For knowledge meant awareness of the inconclusiveness of human theories and plans. The source had to lie in faith. Indeed, any attempt to justify a conviction by arguing for its basis in knowledge only demonstrated lack of faith. Thankfully, the faithful were in some ways easier to work with than the rational, for the faithful already understood the uncertainty that Dewey insisted was the essence of life. Their faith humbled them, if they were truly faithful. But Dewey thought that rational people were slow to accept his pragmatic conclusion that all human quests, even scientific ones, led to uncertainty. Rational people were still trying to blaze a trail to certainty, still hoping that scientific inquiry would work out better than the old religious trail they had rationally abandoned. Dewey had to try simultaneously to disabuse them of any such millennial hopes and to generate in them a self-sacrificial commitment. He had to find a way to inspire enthusiasm for pursuits he could not himself be enthusiastic about. As his biographer Robert Westbrook puts it, "moral faith," for Dewey, "carried no guarantees; it was a faith in the possible not the actual or the necessary or the inevitable."[31]

Dewey could deny, or be agnostic about, the truth claims made by religion and still say that religion was "real."[32] He did not mean "real" merely in the sense that sociologists and anthropologists say that the practices and paraphernalia of religion are real. Religion's *ideals* were real, Dewey's pragmatic test showed, even if (a not-so-subtle equivocation here) those ideals were not necessarily real in the way that their adherents believed they were real: "The reality of ideal ends as ideals is vouched for by their undeniable power in action."[33] Ideals were forces in social life. Dewey even appealed to the socially liberal senator George Norris of Nebraska, asking Norris to join a new party aimed at "a more just society and that peaceful world which was the dream of Him whose birthday we celebrate this Christmas Day."[34] It is unclear whether Norris thought Dewey was taking the Lord's name in vain. At any rate, Norris had ample pragmatic reasons to decline the appeal and remained a Republican.[35]

It is hardly surprising that Dewey never worked out the problem of securing the blessings of faith to his secular program. He wanted reasonable, human control of society, not an awed appreciation of powers beyond comprehension.[36] Still less did he find a way to make a hybrid of faith and atheism popular to Americans, who since the late eighteenth century have been among the most religious people in the world.[37] He tried more thoughtfully and persistently than any of his contemporaries to pull it off. But what is important here is that he shared with so many liberals the feeling that some modern substitute for religious faith was urgently needed.

PULPIT ENVY:
THE VARIETIES OF A SECULAR WILL TO BELIEVE

At the end of the New Deal decade, another key liberal thinker-activist expressed the hunger for inspiration and solidarity in earthier terms than John Dewey. Malcolm Ross, who would become head of the Fair Employment Practices Committee during World War II, one of the first nonsouthern liberals to gain experience in racial politics, ended the 1930s on a weary note. His 1939 autobiography, *Death of a Yale Man*, was the story of a man disillusioned before his time. Ross looked back on his adventures as a reporter in the 1920s, when life had been invigorating. His assignments had included covering Billy Sunday's revivals in Louisville, Kentucky. Of that evangelist, Ross wrote, "There is a certain dignity about anyone entirely engrossed in his profession, and Billy was a knockout at the business of saving, pro tem, the souls of the emotional." Sunday was near the end of his career when Ross spent a cross-country train ride getting to know him. Looking back, Ross remained "pleased to have seen the last of those who could barnstorm America on a hell-and-damnation platform." Then he caught himself and added, à la Sinclair Lewis or H. L. Mencken, that he was pleased "because America has outgrown the stage where storekeepers can subsidize a revivalist to attract crowds into town."

Ross's liberal cynicism about evangelical religion kept him from developing religious commitments of his own. But through his own irony he could yearn, "Lord of Hosts, if thy servant Billy Sunday had been a man with an honest tongue to tell people where they stand and to what cause they should deliver their hearts, what a healthy jolt those meetings might have given Louisville." Ross blamed the storekeepers for allowing only a personal salvation beyond this world to be preached in town. He blamed his own newspaper for being in league with the storekeepers. "I wish now that I had had the inspiration to ask Billy Sunday . . . how he stood on the question of the coal-field battles being fought at the other end of Kentucky. That would really have made a story, and I should probably have been fired for filing it." To Ross, religion's otherworldly diversion from real social problems was not entirely the result of a conspiracy. Ross would not speak pessimistically of the limitations of human nature. Rather, in the liberal fashion, he reflected sadly on the limitations of those less educated than he. That the coal miners' suffering never came up when Billy Sunday was in town, largely because he was in town, "illustrates our traditional preference for emotion over realities."[38]

Dewey's feeling that liberalism sorely lacked a congealing faith, like Ross's specific regret, is a theme that runs through liberal thought.[39] It might be called pulpit envy.[40] The prominent New Deal thinker Thurman Arnold discussed the need for faith more optimistically than Dewey and Ross, but with equal emphasis on its importance. Arnold, a former law professor, joined the New Deal in 1933 as special counsel to the Agricultural Adjustment Administration. He rose to national prominence through his popular books, *The Symbols of Government* (1935) and *The Folklore of Capitalism* (1937). These emphasized that ostensibly unemotional bureaucracies, public and private, advanced or declined according to the "loyalties and enthusiasms" that bound men to them. Organizations required "morale." They could not get that through education and rational persuasion, which were impotent in the face of man's irrationality. Organizations generated morale through symbols, whose mythological character would be obvious to future generations. Franklin Roosevelt, ever conscious of the usefulness of symbols, chose Arnold to head the Justice Department's antitrust division in 1937.

Though Arnold was witheringly skeptical of the "creeds" that drove conservatism and most schemes of reform (including antitrust laws), he saw the value of irrational enthusiasms. Honest and rational students of government always found themselves "confused and ineffective" in real political campaigns, he wrote. In campaigns, "the so-called demagogue has an advantage, because he does not view the control of human institutions under the illusion that men in groups are composed of so-called thinking men." Though most demagogues served conservatism or reaction, irrational enthusiasms might on occasion coincide with a practical idea, like old-age insurance. In that case, irrational enthusiasm for change was the only weapon that could overcome irrational resistance to change. Dr. Francis Townsend was Arnold's best example. Arnold considered Townsend a quack, but in the battle over what became the Social Security Act in 1935, "quacks could lead the most effective campaigns" to uproot the traditional "moral issues" that obscured the practical need. Townsend's popular plan for universal old-age pensions "became a movement which transcended in actual importance all the more sensible schemes of accomplishing the same object." Townsend's scheme softened up the public mind for the rational solution that Arnold endorsed.[41]

Arnold made one exception to his indictment of popular beliefs. For all his skepticism about America's wacky "creeds," he spoke with unselfconscious zeal about the progress of medical science. He held up as a model the "quack" who managed to cure malaria with quinine, and attracted thousands of followers, though the remedy was banned by the learned authorities of the University of Paris, who saw only its inconsistency with their philosophical system. Arnold's enthusiasm for medicine extended to a "new creed called psychiatry," which was bringing "a new sense of tolerance and common sense" to public life. It is sometimes startling to recall the sorts of programs in which liberals put their faith in those days, when they got around to the specifics that Dewey tended wisely to avoid. Arnold wrote that "the psychiatrists, like physicians," avoided theoretical speculation and moralizing: they concentrated on making insane persons comfortable and treated them with genuine interest. "And in this atmosphere curative techniques developed, and men actually learned."

Arnold thought that the psychiatric "creed" could extend into politics, where he hoped it would replace great-man theories of leadership. The notion of "the great man who lived and died for moral and rational purposes"—purposes that kings had dramatized by leading crusades back in medieval times when "nations were holy"—no longer worked. In "modern times," when "governments act in the image of great businessmen" rather than of deities, men needed to find better models in their own experience. Arnold admitted that psychiatry's crusade for the "tolerant, adult personality" had been an insufficient model so far: There was "little in the present conduct of the governments of the world which can by any stretch of the imagination be called adult." Like other liberals, Arnold found more fault in the uneducated masses than in the enlightened few. "Fanatical devotion to principle on the part of the public still compels intelligent leaders to commit themselves, for political reasons, to all sorts of disorderly nonsense." The struggle against irrationality would be long and hard: "So long as the public holds preconceived faiths about the fundamental principles of government, they will persecute and denounce new ideas . . . and orators will prevail over technicians." Still, the new doctors of sense might triumph. At least Arnold thought he might be "permitted to hope." For he had "faith that a new public attitude toward the ideals of law and economics is slowly appearing to create an atmosphere where the fanatical alignments between opposing political principles may disappear and a competent, practical, opportunistic governing class may rise to power."[42]

For all their political differences, the hunger after a fundamental missing faith unified a New Dealer like Arnold with an "independent" liberal like Dewey, who criticized the New Deal for doing too little. This hunger even seemed to afflict the most influential liberal who criticized the New Deal for doing too much. The columnist and public philosopher Walter Lippmann defended liberalism, "the philosophy of [the] industrial revolution," against what he saw as the "collectivism" of the New Deal and of "Totalitarian" states to its left and right. Lippmann urged true liberals to provide society not just with new structures of law and organization but also with the "cultural equipment that men must have if they are to live effectively, and at ease with themselves, in an interdependent [i.e., modern industrial] Great Society." He found liberals stymied by "the science" they had inherited. Liberals were "unable to carry forward their science." Lippmann envied the "collectivists," who had "the zest for progress, the sympathy for the poor, the burning sense of wrong, the impulse for great deeds which have been lacking in latter-day liberalism."

Lippmann complained that America mistakenly endorsed the New Deal because its deep liberal "faith" in individual freedom had been lost. The loss was a necessary consequence of the new division of labor brought by industrial development. (Lippmann thought that concentration of corporate power was merely a "secondary" concern—perhaps his greatest difference with Dewey and with the small faction of New Dealers who believed that control of the radical new institutions of capitalism was an essential first step on the road back to freedom.) Lippmann was the most militant of liberals in his resignation to the "realities" of modern capitalism: "Men may have to pass through a terrible ordeal before they find again the central truths they have forgotten."[43] But he held on to the conviction from his earliest writings that the modern disenchantment of the world (to use Max Weber's phrase) needed to be, and could be, addressed with some positive new, or reinterpreted old, body of "central truths."[44]

At least one other liberal who criticized the New Deal on individualist grounds emphasized society's grave loss of faith from yet another angle. Glenn Frank, one of the most influential Republicans of his day, played a key role both in the GOP's shift toward acquiescence in New Deal spending and in its nomination of Wendell Willkie for president in 1940. A former editor of *The Century* and former president of the University of Wisconsin, Frank had crusaded against racism in the 1920s and was one of the founders of the Citizens National Committee for Sacco and Vanzetti. In the 1930s he advocated a wider distribution of wealth and income to end the depression, proposing confiscatory taxes to achieve this goal if businesses refused to raise wages voluntarily. But Frank grew increasingly critical of the New Deal because it gave too much power to the national state—and perhaps because it stole the liberal and Progressive thunder from his own party.[45]

In his 1935 book, *America's Hour of Decision*, Frank lamented the "exile" of religious leaders from the councils of government. He feared that FDR's method of untethered experimentalism shut out religious perspectives, which, being grounded in fixed principles, could suggest salutary limits. Roosevelt's initiatives were severed from ideological moorings in the name of flexibility. Even if many of these initiatives succeeded, the scattershot techniques of trial and error would yield failures and general disarray. Disappointment would be irresistible to much of the public, Frank feared, especially if poverty continued. The public would then yearn, perhaps uncritically, for some vigorous assertion of principle. Then dictatorial left- or right-wing movements would all too easily fill the ideological vacuum.

Frank specifically feared that American nationalism would fill the vacuum. It would grow into "neo-tribalism." Though he opposed state control of religion—and the efforts of "parson lobbyists" to use the state for religious purposes—he warned that political actors were ignoring religious counsel at their peril. Only by tapping religious traditions, which were repositories of social and institutional wisdom, could America steer between the twin dangers of "extreme laissez-faire" and "regimentation." If America did not steer carefully, it would never achieve the only viable modern form of freedom, "voluntary cooperation." That was the only way to save "capitalistic industrialism."[46] Political leaders who wanted to maintain authority and popular influence had to restore a politically relevant religion, Frank insisted. Religious leaders who wished to enjoy the public's trust and to revive their own sense of usefulness had to join in that restoration. Industrial codes and trade agreements were vital instruments for dealing with the economic crisis, but they were not enough, Frank thought, to restore humane and rational control of society. "How," he asked, "shall spiritual leadership make God again believable to men who have lost all faith in any lordship of life?"[47]

Interestingly, one of the New Deal's wisest and most liberal propagandists, Rexford Tugwell, believed that there was one leader in the crisis of American democracy in the 1930s who had not lost faith: Franklin Delano Roosevelt. Tugwell, a Columbia University economist who became a member of FDR's "brain trust," observed with some wonderment that the president "believed in an external guidance not all of us accept as reality, and he was certain of a commanding destiny most of us have no reason to anticipate." It was "peculiar," and it demanded a biographer's explanation, that FDR "had no adult doubts, no doctrinal difficulties, and only a serene faith which nothing could disturb." Roosevelt said little about this faith, and Tugwell had trouble accounting for it. Tugwell knew only that FDR had "found religion as a boy. If he never let it be questioned, that may well have been because he had found it in circumstances so utterly convincing that reexamination was unnecessary."

Tugwell was sensitive to what he called the "practical consequences" of faith. Roosevelt's persistently "robust spiritual health . . . gave him a sense of balance and perspective capable of supporting him firmly when grave decisions were to be made and when counsels were confused." This faith enabled the president "to sleep long and restfully at night, when he felt that the day had been given to the service of men—who, along with him, were God's children. If the men he served were God's children, they were also his—Franklin's—brothers and worthy of equal sharing in all the opportunities of life. He was not the sort to make this kind of thing explicit, but that he thought of himself as a practicing Christian there is every reason to believe."[48] The biographical accuracy of this speculation is not what matters.[49] It reveals as much about a key New Deal liberal's beliefs—beliefs that persisted long after the crisis had passed (Tugwell published these observations in 1957)—as it does about FDR's own beliefs. Whether Roosevelt was graced with such a bounteous gift of faith or not, observers near and far sensed that he had something that they lacked. They called it leadership, charisma, popularity, the common touch.

Liberals invested FDR, whom they could see and hear, with the faith they could no longer have in anything supernatural. (Social historians have suggested that such faith in FDR spread far among ordinary Americans.)[50] Whatever Tugwell knew or did not know about Roosevelt, his confidence in FDR's faith measures the degree to which key liberals tied their hopes to a single leader. It also measures how severely they would be set adrift—left "rudderless," as Richard Hofstadter observed—when FDR died. Tugwell was inadvertently suggesting a different answer to Dewey's quest: Transferring faith from supernatural to earthly objects—at least to earthly personalities—did not eliminate the hazards of faith.[51]

THE POSTWAR POLITICS OF CULTURE

Liberals' sense of crisis over their lost faith in what Lippmann called "central truths" lived on past the economic crisis of the 1930s. Donald Richberg, a former labor lawyer who advised FDR on policy and came to be known as his "assistant president," said, looking back on the 1930s, that the task of a man of affairs was "the maintenance of a simple faith in the reason and purpose of living, a guiding star that, often lost to view yet ever shining, will save him again and again from the emptiness of despair and a struggle that has no meaning and no end." For some, this simple faith might come from "old-time religion," for others, from egotism or instinct, but it was vital and it was missing.[52]

Not surprisingly, the feeling of a fundamental absence at the core of liberal thought grew more intense after the shocks of World War II. Some liberals saw their postwar troubles with Communists and fellow travelers as a product of their own failure to inspire a devoted and enthusiastic following. Communism, whose millennial roots had long been recognized, could inspire that sort of commitment. That is why liberals saw it as such a great threat.[53]

Lionel Trilling gave voice to the more general hunger in his influential book, *The Liberal Imagination* (1949). The keynote of Trilling's book was melancholy, though it was premised on the complete triumph of liberalism in mid-twentieth-century America. "Liberalism is not only the dominant but even the sole intellectual tradition," Trilling famously wrote. "For it is the plain fact that nowadays there are no conservative or reactionary ideas in general circulation." There were "impulses" of conservatism, but these did not, "with some isolated and some ecclesiastical exceptions, express themselves in ideas." The cultural effect of conservative impulses was limited because these impulses only gained expression "in action or in irritable mental gestures which seek to resemble ideas." Though this state of affairs would "seem to some liberals a fortunate thing," Trilling warned that conservatives' lack of ideas was precisely what made conservatism such a danger, a danger for which liberals were unprepared.

The rise of the Nazis, Fascists, and "totalitarian" socialists in the Soviet Union shaped Trilling's thought, as it shaped the thought of a whole generation of "chastened" liberals who dominated American political culture in the late 1940s and 1950s. It was dangerous for liberals to dismiss movements that had no ideas, Trilling said: "As the experience of Europe in the last quarter-century suggests . . . it is just when a movement despairs of having ideas that it turns to force." And force might be disguised with "ideology," a kind of pseudointellectual program that could be all the more destructive for its lack of intellectual rigor or sophistication.[54] Ideology became a dirty word in these years, and liberals fell all over themselves to show that they had outgrown it—a tendency that culminated in Daniel Bell's popular *End of Ideology* at the end of the 1950s. It was in this era that Americans apparently picked up the habit of pronouncing the word with a short *i*, as though its root were *idiot* rather than *idea*.

To Trilling, Bell, and others, politics was now inescapably cultural and psychological. It was "no longer possible to think of politics except as the politics of culture," Trilling said.[55] Political thinkers who hoped to influence events could not ignore cultural dynamics.[56] Liberalism was at a great disadvantage here: Liberalism viewed the world in a "prosaic" way. What it needed was the "poetic" insight, the Romantic fire that Samuel Taylor Coleridge had brought to English letters.[57] Like all postwar liberals, Trilling was horrified by irrational politics. (Perhaps it was unnecessary to believe in supernatural forces when one had seen the death camps, Stalin's purges, battlefield atrocities in the jungles of the Pacific, deliberate "terror bombing" of civilians, and the advent of atomic warfare. Pointless, unaccountable evil was as vivid and inescapable to the scientific naturalist who read the newspaper as it had been to the imagination of St. John the Divine or Dante.) On the whole, Trilling insisted on the "value and necessity" of liberalism's "organizational impulse," despite the simplification and distortion of human motivation that this impulse required. But he saw it as his duty—as "the job of criticism"—to "recall liberalism to its first essential imagination of variousness and possibility, which implies awareness of complexity and difficulty."[58] He sought, that is, to leaven liberalism, and thus to extend and protect its triumph, with a quasi-spiritual discipline. Trilling's sad tone suggested that squaring this circle would be as difficult as it was desirable.[59]

2

Recovering Optimists

It was a short step from wistful thinking to wishful thinking. In the same year as Trilling's book, Arthur M. Schlesinger Jr. published *The Vital Center* (1949), which became a manifesto of postwar liberalism. It was a more cheerful expression of the "chastened" liberal spirit than Trilling's. But it grew out of the same horror of totalitarianism, the same recoil from recent efforts to make the world conform to utopian ideals. Liberals felt complicit in such utopian efforts. Schlesinger's book was more programmatically political, more organized, one might say more prosaic, than Trilling's. It snatched optimism from the jaws of disillusionment.

Whereas Trilling complained of liberalism's narrowness—and seemed depressed because narrowness was the inevitable product of liberalism's internal logic and of its success in war and Western politics—Schlesinger claimed that a new, improved liberalism already existed. This new liberalism had learned from the mistakes of earlier, utopian liberalism. With more than a touch of hubris, Schlesinger wrote that the formation of his group, Americans for Democratic Action (ADA), "a new liberal organization, excluding Communists and dedicated to democratic objectives," marked "the watershed at which American liberalism began to base itself once again on a solid conception of man and history."[1] Schlesinger provided a way for liberals to worry about their past limitations without calling their very liberalism into question, as Trilling had done. Schlesinger did not mention Trilling, but in effect he answered him.

Schlesinger did mention Reinhold Niebuhr, who had given Trilling's theme a more extended treatment in his *Children of Light and Children of Darkness* (1944) and in his earlier writings, especially *Moral Man and Immoral Society* (1932). Schlesinger claimed to have learned his new brand of liberalism from Niebuhr, and he struck a pose of chastened, disillusioned, Machiavellian "liberalism," which he even called "radicalism."[2]

Yet Schlesinger could never quite make it to the edge of the abyss with Niebuhr (about whom see the next chapter). Niebuhr criticized the naive hope that a new system of education, or a revival of religion or any other human program, would make social conflict unnecessary in the future. Relations between groups, Niebuhr argued, must always be based on force. The owners of capital, in particular, "possess so much power that they win the debate no matter how unreasonable their arguments."[3] No disadvantaged group could hope to win justice through discussion, as liberals hoped; such a group could only hope to wrest away some measure of justice by force or threat of force. Coercion was the keyword of Niebuhr's social ethics.

Niebuhr's lack of faith in voluntaristic cooperation, which to his mind depended on an idolatrous faith in man, was what separated him from the liberals. Even if modern economic development—capitalist, socialist, or mixed—could succeed everywhere at once, it could never cure human societies of their need to force people to get along. To Niebuhr, industrial progress—or any other idol—could not create heaven on earth.

Schlesinger, on the other hand, wrote that although industry inevitably drove the individual "to the wall," regardless of the system of ownership, there were still "common values" between businessmen and liberals. These common values could be the basis of a successful battle against totalitarianism (the threat that lurked in Soviet expansion and in ideologies of perfection at home). Niebuhr rejected both certainty and the notion that human beings could ever be completely free or happy on earth. Yet Schlesinger declared, "I am certain that history has equipped modern liberalism . . . to construct a society where men will be both free and happy."[4]

It may be objected that Schlesinger was making a reasonable compromise, that complete pessimism about human nature is as unrealistic as optimism and at any rate is an impractical basis for a political program. But Niebuhr had already compromised. Niebuhr insisted that he was not "neo-orthodox"; he rejected Karl Barth's pessimism, Barth's Augustinian rejection of this world. Niebuhr sought to engage in political conflict, to fight oppression, and "to mitigate the brutalities" of modern life, even while he held that complete success in such efforts was impossible. His biographers and other students of his work now emphasize that Niebuhr greatly exaggerated his own rejection of liberal theology. He was really criticizing liberalism from within, seeking to curb its excesses, not rejecting its engagement with this world and efforts to reform it.[5] Fundamentalists routinely lumped Niebuhr with liberal theologians; to suggest that he was neo-orthodox, as historians persist in doing, is an equal and opposite error. Niebuhr compromised extensively with both neo-orthodoxy and liberalism. To compromise further with liberalism would be to lose the distinctive features of Niebuhr's thought—the features that made him a significant departure from the previous generation of liberals, whom Niebuhr defined himself by attacking.[6]

The most striking differences between Schlesinger and Niebuhr appear in what they said on race and related subjects. Niebuhr thought that race was a central injustice in American society, a tragedy. In 1932 he expressed the hope (prophetically, it turned out) that the American Negro—*not* the working class—would be the group to struggle successfully against oppression in the United States. He also hoped (again prophetically) that the American Negro would do so by nonviolent force, a technique of struggle that Niebuhr, following Gandhi, understood as having more in common with war than with pacifism.[7]

But Schlesinger, writing seventeen years later—after all the years of agitation and outrage over lynching and the poll tax, after the "rising wind" of black militancy in World War II—had little to say (and nothing original) about race. He did say something about nonviolence—only to dismiss it. The very year that Gandhi's movement succeeded in driving the British Empire out of India, beginning the wave of post–World War II decolonization, Schlesinger claimed that Gandhi's notion of nonviolence was just a form of egotism. To Schlesinger, Gandhi's faith was something that "enthusiasts" follow with "serenity." But in practical terms nonviolent methods were like anarchism and decentralization, which Schlesinger saw as backward yearnings for a "restoration of Feudalism." They could not solve anything except the psychological "complexes" of "the individual who adopts them."[8]

Schlesinger was deaf to what was going on in what became the world's largest democracy. He was deaf to the distinction that Niebuhr, who was influenced by Gandhi as early as the 1920s, drew between nonviolent force, à la Gandhi, and "pacifism," which Niebuhr defined (and denounced) as Tolstoyan nonresistance. (Gandhians understood their technique to be a form of practical politics by which they coerced their enemies to make concessions against their will. They understood that their technique only worked in special circumstances. Tolstoyans, by contrast, turned the other cheek without regard to practical results or political and economic particulars.) After denouncing the arrogance of nonviolence, Schlesinger went on somewhat inconsistently to say that we must defend and strengthen our "free society" against the one power that would *not* be susceptible to Gandhian tactics, the Soviet Union, but we must do it short of war.[9] (Schlesinger's certainty of America's virtues, bordering on arrogance, far exceeded Niebuhr's, even at the height of Niebuhr's "us or them" attacks on the Soviet Union during the Cold War.) As to racism more generally, Niebuhr believed in a power struggle, whereby the Negro would gain ground only through "coercion," Niebuhr's favorite word. Schlesinger, by contrast, took the standard liberal line that "prejudice" would yield to "education."[10]

Arthur Schlesinger Jr., an intellectual leader of post–World War II liberals, claimed to have overcome the utopian optimism that had characterized liberalism since the eighteenth century. But he remained hopeful about human progress in the United States—most of his pessimism he confined to international communism. He later regretted not paying greater attention to the race issue in the 1940s and early 1950s. (© Bettmann/Corbis)

Always more insightful when looking backward than when looking at his own times, Schlesinger revealed in his memoir of 2000 that he regretted not taking an active position against racial discrimination in the South in the 1940s, though he sympathized with black people and was shocked by their condition. Perhaps most illuminating is the record that Schlesinger left of his wartime mission to the South in 1942 for the Office of War Information, which employed him as a "writer-researcher." Schlesinger remembers expressing pessimism about the prospects for racial justice, a pessimism strikingly at odds with his public manifesto of 1949. In the memoir he quotes a memorandum he wrote from the 1942 mission: "The tragedy of the situation is that no improvement would be made by giving more power to the Negro. The southern Negro would abuse power even more than the reactionary southern white." The white northerner, meanwhile, could not act because the white South would react too overwhelmingly. Whether this pessimism lingered after 1942, and he hid it from his 1949 readers, or something washed it away (victory, or the founding of the ADA, perhaps), is unclear. It may simply be that Schlesinger confined his hopelessness to the

South—that backward, recalcitrant sink of ignorance and superstition that had so long been the liberal counterpoint to Pollyannaism about those parts of the world that had the sense to develop modern institutions.[11] That said, the record of Schlesinger's pessimistic statements concludes with the belief that the South had to be left alone—that if anything could help the South, only its few indigenous liberals could. For whatever reason, intervention made no sense to Schlesinger in 1942, despite his outrage at the Negro's plight. His dabbling in the South and in pessimism had exactly the same policy implications as his later optimism.

It would be unfair not to stress that liberals, including Schlesinger, were more receptive to complaints about racial discrimination and racial violence than their main domestic political competitors. And it would be unfair not to grant their point that their main international competitor, the Comintern, exploited America's racial injustices with a staggering opportunism and hypocrisy. The point is not to heap scorn on liberals, but simply to establish that to knock down the racial barriers to the realization of their dream of an open society, liberals needed considerable help from outside their tradition. Their very liberalism blinded them to intractable social conflicts, even as many of them appeared (in the wake of World War II) earnest about facing up to them. For they were intent on regarding such conflicts as products of the mental stubbornness and the overweening expectations of other, illiberal minds. That was more a way of pretending to see social conflicts than of accounting for them in their political plans.

In 1949 Schlesinger seemed to acknowledge the inevitability, the ineradicability, of social conflicts in human affairs,[12] but he did not see great conflict in America, economic any more than racial. Schlesinger did not think— as Niebuhr (and Madison and Tocqueville and Marx) did—that there was a fundamental conflict between rich and poor. According to Schlesinger, the significant "dislike for business" in America "came, not from sour grapes, but from a reasoned analysis of the political incapacity of businessmen." Like most historians of his generation, Schlesinger made much of the failure of European class feeling to survive the voyage across the Atlantic. Discontent in America derived from the ignorance and incompetence of businessmen—their inability to use their power "intelligently"—not from a fundamental conflict of interest or even a fundamental belief in a conflict of interest.

Even on the narrow question of the competence of businessmen to run the world intelligently, Schlesinger had considerable optimism: "The stabilization of economic life has given some business circles, at least, a clearer sense of their responsibility for the general welfare. Indeed, the very withering away of capitalist motivation, while rousing intimations of death-wish in some businessmen, has served as a means of liberating others from the tyranny of the profit motive. The modern American capitalist as a result has come to share many values with the American liberal," including "equality of opportunity." Schlesinger seemed to rejoice in his observation that even Robert Taft, the leader of the right wing of the Republican Party who was "myopic" in foreign policy, still "understands very clearly that the capitalist system must feed human needs in areas like housing, health and education if it is to survive."[13]

In fudging the line between pessimism and optimism, Schlesinger tried to fit not only Niebuhr but also Nathaniel Hawthorne into a soft tradition of *American* pessimism—a pessimism that held that "power, unless checked by accountability, would corrupt its possessor."[14] That is not a pessimistic view, nor is it peculiar to Hawthorne or Niebuhr: it is a nearly universal, commonsense view that holds as well for aristocratic and monarchical theories of power as it holds for republicanism or democracy. A pessimist does not need to add that "unless checked by accountability" clause, a clause conspicuously absent from Lord Acton's famous formulation. Schlesinger had Hawthorne and Niebuhr wrong. Those two more wholeheartedly rejected liberal—and indeed American—optimism: they believed in the classical and Christian fashion that power *always* corrupts.

Niebuhr liked democracy as the best way so far to limit power, but he never put much stock in the magic of accountability (this separated him from Dewey as well as from Schlesinger). Niebuhr had seen too much demagoguery become popular. Far from believing that power had to be unchecked in order to corrupt, Niebuhr put it close to the other way around: it was necessary (not just pragmatically unavoidable, but morally necessary) to corrupt oneself in order to *get* power. One need not wait for the attainment of power, that is, for the corruption to set in. This is the heart of Niebuhr's pessimism. In one of the most disturbing passages of his great work of 1932, Niebuhr insisted that even in a genuine struggle for justice, a truth-stretching propaganda was necessary. "Contending forces in a social struggle require morale; and morale is created by the right dogmas, symbols and emotionally potent over-simplifications."[15] Niebuhr was so intent on avoiding self-righteousness about his own side—so intent on avoiding the error of thinking that benevolent intentions justified cruel and dishonest methods—that he argued that those working to overthrow an unjust order typically had to become more unjust in their methods than those defending it.

Niebuhr, always trying like Jesus to be on the side of the oppressed, said it was unfortunately *more* necessary for the oppressed to stretch the truth than it was for those already corrupted by possessing power. "No class of industrial workers will ever win freedom from the dominant classes if they give themselves completely to the 'experimental techniques' of the modern educators. They will have to believe rather more firmly in the justice and in the probable triumph of their cause than any impartial science would give them the right to believe, if they are to have enough energy to contest the power of the strong." Keeping in mind that capitalists "possess so much power that they win the debate no matter how unreasonable their arguments,"[16] Niebuhr could not escape the implication that honesty was useless to the opponents of Capital. They needed strong propaganda if they were to have a chance; they might beneficially alter the status quo, but they could not do so without dirtying their hands.

Schlesinger saw that man "cannot be trusted" with "absolute power,"[17] but stopped far short of Niebuhr's point, which was that man cannot be trusted with any other degree of power. To Niebuhr, all politics, all group action, involved coercion and therefore, tragically, involved injustice. All power was corrupt and corrupting. Working for a just cause provided no escape from corruption.

But the only thing about which Schlesinger was irredeemably pessimistic was the Soviet Union, which, he said, was a greater danger than Nazism, because it could rally its fifth columns anywhere and because it saw any existing "free society" as a threat. Schlesinger would not compromise his belief in liberty for this: he would not outlaw the Communist Party, U.S.A. But he did encourage the tattletaleism that soon came back to haunt him and other liberals: "Some people feel that it is somehow below the belt even to report on Communist Party activities or to identify its influence. Yet, given the nature of the Soviet drive against free society, given the frightful tyranny implicit in the principle *cuius regio, eius religio*, there is surely no alternative to paying exact and unfaltering attention to the Communists in our midst." Given the ruthlessness of American Communists and their unswerving loyalty to a hostile foreign power, "we would be well advised to take the necessary precautions." He echoed the chest-thumping pronouncements of Federal Bureau of Investigation (FBI) director J. Edgar Hoover: "Counterespionage is no field for amateurs. We need the best professional counterespionage agency we can get to protect our national security."[18] It would be churlish to lay at Schlesinger's door the corruption of that "professional" band of investigators.[19] But his faith in the self-appointed defenders of "free society" in 1949 suggests that he had not been fully chastened by the totalitarian experience.

Postwar liberals like Schlesinger were committed to staying in power. (In that sense, *they* were Niebuhrian, though their thinking was not: they devoted themselves to getting and maintaining power, but unlike Niebuhr they did not articulate a philosophy of power. Their philosophy continued rather to stress what they would do once they had secured power—promote prosperity and free speech, etc.) If the ADA *World*, the biweekly newsletter of Americans for Democratic Action, the liberal faction that survived McCarthyism, had a dominant theme in its first few years, it was the importance of winning elections. It repeated again and again the need to avoid candidates who were too liberal to win. The stakes were high. If liberals did not control government, they could not prevent isolationists from tempting the Russians to initiate World War III. In that event, domestic goals like liberty and prosperity would have no chance.[20]

The goals that ADA liberals highlighted in the 1940s and early 1950s were in foreign policy. (Emphasis on foreign policy became the basis of their surprising identification with John F. Kennedy years later.) Their first major domestic goal, the defeat of Henry Wallace's bid for the Democratic nomination and subsequent independent presidential candidacy in 1948, was an offshoot of their foreign policy goals. The leaders of the ADA saw Wallace as a Soviet dupe. It was no coincidence, they thought, that his opposition to the Truman Doctrine and Marshall Plan matched the Kremlin's. Moscow wanted to divide the Democrats to ensure the election of a GOP isolationist. The danger was that Wallace would draw overly idealistic voters away from an otherwise electable, and internationalist, Democrat.

At this point, before the conventions of 1948, most ADA members still opposed the unpopular Harry S. Truman, as well as Wallace. About one-third of the country's ADA chapters wanted to throw their support to Dwight D. Eisenhower, who was thought to be liberal on many issues, though he had opposed desegregation of the military and federal compulsion of states on civil rights. ADA operatives at the 1948 Democratic National Convention tried to organize a draft-Ike movement. (They were joined in this effort by conservative senators Harry Byrd of Virginia and Strom Thurmond of South Carolina, both of whom found Truman too radical on civil rights.) Many liberals thought Ike was a Democrat or could be induced to become one, as so many liberal Republicans had in the 1930s. The main thing for the liberals was that Truman looked like a loser, and Eisenhower's popularity rivaled that of the late FDR. Only two out of forty-seven ADA chapters wanted to back the incumbent Truman. The liberals joined in introducing the radically pro–civil rights plank in the 1948 Democratic Convention, partly because they believed Truman was going to lose anyway, and the liberals thought they might as well use the opportunity to weaken the southern wing of their party. Some historians have reasonably suggested that the ADA initially supported a strong civil rights plank as a tactic to sabotage Truman's nomination: it would force Truman either to support the plank, thus alienating the southerners, or to oppose it, thus alienating a powerful combination of the northern urban bosses, who needed the black vote, and northern labor and liberal activists. Truman's failure would then open the way to nomination of a popular candidate, such as Eisenhower.[21]

There is also evidence that the ostensibly bold steps that ADA leaders took to push civil rights in 1948 derived from their desire to sabotage Wallace. In April 1948, when Wallace's movement appeared as the main threat to the nomination of an electable Democrat, ADA secretary-treasurer Jim Loeb urged Hubert H. Humphrey, on behalf of the ADA, to take a strong stand at the convention in favor of civil rights. "Whether or not [Truman] is the Democratic candidate, it seems to us absolutely essential that the civil rights issue be defended at the National Convention," Loeb wrote. Any compromise on civil rights would put northern and western liberals in an "impossible" position. If Truman won the nomination, he would be "much stronger if the Convention wins a good fight on this issue." Loeb proposed that the ADA work anonymously to enlist prominent Democrats in a public endorsement of Truman's civil rights committee, whose celebrated report, *To Secure These Rights*, had outraged southern Democrats. It was essential, Loeb said, "both for the moral position of our Party and for reasons of political realism that those of us in the North and West make our position abundantly clear with equal vigor." But the politics of foreign policy clinched the argument. "Any real concessions [to southern Democrats] on this matter would only serve to strengthen the political position both of our reactionary Republican opposition and the Communist-dominated Third-party movement." Loeb thought that the Republicans and Progressive-communists were "united in their efforts to elect reactionary government in the United States."[22]

Thirteen days after Loeb's letter to Humphrey, New York columnist James Wechsler, an ADA supporter, began discrediting Wallace's civil rights credentials. Wechsler noted that Wallace, posing as "a solitary figure battling the forces of prejudice and hate" in 1948, had resisted desegregation efforts while he was secretary of commerce.[23] As it turned out, Humphrey succeeded in pushing the adoption of a radical civil rights plank, and the ADA took a great deal of the credit.

Liberal survivors of the 1948 struggle, considering electability the sine qua non of all liberal hopes, took great pains to avoid alienating southern Democrats after the election. The ADA's southern chapters, much less developed than the northern chapters, showed little interest in initiating action on racial issues in the 1940s and early 1950s. They emphasized instead the need to purge communists from liberal groups and to induce noncommunists to defect from tainted organizations like the Southern Conference on Human Welfare.[24] This is not the place to sort out the degree to which irrational fears of communism drove the ADA away from civil rights, or the degree to which the ADA took advantage of the post–World War II Red Scare to enforce what it considered a more viable, more realistic liberalism. Nor is it the place to sort out the degree to which communists and other leftists embraced racial issues opportunistically to establish their superior courage and integrity as they competed with liberals for the black vote. Suffice it to say that the ADA, North and South, saw the purification of liberal institutions as necessary to further progress, trumping all other issues.

That emphasis reinforced liberals' resistance to any strong support of civil rights after the election of 1948. William Kolb, of Newcomb College, who later became head of the ADA's Louisiana Chapter, wrote to Loeb in December 1948, "Of course if we build into a mass organization we have the racial problem always with us." He believed that the ADA had to lead both the Negro and the worker, but that created a dilemma: emphasis on black rights would alienate white workers. This dilemma—"the crux of our basic problem"—was worsened by the ADA's rivals, Wallace Progressives, who were "ready to let fly at our first slip."[25]

More important in inhibiting liberal emphasis on civil rights was the memory of the 1948 election, which had fractured the vehicle of postwar liberal hopes, the Democratic Party. The party—already strained by the New Deal–wartime concentration of power in Washington, which threatened the party's tradition of states' rights—almost fell apart over the strong civil rights plank Humphrey introduced that year. Truman, surprisingly, won on that platform, but barely, and the party was badly injured. Southern defections to the States' Rights Party of Strom Thurmond hurt the Democrats much more than liberal defections to Wallace (a few liberals also defected to the Republicans). Liberals did not want to repeat the mistake in 1952 and 1956, when they believed a Democrat had a real chance of winning. The civil rights planks of those years were weaker, and the ticket was far less identified with civil rights than in 1948, though liberals had as much clout within the party in 1952 and 1956 as in 1948.

Schlesinger and other ADA liberals were as conscious as FDR had been that any action on civil rights would divide the Democratic Party. Visiting Chattanooga, Tennessee, in 1950 to investigate the possibilities for establishing ADA chapters in the South, Schlesinger found that the civil rights issue was the liberals' "main obstacle in recruiting and organizing." Southern liberals, he found, did not "want ADA to modify its stand" on civil rights (which was not very strong at that point), but anything that would make the ADA "seem exclusively or largely concerned with the civil rights issue" would only make their lives more difficult. Accordingly, Schlesinger suggested that "it might help our organizing in the South if something could be done to make the ADA seem something else than another Yankee liberal outfit." It was especially important that "ADA seem in the South much less a personal machine for the civil rights program of Hubert Humphrey."[26]

Even Humphrey soon offered an olive branch to southern Democrats. In November 1951 he wrote to twenty southern editors stressing his "deep affection" for the South, fondly recalling his years as a graduate student at Louisiana State University. He assured the editors that he did not want to push civil rights too hard. "I know that we frequently place too much trust in the power of the federal government. I know the federal government is not the only government that can deal with the pressing issue of human rights. . . . My program for civil rights places its main emphasis on community activity, individual responsibility, education and moral values, supported by legislative standards." A few years later Humphrey helped Lyndon B. Johnson persuade Senate liberals to abandon their effort to change Senate rules to undercut the southern filibuster, the strongest anti–civil rights weapon. Though that move was an obvious concession to political realism, Walter White of the NAACP denounced it as "abject surrender." Senator Walter George of Georgia volunteered to campaign for Humphrey in 1954 and supported his efforts to win the vice-presidential nomination in 1956.[27] Humphrey and others cooled to civil rights perhaps because they overestimated northern support as much as they underestimated southern opposition.[28]

After Wallace's defeat and congressional acceptance of the Marshall Plan and the Truman Doctrine, ADA liberals could focus more on domestic issues. Still, before the *Brown* decision of 1954 and the Montgomery Bus Boycott of 1955–56, they paid far more attention to economic growth, labor, and civil liberties than they did to racial oppression.[29] When liberals mentioned issues like poverty and housing, they generally did not connect them to race, as post-1960s liberals nearly always did. Pre-*Brown* liberals expressed what seem to be sincere hopes for improvement in the condition of the Negro, but they almost never made him their headline issue.[30] When they did emphasize racism, it was to voice outrage about racial violence. The historian Peter Kellog wisely observed that this emphasis on violence underwrote the basic assumptions of liberal ideology: it allowed liberals to keep thinking of racism as an aberration, as something peripheral rather than central to modern American politics.[31] Liberals treated racism's occasional, and by all accounts decreasing,[32] outbreaks of violence as crimes that could in principle be contained or treated while America went about its business of economic growth and cultural improvement. Liberals did not see these outbreaks the way scholars now tend (like some activists at the time) to see them: as reminders of the brute force on which the southern racial system rested—a system in which terror was so ingrained that, once established, it required only occasional reminders. (For many scholars, the increasing rarity of lynchings is evidence of their effectiveness, not their peripherality. Moreover, according to some, the states' racially concentrated use of capital punishment, which many referred to as "legal lynching," did the mobs' work more efficiently with legitimate power.)[33] Of more immediate import was that liberal emphasis on occasional and declining outbreaks of violence was politically safe. The most conservative and paternalistic white southerners had long been proving their respectability by denouncing lynching—which challenged their power more directly than that of Yankee liberals—and by showing progress toward its eradication. Even southern demagogues deplored mob violence. The only division was that Yankees and the NAACP favored the imposition of federal law, whereas white southerners (with a few exceptions) insisted that they could stamp out what remained of the already illegal practice with their own state power.

Schlesinger and other liberal thinkers supported ADA statements in favor of federal antilynching bills, along with ineffectual proposals for a permanent Fair Employment Practices Committee. But they never put racism or civil rights at the center of their analysis of American society or their proposals for reform. Nonetheless, as black southerners and northward migrants became increasingly assertive, racism became more and more prominent, and liberals had to find ways to deal with it. Their most important source of knowledge on the subject—Gunnar Myrdal's *An American Dilemma: The Negro Problem and Modern Democracy*, published in 1944—created such a sensation that it must be counted as part of the reason that the issue became increasingly prominent.

MYRDALERIE OR MASTERY?
ON THE IDOLATROUS FAITH IN INSTITUTIONS

It is odd that the book that provided post–World War II liberals their guidance on what would, two decades later, become their most significant historical achievement made none of Schlesinger's show of skepticism, of disillusionment, of recovery from naive optimism. A more striking contrast to Reinhold Niebuhr's view of human nature could not be found. Myrdal's was one of the most optimistic books published in the twentieth century. Myrdal did not even struggle with the need that other liberals felt to conjure up a postreligious inspiration for solidarity and sacrifice. The massive report, whose collaborators included many of the most prominent social scientists in America, had 1,117 pages of exhaustive data and analysis. It all boiled down to a prophecy: Americans had a "creed" of equality that contradicted their practice of racial discrimination. In the psychic battle between creed and practice, the practice sooner or later had to yield to the creed. Myrdal was confident that the practice would yield sooner, rather than later, because white Americans, even southerners, were becoming more enlightened and more honest about the practice.

As the historian David Kennedy put it, Myrdal's book promised "a virtually painless exit from the nation's racist history." Black and white Americans alike welcomed it. It became a best-seller. The nation was "more flattered than shamed" by Myrdal's study, Kennedy wrote. It caught on so well because it was so familiar to those who, despite the alleged chastening experience of depression and world war, were determinedly optimistic about their domestic problems. Whether Myrdal was or was not accurate about the moral anguish Americans felt about racial inequality, Kennedy noted that Myrdal tapped into a deep current in American culture that ran back at least to the antebellum reformers: "the simple belief that a factual appeal to the better angels of their nature would induce Americans to do the right thing."[34]

Myrdal's experience with totalitarianism was very different from that of Trilling and Niebuhr. Myrdal found the danger of totalitarianism not in the optimism of those who supported it but in the pessimism of those who submitted to it. He acknowledged that his book was optimistic, saying it had to be optimistic to counter disillusionment. "Mankind is sick of fear and disbelief, of pessimism and cynicism. It needs the youthful moralistic optimism of America."[35] Myrdal believed that disillusionment had pervaded Europe in the 1920s and 1930s, particularly his native Sweden, where it spawned a deadly passivity, even in the face of fascist insurgencies. Myrdal's own brand of liberalism, Swedish social democracy, was in his mind too pessimistic, too resigned. Swedish liberalism was on a different trajectory (or, as Schlesinger might say, in a different phase of its cycle) from American liberalism.

When Myrdal came to America, he interpreted its mainstream social science as being similarly pessimistic. In contrast to the rejuvenating sunniness of popular culture, America's social scientists had a "defeatist attitude."[36] The key to Myrdal's indictment of American complacency was his statement that "the Negro problem" was really a "white problem": the conflict between ideals and practice derived from white practices and tore at white consciences. The white people were the ones who needed to change. He dismissed the idea that white people were merely paying "lip service" to the ideal of equality. The white American was, on the contrary, "strongly and sincerely 'against sin,' even, and not least, his own sins. He investigates his faults, puts them on record, and shouts them from the housetops." Myrdal joined Lord Bryce in observing that Americans "have a boundless faith in free inquiry and full discussion." He had no doubt "that a great majority of white people in America would be prepared to give the Negro a substantially better deal if they knew the facts. . . . I have become convinced also that a majority even of Southerners would be prepared for much more justice to the Negro if they were really brought to know the situation."[37] For that reason, Myrdal did not say much about black culture or black strategies of resistance and protest.

In the major histories of Myrdal's project, both of them sympathetic to Myrdal, Myrdal comes across as dogmatic in his optimistic thesis, with which many collaborators did not agree. He apparently fixated on his notion of an American creed without much reflection or study, before he arrived in the United States. Then he clung to it and imposed it on his collaborators.[38]

A few critics of Myrdal's book, notably Robert Lynd, complained that it was too optimistic.[39] But for the most part these criticisms did not catch on until a general disillusionment with the limitations of civil rights took root in the 1960s. Then radical and conservative critics indicted Myrdal for the shortcomings of the movement, which they associated him with.[40] The most important of these criticisms was probably Ralph Ellison's review, originally slated for publication in the *Antioch Review* in 1944; for some reason, however, it did not appear until Ellison's collection, *Shadow and Act*, was published in 1962.[41] Why thinkers so sharply at odds with Myrdalian optimism, including Niebuhr and W. E. B. Du Bois, let Myrdal off the hook so easily in their reviews is a mystery that would bear historical investigation.[42]

To be fair, Myrdal did not view black Americans as an inert mass shaped by forces of progress and assimilation. He warned of their growing militancy. Though he did not see this militancy the way Reinhold Niebuhr had seen it twelve years earlier — as likely to achieve victory through nonviolent force — neither did he see black people as cooperating with the system of oppression or as having any desire to collaborate with it before it changed.[43]

More striking than Myrdal's optimism was the way he directly contradicted Niebuhr (whom he does not seem to have read, though his reading of American social thought was otherwise vast). Not only would white Americans act better toward black people in the future as individuals, Myrdal wrote: they would become even more generous through collective institutions. Myrdal observed that schools, churches, and the government were growing more sympathetic to black demands, whereas individual white persons were not so bold. This led him to believe that institutions would lead Americans in resolving the conflict between their ideals and reality. Since America, like all modern societies, was becoming more institutionalized, Myrdal's optimism was tied to this belief that institutions were leading the way toward morality.[44] The radical sociologist C. Wright Mills observed that this faith in institutions pervaded modern liberalism: "The seat of rationality has shifted from the individual and is now in the big institution." In Mills's eyes, this turned out to be an excellent way for liberals — once the preeminent individualists — to deal with their own failure to spread liberalism among the masses. "The increase of enlightenment does not necessarily wise up the individual. . . . This modern weakness and irrationality of the individual, and especially his political apathy," had become "crucial" for liberalism.[45]

The thesis conveyed in the title of Niebuhr's greatest work, *Moral Man and Immoral Society* (1932), was precisely the opposite of Myrdal's. Within a general framework of pessimism about human nature, Niebuhr insisted that individuals could and often did respect moral rules. Though one could not depend on morality in the realm of individual action, morality had meaning there. But institutions and other collectives were, by their nature, incapable of being governed by the rules that restrained individuals. Institutions might pay lip service to morality and gain prestige by claiming moral

Swedish social scientist Gunnar Myrdal gave American liberals
a seemingly definitive analysis of their race "problem" in his
influential *American Dilemma* (1944), one of the most optimistic
books of the twentieth century. Here, in 1938, accompanied by
his family, he is about to set out for America to begin his study
of race. (Archives of the Labor Movement, Stockholm, Sweden)

purpose, but whenever it came to a choice between a moral purpose and the interests of the institution or its constituents, an institution had to defend its interests. An individual man, though tainted by original sin and incapable of perfection, was at least capable of moral choice. A man *could* act on the basis of moral principle and even sacrifice his own life for a greater good. History was full of examples. But to Niebuhr it was meaningless to say that a nation or a class or an institution ever chose to "sacrifice" itself for a moral cause. An individual man could be moral; society was "immoral." The greatest mistake liberals made, Niebuhr said, was to think that collectives, even nations, could be compelled to act on the basis of morality. In fact, they only acted on the basis of interest.[46]

Though liberals of Schlesinger's generation never assimilated Niebuhr's pessimism about human nature, they did embrace his notion of amoral group conflict in the so-called realism in foreign policy popularized by George Kennan and Hans Morgenthau and in the interest-group pluralism in domestic policy outlined in John Kenneth Galbraith's *American Capitalism* (1952) and Robert Dahl's *Preface to Democratic Theory* (1956). Realism and pluralism became the hallmarks of liberal political theory in the 1950s and 1960s. They marked the liberals' relief at being released from Wilsonian "idealism," a release many of them credited to Niebuhr. (According to Richard Fox, Kennan could not recall ever having said that Niebuhr was "the father of us all."[47] But that everybody believed that Kennan said it was a mark of liberals' desire to claim Niebuhr as the agent of their maturation.) Ultimately, the notion of a civil rights lobby applying pressure to government on behalf of constituents was assimilated to the pluralist theory to justify and explain civil rights and affirmative action without naive reference to the triumph of ideals.

Post-Wilsonian liberals protested too much. There was an optimism embedded in their new foreign policy realism insofar as America had great power on the international stage at the time. A world ruled by interest would smile on the land of the free and the home of the brave now that its adversaries, indeed most of its friends, had been crippled by world war. Pluralism was downright Panglossian in its assurance that rough justice would emerge from the conflict of interest groups. (Pluralism bore a strong family resemblance to Adam Smith's more individualist notion of an invisible hand ultimately bringing the greatest possible growth out of the market.) But realists and pluralists no longer needed to consider themselves naive about the *mechanism* by which optimistic forecasts played themselves out. (Had they read Smith, to say nothing of David Ricardo and Thomas Robert Malthus, they might not have seen this as such an original development in their thought.) They saw the mechanism that produced utopia as an inevitable and costly conflict of forces.

Realists and pluralists were pessimistic only about the mechanisms by which optimistic forecasts played themselves out. They were not ultimately pessimistic about all attempts to organize life in the City of Man, as Niebuhr was, or at least had been in his prime from 1932 to 1944. Niebuhr's stern warning that collective bodies were necessarily immoral meant for him that they should never be viewed with moral complacency. This part of his message was lost on the realists and pluralists, who, in their release from moral idealism, found relief from constant agonizing about the immoral tendencies of organizations and politics.[48] If anything, liberal complacency about the dangers of politics and war increased with the advent of pluralism and realism: the new superficial pessimism about means to utopia masked liberals' abiding optimism about ends, which continued to breed hubris and lack of restraint among liberals throughout the postwar boom and Cold War, at least until they encountered failure in Vietnam.

Myrdal's report had a more powerful effect on liberal opinion after World War II than anything Niebuhr had ever said about race, which may be another way of saying that Myrdal's report reflected the liberals' uncodified and often unstated impulses better than anything. President Truman's special Committee on Civil Rights drafted its 1947 report, *To Secure These Rights*, as little more than a gloss on Myrdal. The committee altered the report greatly before publication, largely to appease southern critics who disagreed with Myrdal's approach or were offended by his failure to quote them in his report. But the president's committee remained Myrdalian in its basic thrust, speaking of an "American Creed" at odds with the practice of racial discrimination and of the necessary triumph of creed over practice. Roy Wilkins of the NAACP said that the Truman Committee report became "a blueprint that we used for the next two decades." Hubert Humphrey, who was second only to Truman in pushing the Democrats to begin supporting civil rights in the late 1940s, was also strongly influenced by Myrdal, whom he read before entering politics and whom he echoed in key speeches. When the Supreme Court finally ruled on the legality of segregation in 1954, Myrdal's report figured prominently in its decision.[49]

One thing Myrdal's report did not do was inspire liberals to build solidarity and self-sacrificial commitment, whose absence they had been fretting over all along. Myrdal did not provide them what John Dewey identified as the key to their future: "Liberalism that is sincere must will the means that condition the achieving of its ends."[50] Indeed, Myrdal's antipessimism is a great irony; his compensating optimism became a strong justification for inaction. Liberals did not feel the need to *do* anything until the battle broke out in the streets of the South in the mid-1950s—a development they did not anticipate.[51] As the historian Walter Jackson observes, "The last thing that white liberals were expecting in the 1950s was a mass movement among African-Americans in the South."[52] Similarly, Richard King argues that the civil rights movement "failed to fit comfortably, if at all, within the confines of conventional liberal politics"; "the civil rights movement was a great surprise."[53] The proximity of Myrdal's report to the first successes of the movement gave a false notion of its effect and its accuracy. The report was welcomed by the liberals: it was in sync with the thinking of those who acted very little on racism in the late 1940s and early 1950s.

This is not to say, again, that liberals were insincere in their expressed desire to better the lot of black Americans. Historians' obsession with sincerity grows out of the Myrdalian habit of thinking of race as primarily a matter of opinion and attitude, susceptible to education or psychotherapy or sensitivity training.[54] Liberals were sincere. Their concern with the suffering of the Negro in no way conflicted with their desire to get his vote — which liberals did not consider to be much more pressing at the time than other racial issues. It is thus pointless to charge the liberals with opportunism in whatever gestures they made in favor of black rights: opportunism on this issue dictated the same gestures as idealism. The point here is simply that liberals felt the need for other things, especially their own power, much more strongly than they felt the need for civil rights. That sense of priorities is not surprising, and it was probably a good thing for liberalism and a host of worthy programs the liberals supported. But liberals were not the ones who gave civil rights its power as an issue. They were not the ones who made it move.

3

The Prophetic Ideas
That Made Civil Rights *Move*

What about those who did make civil rights move? What were their ideas of human nature? Gunnar Myrdal projected his optimism onto black America. He insisted that most Negroes resisted the influence of W. E. B. Du Bois and others who had become "pessimistic." Most of them had "not lost their belief that ultimately the American Creed will come out on top." Black people had even greater faith than white people in "the magic of education."[1]

It is impossible to say whether Myrdal was right about the black population in general. The major black periodicals of the 1940s display a broad spectrum of attitudes about the future, balancing optimism roughly evenly with pessimism.[2] Two literary best-sellers that bracket the period—Richard Wright's *Native Son* (1941) and Ralph Ellison's *Invisible Man* (1952), surely the greatest black novels of the century—reflect none of the optimism that Myrdal attributed to the Negro masses. Many years later in the twentieth century, Jennifer Hochschild came to the "heart-breaking" conclusion that poor black Americans are a lot more optimistic than privileged black or white Americans.[3] Had Myrdal attempted any survey as precise as Hochschild's, he might have found a lot of optimism back in his day, too, or he might not have: again, it is impossible to say. Myrdal has been roundly criticized for ignoring black culture in his study.[4] But subsequent historians have ignored what may be the most relevant aspect of black culture: the thinking of strategists of direct action in the 1950s and early 1960s.

It is possible to know the thinking of at least some of those strategists—those who acted to bring about the equality that Myrdal said would come more or less automatically. Some of them left a clear record of their conceptions of history and human nature—the sort of record that is detailed enough to test Myrdal's assumption of widespread black optimism. The record may not be representative of the black masses of the South, or even of the minority of those masses who participated in civil rights marches and demonstrations. To examine the record of these few is not to presume that their thoughts are more important than the relatively inaccessible thoughts of the masses. It is not to buy into any great-man or great-woman theory of history. Clearly the few who left a detailed intellectual record could not have accomplished much without the support, perhaps without the inspiration and prodding, of the masses. But the masses were either less articulate or less careful to preserve their articulations than the few. At least that is so on certain key philosophical questions. This means that the record of the few is all we have at present on those questions. As with all historical records, it would be silly to assume that this record is the end of the story. Indeed, it will be examined here in the hope that it may inspire and inform more detailed and creative investigations of the consciousness of the masses, or at least of the consciousness of the many still-unsung participants at the grassroots of the great historic struggle for freedom.

The black strategists who left a detailed record of their views do not fit Myrdal's conception. They did not think like midcentury American liberals. Whereas Myrdal and the liberals were optimistic about human development, especially about human institutions, the intellectuals of the civil rights movement stood out for their rejection of this world and its natural tendencies. They were conspicuous for their unwillingness to let social processes work themselves out and for their lack of faith in the power of education and economic development to cure society of oppressive evils. In their thinking, they were more akin to the Hebrew Prophets, Frederick Douglass, and the Reinhold Niebuhr of 1932–44 than they were to mainstream liberals.[5]

MARTIN LUTHER KING'S ANTHROPOLOGY

Martin Luther King is probably the best place to start, though historians at first exaggerated his influence and have lately been underestimating it. King appeared liberal in some respects and obviously owed a debt to liberal theology. For example, when he applied to seminary and when he later looked back on his call to the ministry, he saw the ministry as a social mission rather than a divine inspiration.[6] But he rejected the liberal optimism of the social gospel. King never became neo-orthodox, but scholars have overemphasized his theological liberalism and have neglected to differentiate the relative significance of his liberal opinions from that of his illiberal ones.

King expressed a strong dislike for what he called the "fundamentalism" of his father and the church in which he grew up. In that sense, he was a liberal. But in his doctrine of man—which is far more decisive in explaining his career in civil rights—King could never embrace liberal optimism. On the subject of human nature, he was closer to orthodoxy than to liberalism. Indeed, on human nature he was close to the modern conservatism of Edmund Burke.[7] Even in his papers at Crozer Theological Seminary (1948–51), before he apparently read Niebuhr, King leaned toward a prophetic pessimism about man.[8] That leaning, along with his tendency to focus his pessimism on racial and economic inequality in the United States, distinguishes him from Myrdal and Schlesinger and postwar liberals in general.

Like vital centrists, King often struck a pose of compromise between opposing views. Many scholars have explained this as a fundamental "Hegelian" disposition. But King's writings do not evince Hegel's optimistic faith in the process of history, with its ideal Freedom unfolding in time and gaining realization in the State. King's debt to Hegel was purely formal: he used a dialectical method, setting up abstract (if not altogether fictional) opposite positions as equally unsatisfying, then moving to a satisfying "synthesis."[9] This is only superficially Hegelian. It is the method of countless earlier philosophers, notably Plato. King had no commitment to Hegel's substantive doctrine, which sees an ideal embodied in human history. Even the formal Hegelianism appears to be a crutch that King leaned on when he had little to say, rather than a philosophical commitment. It is significant that the first time King reveals some originality in his academic work, he breaks from the thesis-antithesis pattern. This first break comes in his 1948 essay on Jeremiah, "the rebel prophet." In this essay, King begins to develop a preoccupation with what he (like Niebuhr) calls a "prophetic" tradition. His professor, James Bennett Pritchard, apparently noticed the shift, telling King that this essay was "written with enthusiasm in a convincing manner!"[10]

In the essay on Jeremiah, King sounds out the keynotes of his later speeches and public writings.[11] First, there is the prophetic belief that the nation is in moral decline. According to King, the nation is in decline partly because the national creed—far from creating the psychic tension that would inspire reform (as Myrdal would have it)—is defective and needs itself to be reformed. Jeremiah, King tells us, "realized that the covenant made at Mount Sinai had failed to accomplish its purpose. . . . Instead of being a spiritual asset it was a snare and a delusion. Instead of leading men to their knees it filled them with foolish presumption, until [they strike] out at the priest and scribe and law." Second, there is the indictment of institutions. Jeremiah "saw that the Temple had been relegated to a position of empty formalism[,] which substituted a superficial reverence for the doing of Yahweh's will." The temple "had become[,] in Yahweh's eyes, a cave for robbers to shelter themselves in," and "functionaries of the Temple . . . drifted into the belief that the Temple was more important than the distinction of good and evil, the sacrifices more vital than sin." Third, there is the recognition that society rejected prophets. Jeremiah "was a failure" by the standards of his contemporaries and "by the standards of the world." Finally, there is the rebellion and renewal motivated by prophetic truth. In articulating the Second Covenant, Jeremiah was correcting the naïveté of the Deuteronomists: For all their accomplishments in organizing their religion, the Deuteronomists "failed to see that religion is not something which can be organized, rather it is a spontaneous outflow from men's contact with a divine spirit." Since the temple was "a national institution, linked intimately with the fortunes of the race," to "attack" it was political and social rebellion. "It took the fortitude and mind of Jeremiah to expose these pressing faults." Jeremiah "seized upon a revolutionary truth": he remained "a shining example of the truth that religions should never sanction the status quo."[12]

King's attraction to Jeremiah put him on the same path as Niebuhr, who in his rejection of both liberalism and neo-orthodoxy came up with "prophetic religion" as the best name for the doctrines he emphasized. King frequently referred to "prophetic Christianity" in his later writings and speeches and cited Jeremiah, Amos, and Isaiah as examples of brave men who sacrificed their social position and standing (if not their lives) when they preached to society of its corruption and insisted on total, rather than incremental, reformation.[13] As King grows closer to Niebuhr, more conscious of his affinity for Niebuhr's thought, he points to the way that "neo-orthodox" theologians of his own day call us back to the message of the Prophets.[14]

The point is not that King got these emphases solely from Niebuhr. Indeed, the rather obvious point scholars lately stress, that King learned most of his abiding commitments in the black Baptist Church in which he grew up, does not conflict with the argument here. The useful things that King learned from that rich and diverse tradition—the things he did not reject as "fundamentalist"—were compatible with what he later learned from Niebuhr. The significance of Niebuhr is not that he invented the prophetic tradition, but rather that he codified its teachings and expressed them for his contemporaries in vivid, arresting language that King understood—indeed understood better than most liberals. King understood the Niebuhrian language and found it useful, partly because of his grounding in black southern Baptist tradition, which had within it a tradition of prophetic resistance to the corrupt tendencies of this world.[15] The historian Robert Franklin identifies King with a distinct "prophetic radicalism" in the black church, a stance that was rare but well enough established to be an obvious option to King. Building on Franklin, Lewis V. Baldwin's studies of King's cultural roots find all the elements of prophetic radicalism in exceptional black leaders such as Richard Allen, Harriet Tubman, and Frederick Douglass: there is no need for a "white" thinker to invent these elements, though it remains impossible to tell where any given black minister first heard or read a convincing version of them.[16] Fortunately, that does not matter. Where King ends up is what matters. King's striving to reconcile prophetic elements from his peculiar tradition with the best of the rest of American Protestantism, and with the best of the American civic tradition, made his thought converge with Niebuhr's.

King's relationship to Niebuhr is not a question of roots—historians have an occupational susceptibility to the genetic fallacy—but a question of affinities. If we hope to appreciate King and his message to America, we need to understand his grappling with Niebuhr's thought. Surely his background in black southern Baptist traditions prepared him to grapple, but that is all it did. Recent scholarship implies, in effect, that everything King needed to know he learned in kindergarten—his spiritual kindergarten, "the" black church. But it was the mature King who communicated with a world beyond his church, who brought much of his church with him into the "mainstream," who reminded his church and the mainstream how much they had in common.[17]

AN "AMERICAN DILEMMA" OR A "THEISTIC DILEMMA"?

King did not comment on Myrdal's *American Dilemma* until long after he finished school (and then only superficially).[18] But he explored something parallel to Myrdal's theme, what he called the "theistic dilemma," in considerable detail at Crozer. In an essay on "the Problem of Evil," King said that theists like himself have a "dilemma": their faith tells them that the power "behind all things is good. But on every hand the facts of life seem to contradict such a faith." As a Christian, King had to believe (as he stated in an earlier essay) in "eschatological hope." But he also had to be realistic about man's life on this earth before the Second Coming. He quoted John Stuart Mill: "Nearly all things which men are hanged or imprisoned for doing to one another are nature's every day performances. Nature kills, burns, starves, freezes, poisons." Time and again, King wrote, echoing Jeremiah and Job, history shows "the just suffering while the unjust prosper." Evil was "rampant" in the universe: "Only the superficial optimist who refuses to face the realities of life fails to see this patent fact." This argument was incompatible with any Myrdalian belief that psychic guilt would compel a nation to desist from evil practices. King insisted that the problem of evil cannot be fully solved, at least not by human beings on this earth.

King's "theistic dilemma" has a greater long-term significance. The same essay shows a connection between his rejection of optimism and his later calls upon his followers for self-sacrifice. Though King considered all "solu-

Martin Luther King Jr., the thoughtful prophet and eventual martyr, became a symbol of the civil rights struggle. His pessimism about human nature made him skeptical of voluntary, liberal progress and led him early in his career to adopt coercive, though nonviolent, strategies to achieve freedom. (© Bob Adelman/ Magnum Photos)

tions" to the problem of evil to be incomplete, he thought that one of them had great merit: the view that "the purpose of evil is to reform or to test." (This was superior to the theory that evil was a punishment for man's sin, since it responded to the Job- and Jeremiah-like objection that virtuous people suffer evil and evil people often avoid suffering.) King asked, following Edgar Sheffield Brightman, "Who can deny that many apparent evils turn out to be goods in disguise[?] Character often develops out of hardship. Unfortunate hereditary and environmental conditions often make great and noble souls. Suffering teaches sympathy."[19] King later encouraged his followers to go into lions' dens and to walk through valleys of the shadow of death. He told them that their sacrifices could force an unwilling system to make concessions, but even if they failed in this act of protest or in this life, "unearned suffering is redemptive." That phrase is a key to King's philosophy of life, one that owes much to the example of Jeremiah and other Hebrew Prophets. It is also King's gloss on the sacrifice of Jesus, his guide to the path of His footsteps.[20]

King's message came to a pragmatic, political point: the long-suffering people must suffer still more to deliver themselves from injustice. That is the crowning injustice of oppression: those who have already paid the price of injustice must pay further to undo it, while the perpetrators and beneficiaries of injustice get off scot-free—indeed, they will probably find a way to benefit from any decrease of injustice. But this is unavoidable. The oppressed are the only ones who will bear the burden of the struggle against their oppression because they are the only ones with an interest in doing so. To expect history to follow any other path is dangerously naive.

King's first known reference to Reinhold Niebuhr appears in an essay in 1949—his second year at Crozer—the same year Schlesinger published *The Vital Center.* King simply cites with approval Niebuhr's line, "It is unwise for Christians to claim any knowledge of either the furniture of heaven or the temperature of hell." The essay is largely a rejection of Karl Barth's neo-orthodoxy, very close to a position on reason as a path to God articulated by Edgar Sheffield Brightman.[21] That same year, King first referred to Gandhi, naming him as one of the persons "who greatly reveal the working Spirit of God."[22]

King's first full-fledged discussion of the doctrine of man (1949–50) is very Niebuhrian; this is significant because it is also the first academic essay to bring in his personal experiences with racism.[23] In the first paragraph, King explains that he is "going through a state of transition," at one time "leaning toward a mild neo-orthodox view of man" and at others "toward a liberal view of man." He suggests that his neo-orthodox moments may "root back to certain experiences that I had in the south with a vicious race problem." Some of these "made it very difficult for me to believe in the essential goodness of man." This is impossible to reconcile with Myrdal's optimistic view of man (or at any rate, Americans), which Myrdal offers as a result of his own immersion in the "race problem" in the South. King admits his "desire to be optimistic about human nature," but says that it is being tempered by experience and by his reading of "neo-orthodox theologians." In "this transitional stage"—King does not say how long it has been going on—he is trying "to synthesize the best in liberal theology with the best in neo-orthodox theology and come to some understanding of man." In this essay, King develops his understanding of Niebuhr, attributing to him the insistence that "men sin through intellectual and spiritual pride." On the basis of that point, King rejects liberal optimism, concluding, like Niebuhr, that "the modern Christian must see man as a guilty sinner who must ask forgiveness and be converted." King, like many casual readers at the time and since, mistakenly refers to Niebuhr as "neo-orthodox," but King's doctrine of man, rejecting orthodox pessimism *and* liberal optimism, is practically identical with Niebuhr's.[24]

Niebuhr becomes more prominent in King's graduate school writings at Boston University from 1951 to 1954. In his notes on Jeremiah in 1952–53, King suggests that "neo-orthodoxy" could help revive a prophetic movement. Neo-orthodox thinkers "call us back to a deeper faith in God" by rejecting, as Jeremiah did, "all forms of humanistic perfectionism." Though objecting to extreme forms of neo-orthodoxy, he finds the doctrine generally useful to "those of us who are opposed to humanism in the modern world" and who seek to make "a rational defense of theism." There is an urgency in these notes: supplanting faith in man with prophetic faith in God is "the need of the hour." This urgency related to the dangers King perceived in social inequality. Rejecting humanism entailed rejecting the rich, who glorified and found success in the City of Man. In notes on the Seventy-second Psalm, King wrote: "Christianity was born among the poor and died among the rich. Whenever Christianity has remained true to its prophetic mission, it has taken a deep interest in social justice." Whenever the church has abandoned the poor, there have been "disastrous consequences." Saving Christianity means reviving its Prophets' interest in the poor. "We must never forget that the success of communism in the world today is due to the failure of Christians to live [up] to the highest ethical ten[et]s inherent in its system."[25]

The scholarly work that has been done to show King's lack of originality (his frequently sloppy documentation and sometimes outright plagiarism) is most illuminating for the Boston years. The editors of his papers reveal a pattern (though they do not comment on it) that King is at his most original and his engagement with his sources is at its most direct—least derivative of the (often unacknowledged) secondary works—when writing about Niebuhr and Niebuhrian themes. King stresses Niebuhr's view that liberalism "vainly seeks to overcome [in]justice through purely moral and rational suasions." He notes Niebuhr's emphasis on the need for "coercion" to achieve justice, "for men are controlled by power, not mind alone. This the liberal failed to see." King follows Niebuhr's discussion of the "law of love," a theme King often returned to in later life. Niebuhr said, King observes, that

> if *agape* were a historical reality in the lives of men, government, ideally, would be unnecessary, since forceful suasions are irrelevant wherever a love for God is perfected. . . . Actually, however, government is very necessary, for men inevitably corrupt their potentialities of love through a lust for self security which outruns natural needs. Men must be restrained by force, else they will swallow up their neighbors. . . . The force of sinfulness is so stubborn a characteristic of human nature that it can only be restrained when the social unit is armed with both moral and physical might.

King never takes this antiliberal view of human nature to be the basis for acceptance of any particular government or of the status quo. Government is a necessity, but "Niebuhr makes it quite clear that government . . . must never be looked upon as divine." King alludes to Niebuhr's belief that Christianity, even orthodoxy, is sometimes subversive: "When government pretends to be divine, the Christian serves God rather than man. The Christian must constantly maintain a 'dialectical' attitude toward government." Quoting Niebuhr, King writes, democracy " 'arms the individual with political and constitutional power to resist the inordinate ambition of rulers, and to check the tendency of the community to achieve order at the price of liberty.' "

King is equally attentive to Niebuhr's insistence that the corruptions of power do not justify all actions of the powerless. "Niebuhr admits that there is risk in arming men with the power of resistance, but he sees the alternative risk as worse." Here King captures Niebuhr's somewhat negative, Churchillian defense of democracy: it is the best that limited, sinful man can do. "Niebuhr makes it clear that a perfect democracy is just as impossible to reach as either a perfect society or a perfect individual. The evils of democracy are patent." (King is distancing himself, perhaps without realizing it, from Dewey's more complete embrace of democracy.) King concludes that Niebuhr's analysis is "profound," and "with it I would find very little to disagree." The one place in the essay that is known to be unoriginal is where King adds that there is "one weakness" that he finds to disagree with. This point he cribs from an article by Walter Muelder (to which he gives substantial though not full credit), rehearsing some Personalist objections to Niebuhr's "inadequate" treatment of "the relative perfection which is the fact of Christian life." Otherwise, the essay appears to be pure King, an honest and direct engagement with the Niebuhrian source.[26]

In addition to being more original, King's work on Niebuhr is far less tainted by the flattery that seems to cloud his references to the only other contemporary theologians who have been identified as influences on King, the Boston Personalists. (These professors belabored the human "personality" that was always central to liberal ideas of man and Jesus. They also tried, with less intensity, to accommodate orthodox Protestant emphasis on God's personality and the intimate, unpredictable, irrational nature of God's relationship to individual Christians.) Some scholars suggest that the leading Personalist, Edgar Sheffield Brightman, is the culmination and synthesis of King's intellectual influences, the closest thing to a single intellectual model.[27] But there is reason to doubt this. The Personalists graded King every semester. King had no practical reason to flatter Niebuhr.

Whatever King's academic attraction to the Personalists, Niebuhr is the thinker King takes most often into his *public* statements, beginning with an essay he read to the Dialectical Society, a group of young intellectuals over which he presided in Boston. This point needs emphasis. Too many works on King offer an uncritical inventory of the ingredients of his mind—there is a little Rauschenbusch folded in with a little Niebuhr, a soupçon of neo-orthodoxy, a dash of Kant and Thoreau, all Hegelized together and suspended in a vast broth of Personalism (later inventories add that all this was superfluous after the primordial influence of "the" black church)—as a substitute for any analysis of *which* ideas make him historically significant. The Personalists loom large in King scholarship, it seems, simply because King spent more time in Boston and cranked out more pages under their influence than anywhere else. But no analysis shows a qualitative influence of the Personalists on King the public man, the leader of a mass movement—no analysis shows that Personalist ideas *matter* in the work King did as a civil rights leader. Do Personalist ideas differentiate King from thousands of preachers nobody has ever heard of? To understand Personalism is to say that that would be highly unlikely: Personalists are attractive because they absorb (and never seem to sort out) so many conflicting perspectives. The point is not that King read or cited Niebuhr more than, say, Brightman. Rather, it is that what makes King a world-historical figure is his Niebuhrian pessimism about human institutions and his Niebuhrian insistence that coercion is tragically necessary to achieve justice.

In 1954 King told the Dialectical Society that "Niebuhr differs from Barthianism." Unlike Niebuhr, King said, Karl Barth rejected the human experience of contact with God in biblical history. (This was somewhat unfair to Barth, but King followed Niebuhr in that unfairness.) "For Niebuhr, the only adequate religious expression of the human situation is a combination of this-worldly and other-worldly hopes." Niebuhr's synthesis "contains a realistic pessimism which balances the initial Renaissance optimism."

King then focused on the matter that had already drawn *him* away from liberalism: "Niebuhr's anthropology," King said, "is certainly the cornerstone of his thought."[28] There can be no doubt that King endorsed Niebuhr's view of man: "Niebuhr's anthropology is the necessary corrective of a kind of liberalism that too easily capitulated to modern culture."[29] In modern culture, which tended to reduce religion to ethics, "Man who has come so far in wisdom and decency may be expected to go much further as his methods of attaining and applying knowledge are improved." King rejected this modern "ethical religion." Despite its "humane" and "lofty" vision, such "ethical religion" clashed irreconcilably with his own knowledge and experience. "This particular sort of optimism has been discredited by the brutal logic of events. Instead of assured progress in wisdom and decency, man faces the ever present possibility of swift relapse not merely to animalism but into such calculated cruelty as no other animal can practice. Niebuhr reminds us of this on every hand."[30]

Since the Dialectical Society was apparently all-black, the charge made by Keith Miller and some black nationalist critics that King quoted "white" thinkers only when he hoped to manipulate white audiences could not apply.[31] (There is, however, no specific evidence to refute the charge with respect to King's references to Brightman and other Personalists in his papers at Crozer and Boston.)[32]

All the themes from the Dialectical Society discussion of Niebuhr recur in King's later work. It is Niebuhr, not Brightman or any other contemporary theologian, whom King quotes in his "Letter from the Birmingham City Jail" (1963) and his explanation of his intellectual sources in his *Playboy* interview (1965) (two public statements that are immune to the questions, often exaggerated in any case, of the influence of ghostwriters on King's thinking).[33] Niebuhr, or—to invoke a broader tradition behind Niebuhr— prophetic Christianity, is more of a key to what happened in King's public life than the mushy generalizations scholars make about "the" black church or "African-American tradition." It is no more useful to say that King was shaped by the black church than to say that he breathed air or was a Georgian. What sets him *off* from the black church is what makes him significant. Much of the time, black churches really did serve as opiates of the masses— as one of King's mentors, Benjamin Mays, coauthor of the long standard work, *The Negro's Church* (1933), complained.[34] What set King off from the black church is what set him off from the liberals—what led him out of both of those Egypts.[35]

BEYOND KING

Though most authors now acknowledge the roles played by Bayard Rustin, Glenn Smiley, Stanley Levison, Harris Wofford, and others in the writing of many of King's major works, Rustin noted that he and Levison were analyzing Martin and saying "how did he view these kinds of problems, what would be the way for him to tackle them?" It was not we directing him so much as we working with him and giving expression to ideals we knew he had or would quickly accept. . . . I don't like to write something for somebody where I know he is acting like a puppet. I want to be a real ghost and write what the person wants to say. And that is what I always knew was true in the case of Martin. I would never write anything that wasn't what he wanted to say.[36]

Again, the point is not the angels-on-a-pinhead question of where King's ideas ultimately came from, but the affinity of his deepest and most firmly held ideas with those of other prominent strategists of civil rights.

When he was not trying to be a ghost, Bayard Rustin exerted a strong behind-the-scenes influence on King and several later protesters. Rustin's philosophy was well established and well known before he joined the civil rights movement. He had been a Communist Youth League member before rejecting the Communists and taking up with the pacifist Fellowship of Reconciliation (FOR) and getting himself imprisoned for draft resistance. He was arrested for his individual protest against Jim Crow in Tennessee in 1942. That year, he saw a crisis coming in race relations. "The average Negro has largely lost faith in middle-class whites," he wrote. "In his hour of need he seeks not 'talk' but dynamic action. He looks upon the middle-class idea of long-term educational and cultural changes with fear and mistrust."

This was the antithesis of Myrdalian faith in the future. Rustin believed that the Negro was "only interested in what can be achieved immediately by political pressure to get jobs, decent housing, and education for his children." For Rustin, the only practical way was nonviolent direct action, in which he had faith because he had seen it work. In his conception there was no moral purism or faith in the oppressor's conscience. "Nonviolence as a method has within it the demand for terrible sacrifice and long suffering, but, as Gandhi has said, 'freedom does not drop from the sky.' One has to struggle and be willing to die for it."

Rustin saw the importance of southern black religious culture in the coming crisis. He cannot have absorbed this sense through childhood experience, as King might have, for Rustin was a northerner and former Quaker. He made little reference to Christian motivations in his theoretical and tactical writings. He later criticized the southern black church for its ties to the white power structure. Still, Rustin was able to discover what King learned about the generally latent but potentially great power of southern black religion. A gifted musician who had toured with Leadbelly and Josh White, Rustin was particularly drawn to what he called the "tragic" voice of black spirituals. The Negro had developed many resources and qualities that gave him strength and a willingness to acknowledge "his own share of guilt."

These resources and qualities, some of them nonreligious, would help ward off self-destructive bitterness. "But above all," Rustin noted, "[the Negro] possesses a rich religious heritage and today finds the church the center of his life."[37]

Rustin yearned to put that heritage in motion. He saw Jesus as a positive example—"this fanatic whose insistence on love thrust at the very pillars of stable society," he wrote in an "Easter Greeting" to supporters in 1952. Everyone saw Jesus as a lot of trouble, but even crucifixion could not get rid of Him. "Easter in every age . . . recalls the imminence of the impossible victory, the power of the impotent weak." Rustin took the opportunity to note that Jesus' followers "need to be reminded that Easter *is* the reality, and that the awesome structures of pomp and power are in the process of disintegration at the moment of their greatest strength." He was surely aware that he was echoing the Prophets' scorn for human institutions. But he could not have known that he was prophetically anticipating a key phrase in a new prophet's greatest speech: "Easter is the symbol of hope resurrected out of a tomb of hopelessness."[38]

Rustin worked with A. Philip Randolph's March on Washington Movement on and off in the 1940s–50s and participated in the Congress of Racial Equality (CORE—formed in 1944 by Rustin's rival in the Fellowship of Reconciliation, James Farmer). With CORE and FOR, Rustin helped organize the first Freedom Ride, the Journey of Reconciliation, through the upper South in 1947. This earned him a twenty-two-day sentence on a chain gang in rural North Carolina. He memorably justified the "higher law" motive in civil disobedience, citing Supreme Court Justice Robert Jackson at the Nuremberg trials to the effect that "men are individually responsible for their acts, and are not to be excused for following unjust demands made upon them by governments."[39] He emphasized again and again the necessity of sacrifice for peace and freedom: neither came without a price. As a not-too-well closeted homosexual before the 1970s, Rustin had insight from another perspective into the pariah status that was part of the sacrifice of prophets. Identifying himself with "the 'now group,' the group which insists that change for the better must take place immediately and far-reachingly," he told his friend Selma Platt that he always had a "wonderful experience" when he was "associated with people who take an all out position." Historically, "the gadfly . . . has stirred men into action," but "we must be prepared to be looked upon as queer." Socrates, Luther, Lincoln, and Thoreau were "looked upon as queer": their contemporaries saw them as "foolish, unrealistic, idealistic, premature, and doing more harm than good."[40] There was a practical side to this, however: "Only extreme behavior," he wrote A. J. Muste in 1950, "can reach to the real conscience through the veneer of fear, cynicism, and frustration today."[41]

In 1955 Rustin helped produce a famous pamphlet on active, as opposed to passive, nonviolence, entitled *Speak Truth to Power*. Rustin wrote most of the pamphlet but removed his name from the list of authors out of fear that his recent arrest on a morals charge would impair its reception.[42] Its acknowledged authors were A. J. Muste, Stephen Cary, Amiya Chakravarty, and other members of the American Friends Service Committee's executive board. Rustin seemed to be writing the pamphlet at them as much as for them, wishing to shake up the staid, often aloof and self-righteous world of pacifism. That was almost as important to him as shaking up the churches and other structures of modern oppression. The worshippers of peace, like the worshippers of progress, were in need of a chastening. For a time, some of them seemed to get it from Rustin.

Speak Truth to Power began by quoting the gloomy predictions of Jacob Burckhardt and Henry Adams, suggesting that their nightmares—the worst nightmares of the nineteenth century—had already come true. The argument was antitriumphant. The main result of World War II, Rustin wrote, was the "inevitable" conflict between the expansionist imperial powers of the United States and the USSR. "This is an age of violence. . . . Centralized authority, rather than individual conscience, is the dominant force in large segments of East and West alike. . . . The new technology has been perverted to the deification of the state at the expense of the individual, and for millions there is neither bread nor freedom."

With that opening, the pamphlet went on to acknowledge the practical and moral necessity of coercion and force. The authors adopted a "revolutionary policy of peace." Sticking to their nonviolent guns, they faced "the possibility that hatred has gone so far, and injustice has penetrated so deeply, that even a revolutionary policy of peace"—a policy that included aid to the revolutions that were breaking out all over the world—"could not prevent international aggression." Faced with aggression, a nation that disarmed according to the authors' new policy would not "abjectly surrender and let an invader run over and enslave it as is often alleged." On the contrary, it would resist. Gandhi's India was not the only example of nonviolent resistance that worked. But not all circumstances would allow such resistance to succeed. However slim nonviolent resisters' chances were in general, they were better than those of policymakers who thought only of violent responses in a world of nuclear weapons: "Victory in any ensuing holocaust is clearly impossible for anyone." Victory, as a practical matter, had become meaningless. Its moral preferability was beside the point. (Since the Middle Ages, Christian doctrines of "Just War" had emphasized that peace was morally preferable to war, but once war had become unavoidable, a commander's duty to avoid defeat was moral as well as practical.)

The authors were not "suggest[ing] that everything would proceed in idyllic fashion and that no suffering would occur in a non-violent resistance campaign. We have tried to make clear that readiness to accept suffering—

rather than inflict it on others—is the essence of non-violent life, and that we must be prepared if called upon to pay the ultimate price." Indeed, wherever there was no "readiness to sacrifice . . . non-violent resistance cannot be effective." But if men all over were "willing to spend billions of treasure and countless lives in war, they cannot dismiss the case for non-violence by saying that in a non-violent struggle people might be killed!" Nonviolent resistance demanded "greater discipline, more arduous training, and more courage than its violent counterpart." A passive, comfort-seeking pacifism "will fail just as surely as an untrained and undisciplined army would fail in war." Nor could active nonviolence, if ever attempted on a national scale, entertain illusions of economy: "A people ready to pour billions into military preparations" would have to be prepared to put "research and training" into the other mode of fighting, too. *Speak Truth to Power* did not try to con society into peacefulness by arguing that peace would be cheaper than war.[43]

The pamphlet was greeted as an original and invigorating contribution to discussions of war and peace in the new Nuclear Age. Among those to join the lively debate in the *Progressive*, where it was first published in October 1955, were Niebuhr, George F. Kennan, Hans Morgenthau, Lewis Mumford, and Dwight Macdonald. They were generally unconvinced by its argument. But some of them were able to acknowledge a difference between Rustin's views and what most of them had long disdained in pacifism.[44] Rustin had little time to get caught up in—or to worry about missing out on—that debate. A few days after the boycott broke out in Montgomery in December 1955, the liberal white southern novelist Lillian Smith wrote King to say that Rustin, whose knowledge of Gandhian tactics might be useful, was coming to town. At that point, King claimed that he knew almost nothing about Gandhi and nonviolent tactics.[45] But the philosophical affinities between King and Rustin could not have been stronger, and Rustin's organizational and promotional talents served King greatly for the rest of his life. Scholars have underplayed these strong initial affinities, it seems to me, because they focus too much on the technical issue of nonviolence and not enough on the deeper philosophical convictions that made the particular *kind* of nonviolence that King embraced appear to be irresistibly close to him. The philosophical convictions also explain why King adapted to coercive nonviolence so quickly and became such a virtuoso practitioner of it.[46]

An article written by Rustin but published with few changes under King's name in April 1956 (King's first publication, unless one counts a youthful letter to the editor in 1946) explained the movement.[47] Though Rustin did not mention Gunnar Myrdal by name, he refuted the core of the Myrdal thesis. He began by accepting Myrdal's first two premises: fundamental American values conflict with the pervasive practice of discrimination, and this creates psychic stress. In Rustin's words, "In their relations with Negroes, white people discovered that they had rejected the very center of their own ethical professions. They could not face the triumph of their lesser instincts and simultaneously have peace within." But Rustin's conclusion was diametrically opposed to Myrdal's: the practice won out over the ethical professions, and ultimately the ethical professions disappeared. To Rustin, white people "rationalized" their dehumanization of black people, "insisting that the unfortunate Negro, being less than human, deserved and even enjoyed second-class status. They argued that his inferior social, economic, and political position was good for him." White people came to believe that the Negro was exempt from their belief in progress. And any cognitive dissonance that white people may once have felt disappeared. "White men soon came to forget that the southern social culture and all its institutions had been organized to perpetuate this rationalization. They observed a caste system and quickly were conditioned to believe that its social results, which they had created, actually reflected the Negro's innate and true nature."

To Rustin—and to King, if King's agreement to publish Rustin's argument over his own signature has any meaning—what made the situation unstable was not the mental conflict within the white mind. Rather, it was a change on the other side of the racial divide. "Gradually the Negro masses in the South began to re-evaluate themselves—a process that was to change the nature of the Negro community and doom the social patterns of the South. We discovered that we had never really smothered our self-respect and that we could not be at one with ourselves without asserting it. From this point on, the South's terrible peace was rapidly undermined by the Negro's new and courageous thinking and his ever-increasing readiness to organize and to act." In the face of all this, "the white South desperately clung to its old patterns." The Negro's reevaluation of himself was "revolutionary."

FORCE, NOT MERELY SUASION

Black thinking was now "revolutionary," according to Rustin, because black people were abandoning faith in white people's struggles of conscience. And they were abandoning faith in the NAACP's Chinese water torture of incremental gains. Against Myrdal's gradualist prescriptions and his belief that most black organizations rejected immediatism, Rustin wrote: "Our Church Is Becoming Militant." Whereas Myrdal favored the NAACP over rival black organizations, insisting that "revolutionary" organization would only hurt the Negro, Rustin embraced "revolutionary" organizing; he found it eminently practical. Under the heading "Economics Is Part of

Our Struggle," he wrote, "We have observed that small Negro shops are thriving as Negroes find it inconvenient to walk downtown to the white stores." White folk changed as a result of such concrete, forceful demonstrations, not because of internal tensions or moral appeals to their better half. White merchants—not white moralists or preachers or liberals—soon developed greater respect for Negro customers, Rustin wrote, and Negroes themselves found "a new respect for the proper use of our dollar." Nonviolence, to Rustin, was not primarily an educational medium but an instrument of coercion. It might, to be sure, shine a new light on the error in white people's thinking, but it was also "a new and powerful weapon."[48]

Rustin's picture of the southern liberal, "the enlightened white southerner," clinches his disagreement with Myrdal. According to Rustin, liberals were discovering that their "gradual approach" of "putting straws on a camel's back" was "dangerous." Their approach ultimately had "revolutionary implications," but the "violence" that came in reaction to the boycott had unfortunately "immobilized the liberals and most of the white church leaders." Unlike the civil rights protesters, who accepted that they would provoke violent retaliation when they took a stand against powerful interests, the liberals "have no answer for dealing with or absorbing violence." Liberals, including William Faulkner, only end up, Rustin observed disdainfully, "begging for retreat, lest 'things get out of hand and lead to violence.'" Rustin found such hypocrisy, which he seemed to think was inextricably linked with liberalism, intolerable. Faulkner was encouraging Negroes "to accept injustice, exploitation and indignity for a while longer," Rustin said. "It is hardly a moral act to encourage others patiently to accept injustice which he himself does not endure." In contrast to the liberal counsel of delay and retreat, Rustin's coercive nonviolent method could "absorb the violence that is inevitable in social change wherever deep-seated prejudices are challenged." It alone "permits a struggle to go on with dignity and without the need to retreat."[49]

Rustin's most famous public statement came in 1965 with his "From Protest to Politics," published in *Commentary*. Rustin referred to what had happened in the South in the previous eleven years as a "revolution" that could no longer be contained there. In the recent battle of Birmingham (1963–64), the region's most industrialized city, the civil rights movement began attacking "areas of discrimination which were not so remote from Northern experience as were Jim Crow lunch counters." Now the movement, moving northward, would concentrate on de facto segregation "in our most fundamental socio-economic institutions." Rustin again refuted Myrdal's prediction, without mentioning Myrdal: in these institutions, he said, things had gotten worse. "More Negroes are unemployed today than in 1954, and the unemployment gap between the races is wider."[50]

In 1965 Rustin still had hope, but in getting to his hope, he had to dis-

Bayard Rustin, strategic planner, shared King's view of man but could not abide what he called King's "fundamentalist" view of God.
(AP/Wide World Photos)

pense with what he saw as the exaggerated forms of liberal idealism that had become fashionable among baby boomers. This may have been the most penetrating critique of Myrdalian optimism expressed in the 1960s. Rustin thought that gestures of extreme radicalism were nothing but a naked form of such optimism. Some vocal civil rights activists, he observed, concluded that "the only viable strategy is shock." By shock, these activists aimed above all to expose "the hypocrisy of white liberals." The advocates of shock "are often described as the radicals of the movement, but they are really its moralists. They seek to change white hearts—by traumatizing them." These pseudo-radicals applaud Malcolm X because "they think he can frighten white people into doing the right thing." They are apparently convinced that "at the core of the white man's heart lies a buried affection for Negroes." All they had to do, they seemed to think, was push the white man closer to his own true core of feeling. For Rustin, however, "hearts are not the relevant issue; neither racial affinities nor racial hostilities are rooted there. It is institutions—social, political, and economic[—]" that need to be "reconstructed *today*[,] and let the ineluctable gradualism of history govern the formation of a new psychology." [51] Reality had to change first. And reality had to be changed by coercion. Hearts and minds would follow. Rustin's causal arrow pointed in precisely the opposite direction from Myrdal's.

The irresponsibility of his fellow protesters, their "lack of political sense," led Rustin to his most original and most poetic observation about the demands of public life. He looked at the other side of the question Arthur Schlesinger had fudged with his notion of power checked by "accountability." Rustin observed, "There is a strong moralistic strain in the civil rights movement which would remind us that power corrupts, forgetting that the absence of power also corrupts." This is Niebuhrian. Niebuhr never put the point so strongly, but he often articulated this idea, a counterpoint to his main theme that power among groups is amoral. Niebuhr insisted that although power corrupts, it is morally necessary to use power to fight injustice—as pacifists (by his definition of the word) failed to do. In fighting against injustice, the oppressed would inevitably create injustices of their own. But the only alternative to dirtying one's hands—bloodying one's hands—with power was morally worse. To be complacent about automatic progress was dangerously naive. To withdraw from the clash of ignorant armies into moral purism was prideful as well as irresponsible. [52]

Looking back on the civil rights movement's religious dimensions years later, Rustin, who was never comfortable with enthusiastic Christianity, made a pragmatic, almost apologetic point about it that echoed Niebuhr's uncomfortable stress on the need for "emotionally potent oversimplifications." "The high moral tone of the Baptist preacher," Rustin said, "well suited the movement. . . . The movement needed an emotional dimension to whip up the enthusiasm of people who might soon be faced with economic hardship or physical danger. And no one could bring a crowd to an emotional pitch like the black preacher." The preacher's "perseverance and courage" became "more important than intellectual or political analysis" in protest. Nothing like the movement had ever happened before in America, and probably nothing like it would ever happen again.[53]

NONVIOLENCE IS NOT NECESSARILY
THE HEART OF THE MATTER: MODJESKA SIMKINS

Before King and Rustin came together, Modjeska Simkins, secretary of the NAACP branch in South Carolina in the 1940s, was doing her all to arouse the black masses of her state. She, too, had a catastrophic, pessimistic view of human history. Simkins denounced her fellow Carolinians' confidence in the normal evolution of society and urged extreme self-sacrifice to alter history's course. Like Rustin, King, and Niebuhr, she had little faith in moral suasion and emphasized the necessity of coercion. Interestingly, she said nothing about nonviolence. Her witty, withering denunciations of white gradualists and the black "'ain't ready yet' conclave" are prophetic in tone, often self-consciously so. The model activist she holds up is not Jeremiah or Amos or Isaiah, but Job, whose story is in some ways more prophetic, more pessimistic, than that of the Prophets proper. To Simkins, Job was a "minority of one" (a figure George Orwell also used repeatedly). Job kept his faith in the face of the most overwhelming tragedy and defeat. Simkins holds up Job—and occasionally Jesus and other biblical heroes—as admirable and even realistic models.[54]

Though a representative of the secular, bureaucratic NAACP—the kind of institution in which Myrdal had faith—Simkins was a deeply religious, deeply radical leader. As such, she was part of a pattern historians have noticed recently of divergence of the NAACP's national office from the tone and tactics of many local NAACP activists.[55] (The national office tried to restrain Simkins, and by 1957 she left the organization.) Like most prophets, Simkins was as hard on ordinary religion as she was on outright unbelief. She denounced "the made-in-America brand of 'Christianity,'" which "smell[s] to high heaven. Living here in the 'Bible Belt,' we surpass the rest of the Nation in 'stomping' the church floors and desecrating our highways with Bible verse signs. Inscribing these verses on the tables of our hearts and living them daily are white horses of another color." She punctuated this lesson by quoting God's rebuke of Cain (Genesis 4:10): "'The voice of thy brother's blood crieth unto me from the ground.'"[56]

In dangerous times like hers, Simkins had no patience with liberal gradualism. In 1947, referring to a rare moderate among prominent South Carolina newspapermen, she wrote, "George A. Buchanan of the Columbia Rec-

Modjeska Simkins, fiery speaker, columnist, and secretary of the South Carolina branch of the NAACP, excoriated the "black Quislings" of the "ain't ready yet conclave," along with white segregationists. (Modjeska Monteith Simkins Papers, Modern Political Collections, University of South Carolina)

ord, a man of great stature and without a peer as an editor, became quite upset the other day." Buchanan seemed to want to agree with the spirit of the report of President Truman's Committee on Civil Rights (which provoked the Dixiecrat effort to secede from the Democratic Party). Instead, he wrung his hands over its "Poor Timing." Buchanan thought that the report would backfire, like so many immoderate gestures for Negro rights. The report came out just in time to become a campaign issue in Mississippi, where demagogues like John Rankin, "who have been trying to make 'white supremacy' the issue," had until recently "been having hard sledding. Now the civil rights committee's report has gone for to do what Rankin, himself, couldn't do, handicapping those Mississippians who have been working to secure the election of a man who may represent the state with dignity and fairness." Simkins's response was curt: "Well, any time may be the wrong time for weak and unprincipled people to do right. The thing to do with the residents of Bilboland . . . is to give them the works and let them, in plain defiance, elect whom they choose. If they are willing, for spite, to suffer the embarrassment and disgrace that comes from representation by buffoons, bombasts, boneheads, and bullies, 'let the driver roll!' The petting time is over!"[57]

Simkins saved her most caustic venom for the "false leaders" of her own race. Writing about the Palmetto State Teachers' Association, which had recently abandoned its gradualism and "thrown its full strength behind the

S.C. Conference of the NAACP in its fight for first-class educational opportunities for all," Simkins rejoiced in the triumph of her allies over the complacency and complicity of ordinary Negro leaders. Now led by "able and fearless men," the teachers' association had been "lifted" out of the "quagmire," where it had been "held for years by the diabolic maneuverings of the 'ain't ready yet boys—and girls' [—] and certain officials in the state education set-up." False leaders had gotten too comfortable. "As long as the 'misleaders' were fat and warm, and smart enough to keep the blinders on jittery, half-paid, hungry teachers, they just knew that everything was 'copesetic.'" But now "the fog" of the "misleaders" had cleared. Now the "fifth-column" had been exposed. She elsewhere referred to such Negro leaders as "black Quislings," and she took a certain delight in outing them. "Smoking out the 'misleaders' and 'sell-outs' was not easy, but it was most stimulating and satisfying sport." Purged of traitors, she said, the new leadership "can become invincible."[58]

A speech Simkins made in 1948 on the economic plight of Negroes and the need for "strong leadership in the churches"—an institution also plagued by Quislings—conveys her Jeremiah-like tone. The general trend of events was no cause for optimism, she emphasized. Rather, it called for extreme action. She believed it a great sin to let historical development take its course:

> Why do we chafe and lather ourselves on issues that face us . . . in the South and in the Nation today[?] We could sit nonchalantly by and let things go as they will. But—one who can look into the trusting bright eyes of little black children and do nothing about the problems that they face from birth is not fit. We know that countless generations must pass this way.
>
> EIGHTY YEARS AFTER—in the early part of the FOURTH GENERATION removed from physical bondage, we are all free-born American citizens, MOST MISERABLE in status. But that is not the most pathetic thought. Too many of us are of all American souls, most satisfied, satisfied to move slowly along like contented cows, swishing flies and chewing cud and following the beaten path of the common herd.

Simkins's notes indicate that her speech climaxed on the great choice: "GRADUALISM VS PROGRESSIVISM." In this and other speeches, she repeats, in the King James idiom, *"the old order changeth."* But she rejects the idea that it changeth automatically or gradually: "We must work for change, we must welcome change, we must profit by change. We are in an era of radical revolution of thought. Thinkers who are 'hide-bound' have no place in the present scheme of things." Again, she was ruthless in rooting out traitors and defeatists in her own race: "We must keep the EAGLE EYE out for 'misleaders' within our own racial ranks. There are demagogues, self-seekers, and crooks in every race. We must BEWARE—and summarily OSTRACI[Z]E those who would sell out their own race to attain or to keep places of prestige, power, and profits for themselves. (High paid teachers and principals who 'brag.')"[59]

In a later speech (ca. 1960), Simkins likened black people as a whole to Job and other suffering knights of faith. Her outline read:

> Like ourselves—Job in great struggle against power. In Ephesians 6:12 we find, "For we wrestle not against flesh and blood, but against principalities and powers, against the rulers of darkness of this world, against spiritual wickedness in high places.["] Make no mistake. That is where we are tonight. Wrestling against evil in high places—against poor, disfranchised, various forms of racial and sexual abuse, obvious and subtle. . . . We are striving to exist in an alien society.

For all her rhetorical thunder and lightning, Simkins had a Machiavellian pragmatism about power, developed through years of organizing "Negro work" in the Tuberculosis Association, as well as civil rights activity. She stressed the importance of "coalition and confrontation." She even spoke of "HOSTAGES," though it is unclear whether she meant that her followers should plan to take hostages or that they were being held as hostages. She gave no false assurance of easy victory. A battle against "OBSTINATE OPPOSITION" and "BLACK QUISLINGS" demanded "FULL DEDICATION TO CAUSE * NEVER TIRING * STRIVING ALWAYS TO BE ON TARGET." To win, God's warriors would not only have to change the way people think, but also to make the changed people vote: "Realize that politicians cannot be changed." God's warriors would also have to develop power through self-discipline and sacrifice: "We must build economic strength—security—develop thrift."[60] Simkins spent much of her life practicing and perfecting such tactics. With King, Rustin, and God knows how many less visible figures, she left a legacy of thought and experience that later rebels drew upon.

4

Prophetic Christian Realism and
the 1960s Generation

Though it is harder to draw a bead on the younger activists in the
Student Nonviolent Coordinating Committee (SNCC) who flooded
the civil rights movement after 1960,[1] it is nonetheless clear that many of
the important ones had prophetic ideas about human nature similar to those
of the older generation and based their strategies on those ideas. The SNCC
activists drew their views from a variety of sources, some of which are difficult to trace. Bayard Rustin remained a strong influence on SNCC for many
years. The *Student Voice*, SNCC'c newspaper, quoted Rustin approvingly on
many occasions and noted his appearances and speeches at SNCC retreats
and strategy workshops. Rustin stands out as having influenced both the
older movement, centered around Martin Luther King and the Southern
Christian Leadership Conference (SCLC), and the shorter-lived but generally more visible student movement.[2]

JAMES LAWSON

James Lawson had a more sustained and direct influence on SNCC, or at
least on one of its major subgroups, than Rustin.[3] A veteran of the nonviolent struggles of the 1940s, Lawson was stewarding a group of students in
Nashville, Tennessee, who were waiting for an opportunity to apply nonviolent force, when the sit-ins broke out in Greensboro, North Carolina,
in 1960.[4] Better prepared and organized than most other young people who
flocked to the movement, the Nashville students had an authority and prestige in SNCC's early years that made them prime movers. Lawson's overall
influence on SNCC was second only to that of Ella Baker, whose contributions were by all accounts organizational rather than philosophical or strategic.[5] Lawson, though a year older than Martin Luther King, probably had

a greater intellectual influence on SNCC than any other figure.[6] The historians Francis Broderick and August Meier go so far as to say that Lawson was "largely responsible for the moral fervor, philosophical sophistication, and exemplary courage that made the Nashville group the most dynamic student movement between 1960 and 1962."[7]

Lawson was a devoted student of philosophy and theology, as well as a veteran of nonviolent warfare. In 1960 he drafted SNCC's original "Statement of Purpose": "the philosophical or religious ideal of nonviolence [is] the foundation of our purpose, the presupposition of our faith, and the manner of our action." This faith grew "from Judaic-Christian traditions" and sought "a social order of justice permeated by love." Racial integration was only a first step toward this order. In the short run, the technique would embolden oppressed peoples to action: "Through nonviolence, courage displaces fear; love transforms hate . . . hope ends despair . . . faith reconciles doubt. . . . The redemptive community super[s]edes systems of gross social immorality." Though Lawson emphasized moral suasion or "appealing to conscience," and was more effusive than many predecessors about "love," which he called the "central motif" of his philosophy, he attended to the practical aspect of nonviolent force, as Rustin and King and Niebuhr had done. Nonviolent action, he said, "matches the capacity of evil to inflict suffering with an even more enduring capacity to absorb evil."[8]

Despite his emphasis on love, Lawson had a fighter's assertiveness and dissatisfaction with the world. His father, a pistol-packing AME-Zion minister who preached a gospel of liberation in this life and promoted the NAACP and Urban League in Alabama and South Carolina, taught his sons to fight anybody, even bigger kids, who called them "nigger." But after Lawson's victory in one such encounter, his mother persuaded him that winning fights did not do any good. He later referred to this discussion with his mother as a kind of revelation or conversion. He did not acquire the vocabulary of nonviolent resistance until college in the late 1940s, but the core of his faith was formed that day.[9] In his freshman year at Baldwin-Wallace College in Berea, Ohio, Lawson was exposed to the work of A. J. Muste, Glenn Smiley, Bayard Rustin, and James Farmer. He subscribed to the Fellowship of Reconciliation's monthly magazine, *Liberation*, and read Gandhi's autobiography and Niebuhr's *Children of Light, Children of Darkness*.[10]

Lawson was in India when he read about the Montgomery Bus Boycott of 1955–56. After returning to the United States in 1956 to study theology at Oberlin, he met Martin Luther King, who urged him to move south and work for civil rights. Lawson took a job as field secretary for FOR in Nashville, where he began organizing students and helped to set up the first affiliate of the SCLC.[11] In 1958 Lawson joined King and the white southern minister Glenn Smiley (Rustin's replacement from FOR) in traveling around the South, establishing SCLC chapters and teaching strategy.

After enrolling at Vanderbilt to complete his theological studies, Lawson, who had participated in FOR sit-ins in the border states years before, organized practice sit-ins in 1959 among younger fellow students. These included future SNCC leaders Diane Nash, Marion Barry, John Lewis, and James Bevel. Their plan was to stage sit-ins in downtown department stores. They began acting on the plan immediately after the Greensboro sit-in captured headlines in February 1960. In April 1960 King identified Lawson's students as the most disciplined and organized in the movement. By then, all of Nashville's downtown stores had agreed to desegregate and Vanderbilt had expelled Lawson for his political activities.[12]

The radical dissatisfaction with the status quo in Lawson's "Statement of Purpose" for SNCC—like the love he preached—was in his own words "extreme." Like King and Niebuhr, but unlike liberals, Lawson believed that the normal course of human society was corrupting, sinful. Normal life was so morally offensive that it required extreme action. In his address to the founding conference of SNCC in Raleigh, North Carolina, in April 1960, Lawson suggested an answer to the liberals' yearning for the commitment and excitement that their own humanistic faith lacked. He began by noting the sudden change in the visibility of the younger generation. Before February 1960, young people had been written off as "'silent,' 'uncommitted,' or 'beatnik.'" But now it was clear that black students were no longer going to take their oppression sitting down. And not just black students: it was also obvious "that all the white American students were simply waiting in suspension; waiting for that cause, that ideal, that event, that 'actualizing of their faith'" that would allow them to "speak powerfully to their nation and world." Not surprisingly, Lawson identified this as a religious event. Students all over were now bearing witness in a way that was unprecedented "in the history of the Negro or in the history of the nation. . . . God has brought this to pass."

The advent of the civil rights movement was, in Lawson's eyes, a reaction against "the insensitiveness of affluent society." The media did not understand this and misrepresented it. The movement's momentum could not be stopped by the "many merchants zealously smothering their Negro customers with courtesy for normal services." The student protesters' "essential message" was not just about police brutality, or the rule of law, or integration. The protesters forced something greater, an "existential moment," on American society.[13]

Segregation, to Lawson, was just one of many sins rampant in America, one of many forms of pride: "The Christian favors the breaking down of racial barriers because the redeemed community of which he is already a citizen recognizes no barriers dividing humanity. The Kingdom of God, as in heaven so on earth, is the distant goal of the Christian." Negroes as well as white folk were guilty of pretending that segregation could be lived

James Lawson, whose study group nurtured the radicalism of students who went on to lead SNCC. He is shown here being arrested at Kelly Miller Smith's church in Nashville, 1960. The marquee featured Smith's sermon, "Forgive them, Father, for they know not what they do." Lawson said that the movement had "convicted us of sin"; it aimed not just at segregation, but at the whole "affluent society." (© Bettmann/Corbis)

with. Sin, evil, demanded complete renunciation and opposition, not grad-ual "progress." Granted, some progress had been achieved, but too little progress had cost too much. The cost was not so much in the sacrifices of the protesters (though those were considerable) as in the lies that well-meaning black and white moderates told themselves about how the grad-ual progress would some day lead to sufficient renunciation of segregation. He said, "The nonviolent effort has convicted us of sin." "Us" meant black or white people who believed that "progress," which usually meant tinker-ing and tokenism, was sufficient.[14] The other side of convicting one's fel-low Americans of sin, Lawson observed, was the movement's assertion that "the pace of change is too slow." He added, with a plaintive flourish, "All of Africa will be free before the American Negro attains first-class citi-zenship."[15] America's "existential moment" embraced far more than racial issues: the sit-in movement was "a judgment upon middle-class, conven-tional, half-way efforts to deal with radical social evil."[16]

IMMEDIATISM AND THE PRACTICALITY OF
RENOUNCING THIS WORLD: FANNIE LOU HAMER

It might be tempting to think that such radical ideas were the sole posses-sion of fanatical clergymen and intellectuals who came into the movement. It might be tempting to think that the ordinary rank and filers in rural Mis-sissippi had more practical, down-to-earth motives, motives related to bet-tering their miserable economic condition and gaining minimal rights of citizenship.[17] And probably many—for all we know, most—of them did.

Yet Fannie Lou Hamer, often regarded (even by historians) as a symbol of ordinary rank and filerdom, warned the northern students who went to Mississippi in the summer of 1964 (about four-fifths of them white) that they would find nothing ordinary in that state. She was an uneducated, poor, black, rural southerner. The students, like subsequent historians, saw in her an authentic representative of the down-to-earth reality they yearned keenly to understand and to redeem. (My own view is that she would stand out as extraordinary in any demographic category, but no matter: that does not mean she was wrong about her fellow poor black Mississippians.)[18] She warned the students that a basic reality they would have to deal with was a religious commitment among the masses they were trying to help, which would seem extreme to them. Hamer knew that the students were not evan-gelical Christians. If they had religious feelings, they were mostly of the modernist, liberal variety. She knew that many of the students were skep-tics: "Don't talk to me about atheism," she told them. "If God wants to start a movement then hooray for God." Whatever the students' own concep-tion of their role, she told them that they represented an answer to the faith of black Mississippians like herself. "Faith is the substance of things hoped for, the evidence of things not seen. . . . Our religion is very important to us—you'll have to understand that."[19]

Hamer gave an interviewer her view of progress in 1965. She had been beaten, jailed, and harassed for her attempts to vote. Each night she wondered whether her house would be bombed. "And [this] is in America, what is called a free society. . . . And . . . they do a little something now that maybe three or four years they'll do a little something else that bring us gradually what's supposed to [have] been ours for one hundred years. You know that's really disgusting. And it's sickening. And that's the reason I stay in my fight." She was not fighting for equal rights, she said: if she were equal with the senators and other officials of Mississippi, that would mean "I wouldn't be as much as I am now because I would be a thief and a robber and a murderer and the biggest liar on earth." The authorities "tell us today that yes, we're having progress. And just year after year we're killed for no reason at all." Only when the white kids were killed in 1964 did things start to change. The country was "sick" and would survive only if people who were "really concerned about human beings" worked at it.

Skepticism about human institutions was part of Hamer's skepticism about progress. Mainstream civil rights organizations were not sufficiently cut off from the divisive ambitions of their leaders. The NAACP, she declared, stood for the National Association for the Advancement of Certain People. "They like important roles and any way they can squeeze themselves in the machine." NAACP leaders tried to buy her out and control what she said on speaking engagements. "So that's the way I work," she explained: "I have to stay without money." Nor were churches a comfortable place for prophets like her. There is no reason to think that she was merely referring to the white church when she said that the church "played the role of the church for the past hundred years and failed to do what th[e] church should have done." The normal kind of leadership, black and white, "has mostly been bourgeois," she said, too willing to compromise. Speaking of the young people who went to Mississippi with SNCC, she said that she had "seen more Christianity there than I've ever seen in the church." The SNCC activists were scorned and reviled, but they "were willing to go into areas and . . . [be] cut off in the area, in the rural area and they work right with the people. They work with the people that's poor, they work with the people that's never had a chance to be treated as a human being." Some had "given their lives for the cause of human justice. There's not many Christians in these churches that's willing to do that." The churches generally "have failed." She cited Luke 4:18: "'The spirit of the Lord is upon me because he has anointed me to preach the gospel to the poor.' It was his purpose here, was speakin and preachin to the poor. So mostly what the middle class, bourgeois white and black, cause I've seen white Toms and Negro

Toms. They concerned about the person who's already got somethin. . . . And that's the hypocrisy of this country." Building on the adage that the most segregated hour in America was ten o'clock on Sunday morning, she observed that that was the hour "when you see black and white hypocrites goin' to church from all over the country." White people would support change but not let a black person sit next to them: That "couldn't be Christianity because the 17th chapter of Acts in the 26th verse there it has 'made of one blood all nations.'" It was "really time for America to wake up."[20]

Hamer was not surprised that the nation failed to look gratefully at the people who devoted themselves to waking it up. It bashed them as it would an alarm clock. Asked if hers was a new kind of religion, she referred to the Beatitudes in Matthew 5, which her transcriber rendered as: "When men shall revile you and they shall prosecute you and shall say all manner of evil against you falsely for my sake, rejoice and be exceedingly glad for great is your reward in heaven for so they prosecuted the prophets which was before you."[21]

In another interview in 1965, Hamer explained her prophetic compulsion to renounce and denounce the sin-tainted world altogether and everywhere. "The only thing I really feel is necessary is that the black people, not only in Mississippi, will have to actually upset this applecart. What I mean by that is, so many things are under the cover that will have to be swept out and shown to this whole world, not just to America." Minutes later she added, "Actually, the world and America is upset and the only way to bring about a change is to upset it more." Though she did not mention Gunnar Myrdal by name, she said that American professions of freedom were hollow. "This thing they say of 'the land of the free and the home of the brave' is all on paper. It doesn't mean anything to us." Liberals' faith in gradualism, voluntarism, compromise, and the like was false to her: "The only way we can make this thing [freedom] a reality in America is to do all we can to destroy this system and bring this thing out to the light that has been under the cover all these years." To illustrate, she quoted Luke 12:3: "The things that have been done in the dark will be known on the house tops."[22]

Hamer's biographer Chana Kai Lee writes that the great turning point in Hamer's life—her decision to confront rather than run away from oppression—was "somewhat akin to a religious conversion."[23] The most baffling aspect of Hamer's faith was her renunciation of hatred of white people. Her faith, like that of most extremely religious people, was not separable from her practical conception of action in the day-to-day world. In that sense, she was premodern or antimodern. She knew evil well, one might say intimately. As Lee notes, Hamer understood that some white men oppressed her not simply to serve their political or economic interests. They often derived pleasure, including sexual pleasure, from torturing her.[24] Yet she would not hate the white man, any more than she would try to cover his sins

Fannie Lou Hamer, the extraordinary lay preacher who inspired local activists and many who traveled to her native Mississippi. Like Modjeska Simkins, she thought that normal religion, black and white, was part of the problem, not part of the solution. (© Bettmann/Corbis)

with sentimentality: "The white man is the scardest person on earth. Out in daylight he don't do nothin'. But at night he'll toss a bomb or pay someone to kill. The white man's afraid he'll be treated like he's been treating the Negroes, but I couldn't carry that much hate. It wouldn't have solved any problems for me to hate whites because they hate me. Oh, there's so much hate! Only God has kept the Negro sane."[25]

Like most people who questioned the notion of automatic progress, Hamer believed that force was often necessary. Though she renounced hatred as self-destructive, she once lashed out at fainthearted black farmers who were reluctant to join the Mississippi Freedom Labor Union's attempted labor strike in the Delta. Like Modjeska Simkins's devotion to nonviolence, Hamer's was not dogmatic or absolute: "We got to stop the nervous Nellies and the Toms from going to the Man's place. I don't believe in killing, but a good whipping behind the bushes wouldn't hurt them." In her 1967 memoir, she explained why her house never got dynamited: "I keep a shotgun in every corner of my bedroom," and she made the gun's presence known to at least one "cracker" who threatened her.[26]

Armed or not, Hamer's basic philosophy of coercion was the same as that of King and Rustin: "We learned the hard way that even though we had all the law and all the righteousness on our side—that white man is not going to give up his power to us. . . . We have to build our own power. . . . We have to take for ourselves."[27] In her situation, however, she did not say that armed struggle was an effective form of mass politics. She confined her support of violence to the level of individual defense.

For all Hamer's devotion to Christian love, she stated in 1965 that Malcolm X "was one of the greatest men that I ever met in my life cause he told exactly how every Negro in this country feels and didn't have the guts to say it." People had been patient too long and were fed up. At that point she doubted whether even Martin Luther King believed that nonviolence would work.[28] She admired Malcolm's self-sacrificial devotion to the telling of discomfiting truths and shared his (and perhaps King's—or Gandhi's or Jesus') frustration with nonviolence. But she never embraced black separatism, even after many participants in the student movement embraced it. In a 1967 interview for a SNCC publication, she said that she felt "100%" the same as she had when she began working for integration, which had the same justification it always had. "I still believe and people make fun of me for saying this, but I believe in Christianity."

Though by 1967 Hamer's faith isolated her from many in the movement, it was still her source of pragmatic wisdom. "I was just reading yesterday in the Bible what God don't have no respect for a person, and if he made us all and put us on earth together, then there's no need of you trying to get over there by yourself and you wage your little battle." She could not be content with black people's working for just their own freedom. They had to fight for "ALL the people. . . . There's white that suffer, there's Indian people that suffer, there's Mexican American people that suffer."[29] Her message was as universal as Christianity—not confined to a single nation or tribe.

THE OLDER GENERATION'S LESSONS ARE NOT LOST

John Lewis, the most pragmatic, down-to-earth leader SNCC ever had (also the leader whose career from the 1960s on has been the most stable), began his association with civil rights in Lawson's Nashville cadre. Though a student for the ministry and an effective preacher, Lewis never soared to the rhetorical heights of Lawson, Simkins, or Hamer. Yet he shared their extreme faith. That faith was nurtured in the year he spent with Lawson in Nashville, discussing, as Lewis put it, "The New Testament, Gandhi, Israel, India, Africa, Thoreau, and the whole question of civil disobedience and passive resistance."

Lewis recalled feeling that the first sit-ins, in 1960, were "like a holy crusade." The dinner before his first Freedom Ride in 1961 "was like the Last Supper, all thirteen of us that went on the Ride." The hardest thing about being in jail was explaining to his mother that he was "acting according to my Christian faith and my conviction." Lewis's almost legendary willingness to get up after repeated jailings and beatings and go back for more is hard to account for without that faith and conviction. Partly because of his battle stripes (there was a nonviolent macho in SNCC, where jailings and hospitalizations were tallied as badges of honor), Lewis became chairman of SNCC in June 1963, a post he held through the organization's most productive years until his expulsion in 1966. Though most of his public statements dealt with mundane details of organization and the straightforward publicizing of atrocities, Lewis revealed his philosophical core in interviews.[30]

Lewis shared Lawson's belief that the basic trend of normal society was toward corruption. Also like Lawson, Lewis said in 1964 that SNCC was aiming for "revolution," a "social revolution" that raised more "basic questions" than "the question of Negro rights."[31] Lewis never cited Niebuhr, but he did mention Frederick Douglass (as increasing numbers were doing in those years), who made exactly the same point as Niebuhr made in *Moral Man and Immoral Society*: "I don't think the South and those in power are going to give up their interest without some form of struggle. They're just not going to hand it over. As Frederick Douglass said, 'Without agitation there can be no progress.'" Lewis also stressed, like Niebuhr and King, Gandhi's point that nonviolent force had a lot in common with war and no moral superiority to war:

> I think that somewhere in the history of Judeo-Christian tradition is the idea that there can be no salvation without the shedding of blood and there may be some truth in that. Personally, though, I now accept the philosophy of nonviolence . . . but I think that when we accept non-violence, we don't say it is the absence of violence. We say it is the present assumption—much more positive—that there might be the shedding of blood. You know what Gandhi says: "If I had the personal choice to make between no movement and a violent movement, I would choose a violent movement."

Lewis noted that SNCC was refining its nonviolent policy in the direction of "aggressive non-violent action."[32]

For all SNCC's youthful enthusiasm, the pervasive sense of radical dissociation from the world was not simply an intellectual conceit. It carried over into the strategy that emerged from civil rights activity. From Montgomery on, civil rights groups met resistance from successful black people who had economic ties to white leadership—in particular, presidents of black colleges and schools, and to a great extent teachers, who depended on state or philanthropic support. They found an equal and opposite supportiveness, or at least the possibility of it, in black people with no dependence on white leaders—initially some preachers, but as the need for meeting places and fund-raising networks grew, beauty parlor owners and other

John Lewis said the movement
was "like a holy crusade." He
assumed it might involve "the
shedding of blood," since those
in power would not yield without
a struggle. (© Danny Lyon/Magnum
Photos)

entrepreneurs with an exclusively black clientele.[33] Civil rights leaders often understood and forgave the resistance of those with ties, but in the interests of efficient tactics, they sought out and based their movement on those who had no economic interest in the surrounding society. This was an interesting inversion of the old republican philosophy of associating responsible citizenship with a stake in society.

The notion that the present society was corrupt and unworthy of a Christian's allegiance did not entail disengagement or irresponsibility. Hamer expressed the distinction perfectly when she was asked if her goal was equality with whites. "No," she said. "What would I look like fighting for equality with the white man? I don't want to go down that low. I want that *true democracy* that'll raise me and that white man up."[34]

Nobody in SNCC developed this prophetic philosophy more fully than Bob Moses. This elusive, enigmatic leader took SNCC's anarchistic opposition to leadership to absurd lengths in his efforts to forswear his own importance as the dynamic and charismatic leader he clearly was. Having grown up in Harlem, Moses was one of the few black graduates of the selective Stuyvesant High School in New York. He attended Quaker camps in Europe and Japan before doing graduate work in mathematical logic at Harvard, where he received a Master of Arts degree in 1957. His most important link to the civil rights movement was Bayard Rustin, whom he consulted about resisting the draft after his mother's death and his father's hospitalization forced him to leave Harvard. In his spare time from teaching math, Moses contributed to Rustin's civil rights work in New York, helping to organize the second Youth March for Integrated Schools in 1959. Photographs of the southern student sit-ins the following year filled him with excitement and longing. While visiting his uncle, an award-winning architect at the Hampton Institute in Virginia, Moses "slipped into a crowd" in a demonstration at Newport News in 1960. There he experienced "a feeling of release," he said, from "the kind of self-repression every Negro builds into himself,"[35] and he heard Wyatt Tee Walker preach.

After getting a letter of introduction from Rustin, Moses went to Atlanta in the summer of 1960 to work with the SCLC, where he came under the influence of Ella Baker. Described by everyone as contemplative to a fault, Moses, like Martin Luther King, who had also done graduate work on the banks of the Charles River, had wanted to devote himself to study before he got caught up in the movement. Robert Penn Warren, who interviewed Moses extensively, called him an "academic type." Baker recalled with amusement that on his first day in Atlanta, when he was assigned to lick envelopes, Moses became absorbed in an intellectual discussion with Jane Stembridge. "He and Jane hit it off immediately, both of them being philosophy students, and they talked about Camus, Tillich and Kant all day."

Many people thought Bob Moses's last name was no accident: he was "like Moses in the Bible." His Mosaic humility led him to resist the leadership that was thrust upon him. He believed that the modern, urban life he had had up North was not the proper goal of the struggle, and that winners of civil rights were in grave danger of becoming like their oppressors. (Steve Schapiro/Black Star)

The Atlanta student organizer Lonnie King saw another side: "Bob is so quiet and intense that he must be a communist."[36]

One of the few early SNCC leaders who had a developed intellectual bent, and one of the few who came to his philosophy via secular rather than church sources, Moses left maddeningly little record of his ideas.[37] There was a passivity, a diffidence about him that made him more inclined to read than to write. Whatever he thought, he let others publish and take credit for it. But even those who, like James Forman, disagreed with him admired him and recognized his influence. Speaking of the new society the movement was struggling to create, Forman said, "No one dreamed of that new society more often and more thoughtfully than Bob Moses." Regarding Moses's exasperating refusal to accept the dominant position his followers felt inclined to give him, Forman observed, "Some staff members, including persons close to him, were always pointing out at meetings that he exerted too much influence over people. He shouldn't speak at all, they said, because his words carried too much weight as a result of the enormous respect people had for him and his work. He was made to feel guilty, I think, about his power."[38]

Moses had a keen sense of power, despite his nearly pathological aversion to its use. According to Sally Bellfrage, he said that "no privileged group in history has ever given up anything without some kind of blood sacrifice, something." More specifically, Moses told a rally in Jackson after the unsuccessful "freedom vote" campaign of 1963 that the election "makes it clear that the Negroes of Mississippi will not get the vote until the equivalent of an army is sent here. . . . We don't expect to correct the evils of Mississippi by this snail's pace voter registration, but we do expect to build enough pressure to make it politically impossible for a federal government to remain so indifferent. . . . We expect our efforts to dissuade those who believe that anything less than federal troops will work." For all his aversion to "manipulating" fellow activists, he recognized the need to coerce the enemy.[39]

Though Moses had consulted Rustin before joining SNCC, his greatest philosophical influence was Albert Camus, whom he read in college and later in a Mississippi jail. "The main essence of what [Camus] says is what I feel real close to—closest to," Moses told Robert Penn Warren in an interview. That essence was simply that man had to struggle and, while struggling, had to recognize "in the struggle certain humanitarian values, and to recognize that you have to struggle for people . . . and at the same time, if it's possible, you try to eke out some corner of love or some glimpse of happiness within. And that's what I think more than anything else conquers the bitterness."[40] This was exactly what Martin Luther King drew from his most important philosophical influence. The strenuous Christian command to hate the sin but love the sinner, or as Niebuhr more academically put it, the "spiritual discipline against resentment," was the crucial link between King's insistence on the inevitable evil of all politics and his insistence that political action was nonetheless a moral obligation.[41]

Moses found in Camus's discussion (in *Man in Revolt*) of Russian terrorists circa 1905 a rule that applied to his struggles in Mississippi. Those terrorists "accepted that if they took a life they offered their own in exchange." Camus's rejection of violence did not, as Moses saw it, require "that you just subjugate your self to the conditions that are and don't try to change them." On the contrary, "The problem is to go on from there, into something which is active." This "problem" never let Camus feel morally comfortable in his political activism; it is the heart of Moses's wariness, which baffled so many of his followers. The activist faced a perpetual danger of slipping into the complacent habits of his oppressors. According to Moses, the struggle for Camus was "whether you can cease to be a victim and not be what he calls an executioner. For when people rise up and change their status, usually somewhere along the line they become executioners and they get involved in subjugating, you know, other people." For Moses, the problem was how not to be immobilized by self-awareness and by knowledge of human nature: all power corrupted. The power that the oppressed might achieve in the struggle against their oppressors was no exception. Action in a morally just cause still involved the moral danger of abusing power. Yet inaction against oppression was an equally grave moral danger.

Since Moses conceded that American Negroes were hardly in a position to become executioners in the foreseeable future in any case, Warren asked how Camus's balancing act applied to "inside attitudes." Moses answered that it applied very strongly. "We are going through a big thing right now . . . it's very hard for some of the students who have been brought up in Mississippi and are the victims of this kind of race hatred not to begin to let all of that out on the white staff." Moses saw that local black activists' complaints about the presumptuous, domineering habits of the white staff were often justified. Still, that justified resentment was damaging—more damaging to the black activists than to the occasional white targets of their outbursts. Hatred and anger just kept the old tendency of normal society going. Hatred and anger produced no moral or practical gain for the oppressed. Moses did not want "to integrate into the middle-class white culture, since that seems to be at this point in vital need of some kind of renewal." Again, the essence of moral action was to struggle against easy settlement either into passivity or into morally self-destructive domination and exploitativeness. Only in struggle did that "whole problem of identifying yourself in Negro culture—or of integrating yourself into white society[—]" disappear.[42]

Moses's struggle with Camus's "problem" was related to his condemnation of the normal tendency of society toward corruption and evil. Camus was one of the most absolute rejecters of the myth of progress. Cleveland Sellers recalled Moses saying to a group of volunteers at a training session before the Freedom Summer in 1964: "There is an analogy to *The Plague*, by Camus. The country isn't willing yet to admit it has the plague, but it pervades the whole society. We must discuss it openly and honestly, even with the danger that we get too analytical and tangled up. If we ignore it, it's going to blow up in our faces." Just then, Moses heard that James Chaney, Andrew Goodman, and Mickey Schwerner were missing in Neshoba County (their bodies, hidden by the Ku Klux Klansmen who murdered them, were not found for several weeks).[43] The news vindicated his aversion to a society that seemed depraved beyond redemption.

But Moses did not reject everything. There is a great gulf between him as an engagé philosophy student and the fashionable alienation of, say, the Beats or others who wore their existentialism on their sleeve. "The Beats were left without a people—without anybody they might identify with," Moses told Warren. They were antisocial, "against everything." By contrast, "What happens with students in our movement is that they are identifying with these people—people who come off the land," who voice "the simple truths you can't ignore because they speak from their own lives."[44]

Moses was, or was striving to be, what Leslie Dunbar called an "unalienated dissenter." Reconciling the rejection of middle-class society and the American way of life with the quest for community in a middle-class society (and "really a middle class movement," as Andrew Young observed) was perilous.[45] It was as difficult as reconciling the rejection of violence with the rejection of pacifist smugness, as difficult as reconciling the rejection of being victimized with the rejection of victimizing others. Moses's rejection of American society was no less severe than that of the Beats. His imagined alternative was what differentiated him from them. On these points, Moses and his patron philosopher Camus had almost exactly the same ideas as Reinhold Niebuhr had back in 1932.

One of Moses's greatest fans in SNCC, Mary King, noted in her memoir the most surprising side of Moses's lack of faith in progress. "I remember thinking that, growing up in Harlem, he would not have been able to swing in the shade of a low-hanging tree picking up the golden dust beneath his feet where the grass had worn bare." But perhaps because he had seen the underside of urban life in Harlem, he seemed to prefer the rural South, though so many black Americans had fled from it:

If the emigration to northern slums by people in search of jobs could be slowed, Bob maintained, and if agribusiness could be contained to allow small farmers to survive, life might be qualitatively better in the South. . . . In urban ghettos, Bob argued, families disintegrate from economic pressure; life is filled with the stress of over-crowding, crime, unemployment; no one has any roots, nor sense of community. In Mississippi, blacks belonged. They had built the state. Whatever had been developed in Mississippi was a tribute to them. . . . Bob Moses stood out as . . . the first person I heard to argue that once desegregation had been accomplished in the South, the eventual quality of relationships between the races would be finer and more durable than in the North. Once the traumas of adjustment were past, integration would be more successful in the South, Bob maintained, because whites knew blacks and blacks knew whites, unlike the theoretical relationships between the races and lip service to equality of people elsewhere in the country. The enormous disparity between rich and poor in the United States could also, he believed, be more humanely overcome in the South where black people had a real stake in what had been developed.

Rather than embrace the rural-to-urban migration that was synonymous with "progress," one of Moses's strategic goals was apparently to stop the migration. Instead of finding a way for them to flee, he sought to provide rural black people the education and access to services and credit that would allow them to live in dignity where they were.[46]

ON THE SIGNIFICANCE OF PROPHETIC THOUGHT

This prophetic brand of skepticism about human "progress" reverberates throughout the civil rights movement. I am not merely calling attention to aspects of the movement that have been unappreciated by other writers. I am not merely saying that the conflict between liberal and prophetic ideas complicates the standard progressive narrative of civil rights and American history in general. I am making a claim about historical significance: What makes the civil rights movement *matter* are the prophetic ideas it embodies—not the liberal-progressive elements it also undeniably, inescapably contains.

The liberal idea of progress has right-wing versions, which emphasize the power of unrestrained corporate expansion and spontaneous private charity to create a rising tide that will lift even the poorest boats. It also has left-wing versions, which emphasize the need for public as well as private institutions. For present purposes, the common faith in progress and institutions is more significant than these differences.

The thinking activists in the direct action movement rejected liberals' general optimism. More specifically, they rejected the accelerated optimism that Myrdal expressed about institutions, in particular his optimism about the main liberal civil rights institution, the NAACP. Of all the institutions in black America, Myrdal found the NAACP the most beneficial.[47] But the direct action organizations that built on the NAACP's achievements defined themselves largely by their rejection of the NAACP. "The movement," properly speaking, refers to the moment when groups like the March on Washington Movement and CORE, and new groups like the Montgomery Improvement Association, the SCLC, and SNCC, broke from the established practice of the NAACP and were often condemned by the NAACP for doing so. Aldon Morris's study, *Origins of the Civil Rights Movement*, argues that the legal backlash against civil rights, which effectively outlawed the NAACP in some states, ironically ensured greater militancy, since it allowed black activists who would normally gravitate to the NAACP to be released from the association's restraint. Those activists were then free to band together with discontented elements who had never been drawn to the NAACP's gradualism in the first place. They went on to form a larger, more powerful group than NAACP forces alone could have mustered at the local level. Myrdal had said that the NAACP, as a "nonrevolutionary" organization, was more effective than other civil rights groups: "A revolutionary program would be suicidal for the organization and dangerous to the Negro cause."[48] But Martin Luther King and later activists often spoke of their "Negro revolution" and "non-violent revolution." So, too, southern white enemies of the movement called it a "revolution."[49]

After the rejection of automatic progress, the question that divided SNCC was how to achieve moral victories. (This question divided SNCC much more than other civil rights organizations. The sterile yet incessant, obsessional debate over "nonviolence as a way of life" versus "nonviolence as a tactic" did not plague older activists.) SNCC (and the movement as a whole) is often portrayed as believing in moral suasion and then shifting to a more realistic, coercive politics in the late 1960s.[50] Some former activists themselves claim that they naively hoped that they could change America overnight and became "radicalized" as time went on.[51] Yet there is considerable evidence that SNCC, or at least parts of SNCC, believed in coercion from the beginning, as King clearly did.[52] An editorial in the August 1960 issue of the *Student Voice*, on the political ramifications of the movement's growth, stated that, "as the movement gains momentum, it becomes increasingly important and expedient to realize the rights and duties we have as American citizens to exert political force to improve the conditions of those suffering second-class citizenship and the American community as a whole." It was necessary to "let politicians know forcefully how we feel," and for this, elections were "not enough." The editorial called for direct action on election day.[53] In the same issue, SNCC named at the top of its list of recommended books Richard Gregg's *The Power of Nonviolence*, which is devoted to the Gandhian strategy of compelling authorities to make concessions against their will, through nonviolent coercion. Not incidentally, the second book on the list was King's *Stride toward Freedom*, which contains a Niebuhrian defense of nonviolent coercion, with an analysis of how it had recently worked in Montgomery. Also in that issue, Bayard Rustin called for imposing a cost on the state by "filling the jails" and refusing bail. "Only so many can fit into a cell; if you remain there, there can be no more arrests! This is one of the best ways to immobilize repercussive police apparatus."[54]

The next issue of the *Student Voice* presented the other side, insisting (following Martin Buber rather than Gandhi) that

> nonviolence refuses to manipulate. . . . If we lose sight of this basic concept of non-violence, no matter how nonviolent our external tactics remain, we will lose the ultimate potential of the student movement. For, without this commitment to the validity of the other person, the movement will become an institution and the persons will become things. . . . The South and America will not be worth saving unless there are persons, real selves, left to live there. This retaining and creating of personhood is the great and final goal of the student movement.[55]

This mystical emphasis plagued and often embarrassed those who favored a more organized movement with a more concrete sense of goals and the means to attain them.

Unfortunately for SNCC, people on both sides of the factional split confused the mystical Buberian position with nonviolence. The "Floaters" condemned all political and coercive action as morally impure and therefore inadmissible. Many anti-Floaters ultimately became impatient with the tactical discipline of nonviolence and indulged in headline-ready rhetoric about violence, which they rarely acted on.

A number of prominent members of SNCC—Diane Nash Bevel being probably the most visible—were closer to the Tolstoyan perfectionism of nonresistance than the Niebuhrian-Gandhian embrace of nonviolent coercion. They formed a kind of cult of nonmanipulation, hotly denounced by the other SNCC faction (led by James Forman, Stokely Carmichael, Cleveland Sellers, and others). Both sides in the debate missed the insights of Gandhi and Niebuhr on the use of force. This debate, oversimplified by many members of SNCC and their hangers-on, was doomed to oversimplification in the subsequent literature on the movement.

I am not arguing that there was any coherent intellectual influence binding all the motive forces in the movement together. The key thinkers resembled the Hebrew Prophets, in their condemnation of the normal course of society as corrupt and sinful, and in their belief that society would not yield to mild-mannered meliorism. Beyond that, it is difficult to find a common theological or philosophical thread. Few may have read Niebuhr or cared anything about him. (By then Niebuhr had taken positions and made alliances that made it hard to consider the book he had written in 1932 on its merits.)

What I am saying is that the thinking activists in the civil rights movement clearly disagreed with the coherent philosophy of liberalism expressed by Schlesinger and his followers. And their disagreements were not incidental: they disagreed over points that were central to their motives and their tactics. Liberals accepted the movement's advances more than any other group in society. But liberals' receptiveness did not spring from any similarity of goals or motives. Liberals were receptive, in part, because they longed for the missing elements in their own philosophy—the elements that might engender enthusiasm, solidarity, and self-sacrifice. Yet liberals could not embrace those elements fully without abandoning their own philosophy—without ceasing to be liberals. They assimilated some of the goals articulated by the movement, but they never adopted its determination, its initiative, and its hope.

The movement's hope was something very different from the liberals' optimism.[56] Liberals' bright future was automatic. The moral improvement of their world would come as a function of increased economic growth, scientific discovery, and educational dissemination of new ideas. The movement's hope, by contrast, was forged by years of disappointment. A particularly important shaping experience was the entrenchment of segregation during the years of diversification of the southern economy and the development of modern industry in the region—the very developments that liberals always assumed would bring greater freedom for all. Those developments in the American South, beginning in the late nineteenth century, brought not freedom but a more systematic commitment to racial subordination. Activists in the movement believed, or came to believe, that they had to act. They believed that they had to set themselves off from the general drift of social development, even to identify themselves with otherworldly values, to secure a brighter future. Some brightening could occur in this world—they were not premillennialists.[57] But the brightening would come only through sacrifice and submission to the will of God (or, in the case of atheists, sacrifice and submission to an austere moral principle that happened to resemble the law that the Prophets sought to revive). Their hope was not divorced from works, or rather work, but it was the result of a godly grace beyond their control, a grace that demanded humility and gratitude in return.

Activists' hope for improvement in this world could not be sustained without signs that God was on their side. They needed victories in this life over the forces of evil. We may be as grateful as they were that they got plenty of them. Their victories took spiritual, often ritualistic form.

5

The Civil Rights Movement
as a Religious Revival

Participants often recalled the movement years as a heady, life-trans-forming era touched with divine significance. When Johnnie Carr, one of the principal organizers of the Montgomery Bus Boycott of 1955–56, was later asked why the civil rights movement succeeded, she answered, "Because God sent us that man." She was referring to Martin Luther King. Carr had been praised by many students of the movement who emphasized the role of unsung heroes like her. But she did not think her skills and diligence should take attention from the handiwork of the Lord. "Until He sees fit to send us another," she added, "we won't get any further."[1] R. D. Nesbitt, a member of the Montgomery boycott's finance committee, referred to King as "a modern day 'Moses'" and "truly a God-sent man." Black people in Montgomery were complacent before King came along, Nesbitt said, and fell into disarray after he left in January 1960. "We were united" while King was in Montgomery, and many wanted "to follow him to Atlanta" rather than carry on without him. "Quite a number of folks left."[2] Rufus Lewis, chairman of the boycott's transportation committee, observed that poor people in Montgomery responded to King "just like he was their savior." Lewis could not "see what's different between him and the Messiah. That's just the truth about it," he said, "and I am not a real religious man."[3]

Such testimony suggests that it may be misleading to view the civil rights movement as a social and political event that had religious overtones. The words of many participants suggest that it was, for them, primarily a religious event, whose social and political aspects were, in their minds, secondary or incidental. To take the testimony of intense religious transformation seriously is to consider the civil rights movement as part of the historical tradition of religious revivals, such as the so-called First and Second Great Awakenings, as much as it is part of the tradition of protest movements such as abolitionism, populism, feminism, and the labor movement.

The parallels to earlier revivals are striking. The religious enthusiasm that began in Montgomery in 1955 was not confined to the poor and uneducated. "This was the most stimulating thing in the lives of most of the Negroes in this area," Lewis noted. "[King] lifted them so high they just can't help but think he is a Messiah. They can't help it, no matter how smart they are."[4] Even Stokely Carmichael, the so-called militant leader of SNCC, who challenged King's leadership, recognized this. Carmichael (now known as Kwame Toure) said: "People loved King. . . . I've seen people in the South climb over each other just to say, 'I touched him! I touched him!' . . . I'm even talking about the young. The old people had more love and respect. They even saw him like a God. These were the people we were working with and I had to follow in his footsteps when I went in there. The people didn't *know* what was SNCC. They just said, 'You one of Dr. King's men?' 'Yes, Ma'am, I am.'"[5]

King was not the only charismatic leader who evoked this response, nor was the sense of an ultimate, divine mission mere after-the-fact hyperbole about a martyred leader. The Rev. Fred Shuttlesworth, leader of the civil rights forces in Birmingham, apocalyptically told a crowd in 1958: "This is a religious crusade, a fight between light and darkness, right and wrong, good and evil, fair play and tyranny. We are assured of victory because we are using weapons of spiritual warfare."[6] In a later speech calling upon his audience to defeat Alabama governor George Wallace in 1964, Shuttlesworth drew his own connection to the history of revivals, saying that his and other civil rights organizations gave "the Christian Church its greatest opportunity in centuries to make religion real in the lives of men." He thanked God for the new "awakening of the Religious forces."[7]

Shuttlesworth's fearlessness in nonviolent battle was legendary. It helped to inspire the largest and most sustained challenge to segregation in any American city; his city was referred to as the Belly of the Beast of Segregation, Bombingham, and the Johannesburg of the United States. Though Shuttlesworth often provoked anger and resentment in Birmingham and elsewhere, even his rivals defended his reputation and spoke of his personal power with awe and respect.[8]

The older generation of black preachers had no monopoly on worshipful followers. Bob Moses, the young hero of the student movement that tried to finish what King, Shuttlesworth, and others had started, exercised tremendous influence over his followers, as we have seen. What is important here is that local people had a tendency to spiritualize his influence. Rural Mississippians began to refer to him as "Moses in the Bible." Moses tried to disavow his own significance (following the example of his biblical namesake when God first called him). He even dropped his last name and tried to become known as "Robert Parris."[9] John Lewis, the most pragmatic stu-

Fred Shuttlesworth, the tempestu-
ous leader of the civil rights forces
in Birmingham, said that the "holy
crusade" for civil rights was "using
weapons of spiritual warfare." It
gave "the Christian Church its
greatest opportunity in centuries
to make religion real in the lives of
men." (© Danny Lyon/Magnum
Photos)

dent leader, said that Moses had a "tremendous impact . . . [and] not just in Mississippi." His followers made him "the all-perfect and all-holy and all-wise leader, and I think that's one of the reasons he changed his name."[10] Bill Higgs, a white lawyer from Mississippi, one of the rare "inside agitators" who supported the movement, said that when Moses spoke, "It was really like listening to the Lord, I tell you it was!" Moses "could have been Socrates or Aristotle" in the way he tore into Martin Luther King when King suggested compromise on a matter of principle. Higgs quoted Moses insisting: "We're not here to bring politics into our morality but to bring morality into our politics." When Moses said this, according to Higgs, "King and everybody knew the jig was up"—that the Mississippi Freedom Delegation to the Democratic National Convention in 1964 would never accept a compromise. Black student leader James Forman, who became a rival of Moses and tried to pull the movement away from both politics and religion, referred to the "almost Jesus-like aura that [Moses] and his name had acquired."[11] Amzie Moore, from an older generation of black Mississippians who attempted to develop an organized, indigenous political movement with few ties to the urban-oriented SCLC, made Moses sound like a revivalist preacher, too. Moore said that Moses was "like an Apostle who makes his circles, and he goes to this mission and that mission and the other mission, to straighten them out on anything that they might be confused about. And then he makes the circuit."[12]

Evangelism, or reaching out to those who are not churchgoers, is crucial to the expansion of all revivals. During times of civil rights activity, advertising and excited word of mouth helped expand church attendance in the black South.[13] King's partner, the Rev. Ralph Abernathy, recalled rounding up "sinners" in the pool halls, juke joints, and dives of Montgomery to persuade them by whatever means he could to attend the first meeting of what became the Montgomery boycott movement. It was not enough for those who already had the faith to be there.[14] In 1962 King, Abernathy, and others made a similar excursion through the "Harlem" district of Albany, Georgia. They aimed more to persuade the "sinners" not to disrupt movement discipline (some rock and brick throwing had broken out) than to bring them to the meeting. Still, Abernathy preached to at least one group of Albany's hustlers and sharks, "Close the pool hall and come with us."[15]

The promise that these religious leaders made of a political deliverance, if people would unite in the cause, was similar in form to the traditional revivalist promise that sinners would attain God's grace, if they attended a meeting and repented. The big difference this time was that the promise came partially true on earth, in a way that was objectively visible to nonbelievers, in court decisions and acts of Congress. (When the Supreme Court confirmed that local bus segregation was unconstitutional, King's narrative of the Montgomery boycott quoted one "joyful bystander" saying, "God Almighty has spoken from Washington, D.C.")[16] But the considerable delay before the promise was realized, after a century of setbacks and false hopes, was a measure of the great faith that belief in the promise demanded.

Such credulity-stretching faith was encouraged by talk of miracles. In the first mass meeting of the Montgomery boycott, Abernathy remembered, two ministers "experienced miraculous cures." They had been too ill to preach, but when the crowd "rocked the rafters," singing songs with "no revolutionary overtones," suddenly "the scales fell from Powell's eyes. . . . Huffman's laryngitis had disappeared and he was able to recite a long and remarkably resonant prayer. These were the first of many miracles that would occur over the next fifteen years."[17] In her memoir, Coretta Scott King recalled that her husband was disturbed that the victory at Montgomery came so fast. "People will expect me to perform miracles for the rest of my life," he told her.[18] If not a divine spirit, at least good luck and weather kept up with him. A witness of King's "mountaintop" speech in Memphis in 1968 recalled the miraculous special effects. "I'm not a religious fanatic," Jesse Epps said. "But at some points where there should have been applause there was a real severe flash of lightning and a real clap of thunder that sort of hushed the crowd."[19]

One kind of miracle in particular, the conversion experience, plays a crucial role in consummating most religious revivals. In public recitations of conversion narratives, the converted justify their own actions and draw others into the ritual. Typically, this involves admitting one's helplessness and surrendering to a higher power. King's own narrative, though couched in understatement, is in this tradition. King tells of his realization that he had put his wife and children in danger by challenging segregation. Death threats came by telephone, and he could not sleep:

> I got out of bed and began to walk the floor. . . . I was ready to give up. With my cup of coffee sitting untouched before me I tried to think of a way to move out of the picture without appearing a coward. In this state of exhaustion, when my courage had all but gone, I decided to take my problem to God. With my head in my hands, I bowed over the kitchen table and prayed aloud. The words I spoke to God that midnight are still in my memory. "I am here taking a stand for what I believe is right. But now I am afraid. The people are looking to me for leadership, and if I stand before them without strength and courage, they too will falter. I am at the end of my powers. I have nothing left. I've come to the point where I can't face it alone."
>
> At that moment I experienced the presence of the Divine as I had never experienced Him before. It seemed as though I could hear the quiet assurance of an inner voice saying: "Stand up for righteousness, stand up for truth; and God will be at your side forever." Almost at once my fears began to go. My uncertainty disappeared. I was ready to face anything.[20]

Many revivalists would have left out King's phrase, "It seemed as though," and would not have suggested that God's voice was "quiet" or "inner." But those very mutings make it a revivalist set piece for an unconverted audience.

Fuller-blown public enthusiasm was common. A participant-observer report on the Albany struggle in the NAACP journal, *Crisis*, for example, stated that during a public "prayer vigil" in front of city hall, "One of the older sisters 'got happy,' as they say, and responded to the spirit just as if she were praying in the aisle of the Shiloh Baptist Church." [21] Years later a student who worked with SNCC in 1964 recalled: "There were the times when [movement workers] took me to church, and people would start witnessing and jump up and start speaking in tongues, waving their hands in the air. Some of them would lie down on the floor and roll around. People would be telling me, 'Oh, this is perfectly normal.'" Because he had grown up in the Far East (he was half white and half Chinese), this student's experiences with Christianity had been confined to services like those of the Lutherans and Anglicans. The mass meetings of the civil rights movement presented him with "quite an amazing scene." [22]

According to John Lewis, "Some of the meetings that we had were like revivals, where people would sing and people would make speeches, some of them were fantastic sessions." At the 1965 Atlanta meeting where Robert Moses announced his name change, Lewis said, Moses "stood up and took a soft drink bottle with water—he said it was wine but it was not wine—and started singing and marching around the room with a lot of people. It was like being in a revival where the minister saves the souls of the sick." [23]

Conversion-like experiences worked across racial lines, as was often the case in earlier revivals; that is one of the features that sometimes distinguished great revivals from established, segregated religion. In 1972 the Rev. S. S. Seay, former president of the Montgomery Improvement Association (the boycott organization), told an interviewer: "I spoke in Charleston, S.C., once and had a white woman came to me and she just wouldn't turn loose. Finally, she said, 'The day of atonement is with us. I don't know if we will ever be able to repent for what we've done to your people.' Then she hauled off and kissed me. I meet person after person like that." [24]

A black civil rights leader in Tallahassee, Florida, the Rev. Dan Speed, described King's preaching to an audience that included some "die-hard" racists. Speed saw one of these racists, a news reporter, "get up and whoop and scream. I'm talking about a white woman. . . . A reporter. She forgot her job. I personally had to get her. She said, 'I'm sorry.'" Then another movement leader, the Rev. C. K. Steele, said to the woman, "No, don't feel sorry, just let it come." [25]

The sociologist Aldon Morris, who has done more than any other scholar to illuminate the role southern black churches played in civil rights activity,

Religious expression was integral to the experience
of protest both for the older generation—especially
women (top)—and for the younger generation
(bottom). (© Danny Lyon/Magnum Photos)

explains how the movement of the 1950s, especially Martin Luther King, "refocused" the "cultural content of religion for the black masses" across the South. Throughout the first half of the twentieth century, according to Morris, most black churches served as an "opiate," preaching "a religion of containment," which held that a good Christian was "concerned with perfecting his or her spiritual life rather than with material well being." But in the mid-1950s the church revived a militant tradition, the tradition of Nat Turner, Denmark Vesey, Harriet Tubman, and Frederick Douglass. Morris says that the new mass meetings "resembled revivals," but he does not elaborate on the parallel.[26]

One civil rights veteran, Thomas Gilmore, suggested that there was as much continuity as there was change in the advent of the movement. "I consider myself a little mystical," he said. "I think most of us who came through the movement would say, 'I'm going to do what the spirits say do, because I can't really predict what's going to happen tomorrow. . . .' To me that is the spirit I'd been introduced to when I was younger. That was the spirit my grandmother talked about, the Holy Spirit that would make her shout." The movement gave Gilmore "a kind of inner strength" that he had been searching for. He was not sure whether this strength had been "in the process of becoming awake" in his earlier struggles, when he trained for the ministry and then dropped out, "or had been awakened and was frustrated." But he was sure that he found the strength in the movement: "I got strength from facing the sheriff because he was the biggest man in the county. . . . You really get the feeling that somebody bigger than you is walking beside you, and you feel that, well, man, nobody can hurt you if he wanted to. God is real, like Grandma said." After the protests, Gilmore became the first black sheriff of his Alabama county.[27]

Gayraud Wilmore's history of the black church—a history deeply informed by the spirits of the civil rights movement—develops the idea of a return to the old traditions in the civil rights era by describing what preceded that era (especially during the 1920s and 1930s) as the "deradicalization" of the black church. The civil rights movement of the 1950s and 1960s was a return to first principles, an effort to bring the church back to the path of righteousness from which it had strayed. Wilmore's account shows, though Wilmore does not emphasize the point, that after the "revival" of the 1950s and 1960s, black radicalism became increasingly secularized, to the detriment of both radicalism and religion. Wilmore holds out a fervent hope for another black theological "renewal," which would incorporate more non-Christian elements than the civil rights movement did and thus be palatable to black people who have lost (or never found) faith in Christianity.[28]

Taken out of context, these examples of conversion and belief in miracles may seem to misrepresent the civil rights movement, whose uniqueness derived from its effective strategy and organization. They may have been nothing more than the incidental overflowings of a deeply religious people, whose only way of organizing politics was through the church and whose only available idiom was one in which God or the devil was the hidden subject of every sentence.

But "miracles" played a direct, functional role in the political strategy that allowed the movement to advance. Their magic made excellent public relations, even before the largely secular, northern liberal audience known variously as "American public opinion" and "the nation's conscience." King described an incident in Birmingham in 1963 in which protesters marched toward the city jail, intending to hold a prayer meeting. Public Safety Commissioner Eugene "Bull" Connor, flanked by officers with guard dogs and fire hoses, ordered the protesters to turn back. But the leader of the march refused. Connor whirled around to his men, according to King's account, and shouted, "Damnit. Turn on the hoses":

> What happened in the next thirty seconds was one of the most fantastic events of the Birmingham story. Bull Connor's men, their deadly hoses poised for action, stood facing the marchers. The marchers, many of them on their knees, stared back, unafraid and unmoving. Slowly the Negroes stood up and began to advance. Connor's men, as though hypnotized, fell back, their hoses sagging uselessly in their hands while several hundred Negroes marched past them, without further interference, and held their prayer meeting as planned.[29]

Septima Clark, a black leader from South Carolina who helped organize the Voter Education Project, reported a similar incident in Greenwood, Mississippi, in 1964. This time, a black protester named Ida Holland and her pastor, the Rev. Donald Tucker, were marching to the courthouse:

> The white people of Greenwood decided that they would put the police dogs on the marchers. Rev. Tucker was bitten on the ankle. Ida tried to reach him to bind his wounds and was knocked down by a billy club by one of the police officers. While on the ground she could feel the cold nose of the dog near her eyes. She uttered a silent prayer but knew that the dog would soon bite out her eyes and gnaw her cheek. But for some unknown reason a miracle of not wanting to fight pervaded her troubled spirit and she resigned her body to the fate of the dogs and the officers. The dogs did not bite her and the officer did not hit her again.

Holland's pastor made the experience into a streetside sacrament. "She stood up on her feet and Rev. Tucker pinned a white cross on the left side of her dress over her heart. She had been inducted into the non-violent army."[30]

To be sure, the use of the term "miracle" in instances like these is rhetorical inflation. On the other hand, since its use in other cases can never be taken as literally true, it is difficult to distinguish between inflated uses and more earnest ones. The important thing is that, even when inflated, the use of the term reveals the extent to which religious language pervaded movement consciousness. Its frequency suggests that the minds of many civil rights protesters referred almost reflexively to supernatural forces. The otherworldly idiom of miracles was simply the most convenient one to explain the surprises that so often resulted from nonviolent action.

Particularly important to mass discipline were occasions when a miracle kept the nonviolent army from turning violent. One of the leaders of the Tallahassee boycott, the Rev. King Solomon "K. S." DuPont, said that it was part of God's plan that opponents threatened to bomb his house. He told his son, "Go out and pick me up a box of buckshot shells and bring me a big shotgun." But after DuPont's wife refused to go spend the night at her mother's house with their children, DuPont said, "the Lord spoke to me almost as plain as you talking." The Lord said, "You can't fight those with a shotgun." DuPont pumped out the shells, threw the gun aside, and said: "Now, Lord, every room in this house is yours. These pieces of furniture are yours. The grounds are yours. I'm yours. And I'm going to bed now." Without his knowing it, other armed black men had taken it upon themselves to guard his house, and a suspicious-looking group of white men who passed it eleven times never had "the courage to stop. . . . And it's a good thing they didn't."[31]

There were other pragmatic benefits of the religious enthusiasm that pervaded civil rights activity. SNCC organizer Larry Guyot said that his people were viewed "as the embodiment of the 'messianic expectation,'" because many SNCC members were ministers or had ministerial training. The local perception and the young activists' experience helped them fit in, build local support, and draw on local resources. "The church was an institution supported by black people: it had legitimacy, it had a history of liberation and of leadership development." SNCC leaders drew parallels to "biblical exaltations for liberation" that legitimated their work.[32]

THE WAYS AND MEANS OF A REVIVALIST

There was more than an abstract parallel between the civil rights movement and revivalism. In fact, there was a direct relationship between King and the famous revival leader who was his contemporary, Billy Graham. King and his chief of staff, Wyatt Tee Walker, sought advice from Graham and Graham's staff of tactical experts on how to organize large meetings and build publicity.[33] King appeared onstage in one of Graham's "crusades" in New York City in August 1957.[34] The two men even traveled to Rio de Janeiro together to attend the World Baptist Alliance conference in 1960. Graham, whose audiences were not segregated, often preached against racism and refused to speak in South Africa.[35] King and other civil rights leaders attended to Billy Graham's words as well as his techniques with admiration. Fred Shuttlesworth collected Billy Graham columns, which appeared regularly in many southern newspapers. In one of these, Graham defended his belief in Hell in response to a reader's query: "How can an intellectual believe in such a medieval concept? I really didn't know that any educated preachers believed in hell any more." In another, Graham answered readers who wanted to know where "the colored people come from," since Adam and Eve were white. Graham replied, "We are all so race-bound that we think in the color of our own skins. This is natural, but hardly logical. The race problem will never begin to be solved until we see things through the eyes of the other persons, and other races. . . . The truth of the matter is that people reared in the hot sun of Palestine are of a swarthy color—or light brown—and our Savior must have had a skin color similar to the people of that region."[36]

To Graham, belief in old-time concepts like Hell was just as natural as disbelief in modern concepts like racism. King held similar beliefs and generated uneasiness among his less pious advisers. Wyatt Tee Walker, perhaps sensitive to the suspicions of charlatanism that attended charismatic ministers of the poor, testified to the sincerity of King's beliefs, which was apparent in the frequent retreats of movement leaders, out of the public eye. "People may laugh at this now," Walker said, "but we read the Bible, had prayers, expressions."[37]

Of all the movement's strategists, the one least inclined to religious enthusiasm was Bayard Rustin. When an interviewer asked him whether King "retained that fundamentalist's sense of an active, personal god," Rustin replied, "Oh, yes, profoundly, and I was always amazed at how it was possible to combine this intense, analytical philosophical mind with this more or less fundamental—well I don't like to use the word 'fundamentalist'—but this abiding faith."[38] He could have been talking about Jonathan Edwards or Charles Grandison Finney.

What is remarkable about the civil rights movement, and what makes it most like one of the great historic revivals, is that the enthusiasm moved out of the church and into the streets. The movement also shifted the focus of church doctrine, as revivals usually do, though not always in the same direction as this time: away from eternal salvation and toward attaining justice in this life. In a region where white and black people alike had been reared on otherworldly doctrines, and had seen ample charlatanism, charges of hypocrisy were a frequent reaction to this shift. These charges got considerable play in the press, and, it must be said, they contained kernels of truth. Local segregationist spokesmen said that black preachers were buying Cadillacs while poor people were throwing their bus fare into the collection plate and getting blisters on their feet walking to work.[39] In northern cities, Malcolm X and later black militants made substantially the same charge. The predatory techniques of an Elmer Gantry might seem contrary to the spirit of the civil rights movement, yet they are hard to distinguish from some of the techniques used by the movement. Guilt-mongering for financial contributions was a staple of mass meetings, perhaps had to be, considering how hard-pressed the congregants were. Had the movement failed, the charges of the segregationists and black militants might not sound as churlish today as they do.

There is some indirect evidence that, if civil rights leaders struggled with the worries these charges must have raised, they found a way to live with them. Reinhold Niebuhr's stress on the need for "emotionally potent oversimplifications" in mobilizing any political movement, either for change or for maintenance of the status quo, was replicated in the thinking of King and other civil rights strategists. Niebuhr was not apologetic or optimistic about such simplifications. He warned that any collective action—that is, all politics—was "morally dangerous." But he also believed that political movements always have relied and always will rely on such simplifications—even salutary, morally necessary political movements. It was the part of realism to acknowledge those simplifications and the part of morality to take responsibility for them and not abuse them.[40]

MAKING RELIGION "REAL IN THE LIVES OF MEN"

The question raised by the charges of charlatanism in the revivalist techniques of the civil rights movement, then, is not, Did the civil rights movement, for all its virtuous achievements, indulge in mass manipulation? Rather, it is, Could the civil rights movement break the mold of run-of-the-mill evangelism only by politicizing it? Could it achieve a true revival that suddenly made religion a greater presence in people's day-to-day lives than ever before only by turning religion's means to political ends? So the Albany, Georgia, civil rights leader Slater King (no relation to Martin Luther King) asked in assessing why the Albany movement had broken down by 1965. He complained of "the lack of relevance of the Negro church" but noted "the symbolism" the church nonetheless held "for the average Negro woman." Black churches cost the black community as much as $150,000 apiece in Albany, he said. A crucial question for Slater King was, "How can we make the church more relevant?" Somehow the move-

Andrew Young, pictured here between Fannie Lou Hamer and Martin Luther King in Mississippi, said that the whole atmosphere in the black South became "more religious, especially when people start shooting at you—you do a lot more praying." (© Charmian Reading)

ment had done that. Looking back, the most important thing the movement had accomplished was to give the "blighted lives" of young people "a ray of hope":

> I have looked at the black and white workers in SNCC and felt that if there is any such thing as God working through people, I know that he works through them. For I have seen the hope, the faith and belief which they have instilled into other youngsters' lives. I have seen the new vistas of the heart and mind they have opened up to them; and I have seen the conservatives, black and white, almost go into a state of apoplexy whenever a discussion of SNCC comes up. And for the first time, I can imagine what type of persons the pharisees must have been and I can imagine what type of persons the Disciples must have been— intense, devoted, earthy, erring, but still moving forwards.[41]

Two years earlier, Andrew Young had told a reporter that there was "a resurgence of religious feeling" in the South "because of the civil rights movement." The whole atmosphere became "more religious, especially when folks start shooting at you—you do a lot more praying."[42] Was a shrewd political strategy the key to a successful effort to "make religion real in the lives of men," as Fred Shuttlesworth put it?[43] In other words, was political action the only way to make religion credible in a world plagued by political injustice?[44]

The Movement as a Revival 99

This question is not neatly separable from the issue of the separation of church and state. The civil rights movement brought religious concerns to bear upon local and national law. In doing this, the movement may have been no different from any other effort to achieve moral ends by political means. The state frequently responds to religious pressure, even when that pressure is couched in mild, decidedly unrevivalistic tones. Civil rights activists were more forthright about the source of their moral sentiments than other reformers, at the time and since. They frequently said things like, "I carry my battle with the Bible in one hand and the United States Constitution in the other."[45] The civil rights protesters' patriotism was as sincere as their religious devotion, and they did not see any danger in making the state conform to their religious vision. As Shuttlesworth put it at the end of a public declaration in 1964: "We have faith in America, and still believe that Birmingham and Alabama will rise to [the] height of glory in race relations. And we shall be true to our ideals as a Christian Nation."[46]

But the tainting of religious bodies with the concerns of Caesar was a more difficult issue for civil rights leaders. All political movements, even secular ones that shun any explicit establishment of religious ideas, involve the question of reconciling ends and means. King and other leaders often discussed the question, Can a moral end be achieved by political means, which by Niebuhr's definition are always immoral? Even nonviolent means force people to do something against their will; if the nonviolent means are serious, they create real deprivation and loss of life. (Martin Luther King, Bob Moses, and others followed Niebuhr in insisting that there was no moral superiority in the choice of nonviolent over violent means.) Nonviolent action, even to redress existing evils, involves an element of playing God and is therefore immoral. It is a nettlesome and, Niebuhr suggested, logically insoluble question. Only the discipline of a faith beyond logic could keep successful nonviolent action from becoming unchecked evil, and faith was no guarantee. The question, Niebuhr suggested, had to remain alive—it could never be forgotten or considered answered. Comparison of religious revivals to ostensibly secular political movements may contain the key to how such questions move through the minds of masses of people and are, to use a movement word, overcome rather than resolved.

WHAT RELIGIOUS ENTHUSIASM ACCOMPLISHED AND COULD NOT ACCOMPLISH

Recollections of extraordinary religious experiences are widespread among movement veterans and set that period off sharply, in their minds, from their experience in previous and subsequent years. Even for nonpartici-pants, the movement was extraordinary: charismatic preachers became inescapably prominent in public life for several years in a row. The huge crowds spilling out of the churches into the streets, behaving in ways they never had before, often seemed to outsiders to be under a spell. They upset the routine of their communities for months, in some cases years. They influenced political alignments, employment, and trade. The culture and social relations of an entire region were radically transformed. Over the period from roughly 1955 to 1965, the way Americans in the North and the South thought and felt about such central notions as race, freedom, and equality changed radically.

Perhaps more fundamentally, after a period of widespread apathy in the 1950s, a whole new generation suddenly got the idea into its collective head that wildly idealistic visions of social justice were realistic—and worth the trouble to pursue. Can this be equated with the Second Great Awakening of the mid-nineteenth century, which spurred abolitionism and other radical reform movements?[47]

William McLoughlin, a pioneer in the interdisciplinary study of religious life, writes that great religious "awakenings have been *the* shaping power of American culture since its inception." The difference between the historic "great awakenings" and ordinary revivals is that "awakenings alter the world view of a whole people or culture."[48] If McLoughlin is right, then perhaps what historians frequently call the Second Reconstruction could just as rightly be called the Third Great Awakening.[49]

The movement's habit of drawing on revivalist traditions, and its injection of powerful religious emotions into the public discussion that shaped civil rights legislation in the mid-1960s, raise important questions. One is whether our peculiar modern habit of separating religion from politics is entirely realistic. It is now customary for historians and sociologists to point out the great political effects of revivals in the past. So many scholars are driven by a revulsion with oppression that a major trend in contemporary scholarship—perhaps a unifying theme in the otherwise factious humanities and social sciences—focuses on how oppression succeeds and how resistance to oppression sometimes succeeds against the odds. The political decline of the American Left and the fall of organized socialism in Russia and much of Europe has led to a renewed interest in the role that religion might play in defeating what secular movements have failed to defeat. Scholars of religious revivals have made significant findings along these lines.

Much sociological and historical work explains how revivals often serve to justify social changes to deeply conservative masses of people. Sometimes the changes benefit those masses, often they harm them, but in either case the changes require unaccustomed ways of thinking. Revivals provide and reinforce these new ways with frequent repetition and memorable imagery. In the revivals that are conventionally recognized as such, the political and social results were generally indirect and unintended. But the

The Movement as a Revival 101

civil rights preachers' making such results their explicit goal is no more significant than other changes in doctrine from one Awakening to the next. The massive religious upheaval in the 1740s in New England reaffirmed predestination, for example, and the upheaval of the early nineteenth century repudiated it. But that colossal theological difference does not stop most of us from referring to the two upheavals as the First and Second Great Awakenings.

There is evidence, as Paul Johnson argues in his book about the Second Great Awakening in upstate New York, that religious revivals can produce, in effect, a bourgeois revolution, instilling in the artisans a sense of discipline and self-restraint that makes them amenable to new industrial discipline. Allen Tullos makes a similar case in his book about industrialization in the Carolina Piedmont, which took place during twentieth-century revivals there (confirming, in effect, what Liston Pope argued long ago). There is evidence, as Rhys Isaac points out in his book about the "Great Revival" in colonial Virginia, that revivals can democratize a colony and erase habits of deference to the gentry (confirming Alan Heimert's previous argument). There is evidence, as Karen Fields suggests in her brilliant book about the Jehovah's Witnesses in what is now Malawi and Zambia, that revivals may come closer than explicitly political revolutionary movements of the time (1910s and 1920s) to effecting—if inadvertently—an anticolonial war of independence.[50]

In other words, ostensibly religious movements have political dimensions that deserve the attention they have received in recent years. But the converse is also true. Ostensibly political movements have religious dimensions that deserve equal attention. The most successful struggle against oppression in modern America—the civil rights movement—defies sustained comparison with any nonreligious movement. It is hard to imagine masses of people lining up for years of excruciating risk against southern sheriffs, fire hoses, and attack dogs without some transcendent or millennial faith to sustain them. It is hard to imagine such faith being sustained without emotional mass rituals—without something extreme and extraordinary to link the masses' spirits.[51] It is impossible to ignore how often the participants carried their movement out in prophetic, ecstatic biblical tones. In this age of declining faith in revolution, the tradition of revivalist religion—commonly understood to be the opposite of revolution, indeed the most potent form of the opiate of the masses—might supply the raw materials of successful social change in the future.[52]

But the more immediate problem for participants in the civil rights movement was that they were a minority. However much their faith sustained them, however much God appeared to reward their faith, they were involved in a cultural war for the hearts and minds of the American people. To achieve equality of opportunity, they had chosen the expedient of desegregation. That was a radical change, and the protesters, unlike Gunnar Myrdal, expected it to provoke massive resistance.

By the mid-1950s desegregation turned out to be not such a hard sell among northerners. The movement had by then secured at least the acquiescence, if not the outright support, of public opinion in the North. Why? The goals (freedom, equality of opportunity) that black activists shared with northern liberals (still strong in the Democratic Party and prominent enough in the Republican Party throughout the 1960s) eased the way for the means of desegregation—as long as it was not happening in the North. Northern liberals further eased the activists' way by misunderstanding nonviolence. Civil rights leaders themselves were not above encouraging the widespread assumption that nonviolent meant suasionist, cooperative, or voluntary. That assumption led many liberals to defer concerns about the coercive means that southern black protesters in fact used. Again, northerners could at least defer such concerns as long as the coercive means were being used only against distant, presumptively backward southerners.[53] Competition for allies in the newly independent nations of Africa and Asia also helped the southern black freedom fighters gain northern acquiescence. Russian competition impressed upon liberals and nonliberals alike the need to overcome charges of American hypocrisy in the global fight for "freedom." However unfair, such charges impeded American diplomacy.[54] Finally, the protesters' own nonviolent, prayerful appearance— "dignified" was the adjective that clung to them like a Homeric epithet in press coverage—helped. Though this appearance was under great strain, and probably often feigned, it held up long enough to make it difficult even for nonliberals to sympathize with whoever attacked the protesters. The protesters played the role of innocent lambs. Sympathetic reporters, photographers, and editors magnified the protesters' innocence by capturing white vigilantes and lawmen at their most uncouth and thuggish. Widespread antisouthern stereotypes reinforced the stark Manicheanism of the drama. Those stereotypes may have been less damaging, but they were not much less insulting, than antiblack stereotypes, to which they were historically related.

But the protesters needed much more than the acquiescence of northerners. They did not want to test northern liberals' sympathy, still less to rely on their good intentions. Even when northern liberals were riding high— and in the mid-1950s they were not—their good intentions had produced too little to inspire the faith of a movement that, when it came to human powers, was rigorously skeptical. Black southern protesters were carrying most of the burden of battle on their own. They desperately needed a shift of power on the local, southern front. If they could not marshal a larger or more devoted following among the southern black population, if they could not broaden the right to vote enough to make elections relevant, if they could not drum up sufficient money and weapons to match the resources of their enemies, then they would settle for a reduction of their enemies' power. If white southerners splintered and lost their confidence, the white South's superior resources would not matter. The civil rights protesters had enormous—one is tempted to say miraculous—luck on that count, as the next three chapters will show.

6

Broken Churches, Broken Race

WHITE SOUTHERN RELIGIOUS LEADERSHIP

AND THE DECLINE OF WHITE SUPREMACY

The standard image of the white South in the civil rights struggle is a mob—united in anger against nine black students at Little Rock in 1957 or against James Meredith at the University of Mississippi in 1962.[1] With amazing discipline, southern politicians projected a more organized image of unanimity. All but three of the former Confederacy's twenty-two U.S. senators signed the Southern Manifesto of 1956 denouncing the Supreme Court and vowing to oppose its desegregation decree. (The three who did not sign were from Tennessee and Texas, on the periphery of the South.)[2] But the black minority in the region saw through what turned out to be a veneer of defiance and solidarity. Probably the most important reason they saw through it was that the religious leadership of the white South showed none of the militancy and discipline of the political leadership.

As in the antebellum struggle over slavery, American churches were bell-wethers of the whole society. Mid-nineteenth-century divisions in the Protestant churches foretold the biggest division ever in American politics. The most populous denominations, the Baptists, Methodists, and Presbyterians, all split, North versus South, over slavery—the splits became formal for the Baptists and Methodists in the 1840s, for the Presbyterians in 1861—and the country catastrophically followed their lead.

The churches one hundred years later were equally accurate but more complicated predictors. In the 1950s the white churches were still split between North and South—at least the Presbyterians and Baptists were. (Northern and southern Methodists formally reunited in 1939, a step the Presbyterians did not get around to until the 1980s. The Baptists have still not reunited.) In contrast to the 1850s, however, the southern white churches

Senator Strom Thurmond of South Carolina managed to craft extraordinary unity among southern politicians who faced elections and therefore possible baiting by demagogues. Significantly, however, he toned down the Southern Manifesto to obtain the support of moderates. (Clemson University Libraries, Special Collections)

of the 1950s did not remain unified within their region. There was a split in the white southern church that never became formalized, though it was conspicuous to those involved in it at the time. The split was over how to deal with the racial crisis of the mid-twentieth century. It was not as neat as the North-South split of the mid-nineteenth century, which is probably why it never became formalized. Compound fracture would probably be a better metaphor than split: the white churches of the South broke not into two camps, but rather into hopeless disarray and confusion over racial matters in the 1950s.

Interested observers like Martin Luther King and James Lawson sensed the disarray when they looked at white southern Christians: there was no way these people could measure up to the image of unity and defiance their politicians had created. King and others saw where the weak points were, and they drove in wedges. Scholars, blinded by the abiding racism of most of the white southern clergy, miss this crucial point. The historically significant thing about white religion in the 1950s–60s is not its failure to join the civil rights movement. The significant thing, given that the church was probably as racist as the rest of the white South, is that it failed in any meaningful way to join the anti–civil rights movement. Though King and others got rhetorical mileage out of the white southern clergy's failure to join hands with militant black Christians in the streets, they probably were not surprised by it. When in history have members of the clergy—white or black—led a social revolution against the privileges of their parishioners?

The historically significant failure of white southern churches was their inability to live up to the militant image that southern politicians had shown. The churches failed to elevate their whiteness—the institutions and customs that oppressed black folk—above their other concerns. That is what they needed to do to defend those institutions and customs effectively. Members of the churches were a pretty good cross-section of the white South. They loved feeling superior to black folk and they loved segregation; every election and opinion poll makes that clear. But the civil rights militants perceived something that opinion polls and, so far, historians have not examined deeply enough to grasp: that white churches were unwilling to make sacrifices to preserve segregation. They loved other things— peace, social order—more. They could not make defense of segregation the unifying principle of their culture.

Some prominent white southern religious leaders *tried* to achieve unity on the question of segregation—and were for a time confident that they could get it. But they were on the other side.[3] Before the Supreme Court's desegregation decision of 1954, the southern Presbyterians, known as the Presbyterian Church in the United States (PCUS), and, shortly after the decision, the Southern Baptist Convention (SBC) overwhelmingly passed resolutions supporting desegregation and calling on all to comply with it peacefully. People—even historians—are surprised to hear this. The pro-integration resolutions were reiterated later.[4] Both southern denominations elected presidents who were viewed as strong opponents of segregation.[5] Both desegregated their southern seminaries well ahead of most public schools. (By 1958 all SBC seminaries accepted black applicants.) Of course, there was dissent and conflict within the white southern denominations.[6] They were not as unified for compliance with desegregation as their senators were for defiance. Still, it is striking how, initially, the South's religious assemblies sharply opposed the position taken by its elected politicians.

This is not to suggest that the assemblies supported the civil rights movement. They were in their own eyes expressing cautious respect for the duly constituted authority of the Supreme Court. To them, and to us, that may have been a moderate, even conservative, gesture. But the South's political spokesmen believed, at any rate they consistently said, that the high court had abrogated the Constitution and tried to impose a dangerous and insulting revolution on southern society. The battle over forced desegregation in the 1950s began with the white South's religious bodies lined up on one side and its politicians on the other.

Civil rights activists criticized the southern white churches for not doing enough to promote desegregation or to prevent violence. Historians have echoed that criticism. But at the time segregationists were often much more caustic in criticizing those same churches. When white southern Baptist leaders protested that they did not mean to promote any radical or immediate change, angry segregationist leaders answered: "I don't care what you say, I am convinced that the leadership of the Southern Baptist Convention is *fighting* for integration, and we have got to put a stop to it."[7] A Baptist pastor in Mobile wrote that "extreme segregationists" among his parishioners were alarmed by reports accusing the SBC president of direct complicity with integrationists in his home city, Little Rock. (President Brooks Hays was a member of the local Urban League. So was Daisy Bates, organizer of the black students who desegregated the high school there in 1957.) The pastor tried to explain to the extremists that the SBC president had nothing to do with SBC agencies that were distributing integrationist literature, "yet they maintain that if he is our president that we[,] as a denomination, are backing integration."[8]

DEGREES OF SEGREGATIONISM

In opposition to the denominational resolutions, there were occasional fiery statements from southern white clergymen, such as the Rev. Carey Daniel, whose First Baptist Church of West Dallas became a platform for paranoid extremism. Daniel, also executive vice president of the Dallas Citizens' Council, said that Christians had a duty to disobey the Supreme Court, for the Court, in ordering desegregation, had unaccountably contradicted its long established tradition of approving segregation laws. He conceded that the Bible and Baptist tradition commanded men to obey civil authority (to render unto Caesar). But "Which is the more loyal and patriotic American Citizen," he asked, "the one who says that our Supreme Court was right five times and wrong once, or the one who says the court was wrong five times and right once?" Daniel also admitted that God made all souls equal—all equally sinful and "equally in need of being changed by Christ and the new birth." There would be no racial segregation in heaven—and "neither will there be any marriage or child-bearing there (Matthew 22:30), nor any soul-winning there, nor even any church or temple of worship there (Revelation 21:22)," because there would be no need for those things. "There are some things which are perfectly right and proper on earth which would be wrong in heaven, including racial segregation."[9]

Another militant segregationist, the Rev. Leon Burns of Columbia, Tennessee, was less interested in the Bible, which he did not get around to until the end of his speech, than he was in sex:

> The average Negro who wants integration is not interested in equal educational and economic advantages with the White race, and when these things are dangled before him by the NAACP he is unmoved, but when they whisper in his ear that someday he will be able to live with a White woman he is very interested. In a survey made among several thousand Negroes a few years ago, it was found that the secret desire of almost every Negro man questioned was to be able to sleep with a White woman. Several flatly stated that they would risk death in the electric chair to do it.[10]

There are other examples of this sort of militant and dishonest rhetoric from clergymen, but they are rare.[11]

Only a few preachers appear in segregationist periodicals and in the widely circulated segregationist pamphlets.[12] Conversely, most secular segregationists avoided discussion of religious themes. Of the small number of southern white ministers who identified themselves with the segregationist cause, most were much less decisive, much less defiant, than Daniel or Burns.

It is necessary to attend to the tone of segregationist clergymen's statements, and to consider them in the context of the aims of segregationist rhetoric. The segregationists' main problem was not convincing people to agree with them: again, white southerners showed an overwhelming preference for segregation in practically every opinion poll and election in which segregation was an issue. Their problem, rather, was to overcome the apathy, complacency, and overconfidence of white southerners. Segregationist leaders had to fight their own supporters' false sense of assurance that segregation, being so widely supported, was secure. They had to overcome the white southern masses' apparent belief that segregation did not require extraordinary efforts to defend it. These leaders constantly complained about the white South's unwillingness to shoulder the burdens and make the sacrifices of time and money to protect their beloved institution.[13]

The lack of commitment among white southerners who nominally favored segregation was what made clergymen's statements so important. The most widely published and often-cited segregationist preacher was the Rev. G. T. Gillespie of Jackson, Mississippi. He was known for a single speech in 1954—his only known segregationist statement, much reprinted but apparently never developed. (He died in 1958.)[14] Gillespie said, "While the Bible contains *no clear mandate* for or against segregation as between the white and negro races, it does furnish *considerable data* from which valid *inferences may* be drawn in support of the *general principle* of segregation as *an* important feature of the Divine purpose and Providence throughout the ages" (emphasis added). The most obvious inference to draw from Gillespie's hesitant language was that even committed segregationists were unwilling to claim biblical sanction.[15] Most of them saw no point in trying to be dishonest about that. Gillespie could never articulate a fighting faith for his parishioners. He was hedging segregationists' bets, not exhorting them with a vigorous call to arms.

The most decisive statement Gillespie made was: "Concerning matters of this kind, which in the inscrutable wisdom of God have been left for mankind to work out in the light of reason and experience without the full light of revelation, we dare not be dogmatic."[16] Similarly, in a segregationist collection of essays, the Rev. Edward B. Guerry, an Episcopal priest in Charleston, South Carolina, wrote: "We should endeavor to respect the sincere convictions of those who disagree with us. No one can assume for himself an attitude of infallibility on a matter so complex as this racial question."[17]

Other than careful, respectable, and nearly unassailable arguments like Gillespie's (if they can be called arguments), segregationist publications rarely gave space to clergymen or to religious appeals. Segregationist preachers who deviated from the careful, not very helpful pattern of Gillespie and Guerry tended to be even less useful to the cause. They showed little interest in disciplined strategy or unity behind a party line.

For segregationist leaders who were trying to maintain their authority and respectability, if it was not dangerous to indulge zealots like Carey Daniel and Leon Burns, it was probably not worth the trouble. The Rev. T. Robert Ingram of Houston, a "born-again" Episcopalian, herded Guerry and four other "born-again" southern Episcopalians into a little volume of essays that poured cold water on religious agitation for civil rights in 1960. But Ingram had a far more ambitious agenda than most segregationists. He seems to have been more interested in the publicity surrounding segregationism than in segregation itself. In August 1960 he laid out his scheme in a letter to Thomas Waring, editor of the influential segregationist newspaper, the *Charleston News and Courier*:

> Briefly, my plan is this: I am in the process of organizing a propaganda drive to explain how the system of law in the United States and all Christian countries . . . is rooted and grounded in the Ten Commandments. Further, to show that each of the Commandments is under attack by an organized movement of liberals and socialists, the spearhead of which is for the abolishment of capital punishment. . . . I am persuaded that my propaganda drive will tie all the loose ends together for Christian people and throw the liberals into [a] position of attacking not [s]imply a series of isolated issues but the whole law of God.[18]

This is the kind of grandiosity that sensible propagandists like Waring eschewed. For all his racism and fear of federal encroachment, Waring was a practical man who knew the importance of concentrating one's fire.

Most segregationist clergymen felt more compelled to act like Waring than like Ingram. The urge to appear moderate and reasonable while proving their segregationism, however, made them unreliable. The Rev. James Dees—an Episcopal priest from South Carolina who would break away from his denomination in 1963 and start his own, the Anglican Orthodox Church—made flexible as well as rigid statements on segregation. In 1955 Dees published a pamphlet, circulated widely in the South, renouncing all gradualism and defeatism and vowing to oppose integration to the bitter end. Yet at the end, Dees admitted:

> There are certain areas where I think that segregation is not practicable [or] sensible. I am glad to note that at the professional level, the races are coming together for what I believe is for good. I observe that the State Medical Society has voted to admit negro doctors. It has long been a practice for ministerial associations to be inter-racial. I think that it behooves the seminaries of our Church to receive negro students, since it would not be practicable to try to provide a separate seminary for the mere handful of negro seminary students that we have.[19]

Most segregationists thought that concessions like these only legitimated the principle of integration.

It is surprising how little southern white clergymen contributed to the record of the segregationist cause, considering how important religion was in the white South in the period. One reason may be that the Bible, which had so much slavery in it, offered so little objective support for postemancipation racism. There was no biblical equivalent of legal segregation or disfranchisement. There were separate nations and tribes in the Bible, but these were not defined the way race was in the modern South: by laws based on biological concepts. The nations and tribes in the Bible were defined by linguistic and cultural divisions. But the two "races" in the modern South both spoke English and practiced evangelical Protestantism.

For whatever reason, the few prominent religious figures associated with segregationism rarely emphasized the Bible, and when they did mention it they betrayed a complete lack of confidence in its usefulness. Generally they aimed to show only that Scripture was ambivalent on equality and brotherhood on this earth, not that it offered any positive warrant for segregation. Dr. Medford Evans ("an active Methodist layman" and former Sunday school teacher), writing in the Citizens' Council organ in January 1963, outlined St. Paul's insistence on certain earthly social distinctions. He thought that these distinctions might be loosely analogous to race, but he was careful to hedge the analogy: "Whether these injunctions of St. Paul are literally binding on Christians today or not, they certainly prove that St. Paul's statement that we are all one in Christ cannot be used to require indiscriminate integration" on earth. Evans cannot have expected such anticlimactic residues of his exegesis to be very useful in rallying apathetic white southerners. Yet his was typical of would-be religious leaders' statements.[20]

A few lay segregationists and occasional clergymen invoked Acts 17:26, where God created the "nations of men" and determined "the bounds of their habitation." But this was selective quotation of a verse that worked better for integrationists: that verse also said (as Fannie Lou Hamer emphasized) that God "made of one blood all the nations of men."[21] It was not a verse that segregationists could rely on or articulate forcefully. Evans avoided it altogether. Gillespie conceded the main point, emphasized not only in Acts but also elsewhere in the Bible: "Paul affirms the unity of the race"—meaning the human race—"based upon a common origin, concerning which there can be no difference of opinion among those who accept the authority of the Bible."[22] He did not mention that popular scientific arguments for racism required a rejection of biblical monogenesis.

Gillespie's position, like that of most literate ministers who supported segregation, was hesitant and inconclusive as to its biblical bona fides. There were references in the Old Testament that he found useful, especially the curse laid on Noah's son Ham after the Flood (Genesis 9:18–29). The point is not that the curse on Ham was universally understood, by anybody literate in biblical studies, to have nothing to do with racial distinctions. Rather, the point is that Gillespie himself could not do much with it. The story of Ham showed that Providence must have been "responsible for the distinct racial characteristics, which seem to have become fixed in prehistoric times, and which are chiefly responsible for the segregation of racial groups across the centuries and in our time." This was not enough to fuel propaganda. In a sense it was not even relevant, since no one was fighting "racial characteristics." Gillespie needed a justification for man-made legal barriers — barriers that applied even to those who had no distinct racial characteristics, who passed for white. Gillespie was on slightly firmer ground in drawing analogies to Old Testament restrictions on intermarriage and cross-breeding of crops. But his qualifications show that he was on the defensive and not entirely confident even there: the permissibility of modern racial laws was "a possible though not necessary inference" from the ancient Hebrew restrictions.

At any rate, when he got to the New Testament, Gillespie nullified what little support he had shaken out of the Old: "There is no question but that the emphasis placed by Our Lord upon the love of God for the whole world (John 3:16 and other passages) was intended in part at least as a rebuke to the bigotry and intolerance of the Jewish leaders, and to counteract the attitude of contempt and indifference which the Jewish people as a whole manifested toward the other peoples of the world." The best Gillespie could do was to argue, with many qualifications, that the New Testament did not *prohibit* segregation and did not positively *require* integration.[23] So, too, Gillespie's colleague at Bellhaven College, Morton Smith, concluded, "We would have to say first of all that the Bible does not condemn segregation. On the other hand it does not necessarily condemn integration. This being the case this whole matter falls into the realm of Christian liberty. Where the Bible is not clearcut . . . the individual must decide . . . on the basis of his own conscience."[24]

On the fringes of the segregation movement, a few clergymen made more out of the curse on Ham, attempting to claim that God created and intended to maintain racial distinctions.[25] But literate ministers either avoided biblical references or, in the manner of Gillespie, qualified them into uselessness. Again, Carey Daniel was exceptional. The *way* Daniel used the Bible seems to make it clear why he was exceptional. Not content with the curse on Ham or God's setting the "bounds of habitation" of nations, Daniel constructed an obsessive reading of Scripture, entitled "God the Original Segregationist." This took racial segregation to be the central idea of God's plan. Its section titles included "Moses the Segregationist," "Jesus the Segregationist," "Paul the Segregationist," "Nimrod the Original Desegregationist."[26] Christians could be deeply committed to segregation and still not stomach such a distortion of God's sense of priorities. Whatever comfort they might draw from such a reading in private, most were too embarrassed to be associated with anything of the kind in public.

It must be stressed that in public was where it mattered. It is not in dispute that white southerners held deeply racist views (though one might wonder at the strength of a commitment that required such contortions as Daniel's). The question is whether they could organize themselves effectively—publicly—to defend a way of life built on those views.

The Rev. W. A. Criswell, the most celebrated and popular segregationist minister, in a famous address to the South Carolina legislature (again reprinted much but apparently not developed later), mentioned the Bible only once, in passing—not in his actual discussion of segregation, but in the warm-up jokes he told to ingratiate himself with the audience. "You know," he said, "Paul . . . was a Southern Baptist. All through those letters in the Bible he says, 'You all'—y'all. That's in the Bible." And as a Texan visiting South Carolina, he added that "we" also know, however, that Paul "wasn't a South Carolinian . . . , for he also said 'I have learned that in whatsoever state I am therewith to be content.'" (The joke was, it was unthinkable that a South Carolinian could ever be content in another state.) That is all Criswell said about the Bible.[27] Criswell made a ringing if somewhat incoherent defense of segregation, drawing on common notions of social traditions, animal breeding, and so forth, but like most segregationist clergymen he contributed little that drew on his expertise. It certainly helped the segregationist cause that men of the cloth lent their authority to commonsensical, pragmatic, traditionalist, or scientific justifications of segregation. But these justifications were not ones that men of the cloth were specially qualified to provide, or were very good at providing.[28]

The question remains whether a significant number of local ministers, especially in the unaffiliated Baptist congregations and independent sects, might have preached segregation more wholeheartedly (and dishonestly) or, when the Word failed them, might have contributed to segregationist militancy by winks and blinks and nods.[29] The printed evidence reveals two things: segregationist organizations and leaders felt a strong need to add religious authority to their cause (else they would not have pulled the tentative ruminations of Gillespie, Evans, and others into their propaganda at all), and they could not find anything more decisive than what these writers offered (else they would naturally have printed it in their periodicals and pamphlets).

On occasion Criswell—and other preachers—may have indulged in some hocus-pocus to show that the Bible sanctioned segregation.[30] Virtually every historian who has touched on the matter assumes that this went on, though no one has produced much evidence. In his published speech on

The Rev. W. A. Criswell, minister of a Dallas church reputed to be the largest in the country, could not make a biblical case for segregation but allied himself with the segregationists on secular grounds. By the time this photograph was taken (1969), however, he had repudiated his segregationism and had become president of the body long denounced by segregationists, the Southern Baptist Convention. (Southern Baptist Historical Library and Archives, Nashville, Tennessee)

the matter, at any rate, Criswell did not stoop to claim that the Bible sanctioned segregation. Interestingly, it only took him until 1968 to repudiate segregationism altogether, at which time he made a point of admitting that his earlier position had never been justified biblically.[31] Nor did the Rev. Albert Freundt, a prominent segregationist Presbyterian in Mississippi, bother with the Bible in the article he published for the Citizens' Council.[32]

Segregation's biblical sanction was a matter of deep concern that should not be underestimated. The South was the Bible Belt: inerrantist and literalist views ran high. The question of the biblical provenance of their taboos and traditions was, for many white southerners, a subject of great soul-searching.[33] It was not simply propaganda. The soul-searching required honest and literate segregationists to drop any pretensions of conservative views on biblical interpretation: they would have to become radically unbiblical in their derivation of moral support for, let alone commands to maintain, their political institution. It is necessary to read carefully the anguished writings of the moderate segregationists, and would-be segregationists, on the matter.

During the historic struggle in Little Rock in 1957, some of the city's fringe churches had hitherto obscure preachers (Wesley Frank Pruden, for example) making cases for segregation. But two days before the crisis erupted at Central High, the Rev. Dale Cowling, a prominent local minister strongly connected with and supported by the SBC, preached at Second Baptist Church of Little Rock (the church of Congressman Brooks Hays, who later became president of the SBC). Cowling said: "Those who base their extreme opposition to integration upon their interpretation of the Scripture . . . are sincere beyond question. They are simply greatly mistaken in their efforts to prove that God has marked the Negro race and relegated it to the role of servant." Cowling dismissed the segregationist interpretation of Noah's curse on Ham: "A serious study of this section of scripture and History" would reveal that the imputation of Negro descent to Ham's line "is only the conjecture of man. We might as well reason that the Negro is the descendant of any other Old Testament character." Cowling also confined the strictures against intermarriage in Leviticus to the Old Testament dispensation: "Since the coming of the Savior, the clear insistence of the Word of God is that 'in Christ there is neither bond nor free, Greek [n]or Hebrew.'"[34]

The white pastor of First Baptist Church in Poplarville, Mississippi, the Rev. Clyde Gordon, who dissociated himself from "northern agitators" and did not think "immediate" integration was practical, still condemned race prejudice as unbiblical and wrong. "There are some false impressions and conceptions that we need to fight bitterly today. Some of our writers try to take the Bible and prove by it that God is color conscious and, in such an attempt, reveal a staggering ignorance of God and His word." One example sufficed: "Some say that Noah placed a curse on Ham and he became black. That is not truth. It is not so stated in the Bible. . . . The Negro race, along with every one of us, had its beginning back there in Eden." The Negro "is a human being made in the image of God."[35] Gordon did not want to attack segregation; he simply wanted its defenders not to blaspheme themselves.

Such statements infuriated the segregationists but put them on the defensive. Though it is probably impossible to make a complete tally of biblical references, it seems that antisegregationists and moderates refer to Bible stories like the curse on Ham more often than prominent segregationists do. Segregationists' enemies used the curse on Ham story as a foil. It was an opportunity to ridicule the segregationists, to expose their ignorance and failures of reason. Segregationists, in turn, were sensitive to the way people like Carey Daniel exposed their weaknesses, perhaps made segregationist ideology appear weaker than it was. Historians have tended to follow the example of the integrationists and moderates, exaggerating the pervasiveness of Hamidic and other biblical arguments. The point is not to rescue mainstream segregationists from the condescension of posterity; they may well deserve that for other reasons. Rather, it is to establish a sense of realism and balance in historical understanding.

CONSERVATIVES CANNOT
LIVE BY SEGREGATION ALONE

Cowling, along with officials at SBC headquarters in Nashville who answered inquiries on segregation, like Clifton Allen, head of Sunday school publications, gained reputations as liberals—as did the SBC and PCUS hierarchies generally. But one of the most important conservatives in the southern church was quite frank about the matter, too. "Christians should recognize that there is no biblical or legal justification for segregation," said L. Nelson Bell, editor of the *Southern Presbyterian Journal*,[36] in a public forum run by *Life* magazine in October 1956. Bell publicly as well as privately opposed church statements advocating civil rights. His private correspondence makes it clear that he favored segregation and white supremacy. Still, early in the struggle, he said publicly, "It can be safely affirmed that segregation of the races by law is both unchristian and un-American."[37]

Bell was always struggling to maintain the support of his more bigoted allies while differentiating his position from theirs. His issue was freedom, in the sense of individual rights. He objected to coerced desegregation by government or by the church hierarchy but did not claim any authority over individuals who chose to mix with individuals of another race.[38] Bell believed that segregation occurred spontaneously, and that once the political furor died down, segregation would reassert itself. For it was the natural condition that both black and white southerners preferred. Bell's confidence in segregation, and his individualism, meant that he could only go along so far with extreme segregationists. They wanted to marshal the white South into a united fighting front; he wanted to allow nature to run its course. They wanted to maintain segregation by force; he wanted to maintain freedom of choice.

Bell tried to mollify his extremist supporters, but the strain wore him down and ended at least three important friendships. One of his longstanding supporters, the Rev. Arnette Gamble of Hollandale, Mississippi, began arguing with Bell in 1955. Bell thought that Jim Crow laws should be allowed to die: they were no longer needed, if they ever were, to enforce a natural division between black and white. But Gamble insisted, "To think that segregation could or would be maintained without segregation laws, is to be quite unrealistic." Removal of the laws would "inevitably result in miscegenation, . . . a development I believe God disapproves." Gamble

L. Nelson Bell, intellectual leader of conservative southern Presbyterians, tried to build a broad, ecumenical movement devoted to social and theological conservatism. Bell frankly stated that segregation had no biblical sanction. Extreme segregationists resented Bell's strictly "voluntary" segregationism, which they saw as de facto endorsement of integration. (Billy Graham Center Archives, Wheaton, Illinois; courtesy Virginia Somerville)

hit upon the inadjudicable difference that split segregationist ranks everywhere: "The people of Mississippi know" that racial barriers "can only be maintained by force."[39] But Bell believed that he was the true friend of racial customs. Whereas more extreme segregationists doubted the strength of those customs, Bell had confidence in their moral attractiveness to black and white southerners. True segregationists did not need to resort to any tacky imposition of state power, Bell implied.

Bell and Gamble were old partners in promoting social and theological conservatism.[40] But after going back and forth with increasing heat over segregation, Bell finally snapped: "Arnette, let me suggest that you stop trying to live in a world which no longer exists. I am as loyal to the South as any person, but there are higher considerations than any regional loyalty, and those considerations have to do with the gospel of Jesus Christ and our obligation to preach and live it." Bell made a note to himself at the end of Gamble's last letter to him, in 1962, that "I did not answer his letter as he is much like Carl McIntire" — Bell's bitter rival, a fundamentalist who was trying to make America embrace a conservatism very different from Bell's — "Nothing I might write would please him."[41]

Bell had a similar breakdown with J. F. Gallimore, of Tryon, North Carolina, who added anti-Semitism to his extreme Negrophobia. Bell stressed that it was wasteful to "divert our emphasis" from the project of winning souls to Christ by going after particular groups. For a long time, Bell wrote encouragingly to Gallimore, trying to bring him into a reasonable—and viable—conservative movement. But finally Bell could bear it no longer: "I know you and love you well enough to tell you frankly that I *heartily disagree* with your anti-Semitic position and with the literature which you enclosed. Above all else, I do not believe that this position can be sustained by Scripture." The "most important" thing of all was that, "when we have hate in our hearts for *any* people, it does something to us rather than to them"—a point that, incidentally, Martin Luther King had been making, though Bell did not mention that. Bell told Gallimore: "My dear brother, get this hate out of your heart! It cannot hurt the Jews, and it certainly can hurt you."[42]

It is important to view Bell's exchanges with his fellow conservatives in the context of debates and developments that were, in the minds of most Protestant leaders in the white South, more important than segregation. Bell was part of a conservative insurgency within southern Protestantism that came to be known as Evangelicalism—with a capital *E*, to distinguish it from the more general enthusiastic variant of Protestantism that flourished in America, without consistent association with any particular theological doctrine, at least since the 1740s. The Evangelical movement emerged during World War II as an aggressive effort to reestablish the legitimacy, popularity, authority, and institutional strength of conservative doctrine. After the political defeat of fundamentalism (a movement that began about 1909) in the Scopes Trial of the 1920s, many educated Protestant conservatives felt discredited and dishonored. Still, they believed that their social values and interpretations of the Bible were closer to those of the American public than were those of either theological liberals (associated with the Social Gospel and other postmillennialist movements) or neo-orthodox thinkers. (While Evangelicals saw fundamentalism as vindictive and divisive, they rejected neo-orthodoxy as an inadequate response to liberal modernism, viewing their own movement as a distinct fourth choice.) The Evangelical movement grew tremendously in the postwar years, while fundamentalism as such—bogged down in esoteric disputes that often seemed to turn on the personal rivalries of its leaders—seemed to stagnate.[43] The Evangelicals' growth was in part the result of the self-conscious determination of leaders like Bell to learn from the fundamentalists' mistakes.

In Bell's mind, the Evangelical project depended on avoiding the self-righteous tribalism of the fundamentalists.[44] Many schismatic Protestant movements in history, Bell knew, suffered from the same limitations. Pursuit of perfectionist and separatist strategies conflicted with what Bell considered to be the primary duty of a Christian: to spread the gospel as widely as possible. To increase the appeal of their version of the gospel, Evangelicals often tailored it to accommodate the existing beliefs of the largest number of potential converts (as missionaries have generally had the sense to do). Evangelicals believed that their social and theological conservatism had broad democratic appeal.

Not so their racism. To go down the segregationist road, Evangelicals thought, would be dangerously narrow and exclusive—even if they confined their strategic targets to the white South, which few Evangelicals were content to do. Smart white southerners like Bell knew that segregation, whatever its social advantages and moral virtues, was just not popular enough to build an empire on, even in the South. It was with the larger goal of winning souls over to his doctrines, and with increasing exasperation, that Bell tried to rein in fellow conservatives who deviated from his line in an extreme segregationist direction.[45]

Bell's task was the more difficult because he was also trying to hold on to racial moderates and even moderate integrationists. Many on that side of the political fence were with him, or at least willing to listen to him, on social and theological conservatism. Bell tried to dissuade moderates from ruining their ministries with diversionary social action crusades.[46]

He could not sustain the stretch: the committed segregationists took Bell to task in ever stronger language for his efforts to moderate and restrain them. They wanted a church militant. Another of his fading segregationist allies, T. R. Miller, in the heat of one of their exchanges, told Bell, "In my book, there is no such thing as middle ground or moderation in the matter."[47] Previously Miller had seemed almost to worship Bell: "I agree with you on practically every stand you have taken, that has come to my notice, except not quite so on the race question." On that one, Miller said, "I do not believe there is any room for moderation." Whereas Bell shunned the charge of extremism at all costs, Miller embraced it: "While I am an extremist," Miller asserted, he was in good company. After all, he reminded Bell later, "you and I are radicals and fanatics, and so was our Lord and savior. . . . He came to bring the sword and not peace." Miller spoke defensively about the standing of fellow extremists as Christians and gentlemen, adding, "Gradualism is the most dangerous attitude to take with regard to mixing of the races."[48]

Not surprisingly, Miller got so fed up with his church's moderation that he resigned his position as an elder and threatened to quit altogether. Bell, in turn, got fed up with Miller. In what he called a "brutally frank" letter, Bell called Miller's attitude "utterly childish" and said that he hoped to "shock" Miller and "bring you to your senses." Bell asked, "What kind of 'Christianity' can lead you to turn in bitterness from your Lord?" Reminding Miller that there were no perfect men or churches in this world, Bell begged him in Jesus' name to "desist from your folly. . . . I am ashamed of you—and I believe that you are ashamed of yourself." He urged Miller to "read the Bible more" and to read "less of the flood of 'anti' literature"— this for the sake of their shared conservatism. "Once we get involved in always attacking people, something goes out of our life and Christian witness. Don't let the Devil get you down. Go back to your church and get the blessings of God from fellowship with those who know and love you."[49]

ON THE DEFENSIVE:

NO "POSITIVE GOOD" ARGUMENT FOR SEGREGATION

Miller's principled, uncompromising stance was rare among the segregationists who were deeply involved in religion. Whatever they thought in private, most segregationists' public rhetoric maintained not just courteous respectfulness, but a pleading, defensive tone. The Rev. Dees said that, as a segregationist clergyman, he always had to work uphill against prevailing assumptions:

> It seems generally the case when discussing this question, that when religion is brought in to the question, it seems to be tentatively assumed that segregation must be done away with, and that it is the will of Jesus to do so. Because He said that we must love one another, racial distinctions and racial barriers must be destroyed. Religion is so intimately tied in with . . . brotherly love and concern for the underprivileged that many people seem to assume without question that desegregation should be the position of the Church, and that . . . they should do all they can to support it, or . . . at least not oppose it.[50]

Similarly, although the elders of Montgomery's Trinity Presbyterian Church forthrightly affirmed the virtues of segregation in a petition to the PCUS Board of Christian Education, they hedged. They sought to prevail on grounds other than the intrinsic merits of their argument. The best they could do was to insist on keeping the question open, on not accepting the popular assumption that Christianity conflicted with segregation. Most segregationists seemed to believe that this assumption was widespread in the southern white churches as well as in the rest of the country. The Montgomery elders said, "There are strong and sincere differences of opinion on the part of equally sincere and devout Christians. We recognize the right of some of our brethren to differ from us . . . and we ask that we be accorded the same Christian courtesy in our views. We see no reason why this question of race relations should be continually injected into our literature and programs and presented in such a manner as to leave the impression that to believe and think otherwise is un-Christian."[51]

Belief that they were bucking the trend in their own southern white denominations inhibited the segregationists. Rarely did religious leaders seek to persuade their assemblies to adopt resolutions of outright support of segregation. Nobody seems to have articulated anything equivalent to the "Positive Good" position of antebellum slaveowners. As the slaveowners became more confident, they argued that slavery was not merely permissible or inevitable, but also morally superior to the northern labor system, which they regarded as anarchic and irresponsible. A century later, segregationists loved to point to the crime, poverty, and rioting in northern ghettoes, and to blame it all on integration; but their propaganda about their own region remained undeveloped and defensive.

Rather than use religion to justify their peculiar institution, segregationist clergymen cleaved to a safer, more modest position. Their pleadings coalesced around opposition to social and political preaching. This safer position had a long and legitimate pedigree in their churches—which legal segregation, as a new, modern institution, did not. In reaction to other southern ministers who urged the white South to repent of racial violence, the Rev. Albert Freundt wrote in a Citizens' Council statement: "The ministry of preaching should be reserved for the word of God. Our Presbyterian Confession of Faith, for example, says that Churches 'are to handle or conclude nothing but that which is ecclesiastical, and are not to intermeddle with civil affairs which concern the commonwealth.'" The Rev. Morton Smith, a co-conspirator of Freundt and Gillespie in the Central Mississippi Presbytery, also rested his argument on this injunction against mixing religion and politics from the Westminster Confession of 1647. (The defining statement of Presbyterianism, this Confession was also echoed by many early Baptist declarations.) "Jesus, our King," Smith explained, "did not seek social reform, but salvation of sinners." This line became a mantra for segregationist Presbyterians; they usually omitted to mention the next line of the confession, which outlined exceptions to the rule.[52]

Baptists also cited their denomination's history of jealously policing the separation of church and state and insisted on the paramount importance of saving souls through individual conversion.[53] In 1957 one mildly segregationist pastor criticized the SBC's focus on race. Given the deep division over segregation in the church, he said, it would be better if SBC agencies "gave more time to the alcohol problem and so forth." Most of the Rev. Ingram's "born-again" Episcopalians were committed to that idea as well.[54]

In the late 1950s, when a number of small, rural churches bombarded the SBC with resolutions opposing its support of the Supreme Court's desegregation decision, many of the churches simply asked for political neutrality. In South Carolina, for example, Manning Baptist Church felt that the SBC's position was "extremely extraneous to the proper agenda of a religious convention." First Baptist of Olar complained that SBC leaders were "stressing [the] civil right[s] issue and racial problems too much" and "meddling in affairs that [did] not concern them." Making clear their opposition to integration, the Olar members concluded: "We think that our Senators and Congressm[e]n can handle this. As we all know that this is a political matter." And First Baptist of Camden expressed its "regret" that the SBC "took any part in the political questions arising out of the 1954 Supreme Court decision." The Marigold Baptist Church of Marigold, Mississippi, asked the SBC in the future to "avoid the subject of segregation or integration . . . and . . . use its best efforts to table any discussion of said subject . . . and to avoid much unfavo[r]able publicity which has been exploited by the press in recent months." This last request raises the possibility that some segregationists sought to get the church out of politics as a way to hide how deeply the southern white churches were divided.[55] All knew, at any rate, that if the church were further politicized, things would go badly for segregation.

THE WAGES OF NEUTRALITY

Some historians reasonably consider this safe avoidance of politics to be de facto segregationism.[56] It probably was, for many years. What is more revealing about the 1950s and 1960s, however, is how much the apolitical stance of many segregationist preachers divided them from other segregationist preachers. Segregationists needed more than de facto support: they needed help in rallying white southerners. They needed new methods and new authority to exhort the masses. They needed to get the fair-weather segregationists out of their seats and into the fight. Leon Burns declared, "Something is terribly wrong when we, as American people, are afraid to discuss anything that vitally concerns our way of life. . . . We have all learned that you do not solve problems, or overcome difficulties, by refusing to face them, or talk about them. I am a little bit ashamed of some of my brethren who seem to think we can solve this problem of segregation by playing the game of the ostrich."[57]

Criswell, likewise, complained to the South Carolina legislature that the state's Baptist Evangelistic Conference had tried to muzzle him. Members of the conference had told him "things like this: 'Now this thing of desegregation, and this thing of integration, now we are not to mention that, we are not to speak of that. That is a highly debatable issue, and it is volati[l]e, and it is full of political dynamite and no mention should be said about that.'" Criswell said that he thought to himself: "Well! Isn't it a strange come to pass that a minister of the gospel of the Son of God, whose forebears and predecessors were martyrs and were burned at the stake[;] isn't it a strange come to pass in our day and in our generation—why the minister is [asked to be so] cowardly [as] to circumvent any issue such as that."[58] What is remarkable about Criswell's statement is that it sounds exactly like Martin Luther King's "Letter from the Birmingham Jail." Both men said that white southern clergymen's noncommittal attitude hindered the progress of a moral cause.

How well did segregationist ministers themselves respect the injunction against political preaching? So far, I have been able to track down only one full set of the sermon notes of a segregationist who worked as a full-time pastor: those of W. A. Gamble of Hollandale, Mississippi, who clashed with Bell. The Rev. Freundt named Gamble as one of the segregationist ringleaders of the Central Mississippi Presbytery, perhaps the most reactionary presbytery in the South (Gillespie headed it for many years). It is striking that, in a lifetime of preaching (1937–1971) on every subject and Bible verse imaginable, there is no record in Gamble's notes of a single sermon on segregation.[59]

The reason cannot be that Gamble scrupulously respected the tradition of keeping politics out of the pulpit: he gave plenty of sermons on free enterprise, communism, the Cold War. Of course, it is possible that he threw away the evidence later; the sanitizing of archives is a common enough experience. But Gamble's records show no evidence of a purge— such as gaps in the sequence, or diminution of the number of extant sermon notes during periods of great public controversy over civil rights. It is also possible that Gamble improvised segregationism from the pulpit, leaving no record of what might have been copious words on the subject. On the other hand, his notes seem to be complete scripts rather than outlines or fragments, and improvisation would suggest much less thought than he put into every other subject.

Most readers today would naturally assume that people were more racist than they appear in the fragmentary record. There are, indisputably, more white southerners today who remember being integrationists and moderates than there ever were at the time. On the other hand, it is possible that the silences in the record conceal a less, rather than a more, racist reality than we are inclined to suspect.[60] Gamble may have confined his segregationist ranting to meetings of the presbytery, which might have delegated or pressured him to write the angry letters to Bell. Like many a politician or civic leader, Gamble might have been paying lip service to a cause he felt no deep commitment to. The available evidence does not permit a definite answer. What is clear is that the segregationists' overwhelming preference for arguing against all politicization reflected their lack of confidence in their position.

A major variation on the theme of opposition to political preaching is a startling anticlericalism among segregationists. In Chattanooga, a segregationist denounced the PCUS's pro-integration position: "The sad part of this is that just as the rulings of the Supreme Court and their violations of the Constitution have made so many people lose respect for and confidence in the Courts—so the leaders in our churches are forcing many members to lose respect for and confidence in our churches and its leaders."[61] A month after the *Brown* decision, one of the major segregationist leaders of South Carolina, Congressman William Jennings Bryan Dorn, complained to supporters about widespread southern white acquiescence in the decision. He was "alarmed over the tendency exhibited by many of our church leaders, particularly their influence with youth."[62] Another leader of the South Carolina segregationists, state senator Marion Gressette, told the American Legion and other groups during the election campaign of 1956 that his opposition came from two sources: "a few NAACP Mbrs and Church leaders."[63]

Mississippi congressman John Bell Williams sought help from the head of the Association of Citizens' Councils, William J. Simmons, in financing a new segregationist publishing venture, "The American Christian." Williams urged Simmons to help distribute the magazine in churches, where it "might do much to offset the integrationists' propaganda they are hearing from the pulpits."[64] The Methodist Sunday school teacher Medford Evans led his segregationist "Declaration" by reminding readers that "the Methodist Church was founded because John Wesley rejected ecclesiastical authoritarianism," which had once more become a danger. "Too many of our clergy seem servile toward the episcopacy and supercilious toward the laity." These overbearing clerics used the notion of "freedom of the pulpit" to "stifle criticism." The church needed to balance free pulpits with "freedom of the congregation."[65] An article entitled "Is the South Being Betrayed by Its Ministers and White Church Women?," published by the segregationist *Christian Layman*, claimed that "priests, ministers and white church women are *unquestionably* leaders in the struggle for southern desegregation."[66]

Perhaps the ultimate anticlerical statement came from a fan of Strom Thurmond's in 1955: "By now it should be evident to the pro-segregation forces that their real opponent in the fight to provide for the preservation of the white race in America is the so-called christian religion. . . . It should also be evident that segregation in the U.S. is a lost cause unless the pro-segregation forces organize across state lines, po[o]l their knowledge and resources, and launch a frontal assault on organized religion by telling all men the truth about themselves and the so-called christian religion." This fan wanted Thurmond to organize all leaders of the southern states to expose falsehood, suggesting that he "notify the heads of the various religious organizations sponsoring integration that they will be exposed as [frauds] and their religion as a myth, just so much modern witchcraft."[67]

Governor James F. Byrnes of South Carolina, arguably the most distinguished segregationist in the country (a confidant of FDR's, he had been a U.S. Supreme Court justice and secretary of state), offered some perhaps inadvertent insight into segregationists' rivalry with their errant ministers. "I bow to the ministers of my church when they confine their opinions to religious questions," Byrnes wrote to a supporter. He said he was surprised that "a few preachers in the several denominations undertake to speak for the entire membership." He assured his reader that he had received letters from Methodists, Baptists, Presbyterians, and Episcopalians "criticizing the public statements of the clergy since the recent decision of the Supreme Court." These letters convinced Byrnes that "some of our preachers have impaired their ability to serve their congregations." All the deacons in one Baptist church he knew of had signed a letter to their pastor "severely criticizing him" for speaking for them on segregation. Traditionally, Byrnes added with exasperation, ministers had preached the gospel: "They did not preach that Christianity required integration of the races in public schools. They did not encourage intermarriage," as some had been doing recently. Their sudden change of direction did not come from God but from the Supreme Court, and Byrnes questioned their motives. "There is one thing certain, that the preacher or newspaper editor who is willing to surrender to the NAACP propaganda can be assured of a newspaper headline and of praise from metropolitan newspapers."[68]

The higher segregationists looked in their churches, the worse it got. They blamed preachers more than laymen or laywomen, big-city preachers more than rural and small-town ones, bishops or regional and denominational board members more than preachers. Universities and colleges were, of course, the worst of all. The segregationists spent a lot of time bemoaning the takeover of southern seminaries by integrationists. The *Christian Layman* of October 1958 contained only two references to the Bible. One of them was in an article by Baptist minister Dr. Dan Vial, of the Department of Religion at Wake Forest College, who was an integrationist. The segregationist editors gave Vial a lot of space to denounce racist uses of the "curse of Ham" story, which Vial called "demonic" and "absurd" treatments of the Bible that "support immmoral prejudices." But the magazine did not dispute Vial's exegesis. It simply reprinted it above the following statement: It was "obvious" that Vial "is travelling hand in hand with the National Council of Churches, the NAACP and all other agencies that would destroy Christianity. Southern Baptists, this man is teaching religion in one of your church supported schools. Is this what you want?"[69]

In some cases, divinity faculty were indeed disproportionately outspoken in favor of civil rights. In June 1952, when the trustees of the University of the South (Sewanee) rejected a directive of October 1951 from the Synod of Sewanee Province (fifteen southern dioceses) to admit black students, eight of the ten members of the theology faculty protested. The eight maintained that the trustees' position was "untenable in the light of Christian ethics and of the teaching of the Anglican Communion." Sewanee was one of two Episcopal seminaries in the South.[70] The Episcopal denomination, which had never divided into North-South bodies, backed the faculty.[71] Rumors about moral lapses of three of the protesting faculty, spread by students who were encouraged by Bishop Frank Juhan of Florida, led to one resignation, but eventually all but one Sewanee faculty member resigned.[72] The uproar, covered in the national press, led a majority of Episcopal bishops to ask their candidates to leave Sewanee: 35 of 56 first- and second-year students transferred; about one-third of them were welcomed at the other southern Episcopalian alternative, the recently desegregated Virginia Theological Seminary, despite overcrowding there. In 1953 Sewanee trustees desegregated—despite threats of a major funder, the segregationist Jesse Ball DuPont, to withdraw.[73]

A similar dispute over civil rights at Vanderbilt University in 1960 led to the expulsion of the black divinity student James Lawson—soon to become one of the most famous black religious leaders in the civil rights struggle. Lawson's dismissal produced an angry outcry from several of the divinity faculty. Most threatened to resign if Lawson was not reinstated. To deal with the controversy, university president Harvie Branscomb negotiated with his faculty, but he was constrained. Like Sewanee, Vanderbilt had proud southern traditions, and it had an outspoken segregationist on its board of trustees: James Stahlman, publisher of the *Nashville Banner*, one of the most militant conservatives in the South. Stahlman meddled with amazing energy and persistence, lobbying trustees and university officials to take a hard line against Lawson and his sympathizers. The divinity faculty's resignation threats, which so worried and embarrassed Branscomb and the university namesake's heir, Harold Vanderbilt, provoked Stahlman to tell a confidant, "If I had been Chancellor . . . I would have accepted all those . . . resignations immediately, announced the closing of the Divinity School, turned that section of the campus over to the Law School and converted the Chapel into a magnificent law library." Stahlman believed that "closing up some of the left-wing situations" on campus was long overdue. He would also have accepted resignations from "the dissidents on all the other faculties" and given tainted grant money from the Rockefeller Foundation "back to those boys." He would have "announced that Vanderbilt was on its own, for better or worse." Stahlman was confident that "the alumni would have responded 99.99 per cent favorably and most of the foundation and corporate gifts would have been doubled because the University had the guts to stand up and be counted. Maybe I'm wrong, but that's the way I feel about it."[74]

Far more typical of the segregationists' attitude toward religion than the efforts of Carey Daniel and Leon Burns to find biblical sanction was the banner headline of the front-page article in the *Citizens' Council* in 1958: "Southern Churches Urge Mixing." The *Council* condemned the southern white clergy's general support of integration, which it tried to link with communism. As one subheadline put it, "Reds Increase Influence in Many U.S. Churches." An editorial headline earlier that year twinned the NAACP, "Reds in the Woodpile," with the churches, "And in the Rectory." Two years previously, an editorial was headlined "Pinkos in the Pulpit."[75] As late as October 1957, however, the *Council* was apparently not confident that it could overcome the trend. That month an Alabama Methodist minister wrote to the magazine, "The use of official literature to promote radical programs of racial integration has been a source of embarrassment not only to Methodists but to members of other denominations. How long the rank and file of church members will support church agencies and periodicals whose policies defy individual conviction, no one can say. We do know that there is a growing chorus of protests."[76]

Statements of resentment about religious authority abound in segregationist writings. South Carolina newspaperman William D. Workman was probably the most levelheaded and knowledgeable tactician among the segregationists. He wrote that in the face of pervasive pressure to desegregate, which was coming "with almost nauseating frequency" from clergymen, including southern white clergymen, "the Southerner feels a strain on his religion as well as on his temper."[77] Nelson Bell's fairweather ally, T. R. Miller, wrote, "I have lost practically all the respect I ever had (and it was great at one time) for the clergy of all churches, and for the churches themselves."[78] The Association of Citizens' Councils of Louisiana framed an epigraph from J. Edgar Hoover at the top of its July 1957 newsletter: "I confess to a real apprehension, so long as Communists are able to secure ministers of the gospel to promote their evil work." Inside was a report on how the Southern Baptist Convention, "following the trend of all churches all over the world, . . . unanimously adopted a report . . . recommending an end of resistance to integration of races."[79] A Citizens' Council leaflet blamed racial strife on "preachers who recommend racial 'integration' (mongrelization)." It was not just northern preachers, but those "right here at home . . . in whom we had placed our trust" who enlisted in "the enemy's army. . . . It is a waste of time to study the causes for this sudden change of

Roy Harris, the respected political strategist and segregationist firebrand, broke with his Methodist church over segregation, boasting, "I ain't been to church since" his minister signed a statement rejecting extremism. (Photograph by Charles Walton Reeves; courtesy Richard B. Russell Library for Political Research and Studies, University of Georgia Libraries; used by permission of Walter Harrison Reeves)

attitude of the Preachers—most of them. . . . The 'gentle gentleman of the cloth' has turned out to be a vicious monstrosity, without parallel, and to stop him is the task at hand."[80]

Some followed the logic of anticlericalism so far as to dissociate themselves from religion altogether. Roy Harris, the Georgia power broker and sometime officeholder, was one of the most gifted propagandists in the South. When the Methodist hierarchy dared to send his church a new minister who had signed a statement against closing the schools to prevent integration, Harris boasted, "I ain't been to church since."[81] In June 1954 an Atlanta racist attacked the head of the PCUS, Wade Boggs, who had made forthright statements against segregation. Referring to Boggs's "burning desire to establish a mixed race," the Atlanta racist said, "I *was* a member of your denomination, but left Druid Hills [Presbyterian Church] and the faith along with others when Dr. [Donald] Miller ranted and raved to have the races mixed." He compared clergymen like Boggs with "those Senator Eastland speaks of as 'racial politicians in judicial robes,'" that is, Supreme Court justices, who made "desperate" efforts to force racial mixing by law. "THANK GOD THERE IS NO LAW WHICH REQUIRES CHURCH ATTENDANCE."[82] The best-selling segregationist author Carleton Putnam addressed the southern white clergy with even sterner language: "You watch the federal government take forcibly from the South while you sit with your hands folded in prayer. I'm tired of the sort of combined ignorance and stupidity you have shown. I'm tired of your timid conformity with the popular drift. And finally, I'm tired of your milk and water suggestions that we pass the buck to God while you support a policy which forces the white children of the South against the wishes of their parents into associations they understand better than you do."[83] This sort of rhetoric further divided prominent segregationist spokesmen from the white South's religious authorities, making unity ever more difficult.

7

Pulpit versus Pew

White southerners, even when they were not outright antireligious or anticlerical, still saw a clear division between pulpit and pew on segregation. In a debate over the Gray Amendment, the Virginia legislature's program of evasive maneuvers that stopped short of outright defiance of the Supreme Court, Republican state senator Ted Dalton reportedly stated, "The politicians have lined up almost solidly for the amendment and the preachers almost solidly against it." Dalton would take his stand "with the preachers." The article covering this debate for the National Council of Churches (NCC), written by a local ministerial leader, was entitled "Parson's Revolt."[1]

The Rev. W. G. Foster, minister of First Presbyterian Church in Florence, South Carolina, a segregationist hotbed, told the head of the southern Presbyterians in February 1956 that "the Sessions of the Churches in South Carolina are being bombarded with requests to send up overtures condemning the Supreme Court and the General Assembly [of the PCUS] and asking for a vote in the Presbyteries that will silence the Assembly and all dissenters." Foster opposed the rebellious segregationists, including his own elders, but he warned that the position of clergy was becoming difficult. All over the state, "as ministers do not follow the party line, the rift between the Minister and the Elder is beginning to widen as it did in the case of the union vote."[2] (He was referring to the effort to reunite the PCUS with northern Presbyterians.)

The Rev. J. Wayne Fulton of Shenandoah Presbyterian Church in Miami informed the PCUS leadership that he felt that further statements from clergymen and denominational leaders about civil rights "could result in schisms of catastrophic proportions." Before the Supreme Court's decision of 1954, Fulton observed, "there had been wide tolerance" among white southerners "toward those, particularly of their own clergy, who entertained convictions about segregation different [from] their own." Before the Court's sudden change, when desegregation was a matter of abstract speculation, or happened incrementally, "tolerance had been so much in evidence as to create an entirely erroneous impression in some ecclesiastical circles that the people of the South, by and large, were ready to adjust to a mild desegregation program." No such mild program was imaginable now, after *Brown v. Board of Education*. People now viewed desegregationist ministers as "ecclesiastical Quislings."[3]

Hard-core segregationists saw the same pulpit-pew tension. When Nelson Bell's antagonist T. R. Miller condemned the southern Presbyterians' desegregationist statements of 1954 and 1955, he warned: "A deep cleavage is rapidly coming to pass in our church, especially between layman and minister. . . . It is . . . the same . . . in practically every other church. People are rapidly losing respect for all ministers." Miller referred to his friend, the chief justice of the South Carolina Supreme Court, as an example of an important leader who had ordered his name removed from the membership of the Episcopal Church "because of its activity in the race matters." Miller believed that the influence of ministers was especially poisonous because laypeople tended to "think whatever a preacher says and does is absolutely above reproach." He had no doubt that the majority were coming over to his side: "It is alarming how the masses are losing confidence in preachers and churches, and I have lost just about all I had."[4]

Some integrationists saw drawbacks in the religious tone of their side. An early and vigorous southern white foe of segregation, Virginia's J. Shelton Horsley, wrote in February 1945 to Richmond editor Virginius Dabney: "I am always a little leery of any movement that is dominated by preachers. You recall what a mess they made of prohibition and of foreign missions."[5] Dabney understood but replied, "The trouble about getting persons other than ministers to take the lead in this movement is that so few other people will get out in front." The moderation meetings that Dabney had attended in Atlanta and Richmond were "made up overwhelmingly of teachers and preachers. There is a small sprinkling of professional men, and an equally small sprinkling of newspapermen. Not one single prominent businessman has been willing to take a leading role."[6] Black civil rights leaders were certainly justified in saying that, on the whole, the southern white clergy had not demonstrated courage or martyrdom. But few would have suggested that other professions in the white South had better records. What is interesting is that black civil rights leaders had higher expectations of the clergy.

PURGING THE SUSPECTED INTEGRATIONISTS

The anticlerical tendency bore fruit in celebrated cases of integrationist or moderate clergymen who were driven from their pulpits. In 1958 an official of the white moderate Southern Regional Council (SRC) told a reporter that there was a new generation of DPs in the South, "displaced parsons."[7] A lot of work would be required to balance the cases where segregationists succeeded in expelling moderates and integrationists with the cases where segregationists defected from the major denominations or, like Roy Harris, ceased churchgoing altogether. What is clear is that the expulsions, like the defections, dramatically illustrate the deep divisions within southern white churches.

One of the most revealing instances of expulsion was that of the Rev. Robert B. McNeill. In June 1959 the *New York Times* reported that McNeill, pastor of First Presbyterian Church, Columbus, Georgia, "was summarily removed" from his pulpit because he had advocated contact between Negroes and whites. In his final sermon at the 1,200-member church, McNeill, who had been informed of his dismissal four days earlier, said, "There are those in the church who so overtly despise race prejudice that they are willing to wear a black badge of stigma until all racial injustice is wiped out." After the sermon, the Rev. Frank King, of Valdosta, chairman of a judicial commission of the Southwest Georgia Presbytery, informed a surprised congregation of McNeill's dismissal. One woman cried out, "Mr. King, you have been listening to the wrong people." Another declared, "You dismissed him just because a few people have come down there and told you big lies about him." When McNeill walked out of the church, according to the *Times*, "women members of the choir burst into tears, and several elders and parishioners followed Mr. King [to the pulpit] to denounce the commission's action and [to] demand that Mr. McNeill be kept on."[8]

The controversy had begun two years earlier when McNeill published an article in *Look* (May 28, 1957) condemning segregation and urging southerners not to delay integration until federal-state disputes were resolved. Calling for "creative contact" between the races, McNeill wrote that Negroes should serve "on city councils, grand juries, school boards, medical societies, ministerial associations, and other public agencies."[9] (It is worth noting that this was not radically different from what the segregationist priest James Dees advocated with impunity.) According to the *Times*, only about 50 out of 1,200 members (just over 4 percent) of the congregation opposed McNeill. Nelson Bell, incidentally, sympathized with him and believed that he was advocating a strictly voluntary program.[10] A few of the anti-McNeill elders tried to secure McNeill's dismissal from the presbytery. The presbytery's judicial commission specified that eight church elders initiated the action against McNeill, but that sixteen others did not oppose him. McNeill's opponents also withheld pledge payments and refused to support his budget. The judicial commission had initially dissolved the session (the business meeting of church members) for a cooling-off period and in November 1958 admonished the members to protect the freedom of the pulpit. At that point the commission acknowledged the "prophetic task of a Christian minister . . . to proclaim the word and will of Almighty God which often has the unpleasant sound of stern rebuke and judgment." It continued:

> Prophets of old were oftentimes . . . at cross-purposes with the traditions of men. . . . A minister who voices only the comfort of the Christian Gospel without its accompanying challenge and call to repentance, has ignored his obligation to proclaim "the whole counsel of God" and . . . [quoting Swinburne] "served up half a Christ." And, in the opinion of this Commission, such a minister is not worthy of his Christ nor of his calling nor of his congregation. We are under the strongest possible conviction that the Christian pulpit must never be muffled nor silenced by threats of any description.

On the other hand, the commission reminded McNeill that his parishioners had a "right to differ" with him. Referring to complaints from McNeill's enemies that he was neglecting his pastoral duties, the commission warned him that he must be a priest as well as a prophet: "The priestly role must not be sacrificed on the altar of prophetic zeal and courage."[11]

Seven months later, in June 1959, Frank King, speaking for the judicial commission, explained the apparent reversal of its earlier decision to protect McNeill: "The commission feels that the voice of the pulpit should be the voice of the congregation." McNeill would remain on salary and would be allowed to stay in the manse until September 1, or until he found another pastorate.

The *Times* said that McNeill's opponents in the church refused to comment. The only quotation it could get from that side of the dispute came from Deacon Algie Mosely, a Columbus lawyer: "This is a family situation, and I think the newspapers should stay out of it." Defenders of McNeill, who were quite voluble, seemed to be more confident about the church's public, political character—even though they were losing the battle. Church member Eben Reid rebuked Frank King, within earshot of the *Times* reporter: "If we kick a Christian man and his family out like this, then what hope have we? Mr. King, you and your commission have failed a Christian man and his family."[12]

One Baptist minister who was targeted for expulsion by hostile segregationists in his congregation did not take the threat seriously because his enemies were so divided. In July 1957 Fred Laughon, pastor of the First Baptist Church of Orangeburg, South Carolina, informed the secretary of the SBC's Christian Life Commission (CLC), A. C. Miller, that he faced an insurgency among his deacons. Miller had expressed concern about Laughon's position, but Laughon assured him, "I don't think they feel they can ask for my resignation for they are too busy fighting among themselves."[13] As it turned out, Laughon soon resigned under pressure and sought employment elsewhere. Like McNeill, however, he had good reason to believe that the segregationists were not strong enough to ruin him.

Expulsion attempts elsewhere did not always succeed. When they did, they hardly resembled the lynch mob one might expect. Late in 1955 the pastor of First Baptist Church in Batesburg, South Carolina, notified the SBC that his deacons' meeting—which had a clear segregationist majority—might be asking him to resign soon. He was hoping to find a different flock or other "field of service," since "the relationship here is strained to the breaking point." But he was unsure "which would help the cause of Christian race relations the most: for me to resign before being voted out of the church, or to wait for a clear-cut expression of the congregation." He sought advice on how to proceed.[14] He ended up resigning by the end of the year, according to the *Southern School News*, "because of differences of opinion concerning his stand on segregation."[15]

At this point, it is impossible to estimate whether successful expulsions outnumbered unsuccessful attempts.[16] Another case a few years later illustrates what may have been the pattern. A segregationist minority attempted a coup at Belle View Baptist Church in Alexandria, Virginia. Since there were a number of cases like McNeill's and Laughon's where such a minority succeeded, the segregationists at Belle View had reason to hope. They wanted to dismiss the Rev. Norman Alexander Yance in the mid-1960s because he had moderate views on segregation. But, historian Mark Newman reports, they could not do it because the full congregation gave Yance an overwhelming vote of confidence. "Half of those who voted for my dismissal," according to Yance, "were not at all active in the church; most made no financial contribution to the church. Only two or three could be called active members." In April 1965 Belle View became the first of Virginia's SBC-affiliated churches to welcome black members unconditionally. Richmond's First Baptist followed suit seven months later: 70 percent of the congregation approved the decision to desegregate. Six segregationist deacons filed suit to block it, but they lost.[17]

OTHER SEGREGATIONIST
EFFORTS TO ORGANIZE DISSENT

In various pockets of the Deep South, some churches achieved a consensus in support of segregation.[18] A number of them expressed such consensus in formal protests to the central denominational bodies.[19] There are more of these protests in the SBC files than there are references to attempted or actual expulsions. Some of the protests threatened to withhold the church's regular financial contributions to the central body. Again, it is impossible to estimate how many churches voted to withhold contributions, against how many such efforts failed, against how many churches never even entertained such efforts.[20] Counting all the local resolutions in the SBC files, 8 churches actually resolved to withdraw contributions, and another 19 either threatened to withdraw or requested that their money be earmarked for nonintegrationist activities. In addition to these, 48 churches protested the SBC's integrationism without making threats or withdrawing funds.[21] Needless to say, the total, 75 churches, is a tiny minority of the 31,297 churches in the SBC (less than a quarter of 1 percent). There were 1,438 SBC-affiliated churches in South Carolina alone.[22]

SBC officials did not take the resolutions very seriously. A. C. Miller, the convention's point man on racial issues and something of a lightning rod, wrote to a pastor in Florida in 1957 to calm his concern over the restiveness of local segregationists. Miller had been attending SBC meetings for forty-two years and had seen the group "stirred by many divisive issues." Every time, there were "voices raised expressing fear that the Convention will be divided." But he was sure that the SBC "is not going to divide over this issue, and not many of the churches are going to change their loyalty of giving to missions through the Cooperative Program."[23] SBC officials informed several petitioners that the convention's mail ran 34 to 1 in support of the SBC's stance—a declaration that appears to have been dishonest. (Of the extant letters in the CLC and Executive Committee files—where all such letters seemed to end up—segregationist protests clearly outnumber integrationist and moderate voices, though the balance is close. Of course, it is impossible to know whether many letters were lost or discarded.)[24] Often, officials insinuated that such resolutions appeared to be orchestrated to exaggerate their popularity and that they were concentrated in isolated rural pockets of the Deep South (mainly Louisiana and South Carolina).[25] The officials replied to some segregationist resolutions with skepticism as to the procedures by which they were adopted, suggesting that a small group of zealots organized a strong show of feeling that would not have arisen spontaneously. Many resolutions were obviously boilerplate, taken from a single, possibly intimidating (rather than representative) source.

Official skepticism drew strength from local pastors who wrote to the SBC to dissociate their church from a deacons' committee or lay committee that had sent in a segregationist resolution: the majority of regular members did not attend the special meeting or did not vote, the active segregationists were not regular members, or the segregationist majority was just acting on a fleeting impulse that would not be followed up. The Rev. W. Ray Avant of Cameron Baptist Church in Cameron, South Carolina, for instance, "regretted" his congregation's "impulsive action based on such tragically unsound biblical exegesis and interpretation."[26]

George Ritchey, minister of a protesting church in Mansfield, Louisiana, while vacationing in Mexico, wrote secretly to A. C. Miller, explaining: "We have a situation in our church and in North Louisiana that is difficult to deal with. Many of our best men have become involved in the Citizens Council Movement. This organization is fanatically pushing the extreme segregationist point of view." Ritchey's finance chairman, who was also one of his "most faithful deacons" and a Sunday school teacher, led the local Citizens' Council. The group wanted to stop all contributions to the SBC "until something could be done to correct what they thought was promotion of integration by denominational agencies." But when the other deacons took up the question, "they decided on a milder policy of protesting to those agencies which in their opinion were promoting integration." Ritchey noted that other "large churches" in the area were also "disturbed" about the matter. Like many segregationists, the Mansfield group conspiratorially blamed the Christian Life Commission for imposing its radical views on the whole denomination. "Personally, I am not against the Commission and its works, but this integration matter is explosive now and must be handled cautiously."[27]

The executive committee of the State Baptist Convention of Georgia apparently quashed an attempt to present a segregationist resolution to the whole convention, as the head of the committee reported with satisfaction to the central body in Nashville.[28] Similarly, the pastor of First Baptist in Mullins, South Carolina, though urging the convention to slow down its integrationist activities, reported that the recent SBC meeting in Charleston had rejected a motion "to censure the Christian Life Commission" for its integrationism and instead "went on record expressing its faith in the Southern Baptist Convention and [its] agencies."[29] SBC officials were glad to hear from J. Dan Williams, a pastor in Greenville, South Carolina, who dissociated himself from the segregationist resolution of a nearby church: "This church in Newberry does not speak for all of us in South Carolina." Williams pointed out the obvious factual errors in the Newberry petition and the tendency of its author "to impose his own opinion on his fellow Baptists." He closed his letter with the assurance that "many of us in South Carolina stand with you in the effort to find a sensible and Christian way through these difficult problems facing us in the Southland."[30] When the Utica Baptist Church petitioned the Mississippi Baptist State Convention to withdraw a speaking invitation to SBC president Brooks Hays, on the grounds that Hays had "proven himself to be an avowed integrationist," the state SBC thwarted the attempt, and Hays addressed the Mississippi convention the following November.[31]

Segregationists regarded the SBC's Christian Life Commission as the source of the denomination's integrationism. But SBC officials noted with justice that, in the words of Louisiana's representative to the CLC, "every statement of the Commission has been overwhelmingly accepted and adopted" by the whole convention, and that "Brooks Hays, Chairman of the Commission[,] was just elected President of the SBC [in May 1957] by a big majority."[32] (In the nick of time: Hays was becoming a lightning rod, too. Probably the highest profile Southern Baptist after Harry Truman and Billy Graham, Hays served in the U.S. Congress as a representative from Arkansas while he was an SBC official. Despite his declining popularity as a moderate in his congressional district, which included Little Rock, he was reelected president of the SBC in May 1958. But in the afterglow of the Little Rock school crisis of fall 1957, Hays lost his congressional seat, in November 1958, to an inexperienced write-in candidate whose only credentials were his segregationism.) A. C. Miller, who succeeded Hays at the CLC when Hays became SBC president, told a group of segregationists in South Carolina that the people who disagreed with the Southern Baptist Convention and with the Supreme Court had had ample opportunity to make their case to the SBC. Indeed, segregationists had taken up two-thirds of the debate time in the convention. But "in spite of this prolonged opposition the Convention goes on to vote at a ratio of 100 to 1 in favor of the proposal [to support the Supreme Court's 1954 desegregation order]." Given these overwhelming odds, Miller said with blithe defiance, "why should we fuss about it?"[33] Clearly SBC officials were determined to ride out the storm of segregationist opposition. Just as clearly, they were determined not to push for desegregation in any radical way.

The PCUS had fewer threats to withdraw, though Bell's *Southern Presbyterian Journal* published at least three dissenting statements—from First Presbyterian and Central Presbyterian in Jackson, Mississippi, and Trinity Presbyterian in Montgomery, Alabama—during the great season of resolutions, 1957–58.[34] (For some reason, the resolutions died out after that. Perhaps the segregationists lost confidence after denominational officials called their bluff.) The few segregationist churches that tried to use leverage seem to have been resoundingly rebuffed by the PCUS. The Central Mississippi Presbytery and the Mississippi Synod accepted some segregationist resolutions, but most of the local bodies seem to have maintained a neutral or moderate stance. In 1964, after the siege of Birmingham by civil rights forces, that city's presbytery rejected an overture to remove the notoriously integrationist and northern-based National Council of Churches from the list of charities to which the presbytery contributed.[35] Experiences like these reinforced the segregationists' inclination to let the churches go. It was best for them to organize outside the churches and to keep the churches as apolitical as possible.

The segregationist effort to get the churches out of politics was a gambit by laymen who recognized that secular institutions worked better for their cause, on balance, than religious ones. For every moderate pastor the segregationists could drive from the pulpit, for every congregation they could coax into petitioning the SBC, they feared that the moderates and integrationists would have more pastors and letter writers weighing in on the other side—for compliance with the law, for social peace, for reconciliation, and, deadliest of all, for keeping desegregated public schools open. Segregationists could not afford the vast expenditure of energy and time it would take to convert the churches to active segregationism. Even if they could bring the SBC or the PCUS to heel, which they could not, there were too many southern Methodists, Catholics, and Episcopalians—members of denominations that were dominated by northerners. It was more efficient to shore up the boundary between religion and politics.

No one emphasized the need to curb the clergy more than J. Howard Pew, the Texas tycoon of Sun Oil, a key figure in the broad secular conservatism that was percolating in the 1950s. Pew was a funder not only of *Christianity Today* but also of William Buckley's *National Review* and of Barry Goldwater's presidential candidacy. Speaking at the National Council of United Presbyterian Men in March 1958, Pew tied his theme to a broad defense of individual freedom, which he believed was the central idea of the founders of Presbyterianism and of the pioneering American importer and legitimator of Presbyterianism, John Witherspoon. Presbyterian individualism translated into a "Ban on Secular Affairs," Pew said. A "basic tenet of Presbyterianism is that the corporate Church shall not become involved in matters that are properly the concern of the State. Well did our forbears know that intervention in secular affairs would largely impair the ability of the Church to fulfill its mission." Pew cited the Westminster Confession's provision that "synods and councils are to handle or conclude nothing but that which is ecclesiastical, and are not to intermeddle with civil affairs which concern the commonwealth." This did not mean that individual believers should abstain from politics. Witherspoon himself, after all, had signed the Declaration of Independence and pamphleteered for the Revolutionary cause. "But the determination of right and wrong is solely a matter for the individual, subject only to the Divine authority which speaks to him through his conscience." For, as the Westminster divines had also said, "All synods and councils since the apostles' times, whether general or particular, may err, and many have erred; therefore they are not to be made the rule of faith or practice." Individualist traditions were sacred, fundamental to the identity of the church, Pew declared. "Are we now to regard our Church Constitution as a scrap of paper? Are we to plunge our Church into the issues of international trade and other international relationships?" He admitted that the temptation was not simply or unambiguously evil: "Christian people everywhere are seeking to eliminate poverty and illiteracy, and to care for those who are unable to look after themselves. Seeing such ills and much injustice, the Christian is tempted to invoke the police power of government to correct them. But Christ proclaimed the gospel of love, not of force. Police power produces resentment and ill will, stifles energy and destroys production. It never makes men kind and charitable."[36]

Pew envisioned, and helped to create, a national conservative movement that would one day seize the government of the United States. His main ally in the southern Presbyterian Church was L. Nelson Bell, the intellectual leader of an antimodernist, antiliberal movement that was entrenched in the PCUS. Bell believed in segregation, as Pew undoubtedly did. But, as we have seen, Bell did not want to stake his journal, his evangelism, or his conservatism on segregation's defense. Bell tried to adopt a reasonable conservative stance—one very close, incidentally, not only to Pew's, but also to that of the most influential segregationist editor in the country, James J. Kilpatrick of the *Richmond News-Leader* (see Chapter 8).

Bell's agony in defending this position is evident in his personal correspondence, quoted above. His lost friends and allies were worth the risk, however, because of a crucial factor that has been strangely ignored in the literature of the civil rights struggle. Bell's son-in-law was more important to Pew than Bell was, and more important to Bell than Pew was. Bell's son-in-law was the most famous and most influential minister in the white South—indeed, in the world: Billy Graham.

After some waffling, Billy Graham had taken a firm line from 1954 on that he would not allow segregated seating in his crusades.[37] Like Bell, Graham frankly stated that segregation could not be biblically justified, and he frequently had to deal with segregationist baiting.[38] One of his southern admirers, who had been thrilled by the handsome young minister's work to revive conservative Christianity, was shocked to learn of his position on race. "I think it is most unfortunate that Billy Graham has joined the liberals in the idea of integration," she wrote in 1958. "He is definitely hurting his cause and his standing in the South."[39]

One of Bell's jobs was to help answer the mountains of mail that Graham received. What Bell told one irate segregationist in 1959 conveys the flavor of many letters that went out to defend his son-in-law: "Billy has *not* stirred up racial strife. Apparently you have been reading some of the hate literature—some of it inspired by Communists—which revels in attacking those whom God is using."[40] Bell emphasized to another irate follower that Graham was not forcing integration on anybody: "Billy is anxious to preach the gospel to all who will hear, and in Charlotte there have been a few Negroes sprinkled through the auditorium and a few in the choir, but no one has said anything about it and it seems that a real Christian spirit has prevailed. As a matter of fact, quite a number of Negroes have made professions of faith there. When all is said and done, that is the one and final solution to our race and all other problems."[41] Again, Bell did not need to convince people to *like* integration—he did not like it himself. He just needed to make them think that it was not the most important thing in their lives. For entirely different reasons, that was exactly what the civil rights movement needed to make them think.

Governor George Bell Timmerman of South Carolina, like most successful southern politicians, believed that he had to make segregation the most important thing, at least in campaign rhetoric. He protested Graham's plan to speak on the lawn of the state capital in October 1958.[42] Timmerman ultimately reached a compromise whereby Graham preached to a desegregated crowd nearby. But Graham had won the bigger point, desegregating a major public meeting over the objections of politicians and in violation of state law. Governor George Wallace of Alabama—the most popular and influential segregationist ever—made a similar accommodation with Graham and had a cordial meeting with him, even though Graham desegregated a huge public stadium in Alabama in 1965, shortly after the bloody clashes at Selma. Several segregationists wrote dismayed or angry letters to Wallace.[43]

Being on Graham's good side was a chance that segregationist politicians took, for it was more dangerous to oppose such a popular figure than it was to fudge the hard line of resistance. The great segregationist editor, Thomas R. Waring, discovered this after pulling Graham's column from his newspaper in 1961. Waring and many of his subscribers were infuriated by the way Graham was letting himself be used by integrationists. But the mail asking for Graham's reinstatement far outweighed what Waring had previously received protesting Graham's integrationism.[44]

One of most interesting aspects of Graham's career shows up in the light of newspaper publisher William Randolph Hearst's famous "puff Graham" order to his staff. Hearst had hitched the success of his newspapers to that of the great post–World War II revivalist, a wise business decision. Every newspaper that had a chance at Graham seems to have followed the example. *Ebony* puffed him to the hilt in a 1957 spread entitled "No Color Line in Heaven: Billy Graham."[45] The southern press seems almost entirely to have ignored the integration of Graham's audiences, choirs, and ushering staffs, as it promoted him on an epic scale. Graham's extensive scrapbooks of his crusades contain clippings from all the great segregationist papers of the South, with front-page photographs and tear-out sections of multipage photo-essays on his unprecedented crowds. Yet it is impossible to find a black face in the crowd photos—even in places where segregationists were bitterly pamphleteering and sending letters denouncing the integration that was taking place in those crowds. Even closer-up photos rarely

The Rev. Billy Graham with young black men in Harlem. A few extremists tried to use such images of "social mixing" to discredit the popular evangelist and other prominent southern religious leaders. But mainstream segregationist editors preferred simply to suppress evidence of Graham's integrationism. Nelson Bell was Graham's father-in-law, and W. A. Criswell was his pastor. (Billy Graham Evangelistic Association)

The most famous white southern Baptist in the 1950s, Billy Graham, had an affinity with the most famous black southern Baptist, Martin Luther King Jr., photographed together here in New York in 1957. Graham infuriated many segregationists by sharing his pulpit at Madison Square Garden with King that year. King supported Graham's "crusade" to save New Yorkers from sin; Graham endorsed what he called the "social revolution" King was leading in the South. (Billy Graham Evangelistic Association)

reveal the racial composition of the audience. This cannot have been completely deliberate: in the photojournalistic culture of the 1950s and early 1960s, black people were much less often identifiable as such than they have been in published photographs since the late 1960s. The multimillion-dollar hair-straightening and skin-lightening industries also helped make public integration look less dramatic than it actually was. Photo editors had to want to see integration and to make readers see it. Still, it appears that Graham forced the southern papers into the position of choosing to suppress the news of desegregation.

Graham's people noticed the press's blind eye. During the Charlotte, North Carolina, crusade in 1958, Bell observed that there were about 25 Negroes in the 1,500-member choir, and "there were some Negroes scattered throughout the great Coliseum and when the invitation was given, on many occasions there were Negroes among those who came forward. The newspapers made no mention of this, nor did any of the local people do so publicly."[46] Graham himself once complained of the lack of coverage: The *Alabama Baptist* reported in July 1965, "Evangelist Billy Graham Thursday blasted the national television networks for not reporting his integrated religious crusade in Montgomery, Ala., a race hot-bed in recent months." Graham called his interracial activities in Montgomery "the most strategic and most important of any crusade, yet the least publicized." He said up to 18,000 persons integrated nightly without incident, but the networks did not report this adequately. "It looks as though you must protest something to get news," Graham commented.[47]

Other mysteries in Graham's career may take years to unravel. It is unclear whether Graham influenced Bell on integration or Bell influenced Graham. It is unclear how much Graham may have influenced the man he called his own pastor, W. A. Criswell, or whether the two ever discussed integration. I am unaware of any discussion in either the religious or secular press of the bizarre circumstance—coincidence?—that the most powerful practitioner of desegregation in the southern white church was pastored by perhaps its most notorious segregationist.[48] They were as odd a pair as the major voting blocs in the Democratic Party or, for that matter, as the factions in the Southern Baptist Convention. In 1968, as noted above, Criswell repudiated his segregationism and was elected president of the SBC.

Long before 1968 it was clear that the Southern Baptist Convention could not sustain a strong commitment to segregation. The smart money in the SBC was on Graham's strategy of inspiring massive numbers of new converts worldwide without regard to modern, secular, and parochial distinctions like "race." Like Bell's conservatives in the PCUS and in the Evangelical empire that Howard Pew was helping to create around *Christianity Today*, the SBC wanted to hitch its wagon to Billy Graham.

Segregationist editors like Waring did not need William Randolph

Hearst to tell them to puff Graham. Graham filled the stadiums for weeks, not only in the South but also in Africa, Asia, Europe, and Latin America. He probably took the minds of both black and white Americans off civil rights for a while, but he did so by insisting on desegregation. In truth, there is little evidence that Graham wanted to publicize his desegregationism—he was as shrewd as any politician, entertainer, or editor in publicizing things that could help him and soft-pedaling the same things when they might hurt him.

But it is also true that Graham had greater leeway than any one else to follow biblical, political, or commercial imperatives. It was his luck—or was it Providence?—that all three were in harmony on the race question for the moment (as they were at the crucial moments in the careers of Harry Truman, Martin Luther King, and Lyndon Johnson, all of whom incidentally had deep southern Baptist roots). When Graham desegregated his audiences, for example, his vast popularity shielded him from scrutiny and retaliation. A few irate segregationists pathetically attempted to organize a boycott of his crusades after Graham shared his Madison Square Garden pulpit with Martin Luther King and praised the "social revolution" that Graham said King was leading in 1957.[49]

If King's agreement to appear on platforms with Graham, or to send his staff to seek Graham's advice on the logistics of mass meetings, is any guide, King recognized the huge benefit of Graham's soft-pedaled but persistent initiatives. It was useful to the movement to have a charismatic white southerner who had no apparent ideological commitment to civil rights, and therefore was unlikely to be ostracized, break down racial barriers. Apparently King did not appreciate the similar role played by the South's white rock 'n' rollers—Buddy Holly, Carl Perkins, or Elvis Presley—as historians of a certain age are eager to argue. King, sounding more like Graham, or any other southern preacher, wrote in his *Ebony* column that rock 'n' roll "often plunges men's minds into degrading and immoral depths"; thus it was "totally incompatible" with gospel music.[50] Graham, by contrast, was morally clean. Nonetheless, he was more popular than any musician. Graham drew in the squares and the blue-haired ladies, as well as the teenage hepcats, in record-breaking numbers on six continents, not for one-night stands, but for weeks on end.

NOT ONLY UNEQUAL, BUT ALSO UNSEPARATE:
THE LARGER SOCIAL TRUTH BEHIND BILLY GRAHAM

The Southern Baptist Convention and the Presbyterian Church in the United States, like Martin Luther King, recognized that whatever their reservations about the smooth-talking evangelist from North Carolina, they had everything to gain by being seen with him. But the SBC and PCUS had other reasons to resist the weakening tug of segregationism.

Part of the problem for segregationists was that southern churches were not always segregated—in an important historical sense, they never were. Before the Civil War, slaveowners had maintained their superiority in churches that had black parishioners. Masters could keep their slaves under watch when they had them in church, though many slaves and free Negroes expressed a desire for separate churches. After the war, black parishioners left in droves to join existing black separatist churches or to start their own. Black worshippers made their moves to erect or to reinforce separate institutions under different circumstances, and with different motives, from the white politicians who imposed legal segregation in public spaces. On the whole, they did this before legal segregation was decreed. Black Christians gathered "under their own vine and fig tree," to use historian William Montgomery's biblical phrase, before separation became defined as a form (or a stage) of white supremacy—before separation became "segregation" as such. (The masters' superiority in times and places of slavery had been achieved by much more effective means than separation.) The separation of churches into black and white buildings, with entirely separate denominations for the Methodists and Baptists, was generally voluntary. Black migration out of white-dominated churches, like black migration out of southern states, was an act of freedom.[51]

Separation of churches had never been the same as segregation. It was thus somewhat anachronistic for black leaders, including Fannie Lou Hamer and Martin Luther King, to refer to separate churches that way. Hamer and King scored irresistible rhetorical points when they repeated their line that the most segregated hour in America was ten o'clock on Sunday morning. It was easy, as always, to call attention to the clash between professions of Christian brotherhood and reality, the reality in this case being the cold shoulder that white churches routinely gave to uninvited black guests. But Hamer and King misrepresented the historical fact of separate churches. Segregation was by definition a form of degradation and superiority: segregationists had to lie when they tried to convince the nation that it was just a form of separation. (And lie is what they did, from Henry Grady and Henry Billings Brown, the Yankee Supreme Court justice who wrote Grady's "separate but equal" formula into national law in 1896, to Jimmy Byrnes and Sam Ervin.) But segregationists did not get a chance to separate the South's churches. Though the process was complex and varied, black people were more often evading than accepting white supremacy when they formed separate congregations and denominations.

Even at that, the separation of churches had never been strict. The practice of bringing black maids and nurses to church—to sit with "their" white families—persisted into the 1950s and 1960s. In church, the widespread fact of racial mixing was hard to hide, and therefore it was hard to hide the white lie that segregation meant simply separation. It was hard, that is, for white ministers to justify barring black visitors, or even to explain to themselves why they should bar them, from church. They had not felt compelled to bar them until a few black activists started making "segregated" churches a political issue in the 1950s–60s. The policy of racial nonseparation in modern southern churches (at least, upper-class ones) extended, with all the usual condescension, to clerical gestures of goodwill. White church efforts to mitigate the injuries and insults of Jim Crow were common, if minor. White southern churches often seemed to specialize in such limited gestures. It may have been one of the church's political functions to keep the system from becoming too consistent, too outrageous. As the Rev. Dees had said in his segregationist speech of 1958, "it has long been a practice for ministerial associations to be inter-racial." Albert Freundt, one of the few PCUS clergymen ever to contribute to the Citizens' Council publications, stated that the church he pastored (1956–65) in Forest, Mississippi, as a matter of course allowed black folk to mix into the congregation during weddings and funerals.[52]

This was a basic contradiction in the white supremacy system. Where that system was defined as separation, and separation was defined as bigotry, the segregationists pointed to examples of nonseparation with pride: these examples proved that they were not bigots, that they were not rigid. But the same examples undermined their claim that their society had a tradition of strict separation that needed to be maintained and defended.

More to the point, the widespread examples of racial mixing were signs— revelations—of a basic reality, which all southerners with eyes to see understood at some level. That reality was that the races never had been and never could be strictly separate. The reality of social mixing would not permit more than a few white southerners to enjoy a life of absolute, legalistic separation, let alone make a career of it. The society simply did not have room for many such lives amid all the well-established mixing. The segregationists boxed themselves in by pretending that they wanted separation rather than suppression. They walked into a trap when they started pretending to believe in, and devoted themselves to proving the truth of, the "but equal" formula that the original segregationists had cooked up to put the separation system over in the first place. Anybody who looked at the way white southerners actually lived could see that they were no more interested in being separate than they were in being equal. The NAACP Legal Defense Fund worked hard to make it obvious that the system was in fact unequal, and that became a legal point of great political consequence. But had the Fund cared to, it could also have proved what everyone knew and, when it served their purposes, would point out: black and white in the Jim Crow South were not separate any more than they were equal. The conspicuous nonseparation was as much a burden on the system's propagandists as its unconcealable inequality.

Foreign missions ensured that the future would make strict insistence on segregation even more absurd for southern Christians than the past had made it. All evangelical (small *e*) churches had a missionary interest in what is now called the Third World. The SBC and the PCUS were in a position similar to that of the U.S. State Department: they were trying to win the allegiance of the masses in the newly independent states of Africa and Asia. There newspapers and mass literacy conspired to undermine American propaganda, as they spread word of racial violence and protests in the alleged Home of the Free. For the southern churches, a missionary motive was as powerful as the Cold War motive that is so often cited by scholars who are at pains to explain why the U.S. government turned against segregation, suddenly, in the late 1940s and 1950s.[53] The Truman, Eisenhower, and Kennedy administrations could not afford to alienate the newly independent nations—or their "colored" diplomats, who moved into the southern city of Washington, D.C., and liked to drive farther south for beachfront vacations. So, too, the SBC and the PCUS could not afford to alienate prospective converts in Africa and Asia.

In 1956 the SBC had 248 missionaries in Africa alone, on a budget of approximately $2 million. Equally if not more important were the "missions" within the United States. In 1958, 60 members of the SBC's Home Mission Board staff were devoted to "Negro work," with a budget of $200,000 and growing.[54] The archives of both of the all-southern denominations are full of returning missionaries' reports to their sponsoring churches. Letters and church publications about these visits raise the alarm about international news coverage of racial oppression and violence in America. Late in 1957, CLC head A. C. Miller looked back over a year of changing pressures. At first, SBC officials were urged to avoid controversy: "There was tacit agreement among us that we would not mention the racial issue at all" in reports to the convention in May. "But after the turn of the year of 1957, pressure began to mount" in the opposite direction—"from various Convention leaders, and more especially from our foreign missionaries on furlough and from some [in] their fields, urging the commission not only to include a strong section in its report on this issue, but to prepare a statement that could be adopted by the official action of the Commission."[55] The SBC followed the example of Cold Warriors in the Democratic Party, who saw black voters in the North and new allies abroad as more valuable than the aging, shrinking minority of white southern fire-eaters.

In November 1961 the head of the SBC Executive Committee, speaking to the South Carolina Evangelistic Conference (which had rebuked Criswell five years earlier), made a ringing statement of the urgent need to focus on missionary work. He blended his emphasis on depoliticizing the church with emphasis on reaching out to those of different backgrounds and different races:

> We need to take a new look at this world in which we live. We are going to have a better world only when we have better men. We are going to have better men only when they are transformed by the redeeming spirit of Jesus Christ. The facts are there are seven hundred million more non-Christians today than at the beginning of this century. Out of the population of three billion people, there are only about 350 million evangelicals or Protestants. There are 500 million Catholics. There are 450 million Moslems. There are 350 million Hindus. There are 300 million followers of Confucius. There are 150 million Buddhists, and the balance of animists or pagans of one kind or another.[56]

This was an opportunity and a goad.

Not just the SBC, but also the southern Presbyterians had a strong interest in expansion. For example, in 1960 the Virginia Synod of the PCUS adopted a report noting that "much has been said of our race tension as providing propaganda for communism in its appeal to the uncommitted nations of the world. What is of greater concern to us as Christians is the effect in our mission fields in our appeal to those uncommitted to Christ. The South African situation has damaged the prestige and witness of the Dutch Reformed Church. We must learn from this that our domestic problems [affect] our whole Christian appeal to a largely colored world." Practical reasons made it impossible for them to escape their duty. "Presbyterians, many of whom are in key local positions as civic, business, and governmental leaders, have an opportunity to effect changes in our civil life which will strengthen the witness of our church in its appeal to the Negroes of the South, and to the uncommitted in the World Mission Fields of our Church and others."[57]

The parallels with U.S. foreign policy were many. The Kennedy administration had the Democratic Party around its neck—the party that created and maintained the South's peculiar racial institutions of the twentieth century—as it shopped for new allies. Southern missionaries had a similar albatross—or, one might say, their cross to bear: their increasingly well-known history of racial oppression at home. There was even a parallel to the Soviet Union in the competition for new adherents among the rubble of the great European empires: Catholic missionaries, many of them Americans, were mopping up. American Catholics could claim with some justification to have dissociated themselves from racism—from any particularly southern or American sin.

Baptists and Presbyterians felt the Catholic competition as keenly as

Democrats and Republicans felt the Soviet competition. One might wonder whether their indulgence in anti-Catholic paranoia comforted them as they tried awkwardly to cast off their anti-Negro habits. Perhaps such indulgence gave them some compensation, as though to conform to a cosmic law of conservation of bigotry. The southern Baptists' and Presbyterians' efforts to capture the black converts of Africa and America became their way to foil the international Catholic conspiracy. A 1958 SBC report noted, under "Current Trends among Negro Baptists," not only a disconcerting movement toward the rival (northern) American Baptist Convention, but also "the bid of the Catholic hierarchy for the Negro people and the Catholic gains in Negro membership."[58] Southern Protestants' use of one form of bigotry to justify the fighting of another was a fascinating and perhaps ominous irony, whose effects were adventitiously buried by the election of the first Catholic president in 1960.

The pressure on southern churches got worse. The SBC put out a press release in 1961 about a returning missionary who reported that mob attacks on the Freedom Riders in Alabama were impairing missions abroad.[59] The SBC's annual report in 1961 announced, "We cannot afford to let pride or prejudice undermine . . . either our Christian witness at home or the years of consecrated, sacrificial missionary service among all the peoples of the world."[60] In 1963 Professor Samuel Southard of Southern Baptist Theological Seminary reported: "Missionaries have often spoken against segregation to southern white audiences that have never heard a white man condemn it. They have been listened to because they present racial prejudice as a stumbling block to evangelization of the heathen and a scandal to whites who call themselves Christian."[61]

The missionary motive was far more central to the growth and identity of Evangelical churches in the South than historians have recognized—more important than any attachment to a particular legal system of race relations. In 1958 an SBC pastor in Texas commented: "Either we abandon segregation in principle and in practice, or we must abandon our passion for world evangelism. If we abandon world evangelism, there is nothing else that justifies our existence as a denomination."[62] As human institutions with interests to defend, southern denominations could not afford to be devoted to ideals like white supremacy—any more than they could afford to be devoted to prophetic ideals of self-sacrifice and universal brotherhood. Their ideals had to serve their growth and prosperity.

Antebellum southern clergymen quite rationally—and with heartfelt passion—had defended slavery and the whole "way of life" that made their slaveowning parishioners rich. A century later there was no correspondingly clear-cut reason for southern clergymen to defend segregation, a very different system of keeping the black Christians of the South underfoot. Southern ministers believed that they had to maintain and strengthen their own institutions. Segregation did not generate the profits that slavery had—or the external abolitionist attacks that made white southerners close ranks. White southern clergymen felt too many conflicting pressures and incentives to be consistent or effective segregationists.

THE WORLDLY SOURCES OF

BLACK SOUTHERN CONFIDENCE

Segregationists could not live by politics alone. Especially in an age of demagoguery, which was widely ridiculed and satirized in the South as well as the North, segregationists needed more than elected officials fulminating about their alleged rights and traditions. They needed cultural legitimacy. They needed what black southerners, in very visible, headline-grabbing showdowns, suddenly appeared to have: deeply rooted institutions in their communities that were ready to teach discipline to the masses and to imbue them with a spirit of sacrifice and hard work. The white religious leaders of the South did not care deeply enough about segregation to make its defense the most important thing in their lives. As Nelson Bell remarked in 1956: "The noise made by the white Citizens Councils is out of proportion to the spirit of the South as a whole. There is no question about that."[63]

Martin Luther King and other black leaders were famously dismayed that so few white southerners supported them. But they also observed that few white southerners were determined opponents. As King and his nonviolent field marshals, C. K. Steele and Fred Shuttlesworth, stated in 1957: "We are convinced that most white southerners are prepared to accept integration as the law of the land. On the other hand, a small but willful minority, dedicated to violence[,] is resorting to threats, shootings, cross burnings and bombings."[64]

On May 23, 1960, *Christianity Today* reported that the southern Presbyterian Church "is seriously divided" and somewhat unpredictable on segregation. Still, the PCUS, in its one-hundredth anniversary assembly—celebrating a century of growth since its birth signified the split of the country over slavery—"urged its colleges and other institutions to speed processes of desegregation." Moreover, the PCUS reasserted its 1954 recommendation (made before the Supreme Court decision) to open church institutions to qualified students "without regard to social distinctions." The assembly defeated efforts to soften this language, though the vote was not overwhelming: 208 to 186.

The Southern Baptist Convention was divided, too. The mildly segregationist pastor of Earle Baptist Church in Earle, Arkansas, complained to the Christian Life Commission about its imposition of a pro-integration view. He said that it would be "wise" for the commission "to remember that we are divided on the matter of integration. Many of our brethren are moderate integrationist and others moderate segregationist, brethren that love the Lord."[65] There was widespread alarm that the issue was dividing the white South. In 1957 the Rev. William McLin of First Baptist of Sumter, South Carolina, protested that the CLC's "persistence directed at the race problem did not contribute to unity one iota." He predicted the "breakup" of the SBC over it.[66] A parishioner in Utica, Mississippi, told his pastor in April 1958 that the desegregation question would "split the Southern Baptist Convention wide open."[67]

The divided white churches in the South, for the foreseeable future, could not contribute much to a militant defense of segregation—as politicians seemed ready to do. Segregationists could still win victories. But black activists saw through their show of unity and challenged them, knowing, or at least sensing, that the segregationists' foundations in southern white culture were mushy. The segregationists had popular opinion behind them, but not popular conviction. There were indications that even the most militant segregationists believed that the Negro was indeed a victim of great injustice. Judge Tom P. Brady of Mississippi, author of *Black Monday*, the classic attack on the *Brown* decision, took on a Christian voice when he conceded: "Men of the 'Bible Belt' realize fully that the Negro has not received the treatment which he should have received at our hands. We know, too, that no human being can mistreat another and escape paying a terrific price—that God's law of retribution is fixed and immutable as God's law of gravity."[68]

When Martin Luther King, in his great pulpit at the Birmingham Jail in 1963, rebuked the southern white church for its neutrality, he had some hope of making converts to his cause. He was far more confident in his bid to increase his support among white southern Christians than the segregationists ever were in their bids to increase theirs. Black leaders had seen it all from the start in Montgomery, when King wrote to an incredulous Bayard Rustin that "the effect of White Citizens Council and Ku Klux Klan intimidation and action" was the opposite of what one might expect. In Alabama, the segregationist organizations "have given our people more determination to press on for the goal of integration." It was not that black people felt provoked. "There is a general feeling that these organizations will destroy themselves through internal decay. . . . These organizations are putting as much pressure on white people as they are on Negroes. (The white persons who don't agree with their point of view.)"[69]

While visiting Montgomery, a white southern Methodist minister, Glenn Smiley—one of the rare "inside agitators" who joined King's movement wholeheartedly—reported on the eerie feeling of a city under siege by black Baptists. He sensed then what segregationists later reported, that moderate solutions were not possible. There was bitter talk among white Montgomerians—frustration that looked increasingly brittle, increasingly unable to congeal—while black folk walked around with knowing smiles. "Strange—whites are scared stiff and Negroes are calm as cucumbers."[70]

8

Segregationist Thought in Crisis

WHAT THE MOVEMENT WAS

UP AGAINST

The civil rights movement appeals to the imagination as a story of good triumphing over evil. In that sense it differs from other moral crusades—say, the Populist movement, which was defeated, or the Prohibition movement, whose victory most Americans came to regret. It differs from the mid-nineteenth-century crusade against slavery and the mid-twentieth-century crusade against fascism in another sense: the victory of the civil rights movement did not come at the expense of so much bloodshed and moral compromise. The martyrs to the civil rights cause deserve to be richly mourned. Yet a single day of battle in the Civil War or World War II made far more exhausting demands on America's capacity to mourn. More striking is how lopsided the moral responsibility for the martyrdom was. The victors in the civil rights struggle—the good guys—did engage in some lying and manipulation, some failures of moral discipline, even (if we extend the good-guy category to presidents who sent troops) some coercion by violent means. But by historical standards, the victors did little of all that. The triumph of civil rights was an omelette that broke miraculously few eggs.

To note the relative ease of the movement's victory does not trivialize the sacrifices of civil rights activists or the blood on all segregationists' hands. The costs of victory seem, in historical perspective, out of proportion to the evil remedied, and seem to require explanation. This is not what previous writers have sought to explain. A generation's worth of scholarship has established how long and hard the struggle was for the black southerners who threw themselves into it. Community and state studies depict masses of "ordinary" people showing extraordinary bravery in the face of threats and reprisals, church burnings, bombings, police brutality, and jail sentences years before anyone heard of Martin Luther King. Most of this scholarship is devoted to justifying and commemorating the protesters — showing that their victory was long overdue, that they struggled valiantly even before the mass media (or earlier historians) paid attention, and that the delays and opposition they met were outrageous.

All of that scholarship has been effective. It is no longer surprising to hear that black southerners resourcefully "resisted" oppression all their lives. That is the most conspicuous lesson now conveyed in history courses and mass-media commemorations of the movement. For people who were raised on the grassroots-focused scholarship that has dominated historical work on civil rights since the 1970s, it is now rather surprising to hear that there were ever people who needed to learn that most conspicuous lesson.

Yet there remains a mystery about what happened in the 1950s and 1960s. From the Middle Passage on, African Americans had struggled, but this one time they "overcame" — on their own initiative and largely on their own terms. For about ten years, from the Montgomery Bus Boycott of 1955–56 to the Selma March of 1965, "resistance" to racism was not something that dogged historians could detect after years of research, but a mass public insurgency that had realistic hopes of success in the real world. To understand the hopes of the protesters, we need to know a lot more about what they were up against. Why were the protesters so confident that they could win? We learn from all the scholarly documentation of oppression and resistance that they were morally justified in their protests. But that has little, if anything, to do with their belief that they were being realistic in their protests. Perhaps the most important reason for their confidence that they could win — not in heaven or in the eternal sight of God, but here and now, on this earth — was their recognition that their enemies were weak.

We still know little about the white side of the struggle. Previous scholars of opposition to civil rights — ably led by Numan Bartley and Neil McMillen — sought to explain why white resistance to civil rights persisted so long and slowed the movement down as much as it did.[1] There is an understandable moral outrage in their studies. Bartley and McMillen were appalled by the power of segregationist mobs and demagogues who delayed and diluted the victory of good over evil. Viewed in a longer-term historical perspective, however, the weakness of segregationism is as impressive as its power and persistence. If we compare segregationism with the defense of slavery a hundred years earlier, an illuminating difference becomes clear: both of them failed, ultimately, but the defenders of slavery succeeded in rallying southern white opinion, in generating solidarity and militancy, and in forcing their opponents to pay the ultimate price of war. Why didn't the white South put up a better fight a hundred years later?[2]

The answer to that question is complicated. It turns out that thoughtful segregationists feared other white southerners as much as they feared the civil rights movement or the federal government. They feared the unruly emotional force of white bigots and demagogues who undermined the order and respectability on which they believed their authority rested. They never doubted that they had most white southerners on their side. Opinion polls and election returns show that they had no reason to doubt that: white southerners overwhelmingly endorsed segregation.[3] The question was how to stir the majority to militant and effective action without sacrificing order and respectability. The best minds among segregationists fell apart over that issue. That is the crisis they faced.

It is in the conflicts and fissures, the hesitations and confusions, the illusions and misunderstandings of their best minds that we can find the keys to segregationists' failure. It is by looking at the best minds, too, that we can avoid falling into the trap of thinking that segregation was the cause of semiliterate rednecks and demagogues. Segregation had respectability, but its defenders needed to shore up that respectability. Their ultimate failure has made it easy to forget that segregation's political defeat, at the hands of black civil rights leaders and federal agencies, entailed a cultural fall, too. Today, educated white southerners, even those who call themselves conservative, disavow white supremacy, segregation, disfranchisement—pretending that only "trash" was interested in such things. But in the 1950s and early 1960s, the educated class of the white South was, with rare exceptions, united with the trash on the goal of preserving white supremacy. Fortunately for the black protesters, they were not united on the means to achieve that goal.

HOW TO CLAIM THE HIGH GROUND
WITHOUT ABANDONING THE GRASSROOTS

While racial demagogues and brutal cops captured most of the media attention, the most talented and respected segregationist thinkers articulated noble-sounding aims. On his inauguration as governor of South Carolina in January 1951, James F. Byrnes said, "If we demand respect for state rights, we must discharge state responsibilities." As a constitutional scholar and former U.S. Supreme Court justice, Byrnes knew how serious the legal effort to desegregate the schools had become. He sought to undercut the constitutional argument for integration by making "separate" schools truly "equal." Since "state responsibilities" included the "education of our children," Byrnes urged an increase in school spending. Fifty percent of the construction budget, he said, should go into building Negro schools. "It is our duty to provide for the races substantial equality in school facilities. We should do it because it is right. For me that is sufficient reason."[4] (The eeriest thing about this speech is that John F. Kennedy echoed it—in his famous speech during the Birmingham crisis of 1963—the day he became a supporter of civil rights.) Byrnes led the way in elevating the segregationist cause above racial and sectional self-interest. This required some heavy lifting, and not only for speechwriters.

Byrnes knew that he was asking a great sacrifice of the white South and that his expensive plans would meet opposition. "I do not need the assistance of the Ku Klux Klan nor do I want interference by the National Association for the Advancement of Colored People." Putting the zealots of his own camp on the same plane with the enemy was a shrewd rhetorical move toward the calm, reasonable center that Arthur Schlesinger had recently made fashionable. Byrnes hoped that his plan would draw in a silent majority of white southerners who loved segregation but had no taste for controversy. Whatever risk there was in denouncing the most devoted partisans of the segregationist cause, Byrnes hoped to overcome it by gaining the confidence of the moderates—that is, the white southerners who wanted to defend segregation by strictly legal, respectable means. If the moderates were willing to pay taxes to avoid extremism and violence, they would be able to hold their heads high and to maintain control under his leadership.[5]

Byrnes was not the only segregationist intellectual who felt uneasy about the most visible adherents of his cause. By April 1949 the editor of the *Richmond Times-Dispatch*, Virginius Dabney, a leading southern liberal, had made common cause with the Dixiecrat columnist John Temple Graves of the *Birmingham Post-Herald*. During World War II, Dabney had proposed to end segregation in transportation but soon withdrew the proposal after a hostile response from fellow southern editors. The historian John Kneebone reasonably suggests that Dabney, "perhaps unconsciously, sought such a reaction" to demonstrate the impossibility of sudden change. By the end of the war, Dabney had become a firm segregationist and supporter of states' rights. The key issue for him was keeping white southerners, specifically "respectable," nondemagogic men like himself, under control.[6]

Dabney wanted to prepare a careful white southern resistance to "radical," northern-based action, before such action occurred. This gave him common ground with more wholehearted segregationists like Graves, who sought delay as a means of preserving segregation. For both men, avoidance of extreme imagery was paramount. Dabney urged Graves, in April 1949, to abandon his efforts to keep alive Strom Thurmond's failed third-party candidacy: "I know the complete sincerity of yourself, and others who are a part of it. On the other hand, I do not know how you can get rid of the large group of Negrophobes and Ku Kluxers who have gravitated to your banner." Like many southern liberals, Dabney still believed that states' rights was a "sound" and important cause. What disturbed him was the spectacle of "so many people who pervert and distort States' Rights to be shouting

Jimmy Byrnes, after an illustrious career as a U.S. Supreme Court justice, U.S. secretary of state, and near-miss Democratic presidential nominee, made an important symbolic move back to southern state politics, becoming governor of South Carolina in 1950. He provided intellectual leadership and lent considerable respectability to the segregationist cause. (Clemson University Libraries, Special Collections)

for that cause. I have seen these brethren before, and I know they are not really interested in States' Rights. You might reply that almost every cause has its disreputable backers, but it seems to me that the proportion of such backers in the present instance is too large." Dabney's effort to maintain control depended on keeping disreputable backers quiet.[7]

The segregationists needed national as well as regional respectability, which they understood as a precondition of power and influence. Their great Yankee patron, millionaire Carleton Putnam, spoke with authority on this point: "If, being a Northerner, I may dare to speak one last word to the South, in the utmost sympathy and understanding, I would say, curb your anger as best you can. I am convinced the majority of Northerners are sincere humanitarians who are being unconsciously victimized by a hoax. Work to enlighten them, but do not play into the hands of your enemies, and theirs, by violence. Lynchings and bombings do not destroy these enemies; they destroy you."[8] For a long time, segregationists' hopes rested on Byrnes, whose near-miss vice-presidential bid in 1944 led white southerners to cling to the hope that Byrnes could save the Democratic Party from its growing antisouthern forces. South Carolinians regarded Byrnes "almost as a Messiah," according to one close observer in 1951.[9]

Yet Byrnes's supporters were torn. They understood that their hero's national standing, thus his ability to protect the South, depended on his muting his commitment to the South. Yet if he muted it too much, they suspected him of selling out. In 1951 Graves sketched out the quandary in a letter to Dallas editor Lynn Landrum: "Deeply compromising Byrnes' national position may be the one he has been forced to take on the question of race segregation in the public schools—you have noted that he has said he will close the schools if segregation for them is ruled out by the Supreme Court." Short of violence, there was no more extreme commitment one could make to segregation. Byrnes's endorsement of school closing "makes him all the more the man of the Deep South, but in my travels I am finding how it hurts him elsewhere to be named alongside Hummon [Georgia's demagogic Governor Herman] Talmadge in this." Graves feared that Byrnes's—and therefore the South's—hopes would shatter on the rocks of sectionalism. Graves had long been concerned with what he called the "centripetal force of Southern regional circumstance." Byrnes, like "so many other Southerners who have been national statesmen," would be forced to "come home to sectionalism at last." John C. Calhoun, Henry Grady, and Tom Watson, he noted, "in differing ways were all forced to look homeward." It was comforting to have such company, but also ominous.[10] Calhoun and Watson were failures, and Grady's vision of an economically vibrant New South was not realized until long after his death.

In an age of mass communications, thoughtful segregationists like Graves

Birmingham's Dixiecrat columnist John Temple Graves strove, with other newspapermen of the white South, to keep segregationism free from the taint of violence, lawlessness, and open bigotry. (Birmingham Public Library, Department of Archives and Manuscripts, catalog no. 830.7.1.2.8)

often despaired of their ability to fight a public relations war in an unsympathetic national market. "Disreputable backers" gave segregation a bad public image because they made better copy than reputable backers. Graves complained in his column, in response to John Bartlow Martin's famous series in the *Saturday Evening Post*, "The Deep South Says Never" (later a book), that Martin focused too much on the grassroots and often uncouth members of the Citizens' Councils, and too much on the extremism of Black Belt towns in the Deep South. Martin "left out proud Virginia, heart and home of the never-saying. And North Carolina, Louisiana, North Florida, East Texas." Martin made segregationism look too much like a street fight. He ignored "the real fighting front—the legislative, judicial, congressional and editorial one."[11]

Most of all, Graves resented that Martin ignored the intraracial fight that segregationists like himself were engaged in: "He has credited Citizens Councils with their magnificent holding operation but failed to credit them with their equally important influence against vigilantes and foolish knights within and without their ranks."[12] Graves's friend Thomas Waring, the segregationist editor of the *Charleston News and Courier*, likened Martin's series to the old Negro dialect stories of Octavus Roy Cohen in the *Saturday Evening Post* of yore. But "this time [the dialect] is put in the mouths of Southern white people," whereas most of the Negroes "speak correct if sometimes stilted English." *Richmond News Leader* editor James J. Kilpatrick, the most influential voice among segregationist writers, had the same reaction to Martin's series: "All of the Negro sources talk like Oxford dons, while all of the white people talk like Southern white people." Graves, impressed as most segregationists were with the vast power of black civil rights groups, observed, "The NAACP, of course, doesn't allow Negro dialect in magazines or on radio-television." [13]

This suspicion that the NAACP controlled black images in the national media is part of a pervasive envy in segregationist statements about the NAACP. [14] Like white southerners, Negroes were an impoverished minority in America, but unlike white southerners, Negroes were organized. In the segregationists' eyes, Negroes had an unnatural, uncanny power. They had somehow gained influence over radio, television, the newspapers, and, increasingly, the federal government, the mainline churches, and major corporations. Segregationists glossed over the apparent contradiction between this inflated view of the NAACP and their basic belief in Negro inferiority by convincing themselves that the NAACP was not really a Negro organization but a white-led—in more extreme versions, a Jewish-led or Communist-led—organization. The big national institutions were controlled by susceptible white people who, not being surrounded by black people themselves, could not understand racial problems as well as white southerners could. To fight effectively against such forces, the segregationists would have to cabal, connive, and conspire. They would have to become like their enemies.

Organization was a particularly grave step for James Kilpatrick, whose notion of liberty grew out of a strong individualist temperament. Since Kilpatrick was the most creative and influential ideologue of the segregationist cause, his personal hesitations are worth noting. His friend and fellow Virginian, J. Barrye Wall (editor of the *Farmville Herald*), wrote to him shortly after the *Brown* decision that "force of ideas must be matched with an equal force of ideas. In this case the NAACP has had but one goal, namely integration. It has made a first step by lawful means and apparently carried its point." Kilpatrick would have to take his stand with white southerners, who needed people like him to lead a "lawful" and effective protest. "It can not be done individually," Wall insisted. "It must be done through organization, more ably led, well financed and devoted to singleness of purpose [than the NAACP's effort]."

Kilpatrick resisted. "I am just an inveterate non-joiner," he wrote Wall, "not an Elk, or a Moose, a Rotarian, a Kiwanian . . . not a Lion or an Optimist or a Red Man." In June 1954 Kilpatrick still believed that "the mill wheels of the courts grind exceedingly slow, and we can litigate a long, long time before mixed schools ever become a reality in Eastern Virginia." The dangers of organization, for the moment at least, were greater than the need for it.

Wall sympathized with Kilpatrick's individualism: in a better time, he wrote back, he would favor a moratorium on "jining." If everybody would attend to his own business and leave others to theirs, "many of our problems would solve themselves." But at present, Wall saw "no hope for the idea" of individualism: "Success depends upon leadership. . . . Unless we have the best leadership developed in this matter . . . the wrong type, that you and I fear, may become the recognized leadership of the South." The age of individualism was dead. "As much as it is to be deplored, we have government by pressure groups. This being the case, unless we speak out from the conservative point of view and face the issue practically, the hot-heads will represent us in an untrue light."[15]

Something in the personality of Kilpatrick and some other key segregationist thinkers kept them from organizing. Their resistance to centralized power was psychological, perhaps spiritual, not simply public and rhetorical. Their hopes, their very identity, were tied to it. It almost seemed to add honor and glory to their self-image that theirs was a lost cause. Back in 1949 Byrnes had told Graves that he received "daily confirmation" that "our views on the rights of the States are shared by many people outside the South. . . . Of course they are not organized and I assume individualists make poor organization material."[16] He would probably have been surprised to hear that he was echoing John Dewey's laments about liberals.

The campaign for national sympathy was particularly dispiriting for segregationist intellectuals, but the home front presented difficulties of its own. Byrnes, Kilpatrick, Graves, and others needed to rally the "moderate" leaders—the "respectable" business and professional men—who held increasing power in the South from World War II on. These leaders, some of them New Deal Democrats, often owed their careers to federal patronage and private northern investment. They cared more than the average southerner about their extraregional reputations. They would be too easily alienated by "disreputable backers."

The trouble was that disreputable backers were the ones with the enthusiasm and energy to promote the cause. If segregationists wanted organization, they would have to get in bed with the disreputable. Kilpatrick wrote to a friend who had urged him to help organize an effective bloc of southern voters: "The trouble with 'organization' in a cause of this sort, is that all of the wrong people . . . wind up at the head of the organization. . . . And as sure as some association for the advancement of white people is formed, it ultimately will come under the domination of some red-necks, fanatic apostles of Gerald L. K. Smith, and other trash that decent people would not want to remain in the same room with."[17] The reasonable *via media* was a defensive choice. (As an unabashed conservative, Kilpatrick would not have called his position a vital center, but that is essentially where he located himself in the white South.) Respectable segregationists needed to prove—perhaps to themselves first of all—that they were not fanatical bigots.

The easiest task of respectable segregationists was to distance themselves from the hooded symbol of mob violence. Segregationist papers and organizations frequently trumpeted their opposition to the Ku Klux Klan. Dabney had no trouble directing his heaviest editorial artillery at the violent extremist John Kasper: "We Don't Need His Kind." Dabney was encouraged by the Citizens' Council of Mecklenburg County, Virginia, which had recently "made it clear that self-styled pro-segregation rabble rousers are not wanted." That council adopted a resolution calling Kasper "a troublemaker dispatched to the South by Northern integrationists" who had "accomplished what he was sent south to do—make radicals of decent, law-abiding citizens." To Dabney, Kasper was "as welcome in Virginia as a rattlesnake at a church picnic." Kasper might not be an actual northern *agent provocateur*, Dabney said, but he had done "vast disservice to the cause of southern constitutionalism."[18]

A 1957 editorial distinguishing the Klan from the Citizens' Councils in the *Shreveport Times* was typical. The editorial reminded readers that the *Shreveport Times* and other southern newspapers had fought Klanism in the 1920s, noting that in that era the Klan killed white people in northwestern Louisiana, not black people. "There is no reputable newspaper, civic organization, or public leader in the South today upholding the Klan or Klanism. The Citizens Councils . . . as a whole have fought Klanism openly and have insisted that all southern pro-segregation activities should be based on legality." Though there is a lot of truth in this, the defensiveness of the statement betrays a deep insecurity: "Most of the Citizens Councils in Louisiana are made up of recognizedly reputable citizens who openly give publicity to their identity, their activities, and their objectives. Those of both Jewish and Roman Catholic beliefs are members of some of them, Shreveport's included." The editorial was reproduced and distributed by the Association of Citizens' Councils of Louisiana.[19]

The quest for respectability turned segregationists sharply against the Klan: segregationists had to show that they believed in law and order, in genteel and civilized methods of persuasion. As South Carolina journalist William Workman put it in his manifesto, *The Case for the South*, the Klan and all "its unlovely cohorts . . . substitute muscle and meanness for the intellect which by rights must be the defense of the South." Not only Byrnes, but also Herman Talmadge (whose faction had previously opposed anti-Klan laws) signed bills unmasking the Klan in 1951.[20] All of this was a bid for respectability when the Klan's violence and lawlessness had become a damaging symbol, one that hurt the white South's image across the nation and gave segregationists trouble enforcing order at home.

If only the Klan were the end of the trouble. The Citizens' Councils, segregationists frequently insisted, were "reputable" and "respectable," yet they were difficult to keep clean. The *Shreveport Times* editorial acknowledged that "a few so-called 'White Citizens Councils' have gone the other way and are symbolic of Klanism." One of the worst, Asa Carter's North Alabama Citizens' Council, became a thorn in Graves's side. Graves supported the Citizens' Councils generally but often had to condemn their unruly, violent "element" in his columns, particularly after that element gained national attention by storming the stage and beating up the apolitical and interracially popular black singer Nat King Cole during a performance in Birmingham in April 1956. One of the gang convicted and jailed for the incident was a board member of the Anniston Citizens' Council. In an article for the then devotedly right-wing *American Mercury* in July 1956, Graves referred to Asa Carter's group as "an outlaw and fascist element of the Citizens Councils there [in Birmingham] which has already been denounced by the genuine Councils." When Dabney congratulated Graves on the *Mercury* piece, he went out of his way to assure him that "the unsavory reputation of the North Alabama outfit has been made clear in the Times-Dispatch." Dabney reprinted what he called "the Montgomery Advertiser's blistering editorial" about Carter's efforts to establish an office in Washington and gave it "great prominence" on his own editorial page. The editorial referred to Asa Carter as the "loathesome fuehrer."[21]

Respectability-seeking segregationists had to be on constant guard: Graves wrote confidentially to Byrnes, in July 1955, about Byrnes's plans to speak at a mass meeting in Birmingham in which the American States' Rights Association (ASRA) was involved. Graves warned Byrnes that the head of the ASRA, Olin H. Horton, though "on our side," is "inclined toward extremism" and is "not befriended by your friends." (Horton was closely allied with Asa Carter.) Graves urged Byrnes to insist that his speech not be given under the auspices of Horton's organization.[22] A similar exchange took place between Waring and Graves years later, when Waring warned Graves about the white supremacist G. L. Ivey, who had made overtures to Graves. Waring described Ivey as "an extremist, whom the Citizens Councils have so far kept under wraps. . . . Pay no attention to him."[23]

Extremists were too few to make an effective movement on their own, and they scared white masses away from segregationism as a whole. That was vexing, because at that very moment, what the segregationists saw as black extremists were suddenly, mysteriously, more popular than ever among black southerners and among white northern critics of the South. Roy Harris, the Georgia power broker, publisher, and president of the Citizens' Councils of America, gave succinct expression to segregationists' despair: "You have to hand it to Martin Luther King and his group," he said. "They're willing to go to jail for their beliefs."[24]

Graves spelled out the dilemma of the respectable segregationists, which only got worse as the costs of resistance mounted. To get in the headlines and generate support, they had to take extreme positions of defiance. Yet to maintain realism, they also had to recognize that most white southerners were unwilling to make the sacrifices necessary to maintain every detail of segregation. It appeared to Graves that stalwart segregationist politicians, like Georgia's Senators Richard Russell and Herman Talmadge, "just don't know what to do." (Herman Talmadge, governor in 1947-55, was a U.S. senator in 1956–80.) State leaders had it even worse. "Southern governors here are boxed in on [the school segregation issue] by reason of taking the 'not one Negro ever or for a second' stand." The extremists made it impossible for governors to tell their constituents simply to "endure" some temporary, token integration, "yet they shudder for what will happen if the schools are closed."[25]

School closing was, in practice, the only way for many southern politicians to prove their racial loyalty. Yet one segregationist intellectual, Marion Hutson Sass of Charleston, pointed out the drawbacks of taking that step. School closing was really a form of capitulation to the federal government, Sass wrote, since it meant that the South had to pay an unacceptable price to maintain segregation. School closing would force the South to "secede from civilization." It was better to be occupied by federal troops, for that would put the federal government "on the hook in a most embarrassing situation; and most important of all, [when under siege] our own people were *united*, in deep resentment and firm opposition to the integrationist Federal government coalition."[26]

School closing would be catastrophic and catastrophically unpopular—it would produce a backlash of ordinary white southern parents against hardline segregationist politicians. Yet to Graves, as to Kilpatrick and other strategically minded segregationists, school closing was the only alternative left to the delaying tactic of token compliance with desegregation orders. Graves reminded Waring that white Georgia Tech students had marched against segregationist governor Marvin Griffin, who proposed "to deprive them of a football game in New Orleans for segregation's sake." Griffin had prohibited the participation of Georgia students in the game because the opposing team had a black player. The students' predictable outrage was the sort of "human reaction that could bring on ruin if Georgia mothers and fathers had their schools closed." One had to watch one's choice of words, Graves noted, "in the existing delicate and hot psychology." Waring remembered the Georgia Tech incident all too well: "This is one of the reasons we have not protested the Citadel's playing integrated teams (outside the South, however). . . . I see no point in trying to lead a parade in which nobody marches but a couple of worn out drum majors."[27]

The one place individualists might have been expected to submit to some sort of authority and solidarity, the church, was, for reasons we have seen, disappointing to segregationists, and they were too pessimistic to put much faith in it. Though the Bible never became useful to segregationists, as it had been to the antebellum justifiers of slavery, the Constitution looked a lot more promising. Accordingly, lawyers were far more useful than preachers to the segregationist cause. Many of the South's leading legal authorities confidently and consistently cited *their* holy text in defense of states' rights. They—alone in the mid-twentieth-century white South—match the fervor and confidence of their antebellum ancestors.

In addition to Byrnes, John Satterfield (president of the American Bar Association in 1961–62), Senator Sam Ervin of North Carolina, and legal scholar Charles Bloch (author of the treatise, *State Rights: The Law of the Land*) were among the most influential constitutional segregationists. Probably the only segregationist book that has more than historical interest today is a states' rights tract, Edward P. Lawton's *The South and the Nation* (1963), a wise and eloquent meditation on history. The white South's legal authorities of the mid-twentieth century, unlike its religious establishment, showed as strong a commitment to their region's peculiar racial institution as their mid-nineteenth-century counterparts had shown to theirs. They were the only authorities in the modern white South who matched their proslavery predecessors in brains and devotion. With the aid of this uniquely consistent intellectual elite, modern white southerners generally appeared as confident in the 1950s as they had a century earlier that the Constitution was on their side.

The ubiquitous James J. Kilpatrick, though not a lawyer, was the most important publicist of constitutional segregationism. He built a respectable platform in his Richmond newspaper, to which segregationists increasingly looked for intellectual leadership after Byrnes retired in January 1955. Kilpatrick struggled to find a way to lift what he called the South's "problem above the sometimes sordid level of race and segregation and pu[t] it on a high ground of fundamental principles instead."[28] The only fundamental principles he could find were in the Constitution, which he understood as a contract among several sovereign states.

A struggle to define the Constitution was at the heart of the cultural struggle over civil rights. The NAACP Legal Defense Fund stood upon a broad interpretation of the equal protection clause of the Fourteenth Amendment ("No State shall . . . deny to any person within its jurisdiction the equal protection of the laws"). A few segregationist thinkers, reluctant to concede any constitutional basis for human egalitarianism, ques-

Charles J. Bloch of Macon, one of the most visible Jewish segregationists, helped segregationists ward off accusations of bigotry. He
tried to focus segregationist rhetoric on constitutional issues. His
treatise, *State Rights: The Law of the Land*, was a public bid for
respectability. It advanced what many segregationists thought were
the most honorable and effective reasons to resist the Supreme
Court's desegregation order. (Courtesy Middle Georgia Archives,
Washington Memorial Library, Macon)

tioned the legitimacy of that amendment. They argued that the Fourteenth Amendment had never been properly ratified, that it had been "forced" on the South; therefore the word "equal" only appeared once in the Constitution (in Art. 5): to guarantee the permanent equality of *states* in the Senate.[29] But Byrnes, Kilpatrick, Satterfield, and other southerners seeking to remain in the mainstream of respectable opinion, declined to take that radical line. They accepted the legitimacy of the Fourteenth Amendment.[30] Carleton Putnam, who had earned a law degree from Columbia University but was not a practicing lawyer and did not emphasize legal issues generally, brushed aside "feverish talk about the validity of the 14th Amendment" as part of the South's futile, unrealistic faith in constitutional arguments, which distracted the region from the true issue of race.[31]

A separate question was whether the Fourteenth Amendment applied to schools. Frequently, segregationists pointed out that the same Congress that adopted that amendment also approved segregation in the District of Columbia schools, and that many northern legislatures practiced segregation at the time they ratified the amendment. Therefore, they reasoned, the Fourteenth Amendment could not have been intended to interfere with segregation.[32] But the original intent line remained muted, perhaps because it was clear that the framers of the amendment did intend to override many state laws, even if they did not intend to prohibit school segregation per se. Rather than renounce unpleasant additions to the original (pro-slavery) Constitution, segregationists sought, on the whole, a more positive approach. They defended the parts of the original Constitution that the Reconstruction Amendments did not overturn.

Segregationists were most confident and consistent in standing on the Constitution's various provisions for states' rights, especially the Tenth Amendment, which the Fourteenth Amendment may have qualified but did not annul. They conceded that state laws that conflicted with the Fourteenth Amendment were invalid because of the supremacy clause ("This Constitution, and the Laws of the United States which shall be made in Pursuance thereof . . . shall be the supreme Law of the Land; and the Judges in every State shall be bound thereby, any Thing in the Constitution or Laws of any State to the Contrary notwithstanding," Art. 6). But the Tenth Amendment itself was not affected by the supremacy clause: "The powers not delegated to the United States by the Constitution, nor prohibited by it to the States, are reserved to the States respectively, or to the people." By way of clarification or amplification, segregationists often paraphrased the first part of this: "The powers not *expressly* delegated by the existing States to the new Federal Government." That amendment clearly reserved authority over education to the states, the segregationists reasoned, since the Constitution never mentioned public education as one of the federal government's powers. The segregationists had history on their side, too:

the federal government, in practice, had left education up to the states throughout the life of the republic, except education to serve national military preparation.

Several intelligent people today, from Robert Bork to Garry Wills, have stated that the Tenth Amendment is insignificant.[33] It has been treated that way by many judges throughout its history. But segregationists were making a moral argument, that the Tenth Amendment *should* be significant, since it was part of the original agreement. Without such a guarantee that their turf would be protected, the states would never have abandoned their resistance to the original union with other states. Segregationists wanted to restore the amendment to its original significance, arguing that if the Reconstruction Congress had wanted to destroy states' rights altogether, it could have done so by repealing the Tenth Amendment—along with the proslavery provisions of Article 1, section 2, and Article 4, section 2, which it did repeal.

A GENTEEL EFFORT AT A REBEL YELL: INTERPOSITION

In the segregationists' view, the essence of the American system was the division of powers among the branches of the federal government and between the federal government and the several states. Drawing on the writings of Thomas Jefferson and James Madison, segregationists viewed the Constitution as a provisional grant of specified powers from the existing thirteen individual sovereign states to a new central authority. The limits on federal power in the Bill of Rights and elsewhere were the conditions on which the individual states accepted federation in the first place. Then suddenly, in the 1950s, a handful of federal judges, creatively dictating new policy on the basis of sociological theory rather than the Constitution, statute, and precedent, had usurped the role of Congress. When the federal executive enforced a court order with bayonets, in Little Rock in 1957, it helped the federal courts usurp the powers reserved to the states. According to this interpretation, it was not merely a state's right but an American's duty to resist. Segregationists gained confidence from the Supreme Court's hesitancy to enforce its radical new interpretation of the Fourteenth Amendment and from President Eisenhower's obvious reluctance to contradict his own previous endorsement of states' rights. Literate segregationists clung to this line of argument, which had the force that their religious speculations lacked.

Being right was not enough. How could segregationists use states' rights to give white southern masses confidence to stand united against the Supreme Court? Kilpatrick seized on the historic doctrine of "interposition," which he revived in a series of editorials in November 1955. He borrowed

James J. Kilpatrick, editor of the *Richmond News-Leader*, was probably the most influential segregationist thinker. Like Nelson Bell, he tried to stress voluntary freedom of choice, and like Charles Bloch, he pushed constitutional arguments rather than what he called "sordid" racial appeals. His ideas of how best to defend segregation set him at odds with other segregationists. (Kilpatrick Papers, University of Virginia Special Collections)

this doctrine mostly from Madison's reaction to the Federalists' Alien and Sedition Acts, the Virginia Resolutions of 1798 — one of the great defenses of civil liberties of all time.[34] According to Madison, a state legislature could "interpose" itself between its own population and some federal authority where that authority violated the Constitution. As parties to the contract, individual states had power to enforce its basic terms. Everyone who wrote the Constitution, and all justices who later interpreted it, conceded that basic common-law principle, even shoring it up with Article 1, section 10, which forbad the states from "impairing the Obligation of Contracts."

There was sincere and serious feeling behind this doctrine, adopted in one form or another by several southern states in reaction to the *Brown* decision.[35] Kilpatrick and others hoped that interposition resolutions would delay full implementation of *Brown* — long enough for the Supreme Court justices to "come to their senses," long enough for the North to recognize how strongly the South felt about segregation, or long enough for the competition between the national political parties for the "Negro bloc vote" to die down. More than that, interposition was an effort to provide the crowd-pleasing rebel yell that segregationists felt they needed to rouse white southerners from their complacency. Interposition, with a pedigree going back to the Founding Fathers, was a respectable way to drum up enthusiasm. It gave the segregationists a rallying cry without the disreputable taint of racist demagoguery.

Yet it divided segregationists further. Kilpatrick's hope—that an interpretation of the Constitution would inspire enough southern solidarity and northern sympathy to protect segregation—struck some segregation strategists as naive. At odds with Kilpatrick on this, for example, was the rich and influential propagandist Carleton Putnam, whose *Race and Reason* was the book most strongly and persistently promoted by the Citizens' Councils.[36] Putnam had attracted a huge following with his money and his eloquent open letters to the president, the attorney general, and the Supreme Court, which were widely reprinted in the southern white press. Putnam thought that Kilpatrick's doctrines of states' rights and interposition were sound, but what mattered to him was that they were ineffectual.

Intellectuals and lawyers loved interposition, but a successful businessman like Putnam saw intellectuals and lawyers as a fatally limited market. Putnam wrote to Thomas Waring in 1959 out of a growing concern "over the failure of Southern leadership to face the racial issue." Some segregationist leaders, he noted, "assert that Southerners have agreed to drop any discussion of race and to concentrate entirely on States' Rights and the Constitutional Question. To me this seems a mistake." Putnam identified the central division among segregationist thinkers—a division not over what they believed, but over what they should emphasize. It was a dispute over strategy and public relations. They agreed on what their true principles were but disagreed over the best means to rally their own forces in the South and gain sympathy in the North.

By Putnam's lights, Kilpatrick's elevation of the southern white cause "above the sometimes sordid level of race and segregation" took it too far from fighting words. "If the North and the Supreme Court feel that a burning wrong is being committed in the name of the Constitution," Putnam argued, "they will stretch a long way in their interpretation of that document to correct the wrong." Who could deny that that was a legitimate function of the courts? Putnam insisted that the issue was and must remain the morality, not the technical constitutionality, of segregation. Was segregation a form of immoral oppression, as the NAACP claimed?

If the answer to Putnam's rhetorical question was yes, then who cared a fig whether the South had a constitutional right to maintain the status quo? "If you are looking out of your door," Putnam told Waring, "and you see a man . . . who appears to be murdering a child, it does not impress you very much if he replies that he is within his constitutional rights. But if he answers that he is not murdering a child at all but is only shaking the dust out of a rag doll, this changes your feeling in the matter." Putnam urged the South to stick to expressing its true feelings about what justified its peculiar institution: "The South must win the battle for the mind of the North on moral, not on legal, grounds. It must convince the North that integration is morally wrong because it is destructive of the white civilization of the South. If it fails to do this, then the moral issue immediately moves to the Northern side, and injustice to the Negro becomes the dominant question. In neither case does the Constitutional issue have the slightest moral importance or emotional impact." The white South was shaking a rag doll. The NAACP was murdering a child.[37]

Tempted as Waring was to go along with Putnam's reasoning, he did not think that many other respectable southerners would. Respectable southerners had practical reasons to resist Putnam's urgings, even if emotional concern for their own reputations was not enough. For to go along with Putnam was to devote oneself openly to race, to white supremacy. Putnam and Waring were at that moment engaged in trying to set up a tax-exempt intellectual center to promote segregation. "The rub here," Waring wrote, "is that any college, I fear, would feel obligated to take the high ground —states rights, constitutionalism, etc.—in the present state of affairs. An organization frankly dedicated to defending the moral rightness of segregation might automatically be barred from tax privileges and therefore attract little revenue." Yet Waring's own experience confirmed Putnam's: southern students he spoke to were "demanding justification of segregation on moral grounds" and would not accept his constitutional "line of reasoning."[38] Putnam had also been in touch with Byrnes and with *U.S. News* editor David Lawrence (a supporter of the states' rights position). Waring wrote Putnam: "I am inclined to agree with your feeling that there is more popular pull in facing the facts about race than in purely constitutional arguments. Few of us, including Byrnes and Lawrence, have been willing to grasp the nettle firmly."[39]

TOO LITTLE FORCE TO WIN
OR TOO MUCH TO CONTROL?

The nettle was difficult to grasp: Putnam, like Georgia's Roy Harris, Louisiana's Leander Perez, and countless other segregationist firebrands, had faith that racism was sleeping in the hearts of all white people. If only Kilpatrick and Waring would stop sublimating that basic drive, they could win. There is no doubt that Waring and Kilpatrick had racism in their own hearts. The only question was their confidence in the racism of others. They lacked Putnam's belief that racism was strong enough, that enough people were proud and defiant enough about their racism, to rally around it.

Segregationist Thought in Crisis 171

More than that, Waring, Kilpatrick, and other respectable segregationists feared that racism was a force they could not control: their efforts to organize were all too easily co-opted by demagogues. Byrnes had always been on guard against this danger. In a speech in 1950, anticipating a Supreme Court decision against segregation in colleges, he sought to calm down the alarmism: "The situation calls for more thinking and less talking. The thinking . . . must be done by representatives of the State-supported colleges. . . . What candidates for office say about it will not be of importance." The colleges ought to be left alone to deal with the possible desegregation order, "because that is their business. Their decisions will control the policies of the colleges, not the views of the candidates for office." Secrecy was crucial to Byrnes's idea of segregationist strategy:

> If [the colleges] have a practical plan but in advance should shout it from the stump, negro lawyers [will] argue to the court that these plans were adopted solely to discriminate against negroes and thus would give to the courts additional reason for deciding against the State. . . . It is the duty of the trustees of our colleges to meet and consider policies for the future anticipation of suits. It would be unwise to hold such meetings in public and give aid to those who would give trouble to our institutions.

Segregationists would be as troublesome as black lawyers: "Denunciation of Mr. Truman for asking the Court to decide against all segregation will not help our colleges out of the difficult situation confronting them."[40] It is of some interest that this strategy of avoiding publicity—of keeping the issue out of the press and therefore out of the clutches of opportunistic, rabble-rousing politicians—was identical with that of white southern liberals (and a great many northern ones), such as those in the Southern Regional Council.

Byrnes had been dogged by demagogues all through his career.[41] He fought one of the most notorious race baiters ever, Cole Blease, and later saw his enemies gather around another, E. D. "Cotton Ed" Smith. Both men used the race issue against Byrnes in primary campaigns, declaring that he was too moderate. Richard Russell, too, had been attacked by demagogue Gene Talmadge in Georgia. Quiet, gentlemanly professionals like Byrnes and Russell were essential to the legitimation and defense of segregation. They—as much as the leading liberals—feared and were threatened by demagoguery. This was related to liberals' own belief in reason, by which they meant their own reason, and their dissatisfaction with mass emotions, by which they meant electoral politics that did not go their way. Respectable segregationists had more in common with liberals than they or the liberals were willing to admit.

Even demagogues grew frustrated with the emotional fanaticism of their most faithful supporters. The historian Dan Carter explains how hard it was for George Wallace to rein in the extremists to whom he had hitched his wagon. Wallace dubbed his strongest supporters the "nut cases." In fact, the head of his organization in Montana turned out to be a mental patient who had been expelled from the John Birch Society for his "extremism." A Wallace organizer in Oklahoma confided to campaign staffers that "he had no idea how many 'paranoiac-schizophrenics' were running around loose in the country until he published an advertisement inviting volunteers to work in the Wallace Campaign." When Wallace ran for president in 1968, he tried to tone down his extremist image by choosing former Kentucky governor and baseball commissioner A. B. "Happy" Chandler as his running mate. Chandler had presided over the desegregation of baseball in 1948 and was proud of his moderate record, yet he wanted to get back into politics enough to accept Wallace's offer. In an interview with Carter, Wallace's top aide Seymore Trammell recalled that he had told Wallace: "We have all the nuts in the country. We have all the Ku Klux Klan, we have the Birch Society. We have the White Citizens' Council. [But with Chandler] We could get some decent people—you working one side of the street and he working the other side." The plan went up in smoke when many Wallaceites felt betrayed by this choice. One state campaign chairman resigned because Chandler was an "out and out integrationist." Several others also withdrew. To appease his supporters, Wallace reneged on his offer to Chandler and ran with the more resolutely fanatical General Curtis LeMay—whose extremism, in turn, hurt Wallace's effort to broaden his appeal.[42]

THE FUNDAMENTAL
CONTRADICTION OF SEGREGATIONISM

The most difficult part of the segregationists' quest for respectability was finding black support.[43] To justify themselves, segregationists needed the good opinion of the one group they officially held to be lower than the "disreputable" white bigots. Segregationist leaders invoked Booker T. Washington's faith in separate development. They often touted the more recent segregationism of the great black novelist Zora Neale Hurston. Various Citizens' Councils and southern white newspapers reprinted Hurston's 1959 essay in the *Orlando Sentinel* (originally a long letter to the editor) that denounced integration as an insult to black culture.[44]

In segregationists' eyes, the legitimacy of their cause apparently required Negro endorsement, and they often went to great lengths to secure, or at least to claim, it. In a speech at Bennettsville, South Carolina, at the time of the Little Rock crisis in 1957, Byrnes said that segregationists had his state's respected black leaders on their side. Next to his own equalization plan, he said, the main reason that South Carolina had avoided racial violence was "the splendid attitude of the real Negro leaders in this state." It was a "tragedy" that blood was being "shed in racial conflicts" elsewhere in the South. South Carolinians ought to be thankful. "We can be sure that in every community there are some Negroes, as well as whites, who are natural disturbers of the peace." From outside the state, "some Negro men and women . . . will try to arouse ill feeling in our colored neighbors in an effort to foment strife. But to the everlasting credit of the sane, sensible Negroes, to this day they have successfully resisted these efforts."[45] In their monthly *Councilor*, the Citizens' Councils of Louisiana frequently ran a feature, entitled "But the Negro Himself," quoting black persons who dissented from the NAACP line or supported segregation generally.[46] Sociologist Charles Payne reports that the Citizens' Councils in Mississippi obtained the signatures of several black leaders endorsing segregation.[47]

How much black support for segregation actually existed is hard to tell. A 1955 poll found that only 53 percent of black southerners approved of the Supreme Court's *Brown* decision for school desegregation, but a much higher proportion favored other kinds of desegregation.[48] Much of black segregationism was surely imagined out of whole cloth. Some "endorsements" were obtained through white deception or threat of black leaders. There was probably some spontaneous black deception of segregationist henchmen, too—in anticipation of a payoff or other favor, to avoid possible violence or other retribution, or just in the interests of good neighborly relations.[49]

What is interesting is that segregationists went to all the effort to imagine or fabricate or coerce such support.[50] In a revealing example, in 1955 Marshall Moore, a Byrnes supporter in Greenville, told Byrnes about a "segregation plan" that he had "worked out with 80 colored ministers" in the county. Moore reported that 92 percent "expressed themselves openly in favor of it. . . . I am telling the negro preachers that you do not hate them, but you did the best for both races." An attached letter to the editor, published in the *Greenville News*, described how Moore had met with "a large group of prominent colored ministers, spiritual leaders and teachers." Moore believed that the group "was unanimous in desiring to direct their own schools, equipped with equal facilities, each race managing its schools as it does its own churches, tax money divided relative to average attendance, separate trustees for each school elected by parents," and so forth. In a subsequent letter, Moore asked Byrnes's help in lobbying for a state law "to organize the SAECP, or Southern Association for Education of Colored People, the purpose to divide and conquer the negro and run the NAACP out of the state by substitution. The negro as a race is especially proud of authority and when you give him an honor he will be your slave again."[51]

The effort to represent black support proved too much for honest segregationist writers, who knew that black segregationists were few and that the few were ever more reluctant to buck the new appearance of solidarity on civil rights. Apart from Hurston and the conservative black columnist and novelist George Schuyler,[52] the black opponents of integration tended to be weak in their commitment, unpopular, and, in some cases, easily exposed frauds. Waring apparently gave long consideration to promoting the career of Davis Lee, a black newspaperman from New Jersey who criticized the NAACP and supported segregation. But Waring's check into Lee's background revealed scandal after scandal, including criminal convictions. In any case, the NAACP had the jump on Waring, discrediting Lee in the black press to the point where Waring apparently concluded that it was futile to try to palm him off on literate black Charlestonians.[53] Also, Waring and others must have known of the coercion behind black ministers' pro-segregation statements (though I have not yet found any evidence that they knew of or acknowledged such coercion).[54]

It is hard to gauge the shock and disappointment of men like Waring on learning that the "sane, sensible" Negroes did not, in fact, support segregation. Waring, like Byrnes, expected black southerners to eschew extremism as much as white southerners did. Yet some of the most educated, upstanding Negroes, preachers most shockingly of all, were demonstrating their unwillingness to endure segregation.

The outside agitator myth—the notion that "our" Negroes have no need or inclination to protest—was deeply believed in the white South.[55] It took a tough-minded segregationist to admit that it was a big lie. Waring's star reporter, William Workman—the most careful and realistic thinker among the segregationists—warned his fellow segregationists that southern Negroes understood white people a lot better than white people understood them. "There is little doubt but that Negroes know at all times what is going on in the white community." The maids and cooks kept their eyes and ears open. "The Negroes have an 'underground' organization which is constantly aware of the thinking and of many of the intentions of the white community. When that intelligence service is welded to a determined drive for integration, the combination becomes formidable." On the other side, Workman lamented "the incapacity of the white man to fathom the thinking of the Negro." The worst result of this incapacity was the "dangerous delusion," widespread among white southerners, "that Negroes of [South Carolina] do not want integration. The truth of the matter is that a large percentage of them, and an even larger percentage of their leaders, very definitely do want integration of the races, and as soon as possible." White leaders were making "the tactical error—which could prove disastrous—of underestimating the enemy."[56]

Workman's warning fell on deaf ears. Most segregationists continued to embrace the illusion that "their" Negroes were either too contented or too stupid to organize effectively. Even the Mississippi Sovereignty Commission, the closest thing the segregationists had to an espionage agency, seems to have been thrown off the scent by the fantasy that black people were incapable of leading themselves out of their subordinate status. Journalist Peter Maass quotes Rims Barber, a white lawyer who had been active in the civil rights movement, recalling that the commission's investigators paid too much attention to him. "Their prism was that anyone white who was involved must be a leader, and therefore we must watch them." This meant that "they didn't know what was going on. They missed it. They didn't know who the leaders were because there are more mentions of me than there are of [black activist] Henry Kirksey, and that's just plain wrong. They were looking in the wrong places."[57]

This was the ultimate weakness in segregationist thought: to justify the system, the segregationists had to believe that black people were inferior. Yet to defend that system effectively against the mass movement that emerged in the 1950s, the segregationists would have had to recognize just how formidable their enemy actually was. They would have had to recognize that they faced an enemy with remarkable organizational and public relations skills and a militant commitment to its cause. They would have had to recognize that the solidarity of the black protesters (though subsequent scholars romantically exaggerate it) was deeper and stronger than the solidarity of the white resisters—largely because black people had politicized many of their churches.

RACISM AS A SOCIAL BOND
AND SOUTHERN LUCK WITH LEADERS

The irony goes as deep as the irony the slaveowners encountered when they realized that the only way to defend slavery was to arm the slaves — which would mean they would never be slaves again. In this instance, to prepare themselves for an effective defense of segregation, the segregationists needed to admit that their institution was fundamentally threatened. They needed to recognize that their black neighbors were not content with inferior status and that they were capable of organizing and effectively promoting their cause. In other words, to save a racist system, the segregationists would have had to abandon the most fundamental racist assumptions.

A question remains about class: the segregationists who were most interested in "respectability" were educated. (Educated, in the South, meant upper class until the 1970s or so, when the GI Bill and the demographic-economic boom finally paid off: the college degree was devalued to the point where it became necessary for many manual wage earners.) The educated segregationists sought to avoid guilt by association with crude bigots—the "trash" that James Kilpatrick said "decent people" did not want to remain in the same room with. There were segregationists who seemed to welcome the disdain of Kilpatrick and his ilk. They were not too proud to wear their bigotry on their sleeves. Rightly or wrongly, those segregationists were identified as lower class (i.e., less educated), or else their power depended (like that of Roy Harris or the ax-handle-wielding restaurateur-turned-governor of Georgia, Lester Maddox) on lower-class support. (Much research needs to be done on the social origins of different factions and tendencies within segregationism.) Those segregationists alienated their upper-class allies, identifying themselves (not always honestly) as men of humble origins, as men of the people. Segregationists on both sides of the division over respectability failed to overcome the tension between themselves. Rather, they exacerbated the divisions in southern white society. Racism—though powerful as a destructive force and as a negative campaign tactic—did not give white southerners a sufficient basis for unity in the face of a common enemy. Racism might have unified contending factions of white folk in periodic election campaigns, but it was not enough to gird them for the sustained challenge of the civil rights movement.

Segregationists had a basic difficulty deciding whether they were revolutionaries (subverting the authority of their national government) or conservatives (preserving the authority of their state governments and their "tradition" of racial separation). They failed because they did not do what revolutionists (and Tory Radicals like Disraeli) had done in the past: harness the resentments and energies of the lower classes, who had nothing to lose from social upheaval. The respectability-seeking segregationists could have followed the pattern of the American Revolution, the French Revolution, the revolutions of 1848, and the secession movement of 1860–61 by rallying their (white) social subordinates to their program. There clearly was plenty of raw material to work with: energetic resentments of the unrulier Citizens' Council chapters and the lesser, extralegal white supremacist groups.

But the respectability-mad segregationists would not and did not dirty their hands with such organizations. They could have ruthlessly exploited these "disreputable" elements and then cracked down on them afterward, establishing a new social hierarchy to restrain the class that had contributed the most energy and made the greatest sacrifice to destroy the old order. Previous revolutionaries had done exactly that once they had seized power. But respectable segregationists apparently feared or disdained the lower orders too much to use them. They were too conservative. Or perhaps they lacked confidence (probably with good reason) in their own ability to contain the disorder once they had legitimated it. In trying to restrain their more radical allies before the battle was joined, the respectable segregationists prematurely adopted the posture of postrevolutionary leaders. Their lack of radicalism, as much as their racism, hindered them.

For generations, southern liberals had lamented the lousy leadership of the South.[58] But in this case, lousy leadership was what made progress, or rather a substantial improvement in social and political life, possible. Lousy leadership—leadership incapable of mustering unity among the white folk —allowed a different force, much smaller than the white South, to gather irresistible strength. Lousy leadership among the majority allowed the leadership of a minority to find its opportunity and its nerve for hope. For the white majority, disunity made its leaders' indecision hard to overcome. Indecision, in turn, made white unity even harder to imagine.

It would remain for a later conservative movement, one that sublimated the racism of the southern white masses and built its power within the churches, to hammer together a radical (and largely successful) conservative insurgency. The more recent "Christian Right," led by such propagandists as Ralph Reed and Pat Robertson, swept southern white society and much of the rest of the country. What we see in the earlier failure of the segregationist movement is the failure of racism to solidify a conservative coalition. The conservative masses today may well harbor as much racism in their hearts as they ever did. But they learned the lesson of the civil rights struggle: racism does not work well as a force for overcoming social conflicts within the so-called white race.

Religion, apparently, works better: that was a lesson that black southerners taught white southerners by using religion to overcome the social conflicts within *their* race (for a brief but crucial period of struggle from about 1955 to 1965). A new church-supported conservatism now rarely mentions race (except, as the Republican Party did with David Duke and Trent Lott, to denounce and dissociate itself from explicit bigotry). The triumph in the 1970s and 1980s of that new, church-supported conservatism in the post–Jim Crow South is the measure of how well a new generation of conservatives has learned the lessons of history. Historians need to catch up with them.

Conclusions

GAMALIEL, CAESAR, AND US

The history of Protestantism and secular alternatives to it in the modern West has been full of surprises. One surprise that has not been appreciated is that, in the American civil rights movement, the irrational traditions of prophetic, revivalistic religion served the liberal goals of freedom and equality. The flip side of that surprise is that those traditions did not help the allegedly backward, conservative, southern opponents of liberty and equality. Civil rights activists drew from illiberal sources to supply the determination that liberals lacked, but needed, to achieve the greatest post–World War II victory of American liberalism. Their opponents failed to draw anything similarly useful from similar sources.

My argument is not that the prophetic elements in the civil rights protesters' lives were the only elements that mattered. Again, the protesters sometimes expressed the now standard, largely unquestioned liberal belief in formal equality and freedom as the "right" of every individual; they sometimes invoked the notion of "progress" as blithely as any of their contemporaries on either side of the struggle. There are many books about the civil rights protesters that ignore their prophetic qualities—most ignore the content and character of their thought altogether—but yield solid, significant knowledge. I claim not to overthrow but to add something crucial to that knowledge. My argument is that the prophetic content of the protesters' minds is illuminating, though it has been all but ignored in books and articles about the movement. Prophetic motivations and dispositions explain a lot that previous works do not, and probably cannot, explain. These motives and dispositions are not the only reason the civil rights movement succeeded. Rather, they constitute the important reason that this book seeks to add to historical knowledge about the civil rights battles of the 1940s–60s.

It now seems to me very strange to leave the religion of the protesters out of the picture—to refuse to see their religion as central and distinctive. Leaving religion out did not seem strange to me twenty years ago, when I began studying the civil rights movement. But I have come to believe that it is breathtakingly obtuse to omit it now. Even opponents of religion, it seems to me, err in ignoring religion's persistent and unpredictable power. If they hope to fight off religion's vestiges, or to beat back its apparent resurgence in our day, they need to learn from its wily durability in the past, especially the recent past. Opponents of religion might be surprised to find religion shoring up the modern liberal program at a time when liberals often felt incapable of shifting for themselves. And they might be surprised to find that hidebound clingers to southern "tradition" found religion as annoying and destructive as religion's opponents themselves now find it. If this book is accurate, all that happened not so long ago.

Some readers may think that I am too stringent in what I take to be religious. Am I too willing to belittle the religion of the segregationists and the liberals by contrasting them with the admittedly extreme example of the Prophets? Do I not, in effect, reduce liberalism to a tepid, malnourished secularism—when in reality there were liberals who believed in God, went to church, and took their commandments seriously? Surely, by a similar token, segregationists went to church, believed in God, and found some solace and encouragement in fellowship with like-minded Christians —even if they found their religious representatives annoyingly weak as leaders. The problem seems to disappear with the reminder that I am not talking about religion in general, or even about liberalism or segregationism in general. I am talking about a particular moment, when leading American liberals fretted frequently and eloquently about their inability to inspire solidarity, sacrifice, and commitment; some of them explicitly referred that inability to their insufficient religiosity. I am talking about a particular moment when active segregationists expressed similar frustration. Finally, and above all, I am not talking about religion in general in the case of the civil rights protesters. They had a specific kind of commitment, which, as in the case of Bob Moses, did not even depend on a belief in God. The history in this book is of a particular prophetic stance—not of evangelical Protestantism, or of any Afro-Baptist or southern denomination, or of anything broader.

Whatever this book contributes or fails to contribute to American history of religion, it has something to say about racism. It suggests that this troubling modern form of inequality, ugly and vicious as it has been, is contingent on other forces and ideas. Though disturbingly persistent and protean, racism shows no signs of invincibility. Even in the 1950s and early 1960s, a period of intensive racial conflict and heightened public use of racial rhetoric, racism was not enough to determine the course of politics. Racist politicians and politicians who exploited racial fears for electoral gain were taken by surprise; the civil rights activists had a sounder strategy, at least insofar as the battle was about the preservation of disfranchisement and legal segregation. (Like all human battles, this one was about many things besides the main issues that were conclusively decided by the battle. For instance, politicians and powerful social groups were also fighting opportunistically for their own survival, and those who survived cannot be considered losers in the sense that strict segregationists were losers. Like all social conflicts, this one failed to eliminate oppression and inequality altogether; but unlike most, it succeeded in eliminating *two specific institutional forms* of oppression and inequality.) The strategy on the black side was sounder, and turned out to be more successful, largely because it was based on a more realistic understanding of human nature than the strategy of segregationism.

Civil rights activists were no more taken in by despairing hokum about the irreducible racism of white southerners than they were by liberal hokum about the inevitable triumph of egalitarian ideas. What the activists tested, probably without seeing the issue this way themselves, was the strength of racial categories. Would white southerners maintain racial solidarity under pressure? Was "whiteness" (to use a widespread though imprecise scholarly term) as powerful and overriding as leading scholars, like the extreme segregationists at the time, thought it was? Or was racial solidarity a fiction — a lie — that no group of people could live up to if pushed very hard? On the evidence presented in this book, the answer to the first two questions is no, and to the last question, yes.

To say that, however, is to raise the question of the other shoe: how could black people, or black southerners, maintain racial solidarity? They also were under great pressure. The answer this book suggests is that black people (I have also referred to black southerners and black Christians) maintained nothing of the kind. Scholars are far from admitting how limited a mass movement may be: we do not know, in most instances, how much of the population of any given black "community" participated, or participated actively and persistently, in the civil rights movement. We do not know how extensive disagreement with the tactics, or the goals, of the movement was in key black neighborhoods or in the black South as a whole. But surely the number who actively and persistently participated was a minority. The press generally covered the struggle as black versus white (a racist habit that may, in this instance, have aided the black protesters, in that it made them appear stronger than they actually were). Solidarity, hard to achieve on the white side, was also hard to achieve on the black side. Black protesters managed to convince much of the nation that they represented the black people of the South. But surely there is something to the complaints of Modjeska Simkins and Fannie Lou Hamer about the frequent complacency, and the equally tragic, fear-induced immobility, of masses of black folk.

But black folk did not need complete solidarity. The point can best be illustrated, perhaps, by the old joke about the two friends getting ready to go out in the woods. One is assiduously lacing up his fancy running shoes. The other asks, What are you doing? The first one says, There are bears out there, and I want to be ready to run. The other says, You idiot, you can't outrun a bear. The first one says, I don't have to outrun a bear. I just have to outrun you. In other words, black southerners just needed greater strength and determination than their enemies, who happened at the time to be able to muster little of either. The civil rights movement did not overcome resistance by overwhelming force of numbers. Rather, the weakness of white racism could not withstand the strength of the cultural resources that some black protesters brought to bear on the struggle. Segregationists lost the battle to preserve their institutions. I do not say that they were easily defeated: lies about skin color have proven amazingly powerful, and their power appeared to increase in the election campaigns of the mid-1950s. Though antiracists were not cowed by the power and popularity of those lies, neither were they content with the superior sophistication or righteousness of their own view. They could not trust in the inevitable triumph of truth and fairness. Instead, they had to fight determinedly and intelligently. Given that they could and did so fight, their superior understanding of human nature helps explain their greater strength and performance in battle.

Is it possible to imagine where one might attain such a realistic understanding of human nature if not in the Bible? Of course it is. What leaps out of the language of key black activists as prophetic Christian realism has much in common with other traditions, indeed with just about everything except liberalism. One need not theorize about the possibility of attitudes arising from non-Christian sources: the example of Bob Moses's having been influenced by a secular, rather militantly atheist thinker, Albert Camus, demonstrates that one need not be a Christian, or a Jew, or a Muslim, or a follower of any other faith derived from the original Prophets. If one seeks a tradition behind the protesters at all, a rich and varied line of previous personalities who shared their view, the Prophets seem to me the best approximation, theirs the best name, for that tradition. The prophetic stance has usually been a minority tradition within Christianity (and Judaism and Islam), a minor and generally contrapuntal theme, often entirely dormant. If we seek to make what happened in the civil rights movement part of history—always an act of violence that suppresses some of the uniqueness of the events and personalities involved—we must at least explore the question of its prophetic roots. And perhaps we ought to re-interpret the prophetic tradition through the lens of its most recent and in many ways most successful modern exponents.

I have tried to confine my evidence to things that were actually said and recorded by participants and observers of the relevant events. But I have, through sifting this evidence, come to believe—as most writers do—things about my subjects that they apparently did not know themselves. That is one function of historical perspective, one that must be handled with as much care as any other function. There is a conclusion, perhaps less important than the ones explicitly stated in the chapters, that I have come to think significant, though it is admittedly speculative. Looking back at the civil rights activists, and reading the Bible that so many of them lived by, a pattern becomes apparent that they did not, as far as I know, ever notice.

Like Apostles drunk with new faith, the civil rights activists believed, or at least they found, that among whatever group of Pharisees they faced, there would be a Gamaliel who would warn the other Pharisees: "Take heed of yourselves what ye intend to do as touching these men." For, a Gamaliel would always say, like-sounding prophets came among us in previous days, and subsequent events had vindicated those prophets. And so a Gamaliel, anticipating Pascal, would tell the Pharisees, "Refrain from these men, and let them alone: for if [their] counsel be of men, it will come to naught: But if it be of God, ye cannot overthrow it" (Acts 5:34-40). Like the Apostles, and like Hindu Gandhians nineteen centuries later, the civil rights activists discovered that it was not necessary to convert their hearers—which, they knew, was unlikely to happen in any case. It was enough to get them to pause, to hesitate long enough to allow the Apostles to move on and continue their work. Modern-day Pharisees—the opponents of the civil rights activists in the 1950s and 1960s—were not overwhelmingly defeated but immobilized. They were not so much crushed as they were flummoxed.

Scholars tend to be disappointed that the civil rights movement did not succeed more. It did not make all white southerners renounce their racism—desegregate their hearts—or give up their economic privileges. Such scholars are less realistic than the Apostles, who had to take one victory at a time, one escape at a time. The Apostles' tradition made them realists, or their realism drove them to create their tradition.

To be sure, the civil rights activists, like the Apostles, had larger goals in mind than mere destruction of legal segregation and legal disfranchisement. But living as they did in human history, the activists, like the Apostles, recognized that they were lucky—blessed—to achieve anything at all in the little time they had left in a world ruled by sinners.

Like the most prolific and controversial Apostle, the civil rights protesters had confidence that, when their own compatriots rejected them,
they could "appeal unto Caesar"—if only to spread the news of their persecution and martyrdom further. That is, they took their case out of their
own southern evangelical tribe and laid it before the imperious authority of
a distant capital. In Rome or in Washington, that imperious authority generally preferred to let the local tribe suppress its own rebels and prophets.
But if things got really out of hand, that authority would intervene. The
Apostles of the first and twentieth centuries knew that a bigger law, however tainted and human, might get them off the hook. Or, failing that, the
Apostles' appeal to the bigger law would at least allow them to survive a bit
longer and to spread their message. They could count on that bigger law
when their own tribe failed them. The Apostles knew that the factiousness
in their own tribe—especially the factiousness among their enemies within
the tribe—made the distant authority more likely to intervene. So black
southerners knew that when white southerners betrayed them, Washington
might give them at least a marginally better hearing than they could get at
home. That was especially likely when white southerners were themselves
so fissiparous as to be incapable of ruling themselves, let alone of keeping
an oppressed minority in line. Civil rights activists, like the Apostles, had
a better chance before the distant authority in the capital than before the
tribal authorities with whom they were on intimate terms. The distant authority felt less threatened by the activists—for now, anyway—and was less
furious (Acts 25:11–26:32) with them than with white southern politicians.

It was unnecessary for the imperious authority in the distant capital to
believe in the incredible stories the Apostles told themselves about equality;
about freedom from specific social sins, like segregation; about the universal appeal of their strange "news"; particularly about the appeal of that
news to the poor and other pariahs. Indeed, it was probably better that
Caesar, along with powerful and comfortable sinners everywhere, failed to
believe the news, lest he and his successors see how dangerous the news was
to any worldly kingdom. Persecution of the new faith would fail. But the
wiser strategy of co-opting the messengers, of perverting their message and
watering it down, has had a long record of success. The Apostles depended
on the authority in the capital having its own doctrines, for the moment,
its own law. It was unnecessary for the hearts and minds in the capital to be
with the Apostles.

Neither was it necessary for the authorities in Rome and Washington to
believe anything like the creed that Gunnar Myrdal discovered in America
nineteen centuries later. Myrdal was not imagining things: many Americans, perhaps an overwhelming majority, really did believe in equal opportunity. After all, even Judge Tom Brady recognized that the nation mis-
treated the Negro, and there is no evidence that Brady's sorrow was feigned.

The misunderstanding of history comes not from Myrdal's empirical discovery of an opportunitarian faith in Americans, but from Myrdal's own faith in logical consistency. He failed to weigh the significance of the universal tendency of human beings to believe in contradictory things. Consider "Liberty, Equality, Fraternity." Were there ever three more incompatible things? And what has inspired even more murder and martyrdom than the slogan of the French Revolutionaries? The Christian Trinity, for one; the Marxist program, for another—which claimed to reconcile the skeptical economism of British utilitarians with French Romantic fantasies of socialist bliss. Nor need one live in times of religious or revolutionary fervor to live with inconsistency: mild-mannered feminists in the universities of our own day are content to let equality and difference cohabit peacefully in their highly trained minds. More generally, can anybody contemplate free will and determinism for more than an hour without seeing that the two are incompatible and that each of us believes in both simultaneously? As another example, human beings generally see no diminution of violence and degradation, greed and starvation, sickening luxury and pointless torture in their world. Most of us, as Albert Camus pointed out, do not come to the eminently sensible conclusion of suicide. Most of us, on the contrary, hope for a better day. Most of us are somehow driven to bring new human beings into this god-awful place and to call that an act of love.

Americans have lived with contradictions among their various creeds as blithely and as anxiously as any other people on earth.[1] What they need (to borrow a phrase from the creed of the modern priests of economics) are positive incentives to do something about those contradictions. Or they need to have among them people who feel free to do something about those contradictions, ideally people with nothing to lose. This is not the place to settle questions of relative deprivation and rising expectations that students of rebellion have raised in the face of the general truth that the poorest and most desperate are not the ones to lead revolutions. The civil rights protesters were not generally poor and uneducated—though Fannie Lou Hamer was, and she was as representative of the whole as the relatively privileged and hypereducated Martin Luther King or Bob Moses. They were not in any crude, simplistic way acting to better their interests: I believe there remains some irreducible altruism among the civil rights protesters. But what strikes me as more important than that is their realism: they understood that altruism was not a reliable or overwhelming force— any more than racism was on the other side. They had to get people to do the right thing for the wrong reasons. They could not find enough altruism among "their own" people, let alone among people who enjoyed special privileges at their expense.

Civil rights activists lived in a world of human interest, greed, and materialism. They lived in the midst of a constant struggle for power over and security from others. At any moment, that could turn into a struggle for survival. The activists knew that they could not talk their way to success in such a world. Though they certainly wanted to redeem the soul of America — who doesn't? — they did not need to.

Scholars have worked hard and effectively over the last quarter century to establish that the civil rights protesters were not all headline-grabbing celebrities. Thousands, perhaps tens of thousands, of unsung underdogs were involved. Once-invisible grassroots sprang up all over scholarship in the 1980s–90s, making for many diverting and instructive vistas. I do not think these vistas are inaccurate. I just no longer find them startling enough to be very educational. My generation was raised looking at them, and if we hope to add anything to them we had better stop treating them as news.

What becomes most significant about the civil rights protesters, when one does them the honor of looking at them closely on their own terms, is not how much they resemble multitudes of oppressed persons over the globe who have creatively "resisted" oppression for millennia. This is not the only general point scholars have made over the last twenty-five years, but it is the one they emphasize and belabor. That point is valid but incomplete. The now celebrated "weapons of the weak" — foot-dragging, gossiping, playing dumb, following orders too literally, feigning fright or forgetfulness, and so forth — these were not enough for what became the civil rights movement. The watchword of the weak-weapon-wielder-watchers, "resistance," was not enough, any more than survival was enough. Civil rights activists presumed to seize the weapons of the strong, perhaps not realizing how strong they were until they had those weapons in hand. They organized and entered politics, though they could not vote; waged war, though they knew it would be suicide to wage it with guns. Not content to thwart their enemy's will, they destroyed their enemy's will to resist *them*, for a while.

They succeeded. They put their enemies on the defensive. They did that, I think I have discovered, because of two things beyond the luck they had to be born during a time of political instability created by an economic sea change in rural America (with some help from a Cold War that coincided with a period of decolonization). Both things are cultural or intellectual. One has to do with their own motives, the other with their understanding of their enemies.

As to the protesters' own motives, it was hard for me to nail down their religious enthusiasm. First approaching this story as an atheist, I was surprised and skeptical to hear so many of my subjects — whom I admired from afar — expressing what Bayard Rustin called "fundamentalist" views. Even had I been a believer, in the sense that most modern educated folk use the term, I doubt that any isolated testimony of "miracles" ever could have struck me as worth copying down in my notes. But that testimony began to stick out because it was repeated so much and, perhaps, because it was so foreign to me. So I kept copying it down, and ultimately it appeared, not literally believable, but nonetheless a key to the beliefs, and therefore to the choices, including the strategic choices, of my sources.

From this discovery flowed my inquiry into what these miracles and conversion experiences might have meant to intelligent, thoughtful people who recorded their thoughts at the time, like Fannie Lou Hamer and Modjeska Simkins. What I found among these unusually articulate people ended up as Chapters 3 and 4 of this book. Their understanding could not be perfectly revivalist, but it was related to revivalism. Again, my approach was skeptical and my method simply to copy things down that appeared again and again, focusing on things that I had not already learned from books I had read about these people. Up came the prophetic theme, and its secular cognates in Bayard Rustin and Bob Moses. The prophetic theme came to appear as the missing link that made all existing books on civil rights seem incomplete. It seemed to have a lot to do with why these people resisted the temptation to lead normal, private lives and instead became targets of abuse and sometimes bullets. Not only that, but it seemed to explain the determination that made them succeed at whatever they sacrificed their lives to.

The prophetic common ground of the activists I examine in Chapters 3 and 4 turned out to be related not only to the "miracles" and other transformative psychological experiences that ended up being Chapter 5, but also to other important things.

The most important of those things was the protesters' understanding of their enemies. One of the fundamental assumptions out of which this book grew was that, to understand the civil rights struggle, it was necessary to understand both sides of it. That assumption grew difficult with research, because research revealed that there were really more than two sides. Segregationists were divided against one another. The division among segregationists, and their preoccupation with the division, had been all but invisible in the existing literature. It seemed much more important to the segregationists than to subsequent scholars.

Black desegregationists turned out to be no less complicated: they had to grapple with deep divisions among black southerners (class, denomination, ideology). They had to grapple more intimately within the ranks of committed activists over strategic priorities and over the choice of tactical means to whatever strategic ends they could agree on. On top of all that, they had the massive headaches that their alliance with northern liberals gave them.

Most books and movies on civil rights take both black southern solidarity and liberal support for granted. This book has tried to suggest that both things were on the contrary rare and impressive achievements—which could not be sustained. The pressures of competing political goals and the demands of nonpolitical life, which make full-time political commitments a luxury that few can afford, took their toll on black unity and on the black movement's alliance with northern liberals.

Fortunately, however, during the period of apparent black southern solidarity and liberal support, white southerners failed to achieve the unity their leaders had assumed but rarely tested. The last major previous test, the Civil War, whose centennial was being commemorated all over the South in the middle of the civil rights struggle, had given the white South a false sense of solidarity. The way of life associated with slavery, and the religious and nationalist feelings that were generated to shore it up, added up to something formidable. Three-fourths of white southern families in 1860 had never owned a slave. But they depended on the masters who did own slaves; they deferred to them, looked up to them, and though of course they often resented them, they identified with them. The nonslaveowning white folk certainly found that the masters in their section represented a far better hope of security and prosperity than the vengeful abolitionists who seemed to have gotten hold of the federal government. Planter control of politics and propaganda surely made southern white solidarity easier in the 1830s–60s. But it is doubtful that that propaganda could have fooled all the white people in the region all of the time. The nonslaveowning white southern majority ran off to defend the slave system with enthusiasm and bravery. It took years of grueling battle and economic blockade to get many of them to question their solidarity with the planter minority. White southerners lost, ultimately, but they forced their enemies to pay the greatest price in American history.

Slavery, with the cultural and political system that had been organized to defend it, was nothing like the system of segregation and disfranchisement that rose up in slavery's ashes. It would be an exaggeration to say that the new system—named Jim Crow after an old, unintimidating minstrel character, an unconvincing representation of real life—was only propaganda, only culture, only ideology. It had a lot going for it, including the very real privilege it offered to the worst losers in the white population: they always had better seats, better drinking fountains, better schools, better hospitals; always a more plausible illusion that they had a voice in politics; and always far less chance of being punished for physically abusing any random Negro, than Negroes themselves had. But all that was not enough to impel the worst losers to form strong bonds with other white southerners. Many well-heeled white southerners recognized escape routes from the plight that the worst white losers would be stuck with after desegregation. Many knew that they could escape desegregated schools (along with other urban, Yankee-like troubles) by moving to the suburbs or sending their children to private schools, just as the Yankees did.

More important, I think, white southerners were not attacked in the 1950s the way white southerners were attacked in the 1860s. Black civil rights activists focused on divisions within the so-called white community. They attacked piecemeal, locally, often concentrating on targets where white leadership was unusually reckless and impulsive (such as Little Rock and Birmingham). They did not threaten total humiliation and enslavement of the white population, but a complicated improvisation of compromises that might offend some white folk but offered others a more orderly, more peaceful social life than one disrupted by boycotts; a less notorious reputation in national headlines than the one they currently, however unfairly, had; and a more propitious investment climate than they had had under the leadership of racial demagogues.

Once the black folk organized enough to offer desegregation as a route to peace and order, the segregationists failed to make a convincing case that desegregation would lead, in fact, to an inescapable hell of conflict and calamity. There were not enough committed segregationists willing to sacrifice themselves in perpetual war with black activists. That became clear to the federal government—which increasingly took its cues from the South's temporizing white civic and business leaders, rather than from the bombastic speeches of its political candidates. The candidates could win elections and inspire an occasional riot, but they could not inspire the discipline and self-confidence that white southerners needed to keep up with the black protesters.

Looking at both sides of the movement partially vindicates the basic assumption that has guided most scholarly work in the last quarter century: that the major impetus behind civil rights activity came from local black people in the South. But if my work has any meaning, it will require that basic assumption to be severely qualified.

For one thing, I have come to believe that historians tend to misrepresent the local black southern people involved as "ordinary." They appear, on the contrary, to have been quite extraordinary, and to think of themselves as such. But that is a minor and perhaps somewhat semantic complaint compared to another qualification I wish to add to the grassroots assumption: local people themselves cannot be understood in isolation from their allies and enemies. Looking at them in relationship to their allies and enemies calls our attention to the most important things about them—what makes them different from their enemies and allies and from previous generations of oppressed black people in the South.

Their allies—mainstream midcentury liberals—were incomplete and ineffectual before black southerners, who had different philosophical roots, seized the initiative, and gained a degree of influence over civil rights policy. Their enemies, it turned out, lacked exactly the same thing that mainstream liberals lacked—a basis for solidarity and self-sacrifice. Those enemies were unable to call up anything equivalent to an anti–civil rights movement in the white South to supply what they lacked. We give civil rights activists no great compliment by calling them ordinary. The point of seeing their uniqueness is not to put them unreachably above us on some historical pedestal of greatness. Rather, it is to suggest that if we hope to build on their successes, and to learn from their human mistakes and limitations, we need to work very hard to see them as they were.

Appendix

A PHILOSOPHICAL NOTE

ON HISTORICAL EXPLANATION

I chose to focus on people I call intellectuals, including nonformally educated ones like Fannie Lou Hamer, not because I believe intellectuals are prime movers, but because they are keys to retrospective understanding. They talk more on the record, they tend to preserve their own observations, and they have an occupational interest in being more precise and thorough than their fellows about whatever afflicts them. They are by no means more honest than those who produce other kinds of historical record. So it is obviously necessary to treat their accounts with great skepticism. But they provide an efficient means to get a grip on what happened. They often point to realities that their contemporaries, and later pathologists of their society, failed to see. They often point inadvertently, simply because they talk and write so compulsively. We can see things in their musings that they could not necessarily see. But what is of overriding interest, to me, is that they preserved what they saw with greater vividness, complexity, and durability than those around them. That is what defines them as intellectuals, and that is all, as far as this book is concerned.

Lately there has been a lot of loose talk about "culture" among scholars of twentieth-century ideology and grassroots organizing in America. There has been a lot of reaching for guns among other scholars, who find the very word offensive to their sensibilities.

I am not exactly agnostic in this not exactly well-defined dispute. In fact, I believe that material forces (manpower shortages, declining transportation costs, famines, hurricanes, falling bombs, and the like) are distinct from collective human creations like "ideology" and "religion." I also believe that material forces have a peremptory, overriding quality about them that makes me lean away from idealists like Max Weber and toward materialists like Karl Marx—though I cannot dismiss the idealists altogether. Indeed, I believe that the best materialists, like the best idealists, have improved themselves by listening to their enemies. One thing both sides have to acknowledge is that the line between culture and material reality is not self-evident or consistently clear. We cannot communicate at all, however, if we do not acknowledge some sort of line. A bomb, for example, is in a sense a cultural creation, based on human languages of chemistry and mechanics. But its effectiveness comes from its demonstrated use as a material force. It has a different kind of power from talk, even from threatening talk, when that talk is not backed up by bomblike power. So, too, a famine may be a product of human choices, even deliberate choices. But it affects people in a way that headlines and musical scores and economic theories, by themselves, do not.

Those are distinctions that one need not accept to understand this book. But for the sake of placing this book in larger debates about general and particular things, I offer them as points of clarification. These are the terms and definitions I am using, with all due acknowledgment of their imprecision and their inability to inspire universal assent.

It is not "culture" or "religion," then, that I am pointing to, but a particular kind of religious culture in a particular political situation. I happen to think that the political situation itself was created more by material forces, broadly defined, than by cultural precepts. The economic transformation of the twentieth-century South is well documented and understood. Federally financed consolidation and mechanization of agriculture during and after the New Deal made hundreds of thousands of laborers, especially black tenants and sharecroppers, permanently unemployable. (Many forgotten white people were also affected, but they are important for reasons other than the ones under discussion here.) The ensuing cityward migration had two profound political consequences.

In the North, the new migrants destabilized the balance between Republican and Democrat, forcing both parties to compete for the new voters. Northern urban politicians saw that black voters held the balance of power in areas where competition between the parties was close. If the Democrats could outdo Republicans with patronage and credible promises of other benefits for the new black voters (including benefits for their relatives who remained in the rural South, such as increased safety, economic opportunity, and/or political power), then the Democrats would rob the GOP of a voting bloc. The black bloc, up to the mid-1930s, had been devoutly Republican. It took another thirty years for that bloc, which grew all the while, to become devoutly Democratic—for the Democrats to take it for granted and for the Republicans to give up on it. In that thirty-year interval, black leaders who were bold enough to make demands had a chance that they never had before or since. That was the profound consequence of economic transformation and cityward migration in the North.

In the South, the consequence was more complicated. Just knowing that northern politicians had new incentives to make Negro émigrés happy—the easiest way being obviously to beggar the white South—affected southern politicians. But there were direct consequences to the region itself. In some southern cities, Negro voting, or the lack thereof, became significantly more difficult for the authorities to control. Perhaps more important, the black population became much more concentrated: communication, education, political organization, fund-raising, and various kinds of collective self-defense became easier, more robust. The enhancement of black cultural resources in the South through concentration happened to such a degree that the change was not merely quantitative, in my opinion, but qualitative.

The new concentration paid off above all in the churches. They were not the only social institution in the black South, but by far the oldest, most respected, and most widely supported one. Even if most black churches remained conservative or apolitical, there was an opportunity as never before for a few active, bold ones to flourish, too.

The northern and southern political changes that stemmed from the consolidation of southern agriculture were necessary to the civil rights movement's success. These changes were, however, only opportunities. They did not inevitably produce people who could seize these opportunities and make the most of them. Nor did they dictate the specific strategies and weapons by which actual people could seize them. Nor did they determine the character of the allies that actual people would enlist. Men do not make their history exactly as they please, to reverse Marx's emphasis, but they do make their own history.

Some historians, sociologists, or economists may find the ideas and strategies emphasized in this book to be less important in some grand sense than the "structural" or social changes that allowed those ideas and strategies to become visible. If so, I have no quarrel with them. I have chosen to tell a part of the story that has been left out. In my broader understanding of history, I probably lean further in the direction of materialism and economic determinism than the average humanist or social scientist in the United States since World War II. That said, material and economic determinants appear to me only to impose boundaries and limits—often rigid and durable ones—on human freedom; they do not eliminate freedom altogether. What human beings do collectively, and sometimes even as individuals, within those boundaries and limits, the choices they make, are parts of history that we can learn from.

Not that we could ever abolish material limits: to think that we could is a form of hubris that Marxists, along with American politicians who wear the "conservative" label, inherited from liberalism. I believe, if my beliefs matter, that material forces are prime movers in human history and prime limiters of human motivation. That may still be the most important single idea to keep in mind about human society. What I devote my research to, however, is not necessarily the most important thing I can see. Rather, it is the most important element that is missing from the picture shared by the reading public.

Notes

ABBREVIATIONS

ACMHR	Alabama Christian Movement for Human Rights
ADA	Americans for Democratic Action
ADAH	Alabama Department of Archives and History, Montgomery
ADL	Anti-Defamation League (of B'nai B'rith)
ASRA	American States' Rights Association
BGC	Billy Graham Center, Wheaton College, Wheaton, Illinois
BPL	Birmingham Public Library, Birmingham, Alabama
CLC	Christian Life Commission (of the SBC)
CRDP	Civil Rights Documentation Project, Howard University Library, Washington, D.C.
CU	Clemson University, Clemson, South Carolina
FOR	Fellowship of Reconciliation
LC	Library of Congress, Washington, D.C.
LSU	Louisiana State University, Baton Rouge
MDAH	Mississippi Department of Archives and History, Jackson
MFDP	Mississippi Freedom Democratic Party
MLK	Martin Luther King Jr.
MLKA	MLK Library and Archives, MLK Center, Atlanta, Georgia
MLKB	MLK Papers, Boston University, Boston, Massachusetts
NAACP	National Association for the Advancement of Colored People
NCC	National Council of Churches
NCLC	Nashville Christian Leadership Conference
PCUS	Presbyterian Church in the United States (the southern Presbyterians)
PMLK	*Papers of Martin Luther King, Jr.*, ed. Clayborne Carson et al., 4 vols. to date (Berkeley: University of California Press, 1992–)
SBC	Southern Baptist Convention
SBTS	Southern Baptist Theological Seminary, Louisville, Kentucky
SCHS	South Carolina Historical Society, Charleston
SCLC	Southern Christian Leadership Conference

SHSW   State Historical Society of Wisconsin, Madison
SNCC   Student Nonviolent Coordinating Committee
SOHP   Southern Oral History Project, University of North Carolina,
       Chapel Hill
SPJ   *Southern Presbyterian Journal*
SRC   Southern Regional Council
UA   University of Arkansas, Fayetteville
UNC-CH   University of North Carolina, Chapel Hill
USC   University of South Carolina, Modern Political Collections,
       Columbia
USM   University of Southern Mississippi, Hattiesburg
UVA   University of Virginia, Charlottesville

INTRODUCTION

1 See William Sumner Jenkins, *Pro-slavery Thought in the Old South* (1934; reprint, New York: Peter Smith, 1960); Eugene D. Genovese, *The World the Slaveholders Made* (New York: Pantheon, 1969), *The Slaveholders' Dilemma* (Columbia: University of South Carolina Press, 1992), and *The Southern Tradition* (Cambridge: Harvard University Press, 1994); Donald Mathews, *Religion in the Old South* (Chicago: University of Chicago Press, 1977); E. Brooks Holifield, *The Gentlemen Theologians* (Durham, N.C.: Duke University Press, 1978); Mitchell Snay, *Gospel of Disunion: Religion and Separatism in the Antebellum South* (Cambridge: Cambridge University Press, 1993); Richard Carwardine, *Evangelicals and Politics in Antebellum America* (Knoxville: University of Tennessee Press, 1997); and Christine Leigh Heyrman, *Southern Cross: The Beginnings of the Bible Belt* (Chapel Hill: University of North Carolina Press, 1998).

2 See Liston Pope, *Millhands and Preachers: A Study of Gastonia* (New Haven: Yale University Press, 1942), and Allen Tullos, *Habits of Industry: White Culture and the Transformation of the Carolina Piedmont* (Chapel Hill: University of North Carolina Press, 1989). Bryant Simon, in *A Fabric of Defeat: The Politics of South Carolina Millhands, 1910–1948* (Chapel Hill: University of North Carolina Press, 1998), does not devote as much attention to the role of religion as Pope and Tullos—and he finds a religious vision animating pro- as well as anti-union forces—but confirms the basic point that the workers' churches played a strong role in preaching submission to the bosses' authority (see esp. p. 104).

3 See Mark Newman, *Getting Right with God: Southern Baptists and Race* (Tuscaloosa: University of Alabama Press, 2001), 24, and Joel Alvis, *Religion and Race: Southern Presbyterians, 1946–1983* (Tuscaloosa: University of Alabama Press, 1994), 57–58.

1 Toward the end of his career, Henry A. Wallace joined these pioneers, but he said and did little on racial issues while secretary of agriculture in the 1930s, when he might have made a difference. See Wallace, *The Price of Vision: The Diary of Henry Wallace*, ed. John M. Blum (Boston: Houghton Mifflin, 1973); John B. Kirby, *Black Americans in the Roosevelt Era: Liberalism and Race* (Knoxville: University of Tennessee Press, 1980), 25, 52; and John Culver and John Hyde, *American Dreamer: The Life and Times of Henry Wallace* (New York: Norton, 2000).

2 Nancy J. Weiss's *Farewell to the Party of Lincoln: Black Politics in the Age of FDR* (Princeton, N.J.: Princeton University Press, 1983) remains the most convincing explanation of the shift of black votes. Despite the New Deal's inaction on racial issues like lynching, the poll tax, and job discrimination, and despite its aid to white landowners at the expense of black tenants and sharecroppers, the Democrats' transracial commitment to the poor was more attractive to black voters than anything the competition — Republican or Communist — could realistically offer.

3 Other than Eleanor Roosevelt — whom FDR may have used to secure radical support while he let southern conservatives control racial policy — Ickes was the most prominent New Dealer associated with civil rights. Ickes had been head of the NAACP's Chicago branch in the 1920s; he expressed frustration in his efforts to enliven the quiescent branch and concluded that Chicago Negroes just "have no real grievances" to press. H. A. Watkins, *Righteous Pilgrim: The Life and Times of Harold Ickes* (New York: Holt, 1990), 199–201; see also, 643–45. Ickes's low enthusiasm for the local NAACP in the 1920s was in stark contrast to his energetic and heartfelt work on behalf of American Indians. Graham White and John Maze, *Harold Ickes of the New Deal: His Private Life and Public Career* (Cambridge: Harvard University Press, 1985), 91–92. Even with this relatively strong advocate of civil rights, the issue did not come up much, if one is to judge from *The Secret Diary of Harold L. Ickes*, 3 vols. (New York: Simon and Schuster, 1954), 2:115, 131, and (1953), 1:680.

4 Ickes, *Secret Diary*, 2:115. Ickes also believed that northerners like himself had no basis for criticizing southern customs. "Moreover, while there are no segregation laws in the North, there is segregation in fact and we might as well recognize this" (p. 131); see also 1:680.

5 Some southern liberals, including Virginius Dabney, saw segregation and disfranchisement as liberal programs, hearkening back to the age of Henry Grady and Edgar Gardner Murphy, the pioneering southern liberals who supported Jim Crow. See Dabney, *Liberalism in the South* (Chapel Hill: University of North Carolina Press, 1932).

6 FDR once took a step in the direction of offending that oligarchy — campaigning against southern senators Walter George and E. D. Smith in 1938. He failed disastrously. He dared only one more experiment in that direction, ordering an end of discrimination in military industry in 1941. He was forced

into that move, kicking and screaming, by A. Philip Randolph's threat of an embarrassing mass march on Washington and by a labor shortage that dictated increased hiring of black workers whether the government took any action or not. Randolph also demanded the more extreme step of desegregating the armed forces. FDR met him less than half way, but Randolph backed down. By then, New Deal reform was dead in any case. Whatever FDR did for black urban industrial workers in the name of wartime unity can only with great strain be attributed to liberal impulses.

7   Childs, *I Write from Washington* (New York: Harper, 1942), 17. Childs meant that New Dealers themselves made no direct attack on the poll tax. There were radical black and white protesters who did.

8   On black leaders' frustration with the New Deal's failure to do anything about lynching, see Walter White, "U.S. Department of (White) Justice," *Crisis* 42 (October 1935): 309–10, reprinted in Howard Zinn, ed., *New Deal Thought* (Indianapolis: Bobbs-Merrill, 1966), 332–38.

9   Bowles, *And Promises to Keep: My Years in Public Life, 1941–1969* (New York: Harper and Row, 1971), 174. Presidential aide Clark Clifford—who wrote Harry S. Truman's 1948 speech committing the Democrats to a radical civil rights program—echoed Bowles's perspective. Clifford, *Counsel to the President* (New York: Random, 1991), 204. Bowles's reference to Byrnes and Rayburn as "populists" would be hard for any student of history to swallow today, but liberals of Bowles's generation often used the term as a synonym for southerners and midwesterners who, for ideological or practical reasons, resisted liberal initiatives. For an analysis of how congressional Democrats were forced to end their moratorium on civil rights in the 1950s, see David L. Chappell, *Inside Agitators: White Southerners in the Civil Rights Movement* (Baltimore: Johns Hopkins University Press, 1994), chaps. 7–8.

10 J. Joseph Huthmacher, *Senator Robert Wagner* (New York: Athenaeum, 1968), 338. Wagner was no longer active in politics and retired two years later.

11 Hofstadter, *The American Political Tradition and the Men Who Made It* (New York: Knopf, 1948), vii. The most successful effort to remedy the situation, Americans for Democratic Action, was apparently based on Hofstadter's premise. A cochairman of ADA wrote that in the months after World War II, liberals "discovered that there was no cohesive liberal movement, no broad progressive organization. One man had united liberals of all faiths and political viewpoints. With this man gone, the progressive movement floundered, stumbled in confusion, split wide open and—lost the election." Wilson Wyatt, "Liberals Rearm for '48," *This Month*, April 1947, reprinted as ADA pamphlet with same title, copy in ADA Papers, SHSW, ser. 7, box 80.

12 Alan Brinkley, *The End of Reform: New Deal Liberalism in Recession and War* (New York: Knopf, 1995).

13 Liberals' pre-*Brown* emphasis on individual rights tended to mean civil liberties—the largely self-interested protection of political expression from right-wing attack—more often than civil rights, whose enforcement would have structural economic consequences in the South and major cities in the North.

R. Alan Lawson, *The Failure of Independent Liberalism, 1930–1941* (New York: Putnam, 1971), 172; Stephen Gillon, *Politics and Vision: The ADA and American Liberalism, 1947–1985* (New York: Oxford University Press, 1987).

14 Brinkley highlights the postwar concentration on economic growth and individual freedom, in contrast to the depression-era emphasis on structural reform of capitalism (see *The End of Reform*). Hubert Humphrey summed up the novelty of the ADA's postwar priorities in November 1949. For nearly three years, he said, the new organization had been stating "categorically" "that that government is best which afford[s] the maximum economic security consistent with the freedom of the individual to speak, to worship, to associate, to work, to help elect, etc. I believe that the twin goals of modern liberal action must be to broaden economic security and to strengthen individual freedom." There was nothing about civil rights in this speech. Humphrey, draft of Seattle Speech, November 4, 1949, ADA Papers, SHSW, ser. 2, box 53. The ADA charter appears in an article by ADA cochairman Wilson Wyatt, who put the charter in the context of a choice between "the empty shell of freedom minus bread; or totalitarianism." There is nothing about civil rights in the ADA charter or the article. Wyatt, "Liberals Rearm for '48," *This Month*, April 1947, reprinted as ADA pamphlet with same title, in ADA Papers, SHSW, ser. 7, box 80.

15 See remarks on liberals in the Bibliographical Essay.

16 James was drawn to extreme rejections of reason and empiricism—which he explored more forthrightly and adventurously than Dewey. James's famous essay, "The Will to Believe," expresses this, and what many regard as his greatest work, *The Varieties of Religious Experience: A Study in Human Nature* (New York: Longmans, 1902), especially the key chapter on "The Sick Soul," develops it fully. Where Dewey, one might say more pragmatically, feared the rule of dogma and tradition, James (more in the manner of Nietzsche) thought that there was an at least equal and opposite danger in a "desiccated" culture that depended too much on reason. In *Varieties*, James spoke with something close to derision of the "healthy minded" approach to life. For that approach evaded the heady insights—which gave life (and death) its richness and excitement—that were available to the "sick soul."

17 John Stuart Mill, *Autobiography* (London: Longmans, 1873). Mill was also a central figure in John Dewey's *Liberalism and Social Action* (New York: Putnam, 1935), in Dewey, *The Later Works*, 17 vols. (Carbondale: Southern Illinois University Press, 1987), 11:11, 18–19, 23.

18 For other expressions of the post-Christian need to generate passion and commitment, see the section on liberal fears of self-insufficiency in the Bibliographical Essay.

19 Dewey quoted in Lawson, *Failure of Independent Liberalism*, 116. There are hints of this attitude in Dewey's earlier thought. See his *Democracy and Education* (1916; reprint, New York: Free Press, 1966), chap. 26, 354–60, and *Reconstruction in Philosophy* (1920; reprint, New York: Mentor, 1950), chaps. 7–8. In his 1927 refutation of Walter Lippmann's elitist version of liberalism, Dewey

wrote about the popular thirst for community that accompanied the "mania for motion and speed" in industrial societies. It was hard for people in such societies "to form sustained attachments," yet attachments would be necessary to organize a democracy (or anything else). "How can a public be organized . . . when literally it does not stay in place? Only deep issues or those which can be made to appear such can find a common denominator among all the shifting and unstable relationships." Dewey, *The Public and Its Problems* (1927; reprint, Chicago: Swallow Press, 1954), 140–41.

20 Dewey, *Individualism Old and New* (1930; reprint, Amherst, N.Y.: Prometheus, 1999), 26, 30; see also 32, where Dewey argues that "the sense of wholeness" that people think they get from religion "can be built up and sustained only through membership in a society which has attained a degree of unity." That had to happen first before a credible and effective religion could emerge. It was futile to try to pump an outmoded and discredited religion into a society that had lost the ability to live by it. Most Americans, however, clung desperately to an old morality, which was powerless to affect their lives: "Nowhere in the world at any time has religion been so thoroughly respectable as with us, and so nearly totally disconnected from life" (p. 7).

21 See H. Richard Niebuhr, *Social Sources of Denominationalism* (1929; reprint, New York: Holt, 1957), and Robert Lynd and Helen Lynd, *Middletown: A Study in Contemporary American Culture* (New York: Harcourt, Brace, 1929).

22 Indeed, tying these qualities to supernatural beliefs only inhibited their development and impeded their rejuvenation in the modern world. Dewey sought "emancipation" and "liberation" of these qualities from religion. Dewey, *A Common Faith* (1934), reprinted in his *Later Works*, 9:56.

23 One of the historical errors that Dewey made was to assume that all historic Christianity had been committed to the Calvinist doctrine of election, "to a separation of sheep and goats; the saved and the lost; the elect and the mass." He saw "spiritual aristocracy" as well as "laissez faire with respect to natural and human intervention" as "deeply embedded" in Christian tradition per se. Ibid., 9:54–55.

24 Robert B. Westbrook, *John Dewey and American Democracy* (Ithaca, N.Y.: Cornell University Press, 1991), 419–20, quoting Dewey's *Quest for Certainty: A Study of the Relation of Knowledge and Action* (New York: Minton, Balch, 1929), 244–46. See also Alan Ryan, *John Dewey and the High Tide of American Liberalism* (New York: Norton, 1995), 234–35, 241–42, 262–76.

25 This is the central theme of Durkheim's *Moral Education* (1925; trans. by Everett Wilson and Herman Schnurer, Glencoe, Ill.: Free Press, 1956) and is indeed a prominent theme in European and American thought in the age of Darwin and Nietzsche.

26 See Dewey, "Individualism, Old and New, I: The United States Incorporated," and "Individualism, Old and New, II: The Lost Individual" (1930), in *Later Works*, 5:59–89, and in Dewey, *Individualism Old and New*.

27 Dewey's criticism can be found in such journals as *Modern Quarterly, The*

World Tomorrow, and *Modern Monthly*; see Lawson, *Failure of Independent Liberalism*, 124–25.

28 Dewey, *Liberalism and Social Action* (New York: Putnam, 1935), reprinted in *Later Works*, 11:39, 61.

29 Ibid., 11:51. See also Lawson, *Failure of Independent Liberalism*, 129.

30 The quotations in this and the previous paragraph are from Dewey, *Liberalism and Social Action*, in *Later Works*, 11:24–25, 48, 39, 36, 28.

31 Westbrook, *Dewey*, 422–23.

32 In *Moral Education*, begun in 1903 but published in 1925, just nine years before Dewey's *Common Faith*, Emile Durkheim embarked on a much richer appreciation of religion, particularly of the way it is grounded in "the real"—in a way that might have appealed to Dewey, but apparently Dewey never took it up. On the "reality" of religion, see also Durkheim, *Elementary Forms of Religious Life* (1912; trans. Karen Fields, New York: Basic Books, 1998). Durkheim believed that "religion" is the name we give to a society's effort to account for the "force" that differentiates people in society from individual persons. Whatever that "force" is—whatever it is that makes human groups more than the sum of their individual parts—the society invariably feels compelled to explain it with shared myths and symbols. The definition has a certain circularity, but it is hard to find a definition without circularity or something worse.

33 Dewey, *A Common Faith*, 30, quoted in Westbrook, *Dewey*, 424. Dewey extends the equivocation: "An ideal is not an illusion because imagination is the organ through which it is apprehended." "The only meaning that can be assigned the term 'imagination' is that things unrealized in fact come home to us and have power to stir us."

34 Dewey quoted in Westbrook, *Dewey*, 425, 448.

35 Norris added the modifier "independent" to his Republican designation in 1936, as FDR muted his own partisanship and campaigned as head of an independent coalition. FDR mentioned his own party's name no more than three times in the campaign. William Leuchtenburg, *Franklin D. Roosevelt and the New Deal, 1932–1940* (New York: Harper and Row, 1963), 190–91; Richard Lowitt, *George W. Norris: Persistence of a Progressive, 1913–1933* (Urbana: University of Illinois Press, 1971); George Norris, *Fighting Liberal: Autobiography of George W. Norris* (1945; reprint, New York: Collier, 1961). I thank Richard Lowitt for sharing with me his vast knowledge of Norris's relationships with Dewey and other independent liberals.

36 A succinct statement of Dewey's program to bring modern society—already collectivized by rapacious capitalists—under the control of a democratic and scientific culture is in his "Individualism: Old and New" essays of 1929-30, reprinted in Dewey, *Individualism Old and New*. His dismissal of religion—an obstacle to the formation of such a culture—is more wholehearted here (see, e.g., pp. 73-75) than in *Common Faith* or *Quest for Certainty*. In these essays, Dewey calls for a "positive" new culture, but he declines to spell it out, in-

sisting that the old cultural traditions must be destroyed before anything new can be spelled out.

37 On the beginning of this historical surprise, see Jon Butler, *Awash in a Sea of Faith: Christianizing the American People* (Cambridge: Harvard University Press, 1990). Nathan Hatch provides a more tolerant, sympathetic view of America's Christianization in *The Democratization of American Christianity* (New Haven: Yale University Press, 1989). On America's thwarting the expectation of secularization—its refusal to let go of faith as it became the most technological and materialist of cultures—see, e.g., Will Herberg, *Protestant-Catholic-Jew* (Garden City: Doubleday, 1955); George Marsden, *Fundamentalism in American Culture* (New York: Oxford University Press, 1980); and Robert Wuthnow, *The Restructuring of American Religion* (Princeton, N.J.: Princeton University Press, 1988).

38 The quotations in this and the previous paragraph are from Malcolm Ross, *Death of a Yale Man* (New York: Farrar and Rinehart, 1939), 59–63. Ross's contemporary, Reinhold Niebuhr, put a different spin on the same basic observation in one of his most troublesome phrases: public life depends on "emotionally potent oversimplifications." See Chapter 2, nn. 15 and 16, below.

39 Despair over the loss of faith is most powerfully developed in Joseph Wood Krutch, *The Modern Temper: A Study and a Confession by Joseph Wood Krutch* (1929; reprint, New York: Harcourt, Brace, 1956), and Walter Lippmann, *A Preface to Morals* (New York: Macmillan, 1929).

40 Ann Douglas, in *The Feminization of American Culture* (1977; reprint, New York: Anchor, 1988), 103, uses this phrase to describe educated women in the Victorian era who sought "influence" rather than full power.

41 The quotations in this and the previous paragraph are from Thurman W. Arnold, *The Folklore of Capitalism* (New Haven: Yale University Press, 1937), 10, 87–89.

42 The quotations in this and the previous paragraph are from ibid., 89, 69–70, and Arnold, *The Symbols of Government* (1935; reprint, New York: Harcourt, 1962), 270–71. Hofstadter, who echoed Arnold in many ways, also used "opportunistic" nonpejoratively as a synonym for practical and realistic. See Hofstadter, "Franklin D. Roosevelt: The Patrician as Opportunist," *American Political Tradition*.

43 The quotations in this and the previous paragraph are from Lippmann, *The Good Society* (1937; reprint, New York: Grossett and Dunlap, 1943), 237, 236, 204, 40–41. On the idea that loss of faith was dangerous, see the section on liberal fears in the Bibliographical Essay.

44 These yearnings especially echo Lippmann's *Drift and Mastery* (New York: M. Kennerley, 1914) and *Preface to Morals* (1929).

45 Frank died in a car crash in September 1940. His obituaries noted his leadership of the committee that drafted, in effect, the "new charter" of the Republican Party that culminated in Willkie's nomination. See, e.g., *New York Times*, September 16, 1940.

46 One form of such cooperation might be a "folk movement" to "force" or at

least "pressure" economic leaders to adopt more equitable wage, hour, price, and profit policies.

47 Glenn Frank, *America's Hour of Decision* (New York: Whittlesy House, 1935), 191, 200, 246, 253–54.

48 The quotations in this and the previous paragraph are from Tugwell, *The Democratic Roosevelt* (1957; reprint, New York: Pelican, 1969), 11, 31; see also 210–12, 513–16, 650.

49 Frances Perkins seems to have been less awed by FDR's religious drive, perhaps because, as she said, she shared it. She even told how FDR, by all accounts uninterested in abstract thought, was persuaded to read the pessimistic anthropology of Soren Kierkegaard, which he immediately adopted as his explanation of the inhumanity of the Nazis. Perkins, *The Roosevelt I Knew* (New York: Harper, 1946), 141, 144, 147–48. If accurate, Tugwell's and Perkins's perceptions of FDR's faith as a prime mover in his career and policy seem to have eluded his major biographers—perhaps because, as Perkins said, faith was for him an intensely private matter. Ernest K. Lindley, *Franklin Roosevelt: A Career in Progressive Democracy* (New York: Blue Ribbon, 1934), and Kenneth S. Davis, *F. D. R.*, 5 vols. (New York: Putnam, 1972, and New York: Random, 1985–), barely mention it. Frank Friedel's *Franklin D. Roosevelt* (Little, Brown, 1952), 1:36–40, devotes only a few (though perceptive) pages to religion in FDR's youth and barely touches on it in his adulthood.

50 Bryant Simon, in *A Fabric of Defeat: The Politics of South Carolina Millhands, 1910–1948* (Chapel Hill: University of North Carolina Press, 1998), 88, quotes a millworker who regarded FDR as "a god-sent man" and "a modern day Moses" who would lead Americans out of the "Egypt of depression." Robert S. McElvaine reprints numerous letters to FDR that he claims are representative, to similar effect. See McElvaine, ed., *Down and Out in the Great Depression: Letters from the Forgotten Man* (Chapel Hill: University of North Carolina Press, 1983), 217–29. In her *Making a New Deal: Industrial Workers in Chicago, 1919–1939* (Cambridge: Cambridge University Press, 1990), e.g., 256, 283–85, 332, 359, 498–99, Lizabeth Cohen does not quote the use of many religious metaphors, but she shows working-class Chicagoans expressing equally outlandish faith in the man.

51 Hofstadter, *American Political Tradition*, vii. Dewey never could accept the faith that millions of liberals, not to mention other kinds of people, invested in FDR. Perhaps his reason was eminently pragmatic. For the willing follower, the benevolence of such a leader is entirely a roll of the dice—America got FDR, Germany got the equally self-assured and charismatic Hitler. Dewey could not have faith, finally, because faith was too uncertain a business.

52 Richberg, *My Hero: Indiscreet Memoirs of an Eventful but Unheroic Life* (New York: Putnam, 1954), 5–6. There is a similar tone in the memoir of the impassioned liberal activist and propagandist, James Wechsler. In *Reflections of an Angry Middle-Aged Editor* (New York: Random, 1960), Wechsler even suggested that civil rights later played a great role in supplying the missing faith (pp. 114–15).

53 As one ADA operative wrote, concerning her frustrated effort to purge Pennsylvania's unions of Communists, "Many liberals are inclined to excuse working with communists because 'although we do not like them they are the people who do the work.'" Communist-affiliated union workers gained minority control of election campaigns through devious tactics, this operative said. Liberals might be similarly ruthless, but they could not impel a mass of political operatives to be ruthless on their behalf. Nathalie Panek to James Loeb Jr., September 16, 1947, ADA Papers, SHSW, ser. 6, box 1. David Stebenne, in *Arthur J. Goldberg: New Deal Liberal* (New York: Oxford University Press, 1996), 74, suggests that the liberals held their own in ruthlessness: "The ease with which" the radicals were purged from the CIO, Stebenne writes, "calls into question the view so popular in some liberal circles of the radicals as masters of intrigue and manipulation. In fact, the radicals had been thoroughly committed to building the labor movement, albeit for their own reasons, and its success in the 1930s and 1940s stemmed in part from the energy they had given it. Deftly used by trade union leaders and liberals, the radicals were discarded when the need for them seemed no longer to be so urgent." Liberals expressed more general concern about their inability to inspire political action, even when the majority endorsed their goals. The executive secretary of the ADA wrote, "It is not an easy job to build a liberal movement in America, despite the fact that the country is liberal." Loeb to Humphrey, December 30, 1948, ADA Papers, SHSW, ser. 2, box 53.

54 The quotations here and in the previous paragraph are from Trilling, *The Liberal Imagination* (New York: Doubleday, 1949), vii–viii.

55 Ibid., ix. This is a significant, and as far as I know unremarked, change from the days when liberals like Walter Lippmann and even Dewey hailed a denatured politics of technical skill—an important strain in American Progressivism, at times seemingly the only strain that survived the death of Progressivism in 1917–19.

56 The ability to shape political events is a kind of moral imperative, the core of the "realism" that crept into liberal thought in the 1920s and of the "new radicalism" so loudly trumpeted by liberals after World War II. See esp. Schlesinger, *Vital Center*, and Richard Hofstadter, *Anti-Intellectualism in American Life* (New York: Knopf, 1963).

57 Trilling complained that liberalism in his own day had not come to terms with this. "So far as liberalism is active and positive, so far, that is, as it moves toward organization, it tends to select the emotions and qualities that are most susceptible of organization." Liberalism tried "to organize the elements of life in a rational way." In so doing, "it unconsciously limits its view of the world to what it can deal with, and it tends to develop theories and principles, particularly in relation to the nature of the human mind, that justify its limitation. . . . It drifts toward a denial of the emotions and the imagination." Trilling, *Liberal Imagination*, x–xii.

58 Quotations in this paragraph are from ibid., xii–xiii.

59 Dewey, too, had tried to reconcile the rational with the irrational. Respond-

ing to the charge that liberalism's prime value of "free intelligence" was "cold" and that persons would be "moved to new ways of acting only by emotion," Dewey conceded a lot: "Of course, intelligence does not generate action except as it is enkindled by feeling." This seems the weakest argument in Dewey's strongest book. He says that emotion was virtually the same as "ideas" in action. For ideas in action were "imbued with all the emotional force that attaches to the ends proposed for action, and are accompanied with all the excitement and inspiration that attends the struggle to realize those ends." Yet on the next page, Dewey states that liberalism, so good at dissolving the authority of a preliberal order, "was well-nigh impotent" in the positive project of "organizing new forces" to extend liberalism. Dewey, *Liberalism and Social Action*, in *Later Works*, 11:37–39.

CHAPTER TWO: RECOVERING OPTIMISTS

1 Schlesinger, *The Vital Center: The Politics of Freedom* (Boston: Houghton Mifflin, 1949), 166. A more sober effort to restore liberal confidence came from Samuel H. Beer, *The City of Reason* (Cambridge: Harvard University Press, 1949).

2 Schlesinger's term, "the New Radicalism," refers specifically to the intellectuals who got off the sidelines and accepted their responsibility to be men of action. Though these intellectuals made the moral compromises that idealists always despise, they managed to do some good in the real world. Richard Hofstadter gave these "new radicals" a historical pedigree in his *Anti-Intellectualism in American Life* (New York: Knopf, 1963), which saw New Dealers as the first mature American intellectuals. Christopher Lasch subjected them to bitter criticism in *The New Radicalism in America* (New York: Knopf, 1965). George Packer wryly criticizes them in *The Blood of the Liberals* (New York: Farrar, Straus, and Giroux, 2000), e.g., 205. On Schlesinger's alleged debt to Niebuhr, see Arthur M. Schlesinger Jr., *The Vital Center: The Politics of Freedom* (Boston: Houghton Mifflin, 1949), 45, 165, 170; Marcus Cunliffe, "Arthur M. Schlesinger, Jr.," in Cunliffe and Robin W. Winks, eds., *Pastmasters: Some Essays on American Historians* (New York: Harper and Row, 1969), 363–64; and George Kennan, "The Historian and the Cycles of History," and John M. Blum, "Arthur Schlesinger, Jr.: Tory Democrat," both in John Patrick Diggins, ed., *The Liberal Persuasion: Arthur Schlesinger Jr. and the Challenge of the American Past* (Princeton, N.J.: Princeton University Press, 1997), 54–61, and 67–72, respectively.

3 Niebuhr, *Moral Man and Immoral Society* (New York: Scribner's, 1932), xxi, xvii.

4 Schlesinger, *Vital Center*, 4, xx.

5 Donald B. Meyer, *The Protestant Search for Political Realism, 1919–1941* (1960; reprint, Middletown, Conn.: Wesleyan University Press, 1988). Richard Fox, in *Reinhold Niebuhr: A Biography* (New York: Pantheon, 1985), 160–62, rightly

identifies Paul Tillich's "non-Barthian" influence as far more important in Niebuhr's development than Barth's influence. Fox's essay, "The Niebuhr Brothers and the Liberal Protestant Heritage," in Michael J. Lacey, ed., *Religion and Twentieth-Century American Intellectual Life* (Cambridge: Cambridge University Press, 1989), 94–115, focuses on Niebuhr's (and his more conservative brother, H. Richard Niebuhr's) reaffirmation of "a fundamentally liberal, modernist commitment," demonstrating "the continued potency of liberal Protestantism in the mid-twentieth century—a time when it was supposedly in decline and disarray" (p. 95). Here Fox points out that William Hutchison, in "Liberal Protestantism and the 'End of Innocence,'" *American Quarterly* 15 (1963): 126–36, stressed the continuity of the Niebuhrs with the social gospellers. Christopher Lasch, in *The True and Only Heaven: Progress and Its Critics* (New York: Norton, 1991), 379–80, observes that the most rigorous version of the social gospel "expressly repudiated the views attributed by Niebuhr to the social gospel." Lasch quotes Walter Rauschenbusch saying, "Moral suasion is strangely feeble where the sources of a man's income are concerned," and history offered no "precedent for an altruistic self-effacement of a whole class." Therefore, "intellectual persuasion and moral conviction would never by themselves overcome the resistance of selfishness and conservatism." "Christian idealists must not make the mistake of trying to hold the working class down to the use of moral suasion only."

6 Niebuhr's relationship with liberalism is easy to misunderstand. A socialist in 1932, Niebuhr became increasingly identified with political liberals—the internationalist and increasingly anticommunist liberals who formed the Union for Democratic Action (UDA) in 1941, then ADA in 1947. Though political liberalism often overlapped with theological liberalism (or, more to the point here, with anthropological liberalism), it should not be confused with it. In 1943 Niebuhr, then head of the UDA, told a reporter that his position was one of "general rebellion against the so-called liberal interpretation of life." The reporter went on to note: "He has been classified as a pessimist and he acknowledges that his outlook is rather grim. Until 1926 he was a 'typical religious liberal.' Since then experience and observation have convinced him that pure pacifism is ineffectual, that non-violence won't do as a creed, that in politics the use of force may be necessary." Henry Beckett, "Niebuhr—The Grim Crusader," *New York Post*, magazine section, April 20, 1943.

7 Niebuhr's prophetic remarks on race and nonviolent action are in *Moral Man*: he questioned whether any "disinherited group, such as the Negroes," would ever win justice by negotiating with the dominant group (p. xvii). "It is hopeless for the Negro to expect complete emancipation . . . merely by trusting in the moral sense of the white race. It is equally hopeless to attempt emancipation through violent rebellion." "There is no problem of political life to which religious imagination can make a larger contribution than this problem of developing non-violent resistance." For all his Machiavellian emphasis on the practicality of nonviolent force, Niebuhr argued that "secular imagination" was just "not capable" of developing the "attitudes of repentance which

recognize that the evil in the foe is also in the self"; nor could secular imagination develop the "impulses of love which claim kinship with all men in spite of social conflict." Such attitudes and impulses required "a sublime madness which disregards immediate appearances and emphasizes profound and ultimate unities. It is no accident of history that the spirit of non-violence has been introduced into contemporary politics by a religious leader of the orient" (pp. 252–56). Niebuhr returned to the indictment of racism in *The Children of Light and the Children of Darkness* (New York: Scribner's, 1944), 139–42.

8   Schlesinger, *Vital Center*, 6–7.

9   Ibid., 10. Niebuhr, in "The Way of Non-violent Resistance," *Christianity and Society* 21 (Spring 1956): 3, reiterated his understanding of nonviolence during the Montgomery boycott, which he believed was really about "justice in collective relations" and not about "love": "Those of us who are non-pacifists will be quick to admit that whenever pacifism is not preoccupied with moral scruples about guiltlessness and personal perfection, whenever it does not occupy itself with the problem of contracting out of responsibilities of justice in the name of personal perfection, whenever it seeks justice, it becomes impressive." Niebuhr had no doubt that the boycott was both just and an adequate method to achieve justice. Schlesinger (*Vital Center*, 10, 156) said that we must avoid war because war would destroy freedom almost as surely as surrender to totalitarianism would. Niebuhr's more melancholy defense of the West—it is not so great, but it is usually better than the alternative—is expressed in his *Children of Light and the Children of Darkness* (1944). Niebuhr defended democracy, as apparently the most effective check on human excesses, but insisted that democracy, which exerts a communal control over the individual, cannot be equated with liberalism or freedom, let alone with individualism. Schlesinger altogether ignored the distinction, using democracy interchangeably with freedom, liberalism, and individualism.

10 On his certainty of American virtues, see pp. 146–47, 166. "While we may not be able to repeal prejudice by law, yet law is an essential part of the enterprise of education, which alone can end prejudice." Schlesinger, *Vital Center*, 190. Schlesinger also minified the political conflict over civil rights:

> Most Americans accept, at least in principle, the obligations spelled out in the [president's] Civil Rights report. The strengthened civil rights plank in the Democratic platform helped President Truman win the election. Popular fiction and the movies . . . have enlisted in the battle against racism. Even the revolt of the southern governors against President Truman's request for civil rights legislation, if one is to judge by the subsequent election returns, signified temper tantrums rather than a cry of conscience against civil rights; for, where Truman and the neo-Confederate Thurmond were on the same ticket, Truman ran ahead almost two to one. This result suggests that the South on the whole accepts the objectives of the civil rights program as legitimate, even though it may have serious and intelligible reservations about timing and method.

He goes on in a Myrdalian vein to say that racism conflicts with "the American conscience" and "our highest moral pretensions" (p. 190). Schlesinger did admit that "racial cruelties in the United States or in most areas of western colonialism" gave the Soviets leverage in their propaganda. He allowed that many individual communists had "stood honestly and courageously" in the cause of racial equality; before the "flagrant revival of Russian anti-semitism," Western racial practices "compare[d] unfavorably" with Soviet ones. Racism in the West was a danger because it fueled communist propaganda in the decolonizing nations. But far more important for America's competitive stance against the USSR than domestic civil rights measures was economic and technical aid abroad, in effect, to buy off governments and to eradicate the poverty on which communism might otherwise feed (p. 230).

11 Schlesinger, *A Life in the Twentieth Century: Innocent Beginnings, 1917–1950* (Boston: Houghton Mifflin, 2000), esp. 272–74. By the same token, Schlesinger came to regret not doing more about sex discrimination or what we now call "the environment."

12 Schlesinger, *Vital Center*, 167 ff.

13 Ibid. More important for Schlesinger's immediate purposes, however, was American capitalists' support for the Marshall Plan (pp. 28–29). When Taft famously endorsed federal housing legislation, he was denounced by the real estate lobby as a traitor and "socialist." James T. Patterson, *Mr. Republican: A Biography of Robert A. Taft* (Boston: Houghton Mifflin, 1972), 319. The main carrier of Schlesinger's liberalism was the politician-manager-intellectual type or, in foreign affairs, the "new breed" installed by Cordell Hull and Sumner Welles in the 1930s: "the modern professional diplomat, a close student of history and politics, convinced that the desire of men for freedom and economic security may be as legitimate a factor in foreign affairs as strategic bases or the investments of Standard Oil" (pp. 166–67).

14 Schlesinger (*Vital Center*, 36–37, 41) referred to inactive, irresponsible intellectuals as "doughfaces." The doughface Progressive, Schlesinger said, has "rejected the pragmatic tradition of the men who, from the Jacksonians to the New Dealers, learned the facts of life through the exercise of power under conditions of accountability. He has rejected the pessimistic tradition of those who, from Hawthorne to Reinhold Niebuhr, warned that power, unless checked by accountability, would corrupt its predecessor." Jane Tompkins, in *Sensational Designs: The Cultural Work of American Fiction, 1790–1860* (New York: Oxford University Press, 1985), suggests that the tough-minded Hawthorne was in any case an invention of the twentieth century: in his own day, Hawthorne was lauded in the same language as female sentimental novelists were lauded, and for the same qualities.

15 Niebuhr, *Moral Man*, xv.

16 Ibid., xv, xvii, 221, 255, xxi. Richard Fox has informed me that Niebuhr "reversed himself" on emotionally potent oversimplifications after *Moral Man* was published. It seems to me, however, that Niebuhr made the point persuasively in the book and could not logically abandon it without abandoning the

rest of his realist stance. He was right to worry about his appearing to justify the lies of the Comintern, the Nazis, and others who claimed to speak for the oppressed. On the other hand, they would have lied without his help. To observe that political lying is practically inevitable is not to excuse it, any more than Calvinist insistence on man's depravity excuses other sins.

17 Schlesinger, *Vital Center*, 169.

18 Ibid., 97, 102–4, 115, 128–29. Schlesinger said that the American Communist's motives were purely psychological: "Even America has its quota of lonely and frustrated people, craving social, intellectual and even sexual fulfillment they cannot obtain in existing society. For these people party discipline is no obstacle; it is an attraction. The great majority of members in America, as in Europe, *want* to be disciplined" (p. 210).

19 Schlesinger pled for due process in appeals of dismissals of officials accused of disloyalty. And, for all his vigilance about the Wallace Progressives, Schlesinger declared that the CPUSA was not really a threat *in peacetime* and that revolution was not possible in the United States. In fact, the CPUSA was the great ally of conservatives because it divided and neutralized the left. Ibid., 129–30.

20 *ADA World*, 1949–56 (microfilm). Peter Kellog, in "Northern Liberals and Black America: A History of White Attitudes, 1936–1952" (Ph.D. diss., Northwestern University, 1971), 261, 280, 284–86, 316, observed the same emphasis on winning elections in the major liberal organs, *Nation* and *New Republic*. David Stebenne, in *Arthur J. Goldberg: New Deal Liberal* (New York: Oxford, 1996), 70–71, affords valuable insight into the liberal quandary here.

21 Significantly, Truman opposed the radical civil rights plank that the ADA supported. Probably he aimed first to stem southern defections in the convention, then to return to strong advocacy of civil rights soon after. As it turned out, in the postconvention campaign Truman made a stronger commitment to civil rights than any president since Abraham Lincoln—and followed up on it. Before the convention, too, Truman had identified himself with Negro rights and had done more for them than most ADA members. (He supported extension of the Fair Employment Practices Committee in 1946; was the first president to speak to an NAACP meeting, in 1947; authorized the Justice Department to intervene on behalf of black plaintiffs in the restrictive covenants case, *Shelley v. Kraemer* [1948]; and, most important, at the beginning of 1947 initiated his famous commission on civil rights, knowing that it would probably advocate radical changes.) Donald McCoy and Richard Ruetten, in *Quest and Response: Minority Rights and the Truman Administration* (Lawrence: University Press of Kansas, 1973), 114, 77, reasonably suggest that when ADA operatives pushed the radical civil rights plank in the 1948 convention, they were more interested in sabotaging Truman's nomination than in actual achievement of greater equality. The devotion of many of these ADA operatives to civil rights was clearly negated by the alternative they proposed to Truman: Dwight Eisenhower, a firm believer in states' rights who was on record, as recently as his testimony to the Senate Armed Services Committee

the previous April, as an opponent of military desegregation. The NAACP leader and some of the black press, McCoy and Ruetten note, recognized this and publicly expressed disillusionment with Eisenhower. Alonzo Hamby, in *Man of the People: A Life of Harry S. Truman* (New York: Oxford University Press, 1995), 446, 448, substantially confirms McCoy and Ruetten's skepticism about ADA motives.

22 Jim Loeb to Hubert Humphrey, April 14, 1948, ADA Papers, SHSW, ser. 5, box 7.

23 Wechsler column, *New York Post*, April 27, 1948, quoting an ADA report at length. Copy in ADA Papers, SHSW, ser. 6, box 1.

24 This judgment is based on a reading of the ADA chapter files of Alabama, Arkansas, Georgia, Louisiana, Mississippi, North Carolina, and South Carolina. ADA Papers, SHSW, ser. 3, various boxes.

25 Loeb and other ADA officials did not see Kolb's concerns as terribly urgent, probably because (as Kolb acknowledged) ADA had little confidence in the growth of any liberal organization in the South. Kolb to Loeb, December 15, 1948, and Loeb to Kolb, December 24, 1948, ADA Papers, SHSW, ser. 3, box 17.

26 Schlesinger to Joseph Rauh and Jim Loeb, January 25, 1950, quoted in Stephen Gillon, *Politics and Vision: The ADA and American Liberalism* (New York: Oxford University Press, 1987), 62–63.

27 Humphrey quoted in Allan H. Ryskind, *Hubert: An Unauthorized Biography of the Vice President* (New Rochelle, N.Y.: Arlington House, 1968), 173; White quoted in Carl Solberg, *Hubert Humphrey: A Biography* (New York: Norton, 1984), 169. Solberg describes Senator George's new friendship with and support for Humphrey and his long, fruitless cooperation with Lyndon Johnson (pp. 168, 174–75).

28 Nelson Lichtenstein, *The Most Dangerous Man in Detroit: Walter Reuther and the Fate of American Labor* (New York: Basic Books, 1995), 305–8, 441–43, emphasizes the rise of racism among white working-class Detroiters in the 1940s and its role in undermining support for Fair Deal initiatives. Thomas Sugrue, *Origins of the Urban Crisis: Race and Inequality in Postwar Detroit* (Princeton, N.J.: Princeton University Press, 1996), and John T. McGreevey, *Parish Boundaries: The Catholic Encounter with Race in the Twentieth-Century Urban North* (Chicago: University of Chicago Press, 1996), consider northern urban racism in the context of the breakdown of the New Deal–wartime industrial order.

29 Hamby (*Man of the People*, 366) observes that on the domestic front in 1946–47, civil rights was "far overshadowed, even among the most devout liberals, by the fight for full employment." Peter Kellog's history ("Northern Liberals") of the major liberal organs, *New Republic* and *Nation*, makes clear that racism was not the primary concern of liberals through the early 1950s. David Stebenne (*Goldberg*, 144–46, 118, 185) observes that among the executives of one major union in the liberal coalition, the United Steelworkers of America, the issue of race "emerged" during World War II "when the number of black

steelworkers grew substantially"; but it "did not come up again at a board meeting until the end of 1956" and then only tentatively. (The steelworkers' legal counsel, Arthur Goldberg, had long been convinced, like many in the CIO, that unions could not spread to the South until segregation had been dismantled. Accordingly, the steelworkers filed Goldberg's antisegregation amicus brief with the Supreme Court in the *Brown* case.)

30 This is a summary of the first four years of the *ADA World*, which began publication in 1947. Public policy statements and records of private discussions in the ADA Papers have the same emphasis. Particularly revealing is a memo from the ADA's legislative representative, John Gunther (no relation to the famous author), to its political secretary, Violet Gunther, that sought to distance the ADA from the NAACP, with which it had cooperated previously, especially in the (successful) attempt to include a radical civil rights plank in the 1948 Democratic platform and in (unsuccessful) efforts to create a permanent Fair Employment Practices Committee and to enact federal laws against lynching and the poll tax. Though the NAACP leadership was (like the ADA's) falling all over itself to denounce communism, it often had little control over its established locals. For ADA leaders, even southern ones, anticommunism trumped all issues. Accordingly, John Gunther asserted that ADA's association with the "emergency civil rights mobilization" of 1949 should end as soon as possible because "the mobilization has refused to follow the principle of including only non-Communist organizations." ADA locals had been in an awkward position: they found it hard "to refuse to work with the locals of the participating organizations. Thus, we would run into the difficulty of having the ADA in many parts of the country disassociate itself from the local mobilizations inasmuch as at least one of the major organizations, the NAACP, is Communist dominated in many of its major locals[,] i.e., Pennsylvania, Illinois, New York, Kansas, etc." John Gunther to Violet Gunther, January 25, 1950, ADA Papers, SHSW, ser. 5, box 7.

Equally revealing is the statement by B. F. McLaurin, international field organizer of the Brotherhood of Sleeping Car Porters, an all-black union. The Brotherhood was liberal on most issues and as anticommunist as the ADA. McLaurin noted that in his efforts to fight job discrimination, "many of my good liberal friends and co-workers took issue, others gave support." He believed that "it would be better not to have a federal bill giving aid to education, meeting the needs of health, or relieving the bottleneck of public housing if segregation and discrimination could not be eliminated. To me, there can be no compromise on this issue. . . . Better that all Americans suffer alike than to continue to perpetuate a system that created the difficulties we now face." His liberal colleagues had told him "that it would not be expedient for ADA to take the kind of position I suggested," referring to "the difficult position . . . Senator Humphrey would be called upon to face. My answer to them is that this position is silly and shallow. In the first place, ADA is not a political party. ADA is a band of liberals who have come together to explore truth and to support that truth in spite of difficulties without regard to cost. True liberals should not have to worry about position or strategy." He noted that at the ADA's convention "there were cries of consideration for our southern liberals. I cannot conceive of two kinds of liberalism on this question. Either you are for civil rights, civil liberties and democracy for all, or you are for the American way of life as we know it—discrimination as usual." B. F. McLaurin to William Sturdevant, May 19, 1949, and attachment, ADA Papers, SHSW, ser. 7, box 1. McLaurin's statement was intended for publication in *ADA World* and apparently had been solicited by the editor. A much toned-down version ran under the title, "Principle, Practicality Meet in Anti-Discrimination Fight," *ADA World*, May 26, 1949. The editors inserted a note at the top of the piece saying that McLaurin's was one side of a "pro-and-con" discussion, which the ADA itself had resolved the other way at its recent convention.

31 Kellog, "Northern Liberals."

32 Chris Waldrep, in "War of Words: The Controversy over the Definition of Lynching, 1899-1940," *Journal of Southern History* 66 (February 2000): 75–101, argues persuasively that the lynching data on which everybody has always relied were based on so many conflicting definitions and assumptions that all generalizations—including the universally accepted notion that lynching declined over the mid-twentieth century—are dubious.

33 See George C. Wright, *Racial Violence in Kentucky, 1865-1940: Lynchings, Mob Rule, and "Legal Lynchings"* (Baton Rouge: Louisiana State University Press, 1990); W. Fitzhugh Brundage, *Lynching in the New South: Georgia and Virginia, 1880-1930* (Urbana: University of Illinois Press, 1993); Brundage, ed., *Under Sentence of Death: Lynching in the South* (Chapel Hill: University of North Carolina Press, 1997); and Stewart Tolnay and E. M. Beck, *A Festival of Violence: An Analysis of Southern Lynchings, 1882-1930* (Urbana: University of Illinois Press, 1995). Brundage takes pains to distinguish the effect of legal executions from the effect of lynchings on white lives: white people obviously participated in lynch mobs and witnessed lynchings in large numbers, but the number directly exposed to legal executions (especially after they became private) was negligible. But since mob participants never constituted a majority of the white southern population, this distinction may be overdrawn. Brundage acknowledges that the effect of legal as opposed to extralegal executions on the *black* population is not so easy to differentiate. Tolnay and Beck also differentiate the effect on white lives and note no statistical "substitution effect" of increased legal executions for observed declines in lynchings in the available data. Still, Tolnay and Beck allow that the impact of harsh official justice on the *black* population was similar to that of mob violence. They observe that upper-class white southerners often had reasons to suppress lynch mobs and that lynching increased when those reasons were absent. Again, Waldrep cautions that all data on which such observations are based are highly dubious.

34 David M. Kennedy, *Freedom from Fear: The American People in Depression and War, 1929-1945* (New York: Oxford University Press, 1999), 762.

35 Myrdal, *An American Dilemma: The Negro Problem and Modern Democracy*, 2 vols. (1944; reprint, New York: Harper and Row, 1962), 2:1021.

36 Ibid., 1:19.

37 Ibid., 1:25–49 (quotations, pp. 21, 48).

38 This is the interpretation of David W. Southern, *Gunnar Myrdal and Black-White Relations: The Use and Abuse of "An American Dilemma," 1944–1969* (Baton Rouge: Louisiana State University Press, 1987), esp. 32–33. See also Walter A. Jackson, *Gunnar Myrdal and America's Conscience: Social Engineering and Racial Liberalism, 1938–1987* (Chapel Hill: University of North Carolina Press, 1990).

39 See Jackson, *Myrdal*, 242–43. In the booming scholarly field of "race relations," Oliver C. Cox, in *Caste, Class, and Race: A Study in Social Dynamics* (Garden City, N.Y.: Doubleday, 1948), has been Myrdal's most durable critic.

40 Part of the trouble in the 1940s was that, for a time, American Communists insisted on an equally optimistic line—that wartime production demands would force the American bourgeoisie to grant equality in job opportunities. See Ernest Kaiser, "Racial Dialectics: The Aptheker-Myrdal School Controversy," *Phylon* 9 (1948): 295–302.

41 Though Niebuhr was diametrically opposed to Myrdal's approach—he argued that the basic liberal "creed," which stressed that education and progress could overcome social problems, including group conflicts and inequality, was "sentimental" (*Children of Light*, 33)—he actually gave Myrdal a favorable review. Jackson (*Myrdal*, 243) somewhat cryptically attributes Myrdal's uncritical review to Niebuhr's shift from a "socialist perspective to a liberal viewpoint." Southern (*Myrdal*, 97) is disappointed by Niebuhr's "virtually unqualified praise." Niebuhr's closest readers have struggled to understand why he apparently let down his guard in so many ways after World War II. For contrasting views, see Fox, *Niebuhr*, 219–38, and Christopher Lasch, *The True and Only Heaven: Progress and Its Critics* (New York: Norton, 1991), 369–84.

42 Niebuhr and Du Bois were arguably the most influential American intellectuals of the twentieth century—certainly they would appear in any historian's top ten. David Levering Lewis, in *The Fight for Equality and the American Century, 1919–1963*, vol. 2 of *W. E. B. Du Bois* (New York: Holt, 2000), has this to say about Du Bois, whose review of Myrdal's book was decidedly uncritical: "If he never publicly questioned the Myrdalian concept of moral tension and its muting of economics, there is ample evidence that, privately, he concurred with the sharp criticisms . . . made by Marxist scholars such as Herbert Aptheker, Oliver Cox, and Doxey Wilkerson, who largely dismissed Myrdal's *American Creed* as the opiate of the white liberals" (pp. 452–53).

43 This is especially evident in Myrdal, *American Dilemma*, chaps. 35–44, 2:736–994. See also Southern, *Myrdal*, 68.

44 See Myrdal, *American Dilemma*, 2:1010–11, 1021–24. ADA's national director, former congressman and Nuremberg prosecutor Charles LaFollette, voiced a Myrdalesque love of institutions in a 1950 letter to Roy Wilkins, then acting secretary of the NAACP. On behalf of ADA, LaFollette expressed the "highest admiration" for Wilkins's lobbying and coalition building. He contrasted those activities with the unconstructive lobbying of Communist-affiliated

civil rights delegations in the past that had alienated likely supporters in Congress. For example, a delegation of the National Maritime and United Electrical Workers' unions "was so maladroit, that the evident purpos[e] to destroy support, in order to keep the issue alive, was clearly demonstrated." LaFollette praised Wilkins for preventing similar incidents and gave the ADA credit for supporting the NAACP secretary. "This represents permanent progress," he concluded. LaFollette to Wilkins, January 23, 1950, ADA Papers, SHSW, ser. 2, box 30.

45 I am indebted here to George Packer, who quotes Mills in his fine memoir, *Blood of the Liberals*, 154.

46 This is the main theme of *Moral Man and Immoral Society*. Niebuhr returns to it in other major works, including *An Interpretation of Christian Ethics* (New York: Harper, 1935), esp. chap. 5; *The Nature and Destiny of Man*, esp. vol. 1 (New York: Scribner's, 1941), chap. 8; and *Children of Light*, esp. chap. 2.

47 Fox, *Niebuhr*, 238.

48 On no subject did the future direct-action movement get closer to Niebuhr and further from the liberals than in its general distaste for institutions, which tended to perpetuate themselves at the expense of the moral principles on which they were founded. The movement's distaste may have drawn more on the ecclesioclasm at the roots of Baptist (and Anabaptist) tradition, or in some cases on secular theories of anarchism and existentialism, than on Niebuhr. But the movement's abiding agreement with Niebuhr's view on this, and the liberals' Myrdalian divergence from it, are striking, as will be seen in the next chapter.

49 On the president's committee and Humphrey, see Southern, *Myrdal*, 118–24. Though Schlesinger did not say much about race, Myrdal's study was in sync with his views. As the race issue grew, Myrdal's report, or at any rate its simple thesis, became a motive and a consolation for liberals. Gordon Allport, author of *The Nature of Prejudice* (1954), told the Supreme Court in the *Brown* case that white southerners knew deep down that segregation was un-American. All they needed was for the Court to give them a backbone: "People do accept legislation that fortifies their inner conscience. . . . Let the line of public morality be set by authoritative pronouncements, and all the latent good in individuals and communities will be strengthened." Quoted in Richard Kluger, *Simple Justice: The History of Brown v. Board of Education and Black America's Struggle for Equality* (New York: Knopf, 1976), 719. In 1962 Myrdal's collaborator Arnold Rose, introducing a new edition of the report, stated that the forces generating inequality "will be practically eliminated" and racism reduced to a "minor order" by the year 2000. *American Dilemma* (rev. ed., Pantheon, 1962), xliii–xliv. Even Derrick Bell, who now rejects the Myrdal thesis, does it the honor of admitting that he believed in it back in the days when he was a civil rights activist: "Myrdal and two generations of civil rights advocates accepted the idea of racism as merely an odious holdover from slavery, 'a terrible and inexplicable anomaly stuck in the middle of our liberal democratic ethos.' No one doubted that the standard American policy

making was adequate to the task of abolishing racism. White America, it was assumed, *wanted* to abolish racism." Bell equates this optimism with the view expressed in the song, "We Shall Overcome." Bell, *Faces at the Bottom of the Well: The Permanence of Racism* (New York: Basic Books, 1992), 9, 92, 197, 199. Chapter 3, below, suggests that Bell is wrong about the views of civil rights activists generally, though he may be right about himself.

50 Dewey, *Liberalism and Social Action* (New York: Putnam, 1935), reprinted in Dewey, *The Later Works*, 17 vols. (Carbondale: Southern Illinois University Press, 1986), 9:63.

51 Some liberals dissented from the optimism of fellow liberals. For example, Paul Williams, president of the white moderate Southern Regional Council, seemed to abandon gradualism in his 1950 presidential address: "I cannot share the optimism and single-mindedness of those who claim that education of some unspecified sort is going to bring us to the millennium. I very much fear that those who insist exclusively on the ameliorating effects of education are trying to lull themselves or others into a state of slumbering complacency." Williams, in *New South* (June 1950), quoted in Julia Anne McDonough, "Men and Women of Good Will: A History of the Commission on Interracial Cooperation and the Southern Regional Council, 1919-1954" (Ph.D. diss., University of Virginia, 1993), 475-77. McDonough rightly sees Williams's attempt to abandon gradualism as cutting against the grain of his organization and hence not very effective. She notes that black members of the council, such as Benjamin Mays, were increasingly dissatisfied with the group's gradualism.

52 Jackson also documents liberals' "lack of comprehension" of black America's political dynamism from roughly 1954 to 1960, noting that civil rights was "rarely a central concern of prominent white intellectuals outside the South" over the previous decade. He suggests that "the gulf that opened in the mid-1960s between white and black advocates of civil rights" can be understood by examination of the content of white liberal thought in the period before the movement. Jackson, "White Liberal Intellectuals and Civil Rights, 1954-1960," in Brian Ward and Tony Badger, eds., *The Making of Martin Luther King and the Civil Rights Movement* (New York: New York University Press, 1996), 96-114.

53 King, *Civil Rights and the Idea of Freedom* (New York: Oxford University Press, 1992), 6, 38.

54 The alternative view—that racism is a conscious political technique—appears in such works as J. Morgan Kousser, *The Shaping of Southern Politics* (New Haven: Yale University Press, 1974); Barbara Fields, "Ideology and Race," in Kousser and James McPherson, eds., *Race, Region, and Reconstruction: Essays in Honor of C. Vann Woodward* (New York: Oxford University Press, 1982); and John Cell, *Highest Stage of White Supremacy* (Cambridge: Cambridge University Press, 1982). These scholars argue that, without attentive top-down organization, the universal psychological impulse to identify and dominate some "other," though it may be ugly and occasionally dangerous, remains un-

focused and ineffectual. The psychological impulse by itself cannot deprive or degrade an "other" in the systematic way implied by the common meaning of racism. To achieve such systematic deprivation and degradation requires politics. Though psychologists (and historians who reduce racism to psychology) may have special insight into the raw materials that racist politicians use, racism, in my view, cannot be explained by psychology alone.

CHAPTER THREE: IDEAS THAT MADE CIVIL RIGHTS MOVE

1 Myrdal, *An American Dilemma: The Negro Problem and Modern Democracy*, 2 vols. (1944; reprint, New York: Harper and Row, 1962), 2:799, 884. Two scholars have shown that the black southerners' political emphasis on education was a more complex matter than Myrdal allowed. The politics and economy of the South were so restrictive that education was, like religion, one of the few avenues left open to black southerners with selfish or unselfish ambitions. See James L. Leloudis, *Schooling the New South: Pedagogy, Self, and Society in North Carolina, 1880–1920* (Chapel Hill: University of North Carolina Press, 1996), and Adam Fairclough, "'Being in the Field of Education and Also Being a Negro . . . Seems . . . Tragic': Black Teachers in the Jim Crow South," *Journal of American History* 87 (June 2000): 65–91.

2 See the intellectual journals *Phylon, Midwest Quarterly, Negro Quarterly*, and *Journal of Negro Education*. There is little evidence in other sources to corroborate Myrdal's assumption of pervasive optimism. See section on black opinion in the Bibliographical Essay.

3 Hochschild, *Facing Up to the American Dream: Race, Class, and the Soul of the Nation* (Princeton, N.J.: Princeton University Press, 1995). See remarks on black opinion in the Bibliographical Essay.

4 See Walter A. Jackson, *Gunnar Myrdal and America's Conscience: Social Engineering and Racial Liberalism, 1938–1987* (Chapel Hill: University of North Carolina Press, 1990), and Chapter 2, n. 42 above.

5 John Lewis, describing the Nashville reading group from which many SNCC leaders came, recalled that the group studied "Reinhold Niebuhr and his philosophy of nonviolent revolution." Lewis, with Michael D'Orso, *Walking with the Wind: A Memoir of the Movement* (New York: Simon and Schuster, 1998), 85. Andrew Young, in *An Easy Burden: The Civil Rights Movement and the Transformation of America* (New York: HarperCollins, 1996), 93, recalled reading Niebuhr in 1956; Niebuhr's emphasis on negotiating from strength "struck a chord in me." Niebuhr's stress on realism, on power, resonated with what Young had learned in childhood.

6 See King's application to Crozer Theological Seminary, February 1948, *PMLK*, 1:142–49, and his "Autobiography of Religious Development," Fall 1950, *PMLK*, 1:359–79. The only recorded conversion experience he had came later, during the civil rights struggle. See Chapter 5, below, at n. 20.

7 Not to imply that Ralph Luker endorses this statement about Burke, but he

sees a conservatism running strongly in the social gospel in black and white churches. What Arthur M. Schlesinger Sr. saw in 1932 as an increasingly radical critique of industrial capitalism was, Luker says, in fact a conservative awareness that industrial capitalism was the radical force in society. See Luker, *The Social Gospel in Black and White: American Racial Reform, 1885–1912* (Chapel Hill: University of North Carolina Press, 1991). August Meier makes a good case that the best description of King is "The Conservative Militant," in C. Eric Lincoln, ed., *Martin Luther King, Jr.: A Profile* (New York: Hill and Wang, 1970), 144–56.

8   Kenneth L. Smith and Ira G. Zepp, in *Search for the Beloved Community: The Thinking of Martin Luther King, Jr.* (Lanham, Md.: University Press of America, 1986), emphasize that the Prophets were the most important part of scripture for King, with the possible exception of the Sermon on the Mount.

9   See David Lewis, *King: A Critical Biography* (1970; 2d ed., Urbana: University of Illinois Press, 1978), 39; John Ansbro, *Martin Luther King: The Making of a Mind* (New York: Orbis, 1982), 122–24; Richard Lischer, *The Preacher King: Martin Luther King, Jr., and the Word That Moved America* (New York: Oxford University Press, 1995), 61–65, 95; and Lewis V. Baldwin, with Rufus Burrow Jr., Barbara A. Holmes, and Susan Holmes Winfield, *The Legacy of Martin Luther King: The Boundaries of Law, Politics, and Religion* (South Bend, Ind.: University of Notre Dame Press, 2002), 112, 217, 263.

10   King, "The Significant Contributions of Jeremiah to Religious Thought," for Pritchard's course on the Old Testament, Crozer Theological Seminary, November 1948, *PMLK*, 1:181–95. "The rebel prophet" was the term of T. C. Gordon, one of King's sources. King warned that society "has reacted, and always will react, in the only way open to it. It destroys such men" (p. 195). The tradition of the Jeremiad is well established and well documented as a major theme (some say *the* major theme) in American religious history. See the works of Perry Miller, esp. *Errand into the Wilderness* (Cambridge: Harvard University Press, 1956); Sacvan Bercovitch, "New England's Errand Reappraised," in John Higham and Paul Conkin, eds., *New Directions in American Intellectual History* (Baltimore: Johns Hopkins University Press, 1979), 85–104; and Andrew Delbanco, *The Puritan Ordeal* (Cambridge: Harvard University Press, 1989). Richard Brodhead is working on a history of the prophetic tradition that will place King in a line with Jonathan Edwards and Abraham Lincoln—a tradition that Brodhead reads far more sympathetically and convincingly than Bercovitch. I thank Brodhead for sharing drafts of some of his chapters with me.

11   Even before the scholarly work on Jeremiah, King had spoken out in prophetic tones. The first words he ever published appeared in a letter to the editor of the *Atlanta Constitution* on August 6, 1946 (*PMLK*, 1:121), when he was an undergraduate at Morehouse. The *Constitution* had expressed shock at mob violence but added the characteristic southern liberal warning that any federal law to address it would make things worse. Like Isaiah, King attacked the paper and its readers for evasion and hypocrisy. Whenever "decent treatment

for the Negro is urged a certain class of people hurry to raise the scarecrow of social mingling and intermarriage. . . . And most people who kick up this kind of dust know that it is simple dust to obscure the real question of rights and opportunities." Like Isaiah, King rubbed his readers' noses in their history of sin. Almost all "race mixture in America has come, not at Negro initiative, but by the acts of those very white men who talk loudest of race purity." Though he did not warn of divine retribution, his demand for basic rights, opportunities, and courtesy might have seemed as unbearable as divine retribution to *Constitution* readers. King seems to have found his voice. Martin Luther King Sr. later recalled that he and his wife had "no intimation of [King Jr.'s] developing greatness . . . until as a teenager he wrote a letter to the editor of a local paper which received widespread and favorable comment" (*PMLK*, 1:121).

12 King, "Significant Contributions of Jeremiah." King developed his prophetic streak in a 1951 essay, "Jacques Maritain," *PMLK*, 1:436–39. Jeremiah came up again in King's essay on hermeneutics, *PMLK*, 1:255. The importance of "a higher standard," of "a prophet" who pushes values that are not "socially recognized," returns in an essay on William Kelley Wright's *A Student's Philosophy of Religion* (New York: Macmillan, 1935), *PMLK*, 1:384–89. The emphasis on decline, or "breakdown in moral standards," also returns in his essay, "An Appraisal of the Great Awakening," *PMLK*, 1:335–53. Later King explains how the Hebrew Prophets arrived at their "ethical monotheism" through "national and international disaster. . . . Unlike the Greek who came to monism through intellectualizing on the unity of the world, the Hebrew came to monotheism through the realistic experiences of history." Final exam answers, Old Testament, January 1953, *PMLK*, 2:169–70.

13 The most thorough articulation of this "prophetic" rejection of *both* liberalism and neo-orthodoxy is in Niebuhr's *Interpretation of Christian Ethics* (New York: Harper, 1935), but it is evident in all of his works, even those, like *Moral Man and Immoral Society* (New York: Scribner's, 1932), that regard liberalism as more prevalent than neo-orthodoxy and therefore more in need of criticism. Even the most careless reader could not come away from *Interpretation of Christian Ethics* with any thought that Niebuhr was trying to revive orthodoxy. His brother, H. Richard Niebuhr, gave "prophetic religion" a pointedly antinomian definition in his *Kingdom of God in America* (New York: Harper, 1937), 10–11. Andrew Delbanco has echoed that recently in *Puritan Ordeal*.

14 See, e.g., King's essay on Barth, *PMLK*, 2:106.

15 William Robert Miller, *Martin Luther King: His Life, Martyrdom, and Meaning for a New World* (New York: Weybright and Talley, 1968), 2, provides insight into the religious beliefs and practices of King's elders, whom he called "the black puritans of Auburn Avenue." On the diversity and conflict within "the" black church, see the section on African American religion and politics in the Bibliographical Essay.

16 Franklin, "Religious Belief and Political Activism in Black America: An Essay," *Journal of Religious Thought* 43 (Fall–Winter 1986–87): 63–72; Baldwin,

To Make the Wounded Whole: The Cultural Legacy of Martin Luther King, Jr. (Minneapolis: Fortress Press, 1992), and *There Is a Balm in Gilead: The Cultural Roots of Martin Luther King, Jr.* (Minneapolis: Fortress Press, 1991). Albert Raboteau and Richard Lischer use "prophetic" to similar effect in their treatment of the tradition on which King drew. See the section on the intellectual history of modern black prophets in the Bibliographical Essay.

17   The discussion of theological affinities must remain limited, since King's genius lay in realms other than systematic thinking. He was not a fully developed theologian but rather devoted his scholarly energy and most of his taste for intellectual subtleties to questions of social ethics. (Even in that emphasis he resembles Reinhold Niebuhr.) The effort to reduce King to what he learned as a child seems to date from Joseph R. Washington's *Black Religion: The Negro and Christianity in the United States* (Boston: Beacon Press, 1964), which states that King was "a remarkable product of the South; barely tainted by his academic exposure in the North" (p. 3). This line has been developed by others who follow the lead of the black nationalist scholar James Cone (see n. 31, below). Importantly, King condemned black folk who passively stood on the sidelines, sometimes seeming to suggest that they were as much an obstacle to freedom as active white segregationists. See King's eulogy for the four girls martyred at the 16th Street Church in Birmingham in 1963, in James Melvin Washington, ed., *A Testament of Hope: The Essential Writings of Martin Luther King, Jr.* (New York: Harper and Row, 1986), 221.

18   In April 1956 King made a veiled reference to Myrdal in "Our Struggle," written by Rustin and published under King's name in *Liberation*. Under the subheading, "THE LIBERAL DILEMMA," King warned that boycotters and others might die, because "many white men in the South see themselves as a fearful minority in an ocean of black men." King did not refer to any Myrdalian conflict in the minds of these white men: "They honestly believe with one side of their minds that Negroes are depraved and disease-ridden. . . . They are convinced that racial equality is a Communist idea and that those who ask for it are subversive." Such men were in conflict with forces outside, not inside, their personalities: with unbigoted white southerners. The unbigoted did have an internal dilemma, but it did not behave as Myrdal predicted. Rather than drive southerners to improve their society, "the liberal dilemma" paralyzed them. To King, the liberal dilemma would not lead to a happy ending by itself. "Our Struggle," *Liberation* 1 (April 1956): 3–6, in James Melvin Washington, *Testament of Hope*, 80. See also King, *Stride toward Freedom: The Montgomery Story* (New York: Harper, 1958), 205, and "The Time for Freedom Has Come," *New York Times Magazine*, September 29, 1963, and "The American Dream," Address at Lincoln University, June 6, 1961, both in Washington, *Testament of Hope*, 161 and 208–9, respectively; and Taylor Branch, *Parting the Waters: America in the King Years, 1954–1963* (New York: Simon and Schuster, 1988), 490. King referred to Myrdal in passing in a February 1958 speech to the National Negro Press Association, *PMLK*, 4:363.

19   The quotations in this and the previous paragraph are from "Religion's An-

swer to the Problem of Evil," essay for George Davis's Philosophy of Religion course, Crozer Theological Seminary, April 27, 1951, *PMLK*, 1:416–33. This essay is also of interest for its expression of dissent from Brightman (see section on King's intellectual history in the Bibliographical Essay). The editors of his papers make clear that King closely followed the work of J. S. Whale, *The Christian Answer to the Problem of Evil* (London: Student Christian Movement Press, 1936), and H. F. Rall, *Christianity: An Inquiry into Its Nature and Truth* (New York: Scribner, 1940). They do not make clear that King wound up with a very Niebuhrian notion of order, which he seems to have cribbed from Rall. Order, King says, brings us all that is good and beautiful; but order, which brings, for example, the predictable vaporization of water with heat, inevitably brings "tornadoes, flood and destruction in which the good suffer with the evil." This exactly parallels Niebuhr's emphasis in *Moral Man* that social order, which is better than anarchy, cannot be achieved or maintained without injustice.

20 See King's exam answers on the theology of the Bible (November 1953), which state that Jeremiah and Job "make it clear that the righteous do suffer and the wicked do prosper." Jeremiah was the first to question the Deuteronomic principle that evil in the world was simply "punishment for sin." King also argues that Isaiah's "suffering is not due to something that he has done, but is *vicarious* and *redemptive*. Through his suffering[,] knowledge of God is sp[r]ead to the unbelieving Gentiles[,] and those unbelievers seeing that this suffering servant is innocent will become conscious of their sins and repent and thereby be redeemed." *PMLK*, 2:207–8. The refrain, "unearned suffering is redemptive" appears in King's "Pilgrimage to Nonviolence," in *Stride toward Freedom*, 103. It also appears in "Suffering and Faith," *Christian Century*, April 1960, 510; in "Love, Law, and Civil Disobedience," *New South* (December 1961): 3 ff.; in the "I Have a Dream" speech at the Lincoln Memorial in 1963; and in King's eulogy for the four girls martyred at the 16th Street Church in Birmingham— all reprinted in James Melvin Washington, *Testament of Hope*, 41, 47, 219, and 221–22.

21 *PMLK*, 1:230–36 (quotation, p. 231). His next paper picks up the same theme, vindicating the liberalism that King likes, which he says is "a method not a creed." He means by this simply the use of the historical method with the Bible. King compares the liberal's openness to "the dominant thought pattern of his day, viz., science" to the Thomists' attempt to "wed theology to the dominant thought pattern of their day, viz., Aristotelian philosophy." Here he also refers to the liberal doctrine of man: for the liberal, "there never was a fall of man" but rather "an upward (evolutionary) movement of man." The liberal "sees value in human nature"; he cannot sincerely sing the hymn, "Would he devote the sacred head / for such a worm as I?" King seems to remain more open to orthodox views of man than to orthodox views of of biblical interpretation, on which he clearly favors the liberals (see, e.g., *PMLK*, 1:236–42). In an essay on the divinity of Jesus, however, King comes down squarely in favor of modernist views and rejects orthodoxy. "The Humanity and Divinity of

Jesus," *PMLK*, 1:257–62. He returns to the doctrine of man in a subsequent essay, "How Modern Christians Should Think of Man," again emphasizing a balance between liberal and neo-orthodox views, a view that was, whether King realized it or not, very close to Niebuhr's. *PMLK*, 1:273–79.

22 The book King was summarizing when he mentioned Gandhi, William Newton Clarke's *Outline of Christian Theology*, published in 1898 (*PMLK*, 1:249), cannot have referred to Gandhi, who was born in 1869 but did not gain fame until his South African period, 1907–14.

23 "How Modern Christians Should Think of Man," essay for George Davis's Christian Theology for Today course, Crozer Theological Seminary, Winter 1949–50, *PMLK*, 1:273–79.

24 In his answers to the qualifying exam for the History of Doctrine (1953), *PMLK*, 2:213, King mislabels Niebuhr as "neo-orthodox." Yet even there, he notes that not only Niebuhr but "all of the outstanding Neo-orthodox theologians accept the latest results of Biblical and historical criticism, and yet hold to the most orthodox and traditional theological view." In more thorough considerations of neo-orthodox thinkers, King leaves Niebuhr out of the discussion. See "Contemporary Continental Theology" (1952), *PMLK*, 2:128–38, and Answers to qualifying exam for Systematic Theology, *PMLK*, 2:228–31. He later distinguishes between Niebuhr and "Barthianism" (see n. 28 below).

25 Notecards on Jeremiah and Psalm 72 (1952–53), *PMLK*, 2:165–66.

26 The quotations in this and the previous two paragraphs are from King, "Reinhold Niebuhr's Ethical Dualism" (1952), *PMLK*, 2:141–51. Interestingly, in an earlier outline of this and a later essay, King criticized Niebuhr's apparent "agnosticism" as to the nature of God; his complaint is that Niebuhr is *too* liberal on some questions. "Reinhold Niebuhr" notes (1953), *PMLK*, 2:141. This negative justification of democracy as the least evil of known alternatives differentiates King from Dewey.

27 For the Brightman connection, see Smith and Zepp, *Beloved Community*; John Ansbro, *Martin Luther King, Jr.: The Making of a Mind* (Maryknoll, N.Y.: Orbis, 1982); and Warren E. Steinkraus, "Martin Luther King's Personalism and Non-violence," *Journal of the History of Ideas* 34 (January–March 1973): 97–110.

28 The quotations in this and the previous paragraph are from King, "The Theology of Reinhold Niebuhr," presented to the Dialectical Society, Boston, June 1954, *PMLK*, 2:269–79. Niebuhr rejected, King said, "the easy optimism" handed down from the Renaissance to the Enlightenment to the first three decades of the twentieth century that held that "man had only to be educated and put in agreeable environments in order that the kingdom of Heaven might be realized on earth. Modern liberal or 'progressive' version[s] of the Christian faith readily joined in to sing with the optimistic charms of modernity." He quoted Niebuhr on the "obvious refutations of this view of man" that came from recent history. "Says Niebuhr, 'Since 1914 one tragic experience has followed another, as if history had been designed to refute the vain delusions of modern man.'" Ibid., 278–79.

29 The only thing King had to say against Niebuhr's views was that they were not "as orthodox and Biblical as he assumes them to be." This criticism sounds strained, and King's editors point out that it was cribbed from Walter Muelder. *PMLK*, 2:278–79, nn. 16–18.

30 King praised Niebuhr's "biblical and Christian Anthropology," which he called a "synthesis" of idealism and naturalism, in contrast to the tendency of idealist *and* naturalistic thinkers to cleave to either pole. King emphasized that human power comes through an embrace of one's helplessness, which can invite (though not determine) God's grace. Still, "there can be no real moral progress in man's social, political, and religious life: for good can never triumph over evil in history, due to limitations of human nature." Like the human suffering that King so often emphasized, grace was unearned; it would never be perfectly achieved. *PMLK*, 2:272, 274–78. The issue was replayed later in King's kitchen conversion; see Chapter 5, below, at n. 20.

31 See James Cone, "Martin Luther King, Jr., Black Theology—Black Church," *Theology Today* 40 (January 1984): 411, "The Theology of Martin Luther King," *Union Theological Seminary Quarterly Review* 40 (January 1986): 28, and "Martin Luther King, Jr., and the Third World," *Journal of American History* 74 (September 1987): 455–67; Paul Garber, "Black Theology: The Latter Day Legacy of Martin Luther King, Jr.," *Journal of the Interdenominational Theological Center* 2 (Spring 1975): 16–32, "King Was a Black Theologian," *Journal of Religious Thought* (Fall–Winter 1974-75), and "Too Much Taming of Martin Luther King," review of Smith and Zepp's *Beloved Community, Christian Century*, June 5, 1974; and Keith Miller, "Martin Luther King, Jr., Borrows a Revolution: Argument, Audience, and Implications of a Secondhand Universe," *College English* 48 (March 1986): 249–65, "Composing Martin Luther King, Jr.," *PMLA* 105 (January 1990): 70–82, "Martin Luther King, Jr., and the Black Folk Pulpit," *Journal of American History* 78 (June 1991): 120–23, and review of *The Papers of Martin Luther King* (which criticizes the editors for failing to toe the party line of Cone), in *New York Times Book Review*, March 15, 1992.

32 I do not mean to countenance the racial charge in any form. But there may be some of the unconscious flattery that often appears in graduate students—of all colors—in King's references to Brightman. After Brightman died in 1953, the flattery may have lingered as an uncritical reverence for the dead and/or a living appeal to Brightman's protégé, Harold DeWolf, King's professor and dissertation reader. Brightman, at least, encouraged King to criticize his ideas, and King did criticize Personalism in general and Brightman in particular (e.g., in his 1951 essay on the problem of evil)—in a Niebuhrian tone.

33 "Letter from the Birmingham City Jail" (1963) and the *Playboy* interview (1965) are in James Melvin Washington, *Testament of Hope*, 289–302, 340–77. I must note here, however, the superb work of Jonathan S. Bass, which suggests that King's famous letter was not written in jail or even by King but rather was a collaboration of several of King's advisers, carefully calculated to achieve a maximum public-relations effect. See Bass, *Blessed Are the Peace-*

makers: Martin Luther King, Jr., Eight White Religious Leaders, and the "Letter from Birmingham Jail" (Baton Rouge: Louisiana State University Press, 2001).

34 Mays and Joseph Nicholson, *The Negro's Church* (New York: Institute of Social and Religious Research, 1933); see also Mays, Commencement Address at Howard University, June 1945, *Journal of Negro Education* (Summer 1945): 527–34. The only way to avoid fascism in the United States was to "Christianize" the country, Mays said. But he thought it necessary first to Christianize the churches, for at present "the Church is subservient both to State and to society"; the church must stop being "priestly" and become "prophetic" (p. 528).

35 In an essay on the affinities between King and Thomas Merton, Albert Raboteau wisely argues that the course of both exceptional thinkers could not have been determined by their backgrounds. King stood apart from "the prophetic tradition within African-American religion"—just as Merton stood apart from much of "the contemplative tradition within monasticism." To Raboteau, "it was not traditions per se, but what King and Merton took from them, or better, the ways in which King and Merton were transformed by them, that made all the difference." Irresistible as the wisdom of this observation is, however, Raboteau goes on to show Merton as much more self-conscious and decisive in separating himself from the general run of contemplative monks than King ever was in separating himself from prophets. Raboteau shows King separating himself, in fact, from just about everything *but* the company of prophets—that and God's love for the human race, which is ever looking for ways to murder His prophets. Raboteau, *A Fire in the Bones: Reflections on African-American Religious History* (Boston: Beacon Press, 1995), 169–71.

36 David J. Garrow, *Bearing the Cross: Martin Luther King, Jr., and the Southern Christian Leadership Conference* (New York: Morrow, 1986), 649. See also Stephen Oates, "Intellectual Odyssey of Martin Luther King," *Massachusetts Review* 22 (Summer 1981): 301 ff. In a letter to King about Rustin's work on King's speech for the Lincoln Memorial Prayer Pilgrimage of 1957, Rustin wrote, "Of course you will always speak in your own way." Rustin to King, May 17, 1956, Rustin Papers, microfilm, reel 4.

37 The quotations in this and the preceding two paragraphs are from Rustin, "The Negro and Nonviolence," *Fellowship*, October 1942, reprinted in Rustin, *Down the Line: The Collected Writings of Bayard Rustin* (Chicago: Quadrangle, 1971), 8–12.

38 Rustin, "Easter Greeting," n.d. [ca. 1952], Rustin Papers, microfilm, reel 20.

39 "Civil Disobedience, Jim Crow, and the Armed Forces," April 11, 1948, Thomas Jefferson Award acceptance speech, in Rustin, *Down the Line*, 51. Rustin described his solo Tennessee challenge in "Nonviolence vs. Jim Crow," *Fellowship*, July 1942; the Journey of Reconciliation in "We Challenged Jim Crow," *Fellowship*, April 1947; and his imprisonment in "Twenty-two Days on a Chain Gang" (edited versions of which ran in the *New York Post* and the

Baltimore Afro-American), all reprinted in *Down the Line*, 5–7, 13–25, 26–49. See also Rustin's "Biographical Sketch" in Rustin Papers, microfilm, reel 20.

40 Rustin to Platt, September 3, 1948, Rustin Papers, ibid., reel 20. He also emphasized the necessity of sacrifice to a young friend in a 1952 letter. He counseled the friend to end his quest for security simply by accepting insecurity—an interesting answer to Dewey's quest for certainty, perhaps, and an echo of Mill. Rustin to Steve Smith, May 12, 1952, ibid.

41 Rustin to Muste, February 2, 1950, ibid. Rustin's report on activism for integrated housing in the Chicago area makes clear that, although he believed in love and reconciliation as the ultimate goal, catastrophic changes had to come first. "It cannot be assumed . . . that a Negro family can move into Cicero without causing a ripple on the 'peaceful' waters of the community." Memorandum from George Houser and Rustin, "Integrated Housing in the West Suburban Area of Chicago . . . ," n.d., ibid.

42 Jervis Anderson establishes that Rustin was the main author of the pamphlet and Rustin's reasons for insisting that his name be left off the list of authors. The chairman of the acknowledged authors, Stephen Cary, told Anderson that without Rustin *Speak Truth to Power* could never have been written." Anderson, *Bayard Rustin: Troubles I've Seen* (New York: HarperCollins, 1997), 174–76.

43 The quotations in this and the previous two paragraphs are from *Speak Truth to Power: A Quaker Search for an Alternative to Violence: A Study of International Conflict* (Philadelphia: American Friends Service Committee, 1955), 1–2, 64–66. Since then, the awe of Rustin's generation in the face of nuclear weapons has worn off—partly because those who possess these weapons have indeed found their use impractical.

44 *Speak Truth to Power* originally appeared in the *Progressive*, October 1955, 5–8. Responses followed by Dwight Macdonald, Norman Thomas, Reinhold Niebuhr, Karl Menninger, and George Kennan (pp. 9–18). Stephen Cary and Robert Pickus presented a "Reply to Critics" (pp. 19–24). Perhaps the most interesting reaction was Kennan's statement that when he wrote his famous article on "containment" in 1946, he "did not think of it primarily in military terms" (p. 16). Niebuhr's response was disappointingly thoughtless. Written as an official statement for the ADA, it was more concerned with justifying ADA's Cold War policies—which Niebuhr longwindedly quoted—than in clarifying principles or differences in perspective (pp. 13–14).

45 According to Glenn Smiley, Rustin's replacement from FOR in the Montgomery movement, King said that he had become familiar with Gandhi at Boston University. "He had Gandhi in mind when this thing started, he says." Smiley to John Swomley and Al Hassler, February 29, 1956, Rustin Papers, microfilm, reel 4. In two interviews in June 1969, Rustin discussed his connections with King, including Lillian Smith's role in initiating the contact and their frequent association even after Rustin's public break with King in 1960 (in response to a blackmail threat from Adam Clayton Powell, Rustin resigned as chair of King's defense committee). University of Texas Oral His-

tory Project, Lyndon B. Johnson Library, Austin. See esp. Interview I, pp. 11–20, Interview II, pp. 2–3, 5, 7–12. Rustin's correspondence with King is mostly in MLKB, boxes 53, 55, 56A, 57, 64A, 67. David Garrow (*Bearing the Cross*, 66–73, 83–86, 455, 599, 649 n. 21) unearthed a great deal of what is now known (including what the FBI knew) about Rustin's relationship with King (including ghostwriting for him). Taylor Branch adds perspective to this in *Parting the Waters*, 168–80, 196–99, 208, 250, 264–65, 329, 847. Jervis Anderson's *Rustin*, the first full biography, is also illuminating.

46 David Garrow, the most thorough of King scholars, understands the difference between coercive and passive nonviolence, having read Clarence Marsh Case, *Non-violent Coercion: A Study in Methods of Social Pressure* (1923; reprint, New York: J. S. Ozer, 1972) and other relevant works. But he mistakenly attributes the coercive version to King only after what he sees as King's attempt at "moral suasion" in Albany, Ga., in 1962: "What King believed in and advocated in the late 1950s and the very first years of the 1960s was nonviolent *persuasion*. This was resistance that employed moral suasion upon one's opponents, and it was basically not coercive." Garrow, *Protest at Selma: Martin Luther King, Jr., and the Voting Rights Act of 1965* (New Haven: Yale University Press, 1978), 221. Garrow moderated the sharp dividing line of Albany in his later biography of King (*Bearing the Cross*) but did not abandon the claim that King came to believe in and practice coercion only through experience with failure late in his life. This interpretation conflicts with the evidence I present above of King's ideas. I claim that King believed in coercion from his Boston essays on and practiced it from the Montgomery struggle on. How else are we to view a year-long boycott than as nonviolent coercion? King believed in persuasion, too—not only before Albany, but also after it. But he saw persuasion the way military commanders do: as something that must sometimes be backed up with force. Attempts at persuasion often precede or accompany nonviolent force—as they often precede or accompany violent force. We might call such attempts nonviolent diplomacy. In King's mind, they complemented nonviolent force but did not replace it.

47 The quotations in this and the next paragraph are from King, "Our Struggle," *Liberation* 1 (April 1956): 3–6. Garrow identifies Rustin's authorship of this article in *Bearing the Cross*, 73. For King's youthful letter to the editor in 1946, see n. 11, above.

48 King, "Our Struggle." "Our Church Is Becoming Militant" and "Economics Is a Part of Our Struggle" are subtitles in this article. Rustin claimed that fighting with this new weapon constituted a rejection of migration to the North (a point that Bob Moses developed in the 1960s), which was one of the major avenues of Myrdal's and other liberals' faith in progress. "Montgomery has demonstrated that we will not run from the struggle. . . . The attitude of many young Negroes a few years ago was reflected in the common expression, 'I'd rather be a lamp post in Harlem than Governor of Alabama.' Now the idea expressed in our churches, schools, pool rooms, restaurants and homes is: 'Brother, stay here and fight nonviolently. 'Cause if you don't let

them make you run, you can win.'" Rustin's analysis of white leaders' tactical mistakes shows that he was not as interested in appealing to conscience as in winning concessions through force. Economic pressure hurt the bus company as well as downtown merchants, and white brutality only "further cemented the Negro community and brought sympathy for our cause." Rustin acknowledged the other side's violence and did not shrink from saying that people might die. Far from expecting nonviolent appeals to help resolve conflicts in white people's consciences, he stated: "Many white men in the South see themselves as a fearful minority in an ocean of black men. They honestly believe with one side of their minds that Negroes are depraved and disease-ridden. . . . They believe that their caste system is the highest form of social organization."

49 Ibid. Rustin published his own views in "Montgomery Diary," which appeared in the same issue of *Liberation* 1 (April 1956) and was reprinted in Rustin, *Down the Line*, 55–61.

50 Rustin, "From Protest to Politics: The Future of the Civil Rights Movement" (February 1965), in *The Commentary Reader* (New York: Athenaeum, 1966), 411–22. To Rustin, progress was the cause of black people's immiseration. Black people were more "concentrated in jobs vulnerable to automation than was the case ten years ago." Black median income had dropped relative to white median income. Rustin quoted labor secretary Willard Wirtz saying that "machines have the equivalent of a high school diploma": Negroes who dropped out of high school (57 percent of the black population) "are without a future." While desegregation was moving slowly in the South, segregation was accelerating in the North, along with the growth of slums. The issue was no longer "civil rights" but economic conditions. Recent riots "were not race riots; they were outbursts of class aggression in a society where class and color definitions are converging disastrously." Perhaps the civil rights movement was "misnamed"; certainly it had to change its tactics. The ideal of cultural assimilation prevented "white people of good will" from understanding the issues. The "self-help" notion popularized by Eric Hoffer would not address the plight of unemployed Negroes—or of white people who suffered technological unemployment. Nor would the Black Muslims, whose doctrine had "an ironic similarity" to "the self-help advocated by many liberals": "every prostitute the Muslims convert to a model of Calvinist virtue is replaced in the ghetto by two more." All these problems, though "conditioned by Jim Crow, do not vanish upon its demise. They are more deeply rooted in our socio-economic order; they are the result of the total society's failure to meet not only the Negro's needs, but human needs generally."

51 Ibid., 417–22. Rustin reiterated that "the Negro's struggle for equality in America is essentially revolutionary. Though most Negroes—in their hearts —unquestionably seek only to enjoy the fruits of American society as it now exists, their quest cannot *objectively* be satisfied within the framework of existing political and economic relations." The movement had already done something "revolutionary": it "may have done more to democratize life for whites

than for Negroes." The sit-ins "galvanized white students, banished the ugliest features of McCarthyism from the American campus and resurrected political debate." Protest raised the issue of quality education for all children and probably, "through the resurgence of conscience it kindled, did more to initiate the war on poverty than any other single force."

Rustin wanted revolutionary changes to continue—full employment, abolition of slums, reconstruction of education, and "new definitions of work and leisure." All this would cost America dearly. Rustin criticized nascent demands for affirmative action, not because they threatened equal opportunity, but because they were too conservative. " 'Preferential treatment' cannot help" unemployed black workers: there were too many unemployed. New jobs had to be created. That would happen only after a massive assertion of power, which Negroes could not muster alone, especially not through divisive pronouncements of racial separatism and reparation. The moral purism of many integrationists was as unrealistic as separatism, however. The purists' identification of the hypocritical white liberal as the main enemy of civil rights was simply a "reverse recitation of the reactionary's litany (liberalism leads to socialism, which leads to Communism)." Rustin did not for one minute think that "the Johnson landslide proved the 'white backlash' to be a myth. It proved, rather, that economic interests are more fundamental than prejudice: the backlashers decided that loss of social security was, after all, too high a price to pay for a slap at the Negro. . . . The civil rights movement will be advanced only to the degree that social and economic welfare gets to be inextricably tangled with civil rights."

52   Ibid., 418. Years later Rustin said that "hopefulness" had bound the movement's strands together. Next to A. Philip Randolph, "Gandhi had a more direct influence on the development of civil rights strategy than any other individual, here or abroad." Rustin, *Strategies for Freedom: The Changing Contours of Black Protest* (New York: Columbia University Press, 1976), 14, 20, 24.

53   This may sound like a Myrdalian issue of conscience, where the drama just accelerates the mental conflict in the white mind. But Rustin was ever pragmatic and Niebuhrian in his emphasis on effectiveness, on power: "For protest to succeed, it must produce a feeling of moving ahead; it must force people to take notice of injustice; and it must win new allies." Now, at any rate, the tactic of protest was no longer effective. Rustin, *Strategies for Freedom*, 40, 40–41.

54   In the wake of a 1948 federal decision expanding voting rights, Simkins wrote in her February 6, 1948, column for the *Norfolk Journal and Guide* of the new effectiveness in negotiations: "Columbia's not quite so voteless Negro citizens appealed to city council this week for increased expenditures for recreational facilities. Quite different from the endless series of former 'waitings and prayings' over the years, this week's appeal had a 'kick' in it." Simkins Papers, USC, box 2. Similarly, in 1964 she urged local Masons to join "a widespread determined voter registration drive," since the next election would "be the most important . . . since that of Abraham Lincoln." The Negro's only hope was to compel state authorities: "Our redemption must be bought at the

BALLOT BOXES. . . . Politicians respect votes and VOTES ALONE." Simkins, Speech to M. W. Grand Lodge of Masons, August 1, 1964, ibid., box 3. That year she sent a flyer with a similar message, emphasizing the impotence of mere "talk." She stressed the need to seize power, through "100% Negro registration in every church, secret order, usher board, church choir, missionary society and any other organization. . . . If South Carolina is to be saved in November . . . the Negro vote must be fully employed. . . . America's freedom is at stake in November. But JUST TALKING ABOUT IT IS NOT ENOUGH. . . . Let's neither SLUMBER nor SLEEP . . . *the only way for evil men to prosper is for good* MEN TO DO N O T H I N G!" Two months later she wrote local black leaders that, while their enemies "hanker for DAY BEFORE YESTERDAY, we are envisioning a better life for all men DAY AFTER TOMORROW,—and KING JESUS IS RIDING IN DIXIE!" Simkins to Ministers and Other Leaders, October 24, 1964, ibid., box 3.

55 Adam Fairclough has been particularly strong on this point; see his *Race and Democracy: The Civil Rights Struggle in Louisiana, 1915–1972* (Athens: University of Georgia Press, 1995). See also Charles Payne, *I've Got the Light of Freedom: The Organizing Tradition and the Mississippi Freedom Struggle* (Berkeley: University of California Press, 1995); Stephen G. N. Tuck, *Beyond Atlanta: The Struggle for Racial Equality in Georgia, 1940–1980* (Athens: University of Georgia Press, 2001); John A. Kirk, *Redefining the Color Line: Black Activism in Little Rock, Arkansas, 1940–1970* (Gainesville: University Press of Florida, 2002); and Chap. 2, n. 30, above.

56 Simkins, Column for May 17, 1947, *Norfolk Journal and Guide*, Simkins Papers, USC, box 2. For background on Sinkins, see her interviews with Jacquelyn Hall in the SOHP. I. A. Newby refers fleetingly to Simkins as part of a tradition of "dissidents, from Cato of Stono and Denmark Vesey to Mo[d]jeska Simkins and Cleveland Sellers." Compared to white extremists like Governors James Byrnes and George Bell Timmerman, or Senators like Strom Thurmond, Simkins was, Newby says, a "moderat[e]" black leader of "unusual forbearance." Newby, *Black Carolinians: A History* (Columbia: University of South Carolina Press, 1973), 16, 279. Barbara Woods Aba-Mecha's dissertation and other works cited in the Bibliographical Essay provide fuller treatments.

57 Simkins, Column for November 15, 1947, Simkins Papers, USC, box 2. She rejected liberal gradualism again in her next column, for November 22.

58 Simkins, Column for November 15, 1947, ibid. She lit into the gradualists and temporizers again two weeks later: "Despite the remonstrances and misgivings of the 'ain't ready' conclave, the time to 'shove off' is here. Most Negroes have accepted segregation and discrimination, without [a] second thought, for decades. In theaters, movies, . . . and such, Negroes . . . have received graciously and smilingly the corner set aside for them." Simkins, Column for November 29, 1947, ibid. She later denounced black "women of training, intelligence, means, and with time to spare, [who] gather their finery about themselves and step into their gas buggies, and pass by" all the "outrages"

that were part of everyday life under Jim Crow. They go to their "tittering gabfests where they munch saltines and salads and howl vociferously now and then" without taking action:

> No less guilty are the sisters who go to prayer meeting and pray the same old prayers and sing the same old long metre while imploring God to do something he hasn't a mind to do and they should hope to do themselves.
>
> And the pompous, fat, self-satisfied husbands and papas are no better. They "chew the fat" and shine the chairs, and "get along al[l] right." . . . The Cadillacs, Buicks, Packards, and Dodges (I have one myself) roll up to the schools to keep the little handpicked darlings from getting cold and damp by walking three blocks home, but seldom are their parents found in PTA, NAACP, and civic meetings to see why the high schools are not accredited, why there is such a vast and vicious difference in the curricula and textbooks in the Negro and white high schools and colleges, why their children are forced to use histories that either belittle and underrate or entirely ignore our contributions.

Simkins, Column for December 27, 1947, ibid.

59 Simkins speech notecards, n.d. [ca. 1948] (paragraphing altered from original), ibid., box 5. In this speech she outlined specific tactics, including boycotts and bloc voting. Again in her column for December 13, 1947, ibid., she writes, "But the old order changeth."

60 She returned to the example of Job who faced "FIRE AND FROM HEAVEN — burned sheep an[d] servants . . . Camels slain servants with swords. . . . In this confused, disoriented, suddenly frustrated state, the final blow fell, 'THY SONS AND [THY] DAUGHTERS WERE EATING AND DRINKING IN THEIR ELDEST BROTHER'S HOUSE, AND A . . . GREAT WIND CAME AND STRUCK THE FOUR CORNERS OF THE HOUSE AND IT FELL UPON THEM AND THEY ARE DEAD. . . . Each messenger closed his awful news with the words, 'AND I ONLY AM LEFT ALONE TO TELL THEE.' . . . We do not need great numbers." Speech on back of campaign flyers, n.d., ibid., box 5.

CHAPTER FOUR: PROPHETIC CHRISTIAN REALISM

1 The SNCC records are fragmentary on many matters, including intellectual discussions. Most scholars have followed the lead of Emily Stoper, who denies that there was any significant "intellectual" activity in SNCC: most black members "were not intellectuals and were admirers above all of the non-intellectual virtues of courage and charisma." Many white members were intellectual, but black members expelled them, Stoper claims, "partly because of their intellectuality," which "irritated many of the black members, whose style was action-oriented." (She adds, interestingly, that the white intellectuals' ideas found their way into the "Black Power" movement that emerged after their expulsion.) Stoper, *The Student Non-violent Coordinating Committee:*

The Growth of Radicalism in a Civil Rights Organization (Brooklyn, N.Y.: Carlson, 1989), 105–7, 111–16, 131–33. See the section on the intellectual history of the civil rights movement in the Bibliographical Essay.

2 See "SNCC Schedules Training Conference," *Student Voice* 2 (November 18, 1963): 2, 4, and "D.C. Conference," *Student Voice* 2 (December 9, 1963): 2, 4.

3 David Halberstam's *The Children* (New York: Random House, 1998) provides an evocative narrative, based on interviews with participants, of the Nashville group that revolved around Lawson and then spread his ideas throughout the country. John Lewis, perhaps Lawson's greatest protégé, argues that Lawson, rather than King, was "the man who would truly turn my world around." Lewis felt that Lawson was "God-sent." Lewis, with Michael D'Orso, *Walking with the Wind: A Memoir of the Movement* (New York: Simon and Schuster, 1998), 79, 85, and passim.

4 Background on Lawson's work with Nashville students is in three narratives of the NCLC: Anonymous, Angeline Butler, and Peggi Alexander, in Kelly Miller Smith Papers, Vanderbilt University, box 76. See also Arthur Foster Chronology, James Lawson Collection, Vanderbilt University. The Lawson material in various collections at the Amistad Research Center, Tulane University, has very little on Lawson's work with his Nashville followers and duplicates much of the material available elsewhere. Neither collection is illuminating on Lawson's ideas.

5 It was Baker who pushed the students to separate themselves from the older, church-based, and, to Baker's mind, more conservative generation in SCLC. But she made few speeches and wrote little about what motivated or shaped the students' actions. Baker expressed her ideas about organization in "Bigger Than a Hamburger," *Southern Patriot*, June 1960, and reflected candidly and perceptively on her own role in her interview with Emily Stoper (*Student Non-violent Coordinating Committee*, 265–72). Joanne Grant's biography, *Ella Baker: Freedom Bound* (Urbana: University of Illinois Press, 1999), emphasizes how Baker tried to let students make their own strategic decisions, though she pushed them hard to separate from the adults in SCLC and to be administratively efficient. Baker herself had worked with Rustin (and Stanley Levison) in the 1950s, organizing In Friendship. She, too, believed that the normal tendency of society, and of protest organizations, was toward corruption. See Charles Payne, *I've Got the Light of Freedom: The Organizing Tradition and the Mississippi Freedom Struggle* (Berkeley: University of California Press, 1995), 44, 79–102, 379. Cleveland Sellers, relying partly on Julian Bond, recalls Baker's "Bigger Than a Hamburger" speech at the Raleigh meeting of SNCC in April 1960 as being poorly received (he said that Lawson and Martin Luther King got better receptions), but in retrospect he thought that it was the best speech. Sellers, with Robert Terrell, *River of No Return: The Autobiography of a Black Militant and the Life and Death of SNCC* (New York: Morrow, 1973), 46. Baker emphasized the danger that "adults" would co-opt and manipulate the students if they did not maintain their independence. James Forman, whose ideas of organization were diametrically opposed to

Baker's, nonetheless offers a paean to her selfless, tireless, behind-the-scenes influence, in *The Making of Black Revolutionaries* (1972; reprint, Washington, D.C.: Open Hand, 1985), 215–19. Forman contrasts Baker to King, who, he suggests, was an unwitting tool of the State Department's public relations campaign and who tried to co-opt the students. Clayborne Carson analyzes Baker's role and organizational ideas in *In Struggle: SNCC and the Black Awakening of the 1960s* (Cambridge: Harvard University Press, 1981), 19–26, 71, 202, as does Aldon D. Morris in *Origins of the Civil Rights Movement: Black Communities Organizing for Change* (New York: Free Press, 1984), 102–4, 112–15, 201, 215–16, 218–21, 223, 231, 239.

6 For biographical material on Lawson, see the transcripts of Lawson's interviews in 1968 and 1969 with Joan Beifus and David Yellin, in the Mississippi Valley Collection, University of Memphis; and Byron L. Plumley Jr., "Searching for a Place to Stand: Reflections of Spiritually-Rooted Social Activists" (Ph.D. diss., Union Institute, 1993), chap. 3. I thank Will Campbell, Ed Frank, Peter Kuryla, and James Lawson for help in tracking down material on Lawson.

7 Francis L. Broderick and August Meier, eds., *Negro Protest Thought in the Twentieth Century* (Indianapolis: Bobbs-Merrill, 1965), 274. The most thorough historian of SNCC, Clayborne Carson (*In Struggle*, 22), refers to Lawson as "the most influential of the Nashville leaders."

8 SNCC, "Statement of Purpose . . . Prepared by—Rev. J. M. Lawson, Jr., Saturday, May 14, 1960," in "What Is SNCC? Philosophy," *Student Voice* 1 (June 1960): 2, and reprinted in *Student Voice* 1 (December 1960): 2.

9 Partly through his high school experience on the debate team, he became increasingly interested in world affairs, reading avidly, as his father did, news magazines and journals of opinion. See Plumley, "Searching for a Place," chap. 3.

10 Fellow students considered Lawson a "communist radical." He refused the draft in the Korean War, which led him to form a relationship with FOR and Bayard Rustin. He was imprisoned for a little over a year. He then did a three-year stint as a missionary for the United Methodists in India, where he was surprised to find many Christians who thought Gandhi a threat to Christianity. Ibid.

11 Lawson worked with the Rev. Kelly Miller Smith in setting up the NCLC. The NCLC narratives quote the organization's "Statement of Purpose" from 1959: "If we are to see the real downfall of segregation and discrimination it will be because of a disciplined Negro Christian movement which breaks with antiquated methods of resolving our fears and tensions and dramatically applies the gospel we profess." They also maintain that negotiations failed until protesters engaged in disruptive direct action and applied economic coercion through boycotts. They soon discovered divisions among segregationists, as well as indecisiveness and weakness among previously segregationist white businessmen. Kelly Miller Smith Papers, Vanderbilt University, box 76.

12 Plumley, "Searching for a Place," 50–60; Morris, *Origins*, 124, 162–65, 190;

Glenn Smiley, interview transcript, 1967, CRDP, Howard University. See Smiley, *Nonviolence: The Gentle Persuader* (Nyack, N.Y.: Fellowship Publications, 1991), and Smiley's letters to the author and tape recording (Summer 1989) in author's possession. On Lawson's expulsion from Vanderbilt, see Chapter 6, n. 75 below.

13 The quotations in this and the previous paragraph are from Lawson, "From a Lunch-Counter Stool," address to SNCC conference at Raleigh, N.C., April 1960, in Broderick and Meier, *Negro Protest Thought*, 274–81.

14 "No progress is adequate so long as any man, woman or child of any ethnic group is still a lynch victim." Ibid., 279. Lawson elaborated on his lack of faith in gradualism in his 1968–69 interviews with Joan Beifus and David Yellin. See, e.g., interview III, 6–8, 10, 11; interview IV, 2, 17–18; interview VI, 3–5.

15 Much as rapid change would disturb America, it was a "sign of promise: God's promise that if radically Christian methods are adopted, the rate of change can be vastly increased." Lawson, "From a Lunch-Counter Stool," 279.

16 Ibid., 280. The next year Lawson developed the idea that the normal course of society was corrupt and had to be renounced in toto. Though SNCC had called for federal intervention and protection, he wrote, "we must never allow the President to substitute marshals for putting people into positions where they can affect public policy." No one would hand over such positions voluntarily. The only way to seize them was with "a nonviolent army," which he called upon SCLC and other groups to help "plan, recruit, organize and discipline," with "work camps for training, study, meditation, and constructive work in voting, repairing neighborhood slums, community centers." This army "would cause worldwide crisis, on a scale unknown in the western world except for actual war." In addition to racism, his army would attack "the system and structure of our institutions," for the "American way of life" tended to give segregation "structural support." Lawson, "Eve of Nonviolent Revolution," *Southern Patriot*, November 1961.

17 See the discussions of the "ordinariness" that scholars attribute to civil rights activists in the Conclusion and Appendix.

18 Of course, this does not mean that she was right about them, either. I emphasize Hamer's voice not because it is typical but because I think it illuminates the common ground of prophetic realism about human nature that civil rights activists shared. Again, she may or may not have been representative of the whole of black Mississippi or even the whole of black activist Mississippi.

19 Hamer quoted in James W. Silver, *Mississippi: The Closed Society* (New York: Harcourt, Brace and World, 1966), 341–42. Hamer rejected the move to insulate SNCC from the overbearing influence of educated people and ultimately resigned in protest over the related move to expel white people. See Forman, *Making*, 438.

20 The quotations in this and the previous paragraph are from the Fannie Lou Hamer interview transcript, Project South, Stanford University, MFDP, chap. 55, 4–8, 14–15. In a short memoir first published in 1967, Hamer amplified her dissatisfaction with many black Mississippians, especially in the

church: "So many of our people, though, seem like they don't want to be anything but white. They're these middle-class Negroes, the ones that never had it as hard as the grass roots people in Mississippi. They'll sell their parents for a few dollars. Sometimes I get so disgusted I feel like getting my gun after some of these school teachers and chicken eatin' preachers. I know these Baptists ministers, 'cause my father was one. I'm not anti-church and I'm not anti-religious, but . . . many churches are selling out to the white power structure." Hamer, *To Praise Our Bridges: An Autobiography* (Jackson, Miss.: KIPCO, 1967), 327–28, copy in Labadie Pamphlets Collection, University of Michigan, and reprinted in Dorothy Abbott, ed., *Mississippi Writers* (Jackson: University Press of Mississippi, 1986), 321–30.

21 Hamer, interview transcript, Project South, 6–7.

22 Hamer interview in *Freedomways* (2d Quarter 1965), 234. In the passage Hamer cited, Luke was quoting Jesus at his most prophetic, warning his followers to "beware the leaven of the Pharisees, which is hypocrisy" (Luke 12:1). The parallel passage in Matthew has a slightly different twist: there Jesus was positively encouraging followers to go out and preach to "the lost sheep of the house of Israel" (Matt. 10:27) that the "Kingdom of Heaven is at hand" (Matt. 10:6–7). Jesus was sending them "as sheep in the midst of wolves" (Matt. 10:16). This is also the chapter where Jesus says, "Think not that I am come to send peace on earth; I came not to send peace, but a sword. For I am come to set a man at variance against his father, and the daughter against her mother," etc. (Matt. 10:34–35). Jesus was echoing Jeremiah, who had prophesied that "there shall be lamentation from the House tops" (Jer. 48:38).

23 Chana Kai Lee, *For Freedom's Sake: The Life of Fannie Lou Hamer* (Urbana: University of Illinois Press, 1999), 36. Like Charles Payne, Lee convincingly portrays Hamer as both a moral pragmatist who concentrated on achieving the possible and as a person who was animated by "Christian faith and emotional memories of her parents and grandparents."

24 At the time, Hamer kept her concerns about the sexualization of her torture private. Ibid., 59–60.

25 Hamer quoted in Silver, *Mississippi*, 342. In a 1968 interview, Hamer recalled that, after she and SNCC worker Larry Guyot, who came to get her out of jail, were beaten, she could see why black folk hated white folk. Nevertheless, she said, "I don't hate white [people] because I'm trying to give them a chance." Moreover, "The white people can't destroy me to save their lives; without destroying themselves." Hamer, interview transcript, CRDP, Howard University, 23, 25. King also made the connection between the white man's brutality and the fear that Negroes would do unto him as he had done unto them. See King, *Stride toward Freedom: The Montgomery Story* (New York: Harper, 1958), 215, and *Why We Can't Wait* (New York: Harper and Row, 1964), 50.

26 Hamer quoted in Silver, *Mississippi*, 342. Hamer, *To Praise Our Bridges*, in Abbott, *Mississippi Writers*, 324.

27 Hamer, *To Praise Our Bridges*, in Abbott, *Mississippi Writers*, 327.

28 Hamer, interview transcript, Project South, 0491–6.

29 Quotations in this and the previous paragraph about people making fun of her Christianity and about her rejection of separatism are from Hamer's interview in *Movement*, October 1967, 1, 10. In her 1967 memoir, Hamer voiced sentiments that suggest some sympathy for black separatism. See Hamer, *To Praise Our Bridges*, in Abbott, *Mississippi Writers*, 327–28. But Ed King, who knew her fairly well, wrote in a eulogy that "in the early debates over black power and separation, she affirmed her belief in both black power and integration." King quoted her saying, "I don't believe in separatism—a house divided against itself cannot stand. . . . This is a country of separatists. America is sick, and man is on the critical list." King, "A Prophet from the Delta," *Sojourners*, December 1982, 18–21 (quotation, p. 20).

30 Lewis, interview transcript, in William R. Beardslee, ed., *The Way Out Must Lead In: Life Histories in the Civil Rights Movement*, 2d ed. (Westport, Conn.: Lawrence Hill, 1983), 1–35 (quotations in this and the previous paragraph, pp. 5–6, 8, 10); Carson, *In Struggle*; Lewis, interview with author, Washington, D.C., March 20, 1989.

31 Lewis, interview transcript in *Dialogue Magazine* (Cornell University) 4 (Spring 1964): 3–7, reprinted in Broderick and Meier, *Negro Protest Thought*, 313–21 (quotations, p. 314). Responding to E. Franklin Frazier's idea that black intellectuals were "ashamed" of their heritage and would advance only when they stopped parroting white intellectuals, Lewis said: "The so-called Negro leaders who are part of the American structure are ashamed," but others, less obsessed with their public image, were not (p. 319).

32 Ibid. Lewis repeated many of these points in his March on Washington speech in August 1963, even after toning down his references to Sherman's March and other things that older leaders thought too belligerent. At the Lincoln Memorial, Lewis said, "We are involved in a serious social revolution. By and large, American politics is dominated by politicians who build their careers on immoral compromises and ally themselves with open forms of political, economic, and social exploitation." He called on all listeners to join the "great social revolution." He also stated that "we are not interested in becoming Madison Avenue types." On the background of the speech, see the interview in Beardslee, *The Way Out Must Lead In*, 17. A copy of the sanitized speech appears in *Student Voice* 4 (October 1963): 1, 3.

33 David Garrow and Aldon Morris, among others, emphasize the importance of this stakelessness in the strategy of civil rights. Bob Moses later recalled how SNCC carried this logic to the extreme. By the end of 1961, SNCC leaders had developed

> some general idea of what had to be done to get [a voter registration] campaign going. First there were very few agencies available in the Negro community that could act as a vehicle for any sort of campaign. The Negro churches could not in general be counted on except for under-the-cover help; and, in general, anybody who had a specific economic tie-in with the

white community could not be counted on when the pressure got hot. Therefore, our feeling was that the only way to run this campaign was to begin to build a group of young people who would not be responsible economically to any sector of the white community and who would be able to act as free agents.

Moses in Clayborne Carson et al., eds., *The Eyes on the Prize Civil Rights Reader: Documents, Speeches, and Firsthand Accounts from the Black Freedom Struggle* (New York: Viking, 1991), 176.

34 Hamer quoted in Len Holt, *The Summer That Didn't End* (New York: Morrow, 1965), 143.

35 Moses quoted in Howard Zinn, *SNCC: The New Abolitionists* (Boston: Beacon Press, 1964), 63; and Carson, *In Struggle*, 46–47. Eric Burner also discusses the Moses-Rustin connection in Burner, *And Gently Shall He Lead them: Robert Parris Moses and Civil Rights in Mississippi* (New York: New York University Press, 1994), 19. John Dittmer, in *Local People: The Struggle for Civil Rights in Mississippi* (Urbana: University of Illinois Press, 1994), 102, provides more details on Moses's journey to the South than other studies but leaves out the Rustin connection stressed by others.

36 Warren based his observations on extensive interviews with Moses, quoted at length in Robert Penn Warren, *Who Speaks for the Negro?* (New York: Random House, 1965), 49, 89 99, and passim. Baker, quoted in Sellers, *River*, 41; Lonnie King quoted in Mary King, *Freedom Song: A Personal Story of the 1960s Civil Rights Movement* (New York: Morrow, 1987), 145.

37 Moses's thinking ran toward secular philosophy rather than theology or Christian tradition, but his most frequently quoted statement, smuggled out of jail in November 1961, ends on a phrase from the 118th Psalm: SNCC's action came from "a stone the builders rejected." This statement appears in full in Zinn, *New Abolitionists*, 76; Forman, *Making*, 233; Sellers, *River*, 52–53; and Mary King, *Freedom Song*, 151. The phrase from Psalm 118 — "The stone which the builders refused is become the head stone of the corner," in the King James Version — is echoed in Matt. 21:42 (which replaces "refused" with "rejected"), Mark 12:10, and Luke 20:17.

38 Forman, *Making*, 385, 417–19, 423. Forman, though given to rhetorical outbursts, doggedly tried to rein in the anarchism of other SNCC members. He saw their aversion to hierarchy as part of "that liberal, bourgeois abdication of responsibility" (p. 435), an interesting echo of Rustin. Forman wrote: "We believed in community organizing, in the power of the people to develop their own strength and direction. But this attitude had become a kind of general neurosis in the organization. . . . What had been born as an affirmation became a simplistic negation. Instead of finding ways that people with natural leadership qualities could make their contribution and help to develop leadership in others, this attitude simply said, Curb your leadership" (p. 419). Forman attributed Moses's refusal to lead to "the middle-class element," which

he soon conflates with a new infusion of eighty-five staff members in October 1964, "most of them middle-class and northern, many of them white" (419–20).

It is important to distinguish Moses's attitude—what might be called his cult of antipersonality—from the Niebuhrian or prophetic judgment of King, Lawson, and others: they saw all power as corrupting yet insisted that power had to be assumed to do good work—their only caveat being not to assume that one could maintain moral purity with power. Forman went to the opposite extreme, admitting—exactly like Arthur Schlesinger Jr.—that power *can* corrupt but does not necessarily do so (p. 425). Cleveland Sellers (*River*, 82–83) also emphasized Moses's appeal to people other than the poor rural Mississippians he had come to liberate:

> Bob Moses communicated best with the white students. Most of them had heard about the work he had been doing in Mississippi long before they got to Oxford [Ohio, where training sessions were held]. He was a *culture hero* to them and they talked about him all the time. By the time they had been in Oxford a couple of days, many of the white students had begun to emulate Bob's slow, thoughtful manner of speaking. Others rushed downtown and purchased bib overalls like his. . . . In all fairness, I must admit that Bob had almost the same effect on blacks. There was something about him, the manner in which he carried himself, that seemed to draw all of us to him. He had been where we were going. And more important, he had emerged as the kind of person we wanted to be.

Lewis (*Walking with the Wind*) connected Moses's resistance to leadership with his overall philosophy of freedom. "He had a near-religious attitude toward autonomy and self-direction" (p. 293). Also, though nobody would accuse Moses of a pragmatic sacrifice of principle, Lewis suggested that there was a practical side to Moses's aversion to his own charisma: He avoided the spotlight "partly because of his personal philosophy, and partly because in that part of the country . . . any attention at all from the white community could mean danger or even death" (p. 187).

39 Sally Bellfrage, *Freedom Summer* (New York: Viking, 1965), 33 (first quotation); John Sinsheimer, "The Freedom Vote of 1963: New Strategies of Racial Protest in Mississippi," *Journal of Southern History* 55 (May 1989): 242 (second quotation). Rustin pointed out, approvingly, that by 1965, protesters in Mississippi, "thanks largely to the leadership of Bob Moses," had taken a turn toward a "conscious bid for *political power*." Rustin, "From Protest to Politics: The Future of the Civil Rights Movement" (February 1965), in *The Commentary Reader* (New York: Athenaeum, 1966), 412.

40 Moses interview, in Warren, *Who Speaks?*, 95.

41 This judgment may have been influenced by Christopher Lasch, whose dazzling readings of Niebuhr's predecessors and followers are well rendered in *The True and Only Heaven: Progress and Its Critics* (New York: Norton, 1991), chap. 9.

42 The quotations in this and the previous paragraph are from the Moses interview in Warren, *Who Speaks?*, 95–97.

43 Sellers, *River*, 83–84. Bellfrage tells the same story in *Freedom Summer*, 17.

44 Moses interview in Warren, *Who Speaks?*, 98.

45 Leslie W. Dunbar, *A Republic of Equals* (Ann Arbor: University of Michigan Press, 1966). Young quoted in Lasch, *True and Only Heaven*, 395.

46 Mary King, *Freedom Song*, 152, 335, 544. On the brain drain from black Mississippi and the effort of SNCC's Freedom Schools to deal with it by discussing how to make staying in Mississippi more attractive, see Holt, *Summer That Didn't End*, 113–14. Holt tells how some of the teachers, mostly white and from northern suburbs, "pointed out the drastic shortcomings of the tension-ridden, insecure life of those 'middle class' people (like the teachers' parents) who would have heart attacks if a Jew, Negro or Chinese-American moved into their neighborhoods; who haven't expressed an honest idea in public since the first payment on one of their several mortgages; whose ulcerated, psycho-therapied, martini-drenched lives are composed totally of the deadest, sickest fictions that the most successful Madison Avenue huckster can sell in a world tottering on the brink of ultimate destruction" (p. 115 and cf. p. 122). See also Lewis, *Walking with the Wind*, 187, 242, 250, 283, 293, 295–96, 351.

47 Myrdal's optimism about American institutions did not extend to all institutions that served Negroes. Myrdal had confidence in the NAACP and Urban League and even A. Philip Randolph's March on Washington Movement: he saw all of these as pragmatic, gradualist organizations. But he was pessimistic about "radical" organizations—those that did not endorse his own optimism. Myrdal, *An American Dilemma: The Negro Problem and Modern Democracy*, 2 vols. (1944; reprint, New York: Harper and Row, 1962), 2:814–57. He did not think that radical organizations posed much of a threat, however, since most black people did not support them. The Negro institutions that Myrdal distrusted the most were the much more popular ones: the church and the voluntary lodges and social clubs, which resembled churches in their irrational pursuit of diversion and escape, and which competed with the NAACP for resources (2:825).

48 Myrdal quoted in David W. Southern, *Gunnar Myrdal and Black-White Relations: The Use and Abuse of "An American Dilemma," 1944–1969* (Baton Rouge: Louisiana State University Press, 1987), 66.

49 Use of the word "revolution" was, by scholarly standards, an exaggeration. But it was not empty rhetoric. The direct action movement did not aim to destroy the federal government or capitalism. Many in its ranks surely aimed only to join the bourgeoisie, not to depose and dispossess it. But important strategists at the movement's core consistently expressed a desire to break from existing society immediately and totally; where the NAACP would not help their movement, they broke away from it.

50 Joseph R. Washington, in *Black Religion: The Negro and Christianity in the United States* (Boston: Beacon Press, 1964), offers a useful corrective, suggesting that black leaders' emphasis on "persuasion" and love was largely rhetori-

cal: it served to camouflage the true "coercion" at work in the movement, to maximize white "guilt," and to provide a Christian pretext and incentive for black masses who, black leaders feared, would not participate without a sentimental "religious sanction" (pp. 6–9). On the difference between personal and political nonviolence, see Chapter 3, n. 46, above, and the section on the intellectual history of the civil rights movement in the Bibliographical Essay.

51 See the reference to Derrick Bell in Chapter 2, n. 49, above.

52 The only serious mistake I have been able to find in David Garrow's prize-winning biography and earlier work on King is the insistence that King adopted coercive beliefs and tactics only after 1962. See Chapter 3, n. 46, above.

53 *Student Voice* 1 (August 1960): 2.

54 Ibid., 7.

55 *Student Voice* 1 (October 1960): 2.

56 This difference between optimism and hope is the mainspring of Christopher Lasch's history of the idea of progress, *The True and Only Heaven*. Richard Lischer, in his admirable study, *The Preacher King*, 57, 236–37, sees the same distinction between optimism and hope.

57 Raboteau, in *A Fire in the Bones: Reflections on African-American Religious History* (Boston: Beacon Press, 1995), 34–35, 187–88, 192–95, emphasizes this point with great clarity, using as his text Frederick Douglass's explanation that slaves' song of heading for Canaan was (in Douglass's words) "more than a hope of reaching heaven. We meant to reach the *North*, and the North was our Canaan." Timothy Fulop finds that, among black Christians, premillennialism did not lead to quietism or withdrawal, as it tended to do outside the black church. Rather, "some of the strongest criticisms of white Christianity and American society can be found in black [pre-]millennialism." Fulop and Raboteau, eds., *African-American Religion: Interpretive Essays* (New York: Routledge, 1997), 247–48. On the general issue, see Timothy P. Weber, *Living in the Shadow of the Second Coming: American Premillennialism, 1875–1925* (New York: Oxford University Press, 1979).

CHAPTER FIVE: THE MOVEMENT AS A REVIVAL

1 Mrs. Johnnie Carr, interview with author, Montgomery, Ala., July 14, 1989.

2 R. D. Nesbitt, interview transcript, 22–23, MLKA.

3 Rufus Lewis, interview transcript, 40–42, MLKA.

4 Ibid. Mississippi activist Unita Blackwell (interview transcript, USM, 47) described how King's "charisma" transformed her: "When he walks in a room, you can feel the presence of Dr. King. . . . You would love to get close to him. When another thing was coming out of Dr. King, he was oozing with, what do they call it . . . charisma? But he had love; he truly loved people. And that used to alienate us. Make us mad. . . . But it was so strange . . . you'd be mad with him—because he told them they had to be nonviolent, and that the Lord

would 'buy it.' And I never thought that I would be saying the same things, you know. But he was right."

5 Carmichael quoted in Clayborne Carson, *In Struggle: SNCC and the Black Awakening of the 1960s* (Cambridge: Harvard University Press, 1981), 164. The once-in-a-lifetime feeling is also recalled by a Mississippi movement veteran in John Dittmer, *Local People: The Struggle for Civil Rights in Mississippi* (Urbana: University of Illinois Press, 1994), 271, and cf. 409.

6 Shuttlesworth, Address to ACMHR, June 1958, Shuttlesworth Papers, 1:1, MLKA.

7 Shuttlesworth, Eighth Annual Address to ACMHR, June 5, 1964, Shuttlesworth Papers, 1:1, MLKA.

8 On Shuttlesworth and Birmingham, see Andrew M. Manis, *A Fire You Can't Put Out: The Civil Rights Life of Birmingham's Reverend Fred Shuttlesworth* (Tuscaloosa: University of Alabama Press, 1999), and Glenn T. Eskew, *But for Birmingham: The Local and National Movements in the Civil Rights Struggle* (Chapel Hill: University of North Carolina Press, 1997).

9 Mary King, in *Freedom Song* (New York: Morrow, 1987), 146, also reported that people outside the movement "invariably called him either a mystic or a saint. Local people in Mississippi used to say that he was 'Moses in the Bible.'" Carson (*In Struggle*, 156) notes that Moses shortened his name to Bob Parris in 1965. See also Eric Burner, *And Gently He Shall Lead Them: Robert Parris Moses and Civil Rights in Mississippi* (New York: New York University Press, 1994), 54, n. 59. I am indebted to Burner's fine biography for much of what I know about this enigmatic leader who refused to reveal much about himself either to interviewers or in the records of SNCC.

10 Lewis interview in Emily Stoper, *The Student Non-violent Coordinating Committee: The Growth of Radicalism in a Civil Rights Organization* (Brooklyn, N.Y.: Carlson, 1989), 128, 140. Jack Newfield (*Village Voice*, December 3, 1964, 3, 21) also compared Moses to the original: see Burner, *And Gently*, 204, 277, n. 15. Lewis later said that Moses "was aware of the godlike reverence he was accorded by others. He knew that many of our SNCC staffers saw him as a Jesus figure, all-knowing and all-holy. That made him so uncomfortable he felt like climbing out of his own skin." Lewis, with Michael D'Orso, *Walking with the Wind: A Memoir of the Movement* (New York: Simon and Schuster, 1998), 293.

11 Higgs interview by Anne Romaine, January 12, 1967, in Romaine, "The Mississippi Freedom Democratic Party through August 1964" (M.A. thesis, University of Virginia, 1970), 289–90; in Burner, *And Gently*, 186–87, n. 76; in James Forman, *The Making of Black Revolutionaries* (New York: Macmillan, 1972; reprint, Washington, D.C.: Open Hand, 1985), 420, n. 1; and in Burner, *And Gently*, 200.

12 Amzie Moore interview by Michael Garvey, Oral History Program, USM, in Burner, *And Gently*, 206, n. 23. Sally Bellfrage describes Fannie Lou Hamer altering a verse of "Go Tell It on the Mountain" to make it, "Who' that yonder dressed in red? / Let my people go. / Look like the children Bob Moses led." Bellfrage stayed in the home of an "intensely religious" black family in

Mississippi: "In a corner near a picture of Christ hung one of Bob Moses." The woman of the house "had cut it out of the *Saturday Evening Post*, put it in a frame, and often gazed at it with love. 'When he first come here I'd *cry* for him. I thought sure they'd kill him. . . . I never thought they'd let him leave alive.'" Bellfrage, *Freedom Summer* (New York: Viking, 1965), 14, 81.

13 Black ministers reported a new high in Sunday church attendance, and local police reported a marked decrease in "Negro crime and drunkenness," according to a local white moderate group. Alabama Council on Human Relations, *Newsletter* 2 (February, March, April 1956): 2.

14 Ralph Abernathy, *And the Walls Came Tumbling Down: An Autobiography* (New York: Harper and Row, 1989), 140.

15 Incident reported in Pat Watters, *Down to Now: Reflections on the Southern Civil Rights Movement* (New York: Pantheon, 1971), 213–16.

16 King, *Stride toward Freedom: The Montgomery Story* (New York: Harper, 1958), 160.

17 Abernathy, *And the Walls*, 140.

18 Coretta Scott King, *My Life with Martin Luther King, Jr.* (New York: Avon, 1970), 159.

19 Epps quoted in Joan Turner Beifuss, *At the River I Stand* (Memphis: St. Luke's Press, 1990), 365–66.

20 King, *Stride*, 134.

21 Vincent Harding and Staughton Lynd, "Albany, Georgia," *Crisis* 70 (February 1963): 74.

22 Fred Winyard, interview transcript, 1995, USM.

23 Lewis quoted in William R. Beardslee, ed., *The Way Out Must Lead In: Life Histories in the Civil Rights Movement*, 2d ed. (Westport, Conn.: Lawrence Hill, 1983), 24. Unita Blackwell (interview transcript, USM, 16–18) traced her induction into the movement to a conversion experience, too, though hers did not take place in a demonstration. In 1957 she started hemorrhaging during childbirth: "People thought I was going to die, but I had this experience, and . . . well I choose to call it a visit from God or whatever." She was "in torment" because she "was really a Christian woman" yet was "in the world" just "partying," but then she "got sick" and looked to the Bible and her pious mother's example to try "to find my way back to the Lord. . . . And he visited me in the form of like a cloud came over the bed." And God told her, "'You shall not die, you has work to do.' . . . And then it started to fall into place," because civil rights organizers were looking for workers who knew the community. "I was scared, but still I would do it anyway. . . . That's how I become on the staff of the Student Non-violent Coordinating Committee." The daughter of sharecroppers, Blackwell loved reading and learning but was unable to finish school. She later became mayor of Mayersville, Miss.

24 S. S. Seay, interview transcript, MLKA, 26. Unita Blackwell (interview transcript, USM, 16–18) made a more general observation that white enemies were immobilized by the religious movement: "Cause this movement is bigger than us, bigger than any individual." The authorities would try to "wipe out the

leadership and more would spring up. . . . So everytime they kill off a group, it don't do anything but reinforce. It was like the Christians, you know. Paul was killing Christians, and when he end up, he was one himself, you know."

25 Aldon Morris's interview with Speed, quoted in Morris, *Origins of the Civil Rights Movement: Black Communities Organizing for Change* (New York: Free Press, 1984), 98.

26 Ibid., 96–99. In the Mississippi movement, there was also widespread dissatisfaction with the conservatism of the black clergy on the eve of the civil rights movement. See Dittmer, *Local People*, 65–67, 150–52, 265, 268–69. Richard King, in *Civil Rights and the Idea of Freedom* (New York: Oxford University Press, 1992), 202, 207, also hints at a revival parallel. Albert Raboteau, in *A Fire in the Bones: Reflections on African-American Religious History* (Boston: Beacon Press, 1995), 59, describes the movement of the 1950s as a "revival" with a slightly different meaning but does not develop the parallel. James Finlay, in *Church People in the Struggle* (New York: Oxford University Press, 1993), argues that during the movement a sense of God's presence took root in the northern mainline denominations but then passed out of them.

27 Sheriff Thomas Gilmore, interview, in Beardslee, *The Way Out Must Lead In*, 144.

28 Wilmore, *Black Religion and Black Radicalism*, 2d ed. (Maryknoll, N.Y.: Orbis, 1983), 177. Benjamin Mays, King's mentor from undergraduate days, complained about the otherworldly emphasis of southern black churches in *The Negro's God* (Boston: Chapman and Grimes, 1938). In a report on motivating black people to vote, the Citizen Education Project noted that its leaders were planning a series of conferences for ministers on "The Bible and the Ballot," which would "help to overcome some of the ill effects of a pious, Personalistic religion which has no pro[p]hetic concern for the community. Our experience has been that this gives ministers some theological basis for participating in voter registration." Semi-Annual Report to the Field Foundation, July 1, 1962, to January 31, 1963, SCLC Papers, 136:29, MLKA.

29 King, *Why We Can't Wait* (New York: Harper and Row, 1964), 101.

30 Septima Clark, interview transcript, MLKA, 78–80. Charles Payne does not use Clark's testimony, but his thorough analysis in *I've Got the Light of Freedom: The Organizing Tradition and the Mississippi Freedom Struggle* (Berkeley: University of California Press, 1995), 169–72, was helpful in establishing the context of the incident. The dog biting is also narrated in [signature illegible], Executive Secretary, LeFlore County Chapter of the NAACP, to Curtis Larry, July 20, 1963, copy in NAACP Papers, LC, ser. 3, file C.74. Tucker tells his own story in testimony before the Mississippi Advisory Committee [of the Civil Rights Commission], April 17, 1963, copy in Leadership Council on Civil Rights Papers, LC, box E5, Title I folder, pp. 89–100.

The sacraments were by no means always nonviolent. Unita Blackwell (interview transcript, USM, 39–41) described abuse by jailers in Jackson. She saw the "worst torture that could be done to women." Finally one woman could not endure it: "They grabbed this woman, this is a big woman, and they was going to drag her, and she reached up and grabbed this man between the legs and caught hold of his testicles, and they call him Red. . . . I will never forget that incident, and Red throwed up both hands and lost his stick; she took his gun, everything, Red gave it up, cause she got hold of his testicles, and then we all went to hollering and laughing, cause we couldn't do anything else, and he was trying to scream; the man couldn't say nothing; he was just in a mess, but Red had harassed this woman till she couldn't take no more. . . . And so Red was laid out; he buckled down and went to his knees. . . . You see Red with his eyes, bulged out and going down, and this woman, she was just baptized, she was harassed into doing this violent thing." Jackson was sued for $100 thousand, "and they had to pay off, for their police."

31 K. S. DuPont, transcript of Jackson Ice's interview, 28–29, Florida State University Archives. Unita Blackwell (interview transcript, USM, 38) said that a black man was sent or hired to provoke a fight with her "so he could legitimately shoot me." She attributed her salvation to a voice that came out of nowhere telling her not to argue but just turn away, "and the Lord always takes care of me."

32 Larry Guyot, interview transcript, USM. Guyot, a Catholic, had been very involved in church as a youth.

33 Taylor Branch reports on these meetings in *Parting the Waters: America in the King Years* (New York: Simon and Schuster, 1988), 594–95.

34 David J. Garrow, *Bearing the Cross: Martin Luther King, Jr., and the Southern Christian Leadership Conference* (1986; reprint, New York: Vintage, 1988), 97. See also Edward L. Moore, "Billy Graham and Martin Luther King: An Inquiry into Black and White Revival Traditions" (Ph.D. diss., Vanderbilt, 1977).

35 William Martin, "Billy Graham," in *The Varieties of Southern Evangelicalism*, ed. David Harrell Jr. (Macon, Ga.: Mercer University Press, 1981), 84. See also "No Color Line in Heaven: Billy Graham," *Ebony*, April 1960, and the section on Graham in Chapter 7, below.

36 *Birmingham News* clippings, 1961–65, Shuttlesworth Papers, 4:15, MLKA.

37 Wyatt Tee Walker, interview transcript, CRDP, 78, Howard University, Founders' Library, Washington, D.C.

38 Rustin, in *My Soul Is Rested*, ed. Howell Raines (New York: Penguin, 1983), 57.

39 See, e.g., Montgomery County (Alabama) Citizens' Council, *States' Rights Advocate* 1 (June 28, 1956): 3.

40 Reinhold Niebuhr, *Moral Man and Immoral Society* (New York: Scribner's, 1932), 172–79, 234–56.

41 Slater King, draft article for *Freedomways* with March 1965 cover letter, Slater King Papers, Personal Correspondence, "undated," MLKA.

42 Young quoted in *New York Times*, July 22, 1963.

43 Shuttlesworth, Eighth Annual Address to ACMHR, June 5, 1964, Shuttlesworth Papers, 1:1, MLKA.

44 According to *Newsweek* ("Selma, Civil Rights, and the Church Militant,"

March 1965), the Episcopal suffragan bishop of Michigan declared, "The American Negro, in his travail, is causing the rebirth of the white church." The bishop saw a "revolution" in the church. "More than that," the magazine commented, "there may be a new reformation going on, too—one that may bring the churches closer together rather than tear them apart. In the age of Martin Luther, the churches discovered the individual conscience. In the age of Martin Luther King, the churches may be discovering how to put the individual conscience to work." The article noted that "some thoughtful ministers" saw a "danger" ahead: "that organized religion may fail to recognize that it needs the civil-rights movement more than the movement needs the churches."

45 Interview transcript of a Mr. Johnson, Morehouse College classmate of King's, Montgomery Bus Boycott Papers, folder 64, MLKA. Cf. Fannie Lou Hamer: "But you see you concerned about the real problems of this country, and that's Christianity. And that's the hope of this country." Project South interview transcript, MFDP, chap. 55, p. 0491-12.

46 ACMHR, press release, March 19, 1964, p. 3, Shuttlesworth Papers, 1:15, MLKA.

47 It is commonplace to see the Second Great Awakening in the Protestant churches in the North leading to the great wave of reform movements, especially abolitionism. See remarks on revivals in the Bibliographical Essay.

48 McLoughlin, *Revivals, Awakenings, and Reform: An Essay on Religion and Social Change in America, 1607-1978* (Chicago: University of Chicago Press, 1978), xiii, 1. This important work brings social theory and social science research to bear on the history of religion. See also McLoughlin's standard work, *Modern Revivalism: Charles Grandison Finney to Billy Graham* (New York: Ronald Press, 1959).

49 On the enumeration of "Awakenings" in the American past, see section on the social effects of revivals in the Bibliographical Essay.

50 Paul Johnson, *A Shopkeeper's Millennium* (New York: Hill and Wang, 1978); Allen Tullos, *Habits of Industry: White Culture and the Transformation of the Carolina Piedmont* (Chapel Hill: University of North Carolina Press, 1989); Rhys Isaac, *The Transformation of Virginia, 1740-1790* (Chapel Hill: University of North Carolina Press, 1982); Karen E. Fields, *Revival and Rebellion in Colonial Central Africa* (Princeton, N.J.: Princeton University Press, 1981).

51 Cf. Wilmore (*Black Religion and Black Radicalism*, 186): "No brainwashing appropriation of Marxist dogma or of some other purely materialistic philosophy of social change could have awakened the awe-inspiring sense of mission and prophetic gifts that were released in Malcolm X by his conversion to Islam." Wilmore quoted Malcolm X as saying, "The only true world solution today . . . is governments guided by true religion—of the spirit." Bob Moses noted that mass meetings, with their "testifying" and other expressions of enthusiasm, were the "energy machine" of the movement in Mississippi. Quoted in Dittmer, *Local People*, 131.

52 The role of religion in public life today has been provocatively raised by several authors. Among them, Kathleen Kennedy Townsend, in "Why Are Liberals Afraid of God?" *Washington Post*, March 16, 1982, takes her readers to task for leaving religion to right-wingers, adding the interesting point that "liberals who mock the idea of sin and punishment and find evangelists particularly odious are often able to tolerate and even applaud this type of religiosity among blacks." Michael Ferber, in "A Religious Revival on the Left," *Nation* (July 6/13, 1985), provides examples of religious movements for social change and a compelling argument for converting other movements for social change into religious ones. He does not, however, propose dropping the "left" label, which has long since lost its ability to inspire (or even to describe accurately) commitment to social change. Robert Bellah et al., in *Habits of the Heart: Individualism and Commitment in American Life* (New York: Harper and Row, 1986), accord religion an important role in what still holds some movements for renewal together. Glenn Tinder, in "Can We Be Good without God?" *Atlantic* (December 1989), 69–85, and in *The Political Meaning of Christianity* (Baton Rouge: Louisiana State University Press, 1990), and Stephen L. Carter, in *The Culture of Disbelief: How American Law and Politics Trivialize Religious Devotion* (New York: Basic Books, 1993), plumb the consequences of ignoring and suppressing religion in efforts to remake the world. Ken Leech, in *Subversive Orthodoxy: Traditional Faith and Radical Commitment* (Toronto: Anglican Book Centre, 1992), and Jim Wallis, in *The Soul of Politics: Beyond "Religious Right" and "Secular Left"* (San Diego: Harcourt Brace, 1995), each in different ways suggest how sacrificial religious commitments may engender more than trivial social work. But Eugene McCarraher's bracing history, *Christian Critics: Religion and the Impasse in Modern American Social Thought* (Ithaca, N.Y.: Cornell University Press, 2000), reminds us how difficult it is to translate religious commitments into politics without distorting them.

53 The degree to which northern readiness to take a stand against southern bigotry depends on northern bigotry—demeaning stereotypes of the white South—is a fascinating subject well plumbed by Allison Graham, *Framing the South: Hollywood, Television, and Racism during the Civil Rights Struggle* (Baltimore: Johns Hopkins University Press, 2001). See also Taeku Lee, *Mobilizing Public Opinion: Black Insurgency and Racial Attitudes in the Civil Rights Era* (Chicago: University of Chicago Press, 2000).

54 Historians have finally documented what they always assumed—that a "cold war motive" lay behind much liberal and other federal action in favor of civil rights. See Mary Dudziak, *Cold War Civil Rights: Race and the Image of American Democracy* (Princeton, N.J.: Princeton University Press, 2000), and Azza Salama Layton, *International Politics and Civil Rights Policies in the United States, 1941–1960* (Cambridge: Cambridge University Press, 2000).

1 The title of this chapter alludes to C. C. Goen, *Broken Churches, Broken Nation: Denominational Schisms and the Coming of the American Civil War* (Macon, Ga.: Mercer University Press, 1985). See the section on religious factionalism in the Bibliographical Essay.

2 The Southern Manifesto was also signed by every House delegate from Alabama, Arkansas, Louisiana, Mississippi, South Carolina, and Virginia; by all but one from Florida and Tennessee; by all but three from North Carolina; and by half of those from Texas. For a searching analysis of how this unity was achieved, see Anthony J. Badger, "The Southern Manifesto," unpublished paper delivered at Southern Historical Association Conference, Orlando, 1993, 2; copy in author's possession. The state-level resistance also garnered remarkable unity among politicians. The key vote for "interposition" against the U.S. Supreme Court in 1956 passed the Virginia House 90 to 5 and the Senate 36 to 2; it passed unanimously in the Mississippi legislature. A related though milder resolution of protest received a unanimous vote in both houses of the South Carolina legislature. A stronger nullification resolution passed the Georgia House 178 to 1 and the Senate 39 to 0. See *Southern School News*, March, April 1956. At times even Myrdal saw a unified white South. His optimism about white folk was not seamless: there were exceptions to prove his rule. Like mainstream liberals (see Schlesinger on the South, quoted in Chapter 2, n. 11, above), Myrdal could be pessimistic about the white South—that sink of backward provincialism that figured so prominently in liberal mythology from the 1930s on—as a counterpoint to optimism about the country as a whole, which had the sense to move past the recalcitrant South. He said that white people in the South (but not the North), were "united . . . in a systematic effort to keep the Negroes suppressed." Myrdal, *An American Dilemma: The Negro Problem and Modern Democracy*, 2 vols. (1944; reprint, New York: Harper and Row, 1962), 2:777. Strictly speaking, this does not contradict Myrdal's point (noted above in Chapter 2) that "a majority even of [white] Southerners" (1:48) would support racial justice *if* they were to gain true understanding. Their recalcitrance—like the "pessimism" of what Myrdal took to be a small number of revolutionary Negroes like W. E. B. Du Bois—exempted them from the general rule of optimism.

3 In Virginia, the home of "massive resistance," Baptists appeared unusually tolerant of civil rights. In 1958 Lucius Polhill, an official of the state baptist association, assured the SBC leadership that there was little to fear from Virginia. There had been only one sign of trouble, a request motivated by "pressure groups" to petition the SBC about local church contributions to SBC programs that distributed integrationist propaganda. The request "died from lack of interest and support." Other than that, there were only "a few scattered eruptions." Polhill noted that one of the major speakers at the Virginia convention was Brooks Hays, by then a target (something of a lighting rod)

for segregationist anger: "It was most encouraging to see how the messengers stayed through to the end and gave Brooks their unanimous endorsement." Polhill to Porter Wreathe [Routh?], November 14, 1958, Executive Committee Papers, SBC Archives, box 100. South Carolina, too, became a hotbed of extreme segregationism, but as late as July 1957 the head of the CLC was confident that it would not give much trouble. "I do not believe the [segregationist] movement will spread in South Carolina," he wrote, "and I am *sure* it will not spread throughout the convention." A. C. Miller to Fred Laughon, July 23, 1957, CLC Papers, SBC Archives, box 11.

4 Segregationist William D. Workman summarized the positions of the various southern denominational bodies in *The Case for the South* (New York: Devin-Adair, 1960), 99–101, as did the pamphlet (which also summarized the northern bodies' positions for comparison), *The Churches Speak* (New York: United Church Women, NCC, n.d.), copy in CLC Resource Files, SBC Archives, box 4. See also Samuel Southard, "Are Southern Churches Silent?," *Christian Century*, November 20, 1963, 1429–32; Ed Cony, "More Southern Pastors Plead for 'Moderation' . . . ," *Wall Street Journal*, February 14, 1958; and "Southern Churches Urge Mixing," *Citizens' Council* 3 (May 1958).

5 Brooks Hays, whose presidential sermon supported integration, was reelected in 1958. There was some opposition that year to Hays from a minority, but the vote was not recorded. See *SBC Annual* (1958). I am indebted to Bill Sumners for patient explanations of SBC politics and procedures. Commenting on Hays's reelection, J. Wayne Flynt states that Leon Macon, editor of the *Alabama Baptist*, declined to publish Hays's address because it "called for racial integration" and dealt more with politics than religion. Flynt, *Alabama Baptists: Southern Baptists in the Heart of Dixie* (Tuscaloosa: University of Alabama Press, 1998), 461; see also Mark Newman, *Getting Right with God: Southern Baptists and Desegregation, 1945–1995* (Tuscaloosa: University of Alabama Press, 2001), 151–52. But that was not a step toward segregation even on Macon's part. It was a move toward official denominational neutrality, which, coming from a segregationist in the 1950s, was more an admission of segregationist weakness than an effort to preserve segregation, as will be seen below. Hays was succeeded in 1959 by Ramsey Pollard, who was known for spending more time on evangelism than racial issues. But, again, that means that the SBC only shifted toward a noncommittal course, not a segregationist course. For more discussion of this issue, see the section on segregationists' public religion in the Bibliographical Essay.

Southern Methodists (who reunited in 1939) and Episcopalians (who had never divided) also participated in *pro-Brown* resolutions; only two of the local conferences of Methodists in the South were able to muster segregationist majorities (and even in those, the vote was not overwhelming). See Chapter 7, n. 16, below, and Donald Collins, *When the Church Bell Rang Racist: The Methodist Church and the Civil Rights Movement in Alabama* (Macon, Ga.: Mercer University Press, 1998). Only pockets of opposition to desegregation appeared among southern Episcopalians, though these could get nasty. See nn. 71–75, below, and Gardiner Shattuck, *Episcopalians and Race: Civil War to Civil Rights* (Lexington: University Press of Kentucky, 2000).

6 Yet only three state Baptist conventions appear to have had a significant segregationist presence in their hierarchies: only Louisiana's and Mississippi's state Baptist journals condemned the *Brown* decision; only Louisiana's and Alabama's positively endorsed segregated education. See Newman, *Getting Right*, 24–27, 120. In 1955 the Alabama Baptist Convention hosted its first black speaker, the Rev. U. J. Robinson, who announced, "The world and God does not know us as White and Colored Baptists, 'but Baptists.'" Alabama Baptist officials resisted attempts to politicize their state convention, and the convention demanded that the Baptist Laymen of Alabama (which the officials called the "white supremacy group within our state") "drop the word 'Baptists' from their name." Likewise, an official of the Mississippi Baptist Convention said that a similar breakaway group of segregationists, Baptist Laymen of Mississippi, "has no sanction, approval, or authority from the state convention." Lee Porter, "Southern Baptists and Race Relations, 1948–1963" (Th.D. diss., Southwestern Theological Seminary, Fort Worth, Tex., 1965), 113, 99–104. *None* of the state Baptist conventions supported active resistance to desegregation, let alone violence or law breaking.

As editor of the *Alabama Baptist*, Leon Macon was probably the most highly placed devotee of segregation in the entire SBC. His public segregationism, however, appears to have been more moderate than the kind championed by W. A. Criswell or other renegades quoted below (also more moderate than his own privately expressed views). At first, Macon urged readers to comply with *Brown*: "Southern Baptist[s] are not willing to become rebels again, but to work along quietly and sympathetically to carry out the Supreme Court decision." Though Macon's segregationism seems to have intensified in the years leading up to his death in 1965, his public view was generally that Christians must obey civil authority and that church figures should stay out of politics— unlike the position of militant segregationists, who wanted their clergy to lead aggressively and to preach a moral duty to defy civil authority. Macon did not dare take a public stand against the most prominent and probably most effective integrationist in the SBC, Billy Graham. Also, as Lee Porter, Edward Queen, and Mark Newman point out, Macon allowed free discussion of both sides of the issue in his journal. Finally, on September 5, 1963, Macon instructed his readers to accept federal desegregation orders based on the Bible's command to obey civil authority. (On disestablishmentarian grounds, Macon opposed a segregationist constitutional amendment to guarantee white parents the "choice" of a "private" segregated school supported by tax dollars.) See Macon's editorials, *Alabama Baptist*, May 3, 1956, February 20, 1958, February 26, September 10, 1959, July 14, 1960, April 20, June 8, 1961, September 5, October 3, 24, November 7, 1963, July 23, December 3, 1964, April 1, June 24, 1965; Porter, "Southern Baptists and Race," 98–99; Flynt, *Alabama Baptists*, 456, 460–62, 465, 470–71, 481, 483–84; Newman, *Getting Right*, 28–31, 89, 114, 120–21; and Edward L. Queen, *In the South the Baptists Are the Cen-*

ter of Gravity: Southern Baptists and Social Change, 1930–1980 (Brooklyn, N.Y.: Carlson, 1991), 91–93. Other prominent segregationists in the SBC included L. L. Gwaltney, editor of the *Alabama Baptist* before Macon, and H. T. Sullivan, whose polemics were published in the Louisiana Baptist Convention's *Baptist Message*, edited by the segregationist Finley Tinnin.

7 The Rev. Fred Laughon of First Baptist Church, Orangeburg, S.C. (quoting or paraphrasing segregationist leaders in his congregation) to A. C. Miller, July 15, 1957, CLC Papers, SBC Archives, box 11. Pastor J. I. Jacobs of Duncan Baptist Church, Duncan, Miss., wrote that one of his deacons believed that the SBC had recently passed a resolution approving integration. Though Jacobs was "*sure* that no such resolution was passed," he told the SBC: "We do not want any such issue even though it is false to tear apart the harmony of our church. We have a few who are very radical on this issue of integration and because of their political convictions could injure the church's spirit." Jacobs to Miller, June 10, 1957, ibid.

8 James Wright to Porter Routh, September 4, 1958, Executive Committee Papers, SBC Archives, box 82. Hays was often a target of segregationist ire. See, e.g., "Eisenhower, Nixon Conspiring to Force Race Mixing: Hays Tricks Baptists," *Augusta Courier*, June 16, 1958. Many segregationist resolutions cited in Chapter 7, below, forthrightly accuse the SBC of advocating integration; most of the others take that for granted. W. J. Simmons, president of the Citizens' Councils of America and editor of the *Citizens' Council*, complained to the SBC executive Porter Routh that Routh had denied the active integrationism attributed to him in the magazine. Simmons defended his own effort to out the closet integrationists in the SBC:

> A careful re-reading of the AP article by Mr. George W. Cornell on which our remarks were based conveys the distinct impression that you favor integration and the action of the Southern Baptist Convention in 1954 holding that integration is 'in harmony . . . with the Christian principles of equal justice and love for all men.' It is our purpose to be scrupulously accurate in *The Citizens' Council* at all times. If you do not favor integration and if you do not support the Southern Baptist Convention action in 1954 with respect to the Supreme Court's integration decree, we will hasten to make correction in our paper upon your statement as to your true position. [paragraphing altered from original]

Simmons to Routh, January 15, 1958, Executive Committee Papers, SBC Archives, box 82.

9 Carey Daniel, "God, the Original Segregationist" (emphasis removed), pamphlet distributed by Bible Book Store, Dallas, May 23, 1954, copy in Sam Ervin Papers, UNC-CH, box 340. The pamphlet was advertised in the *Citizens' Council*, July 1957. Other examples of Daniel's work include "Immigration Not Integration Is the Answer," copy in Williams Papers, MDAH, RG 59, RO33-B022-S4-10395—vol. 289, and "God Laughs at the Race-Mixers: 101 Best Jokes on Mixiecrats versus Dixiecrats," copy in Hays Papers, SBC

Archives, box 3. At one point Daniel was president of the Central Texas Division of the Citizens' Councils of America. As a southern Baptist, he informed Brooks Hays that his church planned to cut off all contributions to the CLC, which was making the SBC endorse "the U.S. Supreme Court's unscriptural and unconstitutional amalgamation laws." He had "more Baptist preachers in our local Dallas unit than ministers of all other denominations put together," and "Baptists were the largest church group that voted in the recent referendum in which Texans voted over four to one for interposition and continued segregation. Yet you people continue to try to give the impression that the great majority of Southern Baptists favor race-mixing. If you keep this up you will soon split the SBC wide open—and it SHOULD split before it agrees to making America a mulatto nation." Enclosing his book, he asked Hays to introduce a resolution "CONDEMNING the Supreme Court's mongrelization laws" and noted that the new Texas governor, "an active Baptist" and "outspoken segregationist," was his first cousin, Price Daniel. Daniel to Hays, June 3, 1957, Hays Papers, SBC Archives, box 2.

10 The Rev. Leon Burns, "Why Desegregation Will Fail," speech delivered at West Seventh St. Church of Christ, Columbia, Tenn., March 24, 1957, distributed by Burns, copy in Allen Papers, SBC Archives, no box number. Roy Harris's militantly segregationist *Augusta Courier* ran a summary of Burns's sermon, June 16, 1958.

11 One example is the rhetoric of the Rev. Henry Lyon of Montgomery's Highland Avenue Baptist Church. See Flynt, *Alabama Baptists*, 467, 478. Another is that of the Rev. William Bodenhamer, of Ty Ty Baptist Church in Tift County, Ga., also a leader in the States' Rights Council of Georgia and later candidate for governor. See Newman, *Getting Right*, 58, 158. A third example is that of Wm. Manlius Nevins, "Segregation versus Integration" (n.d., n.p.), copies in Williams Papers, MDAH, RG 59, RO33-BO22-S4-10395—vol. 289, and in NAACP Papers, LC, ser. III.A, box 151.

12 For the sources on which this judgment is based, see sections on segregationist religion and segregation in general in the Bibliographical Essay.

13 Roy Harris, for example, bemoaned the lack of unity and militancy among segregationists. Harris called for a million-dollar southern advertising campaign to sell "the case of the South" up North. "And I tell you we have something to sell." But first, he warned, "we got some missionary work to do at home." If the South were united, "we would not have to spend time speaking to you here in New Orleans again. We should be in Yankee land tonight." Harris urged a boycott of "scalawag" merchants and business leaders in New Orleans. *New Orleans States*, October 31, 1956, copy in Clipping Files, ADL Office, New York. The president of the right-wing American States' Rights Association believed, like most extreme segregationists, that the biggest obstacle to a white supremacist takeover was apathy and passivity of the white South: "Our people (the white people) must be shocked out of complacency." Olin Horton to James F. Byrnes, July 6, 1955, Byrnes Papers, CU, f. 817 (4).

14 According to the records of the Synod of Mississippi, Gillespie retired from

Bellhaven on July 1, 1954. His obituary in the same source states that he was preaching two days before his death on November 18, 1958. He was head of an investigating committee that reported to the synod in 1957 and 1958. Synod of Mississippi Records, PCUS Archives, 124th sess., p. 384, 127th sess., p. 634, 128th sess., pp. 17–19, 129th sess., p. 197.

15 A slightly more subtle inference is that biblical literalism was incompatible with segregationist militancy. This means that it was always hard to reconcile segregationism with another kind of social conservatism then growing in the South: Fundamentalism.

16 Gillespie, "A Christian View on Segregation," address, November 4, 1954 (reproduced by the Citizens' Council, Jackson, Miss.), in Citizens' Councils of America Literature Collection, UA, ser. v., box 146, and in NAACP Papers, LC, ser. III.A, box 282.

17 T. Robert Ingram, ed., *Essays on Segregation* (Houston: St. Thomas Press, 1960), 18–19.

18 Ibid.; Ingram to Waring, August 25, 1960, Waring Papers, SCHS, box 408. Apparently Waring did not reply.

19 Dees's last concession seems odd given that one of the Episcopalians' two southern seminaries, the School of Theology at the University of the South, had recently been the scene of a bitter desegregation battle (see nn. 71–74 below). The Rev. James P. Dees, Address to Lion's Club, Statesville, N.C., "Is It Necessary for a Christian to Support Integration?," copy attached to Dees to Bell, August 5, 1958, Bell Papers, f. 43–12, BGC, and copies in Ervin Papers, UNC-CH, box 340. Dees also contributed to Ingram's collection, *Essays on Segregation*.

20 Dr. Medford Evans, "A Methodist Declaration of Conscience on Racial Segregation," *Citizen*, January 1963, 10–13. This also appeared in *Information Bulletin* 40 (January 1963) of the Mississippi Association of Methodist Ministers and Laymen, a small faction of segregationist Methodists who fought against the Methodist leadership. Copy in Association of Citizens' Councils of Mississippi Files, MDAH, box 1. This was the best that the Citizens' Council could come up with in response to a "widely publicized pro-integration statement by a small group of Mississippi Methodist clergymen." Rather than find positive warrant for segregation, Evans confined himself to questioning the biblical references of integrationists. Whereas they cited Paul's statement that "there is neither Jew nor Greek . . . bond nor free . . . male nor female," etc. (Galatians 3:26–28), Evans pointed out, reasonably enough, that Paul disavowed earthly egalitarianism elsewhere in the Bible, specifically insisting on female silence in church (I Corinthians 14:34) and slave obedience to masters (Ephesians 6:5). No prominent segregationist in the mid-twentieth-century South advocated slavery or the gagging of female parishioners, however, which may explain Evans's swift backpedaling away from the clear implication of these verses. Evans was a John Birch Society official and contributor to the new right-wing *National Review*. See John Judis, *William F. Buckley, Jr.* (New York: Simon and Schuster, 1988), 194–95.

Also confining biblical references to brief attempts to refute integrationism were the Rev. James Dees, Speech in Statesville, N.C., May 9, 1955, reprint from *Statesville Record and Landmark*, May 10, 1955, in Ervin Papers, UNC-CH, box 340, and the Rev. Henry T. Egger, Sermon at St. Peter's Episcopal Church, Charlotte, N.C., September 15, 1957 (biblical references limited to an argument that Paul's statement, "ye are all one in Jesus Christ," does not require "enforced physical proximity" on earth, and the briefest mention of Acts 17:26, on God's separation of "nations"), ibid., box 341. Like Evans's declaration, these speeches are devoted mostly to nonreligious ideas.

21 A resolution from the Santee Baptist Association in South Carolina, which was copied by four or five churches in the area, mentioned the "bounds of habitation" passage, offering one brief, evasive sentence as to its meaning. The resolutions omitted the passage immediately preceding it (arguably the overriding point), that God made those nations "of one blood." They mentioned no other Bible verse. See below, Chap. 7, nn. 19–30, on the protest resolutions sent to the CLC.

22 Quotations in this and the next two paragraphs are from Gillespie's, "A Christian View on Segregation," 1954, in Citizens' Council of America Literature Collection, UA, ser. v, box 146, and NAACP Papers, LC, ser. III.A, box 282.

23 Gillespie's address was reprinted, among other places, in the *SPJ*, June 5, 1957, 7–12, and in the *Natchez Times*, November 22, 1954. (I am grateful to Steven Niven for bringing the latter clipping to my attention.) Gillespie devotes only 5 of his 15 pages to the Bible; the first half of his speech concerns nonbiblical arguments. The obscure Rev. Leon Burns rehearsed the same arguments as Gillespie and Daniel but did not mention them until the end; less than 3 pages of his 16½-page pamphlet relates to the Bible. Burns, "Why Desegregation Will Fail," speech delivered at West Seventh St. Church of Christ, Columbia, Tenn., March 24, 1957, in Allen Papers, SBC Archives, no box number. For a briefer, somewhat less coherent argument using the same Old Testament references as Gillespie, see *Christian Battle Cry* 1 (April 1956), copy in NAACP Papers, LC, ser. III.I, box 21.

Billy James Hargis, the adventurous right-wing evangelist from Tulsa, Okla., relied on Gillespie for pro-segregation exegesis, devoting a whole chapter to Gillespie's argument, beginning with the phrase, "While the Bible contains no clear mandate for or against segregation." Hargis himself is more confident: "It is my conviction that God ordained segregation," he is at pains to insist by way of introducing Gillespie. "It is impossible for me to otherwise interpret Acts 17:26," which he quotes. He reduces the first clause—a resolute statement, much beloved by integrationists, establishing monogenesis—to lowercase (other segregationists omitted it altogether), then capitalizes "AND HATH DETERMINED THE TIMES BEFORE APPOINTED, THE BOUNDS OF THEIR HABITATION." Hargis, *The Truth about Segregation*, published by Hargis, Tulsa, n.d., copy in Wallace Papers, ADAH, box RC2 G320. Another tract that follows Gillespie's pattern is Dr. Charles O. Benham (editor of *National Forecast* magazine of Topton, N.C.), "X-Raying the Racial Issue: Is

Integration Scriptural?" Benham lards his biblical references to separation of *nations* with racist quotations from Abraham Lincoln and Booker T. Washington. He is confident and well founded when he claims (like Evans): "The apostles nowhere give any hint that all linguistic, national or racial differences are to be wiped out in the Gospel dispensation. Paul asserts the unity of all believers *in Christ*" (emphasis added)—not on earth. This is an effective attack on the use of the Bible "by 'progressive' ministers in their endeavor to prove the theory of mongrelization of races" (pp. 11–12, 17), but it is not a positive justification for or defense of segregation. At any rate, Benham's pronounced anti-Semitism marks it as the kind of argument that most respectable and prominent segregationists shunned. Copy in Wallace Papers, ADAH, box RC2 G320.

24 Morton H. Smith, "Bible Study. . . . Lesson 8. Brotherhood and Race" (Women's Work sec.), *SPJ*, July 3, 1957, 17–21. Smith added, "Paul in Romans 14 teaches further . . . that we must . . . not . . . condemn a fellow Christian who . . . may not feel as we do about some specific matter." It is significant that, unlike Daniel and Burns, Smith made no attempt to qualify the Bible's clear position on monogenesis: "The Bible teaches that all men descend from one common pair of first parents"; "again, in the flood we find all of humanity destroyed except for one family. . . . This unity of human kind is further confirmed in the common nature that we all possess. It is seen in the fact that we are all sinners. It is seen in the fact that the Gospel is offered to all men alike." Smith quoted Paul in Acts 17, adding, "Even despite the differences of national and racial heritage among men, they are all one human kind." Whereas the integrationist used such statements to teach "that we are all brothers, and should thus ignore all differences and mix as one race," Smith asserted, "It should be noted, in passing, that the Biblical concept of brotherhood is not primarily that of the physical unity, but rather that of the spiritual unity that Christians . . . know and experience." He argued, correctly, that "the very verse used by the integrationists as supporting their position also speaks of the diversity of peoples." He also referred to the Tower of Babel, cautiously stating that that story "may not be the origin of the races, but it certainly is the Divine separation of peoples into different groups." He mentioned the story of the sons of Noah in Genesis 9–10, which "may well be" where "the origin of the races is to be found." For example, "the descendants of Shem are still known as the Semitic people. Though it is not absolutely demonstrable that the modern races stem directly from these three divisions, it seems likely that the primitive origin of the races is to be seen here." From all this he concluded, in the typical anticlimax of literate segregationists: "It is certain that in the combined accounts of . . . Noah and . . . the Tower of Babel we find God's direct action of separation of different elements of the human race into different groups. . . . [Therefore] it would seem that the principle of separation of peoples or of segregation is not necessarily wrong *per se*." Tacking on a reference to the cutting off of Jews from all others in the Old Testament, he added: "It should be noted that this segregation of Abraham's seed was done

by God ultimately for the purpose of preserving their religious purity, yet it was done by means of racial segregation. This is not the situation that faces us today, but at least the principle of segregation is seen as something that is not inherently evil."

Smith derived "a general principle . . . indirectly from scripture" that "intermarriage" and "amalgamation" would conflict with God's plan. Since God "made the different races as different races it would seem to be at least questionable as to whether man should seek to amalgamate the races. Babel was an attempt to do so." Smith quoted B. M. Palmer, first moderator of PCUS in 1872, to that effect. Even so, Smith entertained qualifications: segregation originated when Negroes "were looked upon as an inferior race, a point that cannot necessarily be upheld today." With respect to the *Brown* decision, Smith repeated the point of an earlier lesson that "the Christian is to be subject to the powers that be," though he went on to countenance claims that the Court had behaved unconstitutionally.

25 E.g., Daniel, "God, the Original Segregationist"; Daniel, "Let's Return Africa to Her Stolen Children . . . a Sequel to 'God, the Original Segregationist,'" n.d., distributed by author, copy in Williams Papers, MDAH, box 289 (f. Seg, 1950s). See also A. A. Hinson, handwritten letter to CLC, "July, 1957," CLC Papers, SBC Archives, box 11, and Frank Garrett Sr., "Christianity Review Segregation or Integration," n.d., copy in Bates Papers, SHSW, box 5. On antebellum uses of the curse of Ham, see George Fredrickson, *The Black Image in the White Mind* (1971; reprint, Middletown, Conn.: Wesleyan University Press, 1987), 88–99. On the broader uses of the same story to justify nonracial subordination, see David Brion Davis, *The Problem of Slavery in Western Culture* (Ithaca, N.Y.: Cornell University Press, 1966), 63–64, 97–98, 451–53, and Paul H. Freedman, *Images of the Medieval Peasant* (Stanford, Calif.: Stanford University Press, 1999), chap. 4. The leading conservative Evangelical magazine ran an article denouncing the segregationist use of the Ham story by a professor of Old Testament at the Southern Baptist Theological Seminary, Louisville, who held degrees from that seminary and the University of Richmond. See Clyde T. Francisco, "The Curse on Canaan," *Christianity Today*, April 24, 1964, 678–80.

26 Daniel, "God, the Original Segregationist."

27 W. A. Criswell, "Christianity and Segregation," address to South Carolina Legislature, n.d. [February 22, 1956], Citizens' Council of America Literature Collection, UA, ser. v, box 146. The probable date comes from correspondence about the speech elsewhere: Porter Routh to Charles F. Sims, April 2, 1956 (box 88), and Criswell to Routh, March 23, 1956 (box 82), Executive Committee Papers, SBC Archives. The speech was briefly covered in *Southern School News*, March 1956. Background on Criswell is in Robert DuCasse, "A History of the First Baptist Church, Dallas, Texas" (M.T. thesis, Dallas Theological Seminary, 1964), and in Leon McBeth, *The First Baptist Church of Dallas: Centennial History* (Grand Rapids, Mich.: Zondervan, 1968).

28 At least one segregationist, Finley Tinnin, editor of the *Baptist Message*, criti-

cized Criswell, saying that his "unfortunate references to the segregation issue . . . [were] deeply deplored by all opposed to cheap and tawdry language in a controversy that calls for clear thinking. . . . It is no time for fanaticism and mudslinging. The battle will be lost when we resort to such crude tactics." Quoted in Porter, "Southern Baptists and Race," 98.

29 Ernest Campbell and Thomas Pettigrew, in *Christians in Racial Crisis: A Study of Little Rock's Ministry* (Washington, D.C.: Public Affairs Press, 1959), found segregationist militancy concentrated in the unaffiliated Baptist churches and independent sects. Paul Harvey is now finding evidence of segregationist folk theology in letters and diaries. How widespread and influential this theology might have been is impossible to say. See, e.g., Harvey, "Religion, Race, and the Right in the Baptist South," in Glenn Feldman, ed., *Religion and Politics in the South* (forthcoming, Tuscaloosa: University of Alabama Press, 2004). The weight of the published record is not at all decisive in favor of segregation.

30 Here are two succinct examples of folk belief in the biblical warrant of segregation. Note how fleeting and undeveloped the references are and how little the argument depends on them. The first is from a letter of protest to Billy Graham:

> I note on your broadcast you have Integration, which I do not think is Scriptural—O.T., Deut., 32—8—and N.T., Acts 17—26; both you and your father [he means, father-in-law] are such good Bible students, you have possibly already compared these two verses from the O., & N.T., of course, we all know about the Tower of Babel, and many other passages. . . . It is my idea, if He had intended Integration, etc., he would have made all of us of one color or race. It is my idea the Old Book does not teach Integration, so I think it is wrong, as integrating, as it has in the North, will in some cases lead to amalgamation; take Mexico, Spain, etc., third or fourth "raters."

Edward Jones to Graham, October 15, 1958, in Bell Papers, BGC, box 15, f. 15. The second example comes from a Houston Baptist and Bible salesman, calling himself "the man WITH the BIBLE," who in 1958 wrote to the SBC president, "I hope you may see fit to bring out the fact that the Bible is for segregation." He thought that Christians should help the Negroes, "but since the Tower of Babel God definitely segregated the races." His own experience taught him that "colored ministers . . . are for segregation as a rule." He had "given the gospel to negroes in hospital work the same as whites and have run errands for them[,] but I believe God is against integration and showed him several scripture references [not specified], with which you are probably familiar." J. Forrest Kelly to Brooks Hays, Hays Papers, SBC Archives, box 3. Three other examples, all using Hamidic arguments, were sent to North Carolina governor Luther Hodges: from Victor Brandon to Hodges, June 1957, and two leaflets, ca. 1957 and 1963, all in Hodges Papers, North Carolina Division of Archives and History, Raleigh, boxes 227-28. The Citizens' Council office in Jackson distributed a curious document, "Is Segregation UnChristian?" This consisted entirely of unannotated quotations from the

Bible, including those from Gen. 9 on the curse of Ham and Acts 17, but offered no explanation as to how these might be interpreted. Only five of the thirty-six quotations were from the New Testament (about an inch and a half of thirteen inches of column). Copy in Association of Citizens' Councils of Mississippi Files, MDAH, box 1.

31 Queen, *Baptists Are the Center*, 92–94. See also Porter, "Southern Baptists and Race," 97, 28, and W. A. Criswell, "The So-Called Social Gospel," *Baptist Standard*, September 22, 1949. Criswell's *Bible for Today's World* (Grand Rapids, Mich.: Zondervan, 1965) lays out his commitment to a near-literalist hermeneutic; it says nothing about segregation or other social issues. Criswell's other books also avoid any serious discussion of racial issues. See Criswell, *These Issues We Must Face* (1953), *Five Great Questions of the Bible* (1958), *Five Great Affirmations of the Bible* (1959), all published in Grand Rapids, Michigan, by Zondervan.

32 Albert Freundt Jr., "Oxford Clergy Wrong in Calling for 'Repentance'!," *Citizen*, October 1962, 4–6. Even Carey Daniel ("God, the Original Segregationist"), drawing an analogy between the Old Testament's Jew-Gentile division and the modern black-white division, recognized how difficult it would be to sustain any such distinction in the Christian dispensation. When he got to the New Testament, Daniel seemed to concede that he had no positive case. In an imaginary dialogue with a skeptical antagonist, Daniel asks himself, "'But can it be proven . . . that Jesus Himself was a segregationist?'" His only answer is, "The Burden of proof, my dear friend, rests with you to prove that He was not a segregationist" (emphasis removed).

33 For example, in February 1956 John Counts, a Sunday school teacher in Huntland, Tenn., sought scriptural references on segregation from Clifton Allen, the editorial secretary of the SBC's Sunday School Board, to teach his fathers' class about the racial issue. His students, he said, "want to say and do the right thing. . . . At present we stand firmly but humbly against inte[g]ration," while feeling love for the Negro "in his place" and believing he should have equal rights but remain separate. Counts insisted that God set black folk "apart. Has God rescinded his decision?" He did not refer to the Bible, attempting only an analogy about different animal species and condemning the physical and moral condition of the Negro. He appealed to Allen, whose radio programs he found helpful, to help him with scriptural references on race.

Allen replied that "the Bible is absolutely clear in teaching that in the sight of God or in the feeling and attitude of God there is absolutely no distinction between races. One of the central teachings of the New Testament . . . is that there is no distinction between the Jew and the Gentile." Jews once thought of Gentiles as dogs, and "we understand their feeling somewhat by thinking of how many people feel toward Negroes now." The Bible tried to teach people to overcome such feelings: "We have inherited a great deal of prejudice. Much of this is unconscious. . . . Social prejudices are deep-seated and hard to overcome. It takes a lot of conscious effort and objective feeling to rise above prejudices." Allen sought to calm fears about the Supreme Court's school desegregation decision, which had prompted teachers like Counts to confront the issue. Like many moderates, Allen dismissed fears that mixing in schools would lead to interracial sex:

> We need to realize that the current consideration of integration in the schools is not to be thought of as amalgamation of the races. . . . In most places where Negroes attend church and school and other institutions with white people, there is less mixing of the races than there used to be here in the South. I think the facts prove that there was more mixing of whites and Negroes during slave days than in any other time. . . . Whatever is wise about integration . . . in our schools—and we ought to remember that the Negroes have just as much rights along educational lines as whites—I am sure that the real solution will have to take place gradually and not be forced. On the other hand, we certainly ought not to fight against it with a mob spirit. Frank and open discussion of the problems in a Christian spirit and gradual cultivation of ourselves to changing situations will work out many problems. Some of the current outbreaks of violence are a reflection upon a true democracy and are a hindrance to all that we ought to do in keeping with Christian principles. If our nation is not willing to be law-abiding, and if citizens are not willing to let the laws of our land be the final authority, we face anarchy, and we will lose our liberty not to the Negroes but to dictators.

Counts to Allen, February 7, 1956, and Allen to Counts, February 9, 1956, Allen Papers, SBC Archives, f. 1956.

In another example, the Rev. G. Jackson Stafford, in a letter to his parishioners at Batesburg Baptist Church in South Carolina, defended himself from the segregationist attack of South Carolina politician George Bell Timmerman. Stafford did not want sudden integration, but he painstakingly demonstrated that many biblical verses justified his decision to support the SBC statement in favor of compliance with *Brown*. Stafford to "Fellow Worker in Christ," with attachments, July 31, 1955, SBC Archives, Baptist History File—Race Relations.

In June 1958 John Davies, a Sunday school teacher in Alexandria, Va., complained to Allen that the Sunday School Board's lesson on race relations did not require his students to do anything—the way lessons on temperance, for example, required them to do things. The men in his class, who already abhorred intemperance, were, by contrast, "not concerned about racial issues because they accept the status quo as the normal way of life." With so much turmoil over race now, Davies thought that the Sunday School Board ought to lead more. Most Sunday school teachers looked to the publications of the board "as a guide in all their teaching," yet there was nothing on race. Many teachers were probably unaware of the principles proclaimed by the SBC:

> I believe that the policy of the Board is to avoid a frontal attack on segregation lest there might be harmful repercussions. But there is much that might be said in a mild, charitable spirit without disrupting the churches. Our people should not object to the editors of Sunday School literature re-

ferring to relevant quotations from Convention resolutions. . . . The . . . Board's policy of just relying on the advocacy of Christian love to ease racial tension means that we must wait a long time to gain relief from the present impasse. What we hear from the pulpit about brotherly love is usually construed as referring to our relations with people of our own color.

Davies noted that Jesus' parable of the Good Samaritan must have shocked the Jews, and that Paul rebuked Peter for refusing to eat with Gentiles. Allen thanked him but regretted that Davies's view was not sufficiently widespread. Davies to Allen and Allen to Davies, both June 4, 1958, Allen Papers, SBC, f. 1958.

34 Cowling, "A Christian Looks at Integration in Little Rock," enclosed with Clyde Hart to "Friend," September 14, 1957, ibid. The state Baptist organ seemed to weigh in decisively on Cowling's side with an editorial entitled "What Would Jesus Do?" He would "not be a part of any crowd committing acts of violence in resistance to duly constituted law and order. . . . He showed that his love knew no racial bound when He led a sinful woman of a despised race, a Samaritan, to accept him as her Redeemer . . . (John 4). He made it clear that the gift of eternal life is for all who will believe in him, with no restrictions as to race or any other circumstance in life (John 3:16)." *Arkansas Baptist*, October 3, 1957, 2. On the same page was a column by the superintendent for Negro Work citing Romans 8:9 as a counsel to practice love and "brotherly kindness" in the "school integration crisis."

When Almarene Outlaw of Webster, Fla., accused Clifton Allen in 1956 of "attempting to prepare your readers for race integration," she asked what Scripture backed up his stance. He replied that in Acts 8, Philip went to Samaria, where the Holy Spirit directed him to lead a revival among people of a different race; he also "led the Ethiopian eunuch to faith in Christ." Allen conceded that segregation was a difficult problem and could not be resolved by force. Outlaw to Allen, May 1, 1956, and Allen to Outlaw, May 16, 1956, Allen Papers, SBC Archives, f. 1956.

35 The Rev. Clyde Gordon of First Baptist, Poplarville, Miss., sermon, "A View of the Race Issue," n.d., copy in CLC Resource Files, SBC Archives, box 4. Gordon associated segregation with the pre-Christian Jews (who "segregated themselves from the Samaritans") and with Hitler. He said interbreeding "is not the fault of the Negro man, nor the Negro woman, nor the white woman, but the white man." Gordon did not mention Acts 17 but seemed to trump it with Acts 24: "God hath given thee all them that sail with thee." He admitted that "a lot of this hullabaloo has been stirred up by northern politicians to put the South in a bad light so that they can elect the next president" and blamed "northern agitators" for much of the recent controversy. (Northerners "want the church to be the 'quarterback' on the political football team. The Church is not going to do it. I am not going to have any part of it.") But he also blamed "agitation" from the other side. "A few, thank God, very few, of the newspapers of this state have preached hatred until their hands are

dripping red with murder now. They are largely responsible for some of the murders that have been committed. There are sections of our state where a Negro can be shot down like a mangy dog and the murderer set free. . . . Also, a lot of half-baked politicians bleat like screaming idiots about the Negro," declaring that they will eliminate or sterilize them. One politician who said such things "took his hearers for fools."

36 There were three southern Presbyterian journals: *Outlook*, the official organ and middle road on most questions; the socially leftist *Bridge*, produced by the PCUS's Committee on Christian Relations; and the *SPJ*, independent of the PCUS, which called itself "conservative" in its opposition to liberal theology and social theory *and* its opposition to Fundamentalism. The *SPJ* changed its name to the *Presbyterian Journal* in 1959.

37 Bell in "A Round Table Has Debate on Christians' Moral Duty," *Life*, October 1956, 160.

38 Bell also feared that extremism was divisive. He believed that "a split in our church is far more likely over the race issue than it was over church union," the controversy over proposed reunion with northern Presbyterians that had recently shaken the PCUS. (The union battle might have been related to race, though Bell did not think so.) Bell to Gamble, February 18, 1956, Bell Papers, BGC, 26-15. On the issue of force, a former southerner (who said, "Once a Mississippian, always a Mississippian") had some insight into the evolution of segregationist resistance. She said, "I shall continue to defend Mississippi's right to decide her own destiny. But I believe, and I'm afraid, her choice is now limited to this: Mississippi must give up segregation by 'law,' or force, or perish." She hoped that would be the way to "salvage all the best of our heritage," which would take "courage" and "grace." "Integration by force is a brutal, beastly, horrible business," she wrote, "but segregation by force is also a brutal, beastly business. The white people of Mississippi are experiencing exactly what we have dished out: intimidation by force. . . . We are trying to maintain something by force that should be kept only as a voluntary custom. We can no longer keep segregation by 'law.' To try to do so is to become lawless." The Civil War had "unfortunately" decided that states could not "maintain a conviction against the majority of the nation at large." Accordingly, "We had better face the necessity of token integration of the public schools and do it gracefully." Emma Knowlton Humphreys Lytle, to Tommy and cc. to others, Association of Citizens' Councils of Mississippi Files, MDAH, box 1.

39 His exact words, quoting Bell: "The people of Mississippi know that 'the barriers which man had no part in making,' and which Mississippians believe should not be destroyed, can only be maintained by force ('segregation by law')."

40 Bell and Gamble could still agree that certain extreme gestures—such as Georgia governor Marvin Griffin's cancelation of a football game with the University of Pittsburgh—was, in Gamble's words, "unwise," though at that point Bell harshly insinuated that Gamble was insufficiently aware of the dangers of rash and demagogic gestures, and was bound to repeat them. Referring

to Griffin's action, Bell observed: "I feel he did our cause a great disservice by trying to stop the Georgia Tech game with Pittsburgh in the Sugar Bowl, simply because Pittsburgh had a Negro on the team. He made the South look silly. . . . It looked like cheap political demagoguery and it hurt what thinking Southerners are trying to do to stem a desperate situation." On the football scandal at Georgia Tech, see Chapter 8, n. 27, below.

41 Gamble to Bell (associate editor) and H. B. Denby (editor) of the *SPJ*, February 10, 1956; Bell to Gamble, February 18, 1956; Gamble to Bell, August 5, 1961; Bell to Gamble, August 16, 1961; Gamble to LNB, August 24, 1962— all in Bell Papers, BGC, f. 26-15. The last quotation is a typed note to file added to the carbon of the secretary's letter sent, in Bell's absence, to Gamble, September 25, 1962, ibid.

42 Bell to Gallimore, December 21, 1961, December 20, 1966, Bell Papers, BGC, f. 26-14. Gallimore sent Bell anti-Semitic screeds (including those of the Rev. Gordon Winrod of Mountain View, Ark., and of J. B. Stoner's notorious neo-Nazi National States' Rights Party). Renunciation of anti-Semitism was a prominent theme in segregationist propaganda. The segregationists needed the support of southern Jews, such as Charles Bloch, one of the segregationists' best legal strategists, and Jews outside the South, such as *U.S. News* editor David Lawrence and the half-Jewish Senator Barry Goldwater. See David L. Chappell, "The Divided Mind of Southern Segregationists," *Georgia Historical Quarterly* 82 (Spring 1998): 56–62, and Clive Webb, *Fight against Fear: Southern Jews and Black Civil Rights* (Athens: University of Georgia Press, 2001).

43 C. Allyn Russell, *Voices of American Fundamentalism: Seven Biographical Studies* (Philadelphia: Westminster Press, 1976); Joel A. Carpenter, *Revive Us Again: The Reawakening of American Fundamentalism* (New York: Oxford University Press, 1997); George M. Marsden, *Understanding Evangelicalism and Fundamentalism* (Grand Rapids, Mich.: W. B. Eerdmans, 1991); Robert Wuthnow, *The Restructuring of American Religion: Society and Faith since World War II* (Princeton, N.J.: Princeton University Press, 1988).

44 For example, in 1960 Bell wrote that he could not blame the ministers of Charleston, W.Va., for "snubbing" a Fundamentalist group:

> The tragedy is that McIntire and his followers are hurting our conservative cause greatly by their use of the half-truth and often of untruth itself. They ride the horse of anti-Communism and conservatism, and in these stands they are correct. The trouble is that they include as their enemies all who do not follow in their own particular camp, and they do not hesitate to smear good men in the process. Like Senator McCarthy, they use a shotgun instead of a rifle [and] hit many innocent people and tarnish many good reputations in the process.
>
> It is men such as McIntire . . . that give the cause of conservative Christianity such a black eye.

Bell to Charles Dickinson, October 31, 1960, Bell Papers, BGC, f. 23-7.

45 An exchange with the Rev. John H. Knight of Opelika, Ala., in 1965 is instructive. Knight asked Bell to try "to put a stop to the constant maligning of the Southern Conservative position that CHRISTIANITY TODAY has been carrying." He was referring to the moderate editorial stance taken after the brutality at Selma. "If this liberal editorial policy does not stop, I am afraid that CHRISTIANITY TODAY will be of little use to many of us in the South." The editorials had grown "especially virulent during the past few months." Like most opponents of free thought, Knight emphasized solidarity in times of crisis: "We conservatives have a great need to work with one another in harmony." Bell replied: "I am not happy about the editorial to which you refer and have already made very clear representation about it. At the same time, I have a feeling akin to 'a plague upon both their houses' with reference to some of the things which have happened in Alabama. Surely the situation in Selma, for instance, was permitted to get out of hand weeks ago, when it could have been handled with far greater wisdom. At the same time, I know that there was deliberate provocation and that the phrase 'nonviolent' is very misleading." Knight to Bell, March 26, 1965, and Bell to Knight, March 31, 1965, ibid., f. 32-4.

46 Bell's exchanges with moderates include Francis Pickens Miller to Bell, July 16, 1958, and Bell to Miller, July 19, 1958, ibid., f. 43-12. See also Bell to C. C. Dikinson (regarding F. P. Miller), August 27, 1957, ibid., f. 23-7, and Bell to the Rev. Zan White, June 9, 1965, ibid., f. 54-18.

47 Miller continued: "Every person should, and I believe will eventually have to be, on one side or the other. Moderation is gradualism, allowing a few interracial marriages this year, a few next year, and so on, and I had rather have it out all at one time." T. R. Miller to Bell, July 8, 1957, ibid., f. 36-10.

48 Miller to Bell, April 26, 1956, January 6, 1961, ibid. Miller continued, "I had rather fight NAACP in its efforts to achieve immediate mixing, or amalgamation, than to have our people put to sleep by moderation and gradualism." His letters were often accompanied by anti-Semitic, anti-Asian, and extreme anticommunist leaflets, and one time Miller quoted Carl McIntire. Miller counted as an ally Thomas Waring, editor of the *Charleston News and Courier*.

49 Bell to Miller, March 1, 1960, ibid. Miller replied that Bell was blind to the virtues of McIntire's group "because your sight is obscured by maniacal prejudice." Miller thought Bell "a fine Christian man" but criticized him for being "an ivy league, ivory tower, silk-stocking Christian" who did not "know the thinking of the people down below." He defied Bell to disprove the propaganda he sent along, adding that "the trouble is today almost nobody has any convictions—or if they have them they don't have the courage to express them." He admired Bell's frankness but wished for the same from other southern white Christians, most of whom he saw as cowardly and hypocritical. Miller to Bell, March 29, 1960, ibid.

50 The title of Dees's address, which appeared in a widely circulated pamphlet, is also revealing: "Is It Necessary for a Christian to Support Integration?" Copy attached to Dees to Bell, August 5, 1958, ibid., f. 43-15.

51 Elders of Trinity Presbyterian Church, Montgomery, to Board of Christian Education, PCUS, June 3, 1957, in *SPJ*, June 19, 1957, 6–8.

52 The Westminster Confession continues, after "commonwealth," "'unless by way of humble petition in cases extraordinary; or by way of advice or satisfaction of conscience, if they are thereunto requested by civil magistrates'" (XXXII, sec. 4). The *SPJ* also printed a statement adopted by First Presbyterian Church, Jackson, objecting to the PCUS's Report to the 97th General Assembly, again quoting the Westminster Confession's strictures against involvement of synods and councils in "civil affairs." The Jackson church added that "the very Son of God did not during his earthly ministry . . . attempt . . . to abolish the social customs and patterns of the day . . . though the Pharisees tempted him . . . to do so." *SPJ*, June 19, 1957, 8–10.

53 Sometimes SBC officials felt forced into this. In April 1956, in the face of accusations that the SBC Sunday School Publications Board was "promoting integration," Clifton Allen wrote: "With regard to . . . desegregation. . . . I . . . assure you. . . . We are aware of the serious problem. . . . We are studiously avoiding the use of material which is inflammatory or partisan." Allen and others frequently insisted that they were only sending information for discussion, that SBC resolutions were not binding on individual congregations, that all congregations and individual parishioners were allowed to dissent freely, etc. Allen to Rev. Don Gambrell, April 18, 1956, Allen Papers, SBC Archives, f. 1956.

54 E. Butler Abington to A. C. Miller, November 8, 22, 1957, CLC Papers, SBC Archives, box 11; Freundt, "Oxford Clergy Wrong in Calling for 'Repentance'!" *Citizen*, October 1962, 5. Ingram's "born-again" Episcopal segregationists (including former bishop Albert S. Thomas of South Carolina) were more intent on this point than any other. Ingram, *Essays on Segregation*, 5, 3. Ingram's volume is a remarkable example of how six conservative southern churchmen could get together to discuss an urgent issue and almost never connect it to the Bible. Ingram distanced his group from the "two extremes"—represented by the World Council of Churches, which claimed that segregation was "abhorrent to God," and "other Christians" who "have gone so far as to declare that segregation is the will of God." Thomas echoed this in his essay (pp. 69–71). Yet all of the authors made clear that their purpose was to defend segregation. One of them, Edward B. Guerry of Charleston, confined himself almost entirely to a discussion of the Constitution in "The Church and the Supreme Court Decision" (pp. 20, 23). The common emphasis of these "born again" Episcopalians was that efforts to change man were misguided, a denial that grace and absolution came from God, not man (pp. 1–2, 61). Their biblical references pertain to this theme, not to race or segregation. This is compatible with the emphasis of the pioneering fundamentalist, C. I. Scofield. On that theme, see Everett R. Taylor, April 21, [1956?], open letter, copy in Byrnes Papers, CU, f. 869 (1).

55 Resolution of First Baptist Church, Camden, S.C., June 14, 1957, Hays Papers, SBC Archives, box 2. In the SBC files, there are either copies of or ref-

erences in letters to approximately 75 resolutions opposing the SBC's stance on segregation. Four of these (Manning Baptist Church, First Baptist Church of Camden, Marigold Baptist Church, and the Elders of Trinity Presbyterian Church of Montgomery, Ala., who were in league with one of the protesting Baptist churches there), ask or demand only that the SBC stop being political. (First Baptist of Camden also expresses hope that the State Convention of South Carolina will dissociate itself from the SBC's integration campaign.) Resolutions in CLC Papers (box 11), Brooks Hays Papers (box 2), and Executive Committee Papers (boxes 1, 54, 66, 76, 73, 82, 88, 100), SBC Archives. See also Chapter 7, nn. 19–31, below.

56   This is the position, for example, of Charles Marsh. See the section on segregationist religion in the Bibliographical Essay.

57   Burns, "The Christian Attitude toward Segregation," September 12, 1954, copy in Ervin Papers, UNC-CH, box 341.

58   The Rev. W. A. Criswell, "Christianity and Segregation," address to the Joint Assembly of South Carolina, n.d. [ca. March 1956], Citizens' Councils of America Collection, vol. 9, UA. Charles Sims, secretary-treasurer of the General Board of the State Convention of the Baptist Denomination in South Carolina, obviously disapproved of Criswell's stance. Sims implied that Criswell was even more belligerently segregationist in speaking to the Evangelistic Conference than he was in the legislature, though no copies of the latter speech were available to Sims or, as far as I know, are available now. Sims wrote to the SBC Executive Committee that Criswell "would have done much better if he had confined his remarks to matters that relate to the great, important subject of Evangelism." Sims to Porter Routh, April 5, 1956, Executive Committee Papers, SBC Archives, box 88.

59   W. A. Gamble sermon notes, 1937–1971, PCUS Archives. (His notes begin in 1926, but only those after 1937 were examined for this book.)

60   At pains to explain the widely lamented "silence" of white southern preachers, Samuel Southard, a faculty member of the SBTS, suggested that cowardice silenced some southern ministers, whereas others simply preferred "working with strategically placed individuals" for peaceful desegregation. Some believed "that premature publicity would wither those efforts as does scorching sunlight a tender plant." (Southard did not make the connection, but that was exactly the position of the racially moderate SRC; see the reference to Byrnes in Chapter 8, just after n. 41, below.) Southard complained that most churches and ministerial associations in the rural Deep South had not taken a stand in favor of desegregation and in many instances had not even spoken out against violence. Yet ministerial associations in Atlanta (November 1958), Birmingham (May 1961 and May 1963), Baton Rouge (June 1961), and Montgomery (November 1962) all urged peaceful acceptance of federal desegregation decisions; "a group of Mississippi Methodist ministers came out openly against segregation January 1963," though their bishop refused to take a stand; Martin Luther King was "warmly received" (in April 1961) by SBTS faculty and students (as far as Southard knew, it was the first time King spoke in a southern,

predominantly white institution of higher learning, though three Alabama churches voted to withhold contributions from the seminary); Florida Baptists declared that those who flouted the Supreme Court rulings were "immature"; Virginia Baptists refused to endorse their governor's call for massive resistance to school desegregation; and Georgia Baptists rejected a report that termed school integration a violation of religious conviction. Southard, "Are the Southern Churches Silent?," *Christian Century*, November 20, 1963, 1429–32.

61 Mrs. Willard Steele to Bell, June 2, 1958, Bell Papers, BGC, f. 47-8. Steele also believed that churches were cooperating with Communist groups: "Having been brainwashed themselves [they] seek to brainwash their members," creating unhappy people and split churches. She wanted to clean "liberal teachers" out of the seminaries. The president of the right-wing ASRA said that the "complacency" of white southerners was "a result of [the] teaching in our schools, colleges, churches." Olin Horton to Byrnes, July 6, 1955, Byrnes Papers, CU, f. 817 (4). The speech notes of a Florida segregationist included the following discussion questions: "Are our Church Leaders Right? Is Segregation Really and Truly UNchristian?" Sam Peacock, "The Illegal Decision of the Supreme Court," speech to Tampa Federation for Constitutional Government, May 21, 1956, in Byrnes Papers, CU, box 839 (2) (3). A Citizens' Council member of Selma, Ala., wrote to a leading segregationist strategist bemoaning the silence and indecision of southern leaders. He planned to speak on the subject at a council meeting: "We are really going to smoke our politicians and preachers out." Alston Keith to Charles Bloch, June 22, 1956, Bloch Papers, Macon Public Library. For other anticlerical segregationist letters, see Laurine Wade Douglas to T. R. Waring, January 6, 21, 1955, Waring Papers, SCHS, box 432.

62 Dorn to his supporters, including Eugene S. Blease, June 22, 1954, Dorn Papers, USC, box 41.

63 This is a subtitle from Gressette's Orangeburg speech notes, June 11, 1956. Two other almost identical sets of notes say "Church Leaders Chief Offenders" for speeches at Cameron, March 11, 1957, and at an unspecified Rotary Club meeting, October 11, 1956. Marion Gressette Papers, USC, box 6.

64 "At least," Williams continued, "it would give the congregation the basis for demanding explanations from 'integrationist' pastors." Williams to Simmons, June 14, 1957, Williams Papers, MDAH, box RO33-BO19-S2-10383.

65 Medford Evans, in *Information Bulletin* of the Mississippi Association of Methodist Ministers and Laymen, Association of Citizens' Councils of Mississippi Files, MDAH, box 1. Evans may have had a point about Wesley, but early Methodism in America was extreme in its hierarchical discipline.

66 *Christian Layman*, October 1958 (emphasis in original), copy in Williams Papers, MDAH, box 10395. I have found only one issue of this publication; it contains mostly reprinted segregationist editorials and speeches. The article cited here quoted a previous article from *McCall's*; it targeted Robert Graetz, erroneously calling him southern. (Graetz was a northerner who pastored an

all-black Lutheran congregation in Montgomery: see David L. Chappell, *Inside Agitators: White Southerners in the Civil Rights Movement* [Baltimore: Johns Hopkins University Press, 1994].)

67 Robert A. Wade, of Hagerstown, Md., to Thurmond, December 23, 1955, Thurmond Papers, CU, f. 1956-12. Where I intrude the bracketed "frauds," Wade used the word "fakirs," but surely he meant fakers. He noted that Christianity was "organized and operating under the banner of the one and only God, the Jewish God, the one and only race, the human race, with justice, equality, liberty, peace and plenty for all regardless of the laws of Malthus and Darwin." Thurmond responded, though briefly and noncommittally. His policy seems to have been to respond to all nut cases except the anti-Semitic ones.

68 Byrnes to Douglas Featherstone, June 29, 1954, copy in Dorn Papers, USC, box 41. Segregationist ministers, perhaps put on the defensive by general anti-clericalism in the movement, were anticlerical too. Leon Burns, for example, found it "strange that Christianity has been influencing the world for almost two thousand years with little thought given by its followers to the matter of segregation one way or another, but with one judicial decree of a civil court the leaders of Christendom suddenly decide that segregation is contrary to Christian principle." Speech at Columbia, Tenn., March 24, 1957, Allen Papers, SBC Archives, no box number.

69 *Christian Layman*, October 1958, in Williams Papers, MDAH, box 10359. The other reference to the Bible was a brief nod to Acts 17:26 in an article by Robert Patterson, which also interestingly condemned the Revised Standard Version as a Communist Bible.

70 Shattuck, *Episcopalians and Race*, 44–50. Philanthropist Jesse Ball DuPont withdrew her funding of the other one, Virginia Theological Seminary, in 1951, to protest its admission of a black student. She threatened to withdraw her funding from Sewanee, too. Some trustees noted that desegregation would violate state law, but one bishop admitted that he feared losing DuPont's funding. Sewanee trustees voted to remain segregated, despite a directive to desegregate in 1952. But in June 1953, a special session of Sewanee trustees, pressured by a survey showing that 80 percent of all Episcopal clergy favored admission of Negroes, voted to desegregate, over the strong protests of a few, including one retired and one sitting southern bishop. But 18 of 20 diocesan bishops present supported desegregation, 14 vowing to remove their students if Sewanee remained segregated. The final vote for desegregation was 78 to 6.

71 This was a resolution of the Protestant Episcopal Church's General Convention, September 1952 (Boston). Arkansas bishop R. Bland Mitchell, then Sewanee chancellor and head of the trustees, stated that the trustees' position was based on practicality rather than support for segregation. Shattuck, *Episcopalians and Race*, 44–50.

72 The one who stayed, Bayard Jones, claimed that his colleagues were not standing on religious principle; rather, they were advocating the indefensible "claim

of the Negro to social equality—and ultimately . . . to the right of intermarriage." Vice Chancellor and President Edward McCrady, who had taught
biology at Sewanee for fifteen years, agreed with Jones, adhering to his belief in the distinctiveness of "the three Great Races (Hauptstrassen)." He re-
cruited and hired five new faculty members to replace the nine who had left—
provoking protests throughout the denomination. Sewanee graduate Albion
Knight (an outspoken segregationist lawyer), Alabama bishop Charles Carpenter, retired South Carolina bishop Albert S. Thomas, and about 80 percent of the undergraduates (in a signed statement) backed McCrady. James
Pike, dean of the Cathedral School of St. John the Divine in New York, published his refusal of an honorary degree in the *New York Times*: he did not want
"a doctorate in white divinity." He said that Sewanee should have challenged
Tennessee's segregation laws. Shattuck, *Episcopalians and Race*, 44–50.

73 Ibid.

74 Stahlman to W. F. Murrah, Memphis, July 1, 1960, Stahlman Papers, Vanderbilt University, box V-3. Clearly Stahlman did not mean that there was any
possibility he could be wrong, but apparently this is the only time that he ever
says he could be wrong. A fascinating book by Melissa Fitzsimmons Kean on
this and the desegregation of four other private southern universities (Duke,
Rice, Emory, and Tulane) is due out soon, based on her fine dissertation, "'At a
Most Uncomfortable Speed': The Desegregation of the South's Private Universities, 1945–1964" (Ph.D. diss., Rice University, 2000), esp. 363–89. See
also Paul Conkin, *Gone with the Ivy: A Biography of Vanderbilt University* (Knoxville: University of Tennessee Press, 1985). A recent forum of surviving participants in the controversy, including Lawson but not Branscomb (who died
in 1998), revealed that for a time Branscomb shared Stahlman's rage, almost
accepting the resignations and giving the divinity building to the law school,
and that Harold Vanderbilt was instrumental in achieving a compromise to
keep the divinity faculty: Lawson was offered a chance to return to finish his
degree; he declined, as many expected he would, but the faculty withdrew
their resignations. Dale A. Johnson, ed., *Vanderbilt Divinity School: Education,
Contest, Change* (Nashville: Vanderbilt University Press, 2001), 131–77. I am
indebted to Mark Noll for directing me to this important source.

75 "Southern Churches Urge Mixing," *Citizens' Council*, May 1958, 1; "Reds in
the Woodpile . . ." ". . . And in the Rectory," editorials, *Citizens' Council*, April
1958; "Pinkos in the Pulpit," editorial, *Citizens' Council*, December 1956.

76 Dr. G. Stanley Frazier, Pastor, St. James Methodist, Montgomery, Ala., to
Citizens' Council, October 1957.

77 Workman, *The Case for the South* (New York: Devin-Adair, 1960), 109. On another occasion, Workman objected to an editorial in the *South Carolina Methodist Advocate*, which tactlessly declared, "By and large Protestant laymen are
lagging behind their ministers in the understanding of the Christian faith"
in, among other things, "race relations." Workman responded: "Such dogmatic pronouncements from our clergy pre-suppose a clerical wisdom and
understanding which is denied us mere laymen. . . . We are told, in effect,

that the poor, benighted layman is incapable of distinguishing between right and wrong UNLESS his views coincide with those of our ministerial mentors." Workman reminded the editor that there had been a Reformation to get away from ecclesiastical control and allow freedom of conscience, an odd point for a Methodist to emphasize. Draft letter to *South Carolina Methodist Advocate*, perhaps never sent, Workman Papers, USC, box 15.

78 Miller to Bell, January 6, 1961, Bell Papers, BGC, f. 36-10.

79 *Councilor*, July 1957, 1, 4, copy in NAACP Papers, LC, ser. III.A, box 282. Stanley Morse, president of the secular Citizens' Grass Roots Crusade, an extreme right-wing group, put the same Hoover quotation atop one of his press releases. April 14, 1954, press release, copy in Dorn Papers, USC, box 41. In a similar vein, the ASRA distributed to its readers an article by Angus H. McGregor, "Has the Methodist Church Gone Mad?" Memorandum to Members, April 14, 1955, in National Association of States' Rights Papers, BPL, file 416.1.2.1.15.

80 C. C. Smith, of Dumas, Miss., "On Which Side Are the Preachers?," copy in Association of Citizens' Councils of Mississippi Files, MDAH, 1954–55. I am indebted to Randy Sparks for calling my attention to this document. The leaflet continued:

> Is it necessary to declare war on the Preachers? Not at all. Simply enlist in the army against Communism and its many, often disguised, 'Fronts,' and you will automatically find the Big Seminary Preachers in the camp of the enemy. The Preachers, 1954 vintage, differ little from the fashionable clergy of Christ's time, when He said: 'You are of your father the devil, and your will is to do your father's desires.' These sons of the Devil crucified Christ, and are today crucifying his followers, on the cross of public opinion.

In a similar vein, segregationist Charles Benham aimed his invective at "the average professional 'Christian' of our time," adding, "These Edomite leaders have the institutions of the church *in their hands*, just as the Talmudist Pharisees had the Temple and Jewish church in control when our Lord was trying to save them." "X-Raying the Racial Issue: Is Integration Scriptural?" (Topton, N.C., n.d.), copy in Wallace Papers, ADAH, box RC2 G320.

81 Harris quoted in *Atlanta Constitution*, February 3, 1960.

82 A. N. S. of Atlanta to Wade Boggs, June 5, 1955, Wade Boggs Papers, PCUS Archives, large box. The "Dr. Miller" to which A. N. S. referred was probably Donald G. Miller, professor at Union Theological Seminary, Richmond, who tore apart G. T. Gillespie's effort to justify segregation in the official PCUS organ, *Presbyterian Outlook*, March 14, 1955. See Joel L. Alvis Jr., *Religion and Race: Southern Presbyterians, 1946–1983* (Tuscaloosa: University of Alabama Press, 1994), 54–55.

83 Putnam in the *Jackson Daily News* and *Jackson State Times*, October 27, 1961. Earlier Putnam had denounced the Catholic bishops' November 1958 statement that "segregation cannot be reconciled with the Christian view of our fellow man." In a letter to Cardinal Spellman, Putnam said that the bishops

were accessories to a "crime against the South." *Citizens' Council* 4 (December 1958). In the same vein, one of Bull Connor's supporters wrote, "I am disgusted with the stand that the preachers have taken." C. B. Gambrell to Connor, January 24, 1963, and Connor to Gambrell, January 25, 1963, Connor Papers, BPL, f. 14-51. Another example—Homer H. Hyde, "'By Their Fruits Ye Shall Know Them," *American Mercury* (Summer 1962): 35–39—asserted that communists had infiltrated the churches and convinced them to support, or at least to refrain from opposing, desegregation. In Connor Papers, BPL, f. 10-27.

CHAPTER SEVEN: PULPIT VERSUS PEW

1 John Marion (an official of the Virginia Council on Human Relations), "Parsons' Revolt," *National Council Outlook*, February 1956, NCC Information Service Newsletter, in Allen Papers, SBC Archives, f. 1956.
2 Foster to J. McDowell Richards, February 27, 1956, Richards Papers, PCUS Archives, box 72. For other letters to Richards reporting the pitting of anti-segregationist attitudes of pastors against the segregationist attitudes of the laity, see, e.g., those from Berryville, Va., February 19, 27, 1953; from Booneville, Miss., February 17, 1953; from Wildwood, Fla., March 3, 1955; and from Charlie King, Houston, February 26, 1953 (all in Richards Papers, box 65).
3 Fulton to J. McDowell Richards, March 15, 1956, ibid., box 72. An integrationist faculty member of Agnes Scott College notified Richards about a segregationist's claim that "'ministers [were] selling the laymen down the river.'" To avert a "split" between clergy and laity, he wanted to persuade ministers and denominational leaders to refrain from issuing further statements on segregation. James Ross McCain to Richards, ibid. The famed white radical Will D. Campbell confirmed that many of the white southern clergy felt exactly as McCain did. Parishioners at Campbell's own first pastorate, in rural Taylor, La., in 1952, initially tolerated his statements on segregation—even found them entertaining (though they were infuriated at his insistence on paying black laborers the minimum wage). It was not until *Brown* that they pressured him out. His rhetoric did not change then, he said, but the context did. Campbell was later expelled from his chaplaincy at Ole Miss for integrationist activity. Campbell, interview with author, Mt. Juliet, Tenn., July 21, 1999, *Brother to a Dragonfly* (New York: Seabury Press, 1977), and *Forty Acres and a Goat: A Memoir* (New York: Harper and Row, 1988).
4 Miller to Bell, May 14, 1958, Bell Papers, BGC, f. 36-10.
5 Horsley to Dabney, February 20, 1945, Dabney Papers, UVA, 7690-a, box VII. Horsley preferred the Hindu view of life after death ("very appealing and much more desirable than flapping around somewhat in the so-called Heaven playing harps").
6 Dabney to Horsley, February 22, 1945, ibid. Dabney added, however, that "one or two [businessmen] have consented to serve on the board of the Southern

Regional Council, Wilson Brown among them. . . . I am not criticizing him. . . . On the other hand he is almost the only businessman in the South who will go as far as he has gone." Horsley was a member of the SRC, along with Dabney, Virginia Durr, and Virginia governor Colgate Darden.

7   Unnamed SRC official quoted in Ed Cony, "More Southern Pastors Plead for 'Moderation'; Many Fight Segregation," *Wall Street Journal*, February 14, 1958. "DPs" was the familiar term for "displaced persons" from World War II —refugees, former prisoners of war, concentration camp survivors, people whose homeland changed governments, etc.

8   *New York Times*, June 8, 1959.

9   McNeill, "A Georgia Minister Offers a Solution for the South," *Look*, May 28, 1957.

10 Correspondence between McNeill and Bell, whom McNeill recognized as a sympathizer, is revealing. Bell congratulated McNeill on his article in *Look*: "I think that it is a courageous article, that it is completely logical, and that it is a thoroughly Christian approach." He apparently gave greater weight than McNeill's enemies (perhaps than McNeill himself) to McNeill's emphasis on what southerners could do while waiting for legal solutions to be worked out. Bell emphasized "again and again" that "the abolition of segregation does not mean integration. . . . A forced integration is one of the most foolish things that people can advocate." Perhaps Bell maintained ties with moderates like McNeill in the hope that he could dissuade them from politicizing the issue. Bell to McNeill, May 13, 1957, Bell Papers, BGC, f. 35-25. McNeill told Bell that his "was the most gratifying letter I received" in response to the *Look* article. "Frankly, I was about to fasten my safety-belt when I realized the letter was from you." McNeill also found Bell's pronouncements on race "states-manlike." When McNeill asked if he could make Bell's support public, Bell agreed. McNeill to Bell, May 30, 1957, Bell to McNeill, June 5, 1957, and McNeill to Bell, June 11, 1957, ibid.

11 "Actions Taken by the Judicial Commission Appointed by the Presbytery of Southwest Georgia to Investigate and Act to Correct the Difficulties in the First Presbyterian Church, Columbus, Georgia," July 22, 1959, ibid.

12 *New York Times*, June 8, 1959. The judicial commission had been running the church since November 30, 1958. McNeill, born in Birmingham, attended Union Seminary in Richmond. In June 1959 he was forty-four. He said that losing his southern prejudices was a difficult process, begun halfway through seminary. As a member of the basketball team at Union, he had refused to play against Virginia Union, a Negro college across town. When an inter-seminary conference was held on campus, he at first declined to sit with Negro delegates but later gave in to moral pressure to do so. "And I discovered that these men weren't so bad after all." He began reading books on race, includ-ing Myrdal. "And then I realized my old attitude on race just didn't stand up." In 1957 and 1958 he drafted two reports for the denomination's Committee on Christian Social Relations "that were hailed as the most liberal statements on racial issues ever put out by a predominantly Southern church," accord-

ing to the *Times*. The presbytery initially gave McNeill a vote of confidence, but at a later meeting it decided by a close vote to turn the matter over to the synod's judicial commission. The commission, in turn, upheld "Freedom of the Pulpit" and the prophetic task of a minister, etc., in its report of November 11, 1958. A similar case in 1965–66 is described by a Baptist pastor from Macon, Ga.: see Thomas J. Holmes, *Ashes for Breakfast* (Valley Forge, Pa.: Judson Press, 1969).

13 Laughon to Miller, July 17, 1957, and Miller to Laughon, July 23, 1957, CLC Papers, SBC Archives, box 11. Miller was confident that the segregationist movement would "not spread throughout our convention. . . . There are spots where it will gain some momentum, but it will gradually lose its force as the actual truth becomes known" about the SBC's work.

14 The Rev. G. Jackson Stafford of Batesburg, S.C., undated memo (refers to an upcoming meeting on November 9, 1955), apparently sent to SBC and elsewhere, Baptist History File—Race Relations, SBC Archives.

15 *Southern School News*, March 1956, 9.

16 Pro-segregation Methodists were similarly incapable of capturing their denominational apparatus, except in pockets. In only 2 southern Methodist conferences (out of 139 nationwide) did the segregationists get a majority to vote against desegregation of their denomination in 1957—and even then the vote was not overwhelming. (In the Alabama–West Florida conference, the tally was 262 to 172 against desegregation; the other segregationist majority was in the Northern Mississippi conference.) Of course, since 1939 southern Methodists had been tied to northerners. But nationwide in 1957, there were only 1,623 votes to maintain segregation (as opposed to 21,148 against it); 1,388 of the votes for segregation were from Deep South conferences in Alabama, Georgia, and Mississippi. Desegregation thus carried comfortably within the southern white Methodist leadership. In the Alabama–West Florida district (which included Montgomery and Selma, but not Birmingham), 6 out of 17 ministers who signed a desegregationist petition in 1958 were driven from their pulpits, though the 6 were all reassigned to other churches in that district, and the segregationists' effort to expel the top minister of the district, Andrew "Doc" Turnipseed, failed—he was resoundingly returned. (The following year, his bishop pressured Turnipseed, who had become a lightning rod for segregationist anger, into transferring to another conference. Turnipseed returned to the Alabama conference in 1973.) See Donald E. Collins, *When the Church Bell Rang Racist: The Methodist Church and the Civil Rights Movement in Alabama* (Macon, Ga.: Mercer University Press, 1998), 47, 44–45, 62; Turnipseed, interview with author, Ramer, Ala., July 13, 1989.

17 Mark Newman, "The Baptist General Association of Virginia and Desegregation, 1931–1980," *Virginia Magazine of History and Biography* 105 (Summer 1997): 257–86 (quotation on p. 279). Samuel Southard reported a similar incident in Albany, Ga. Albany's segregationists—stronger than anywhere else—were able to hand the direct action movement its only southern defeat. But even there, when Brooks Ramsey, pastor of the white First Baptist Church,

became known as a moderate, segregationists were unable to gain a majority against him in his church. Segregationists in his congregation had sought his signature on a petition to write segregation into the church's constitution. According to Southard, Ramsey "vigorously" opposed the petition and "publicly expressed his regret" that ushers had turned away three Negroes who tried to attend a service. In the face of segregationist attacks, Ramsey "sought and received a vote of confidence in his church." Southard also related two other incidents. In the first, Bruce Evans, pastor of University Baptist Church at Louisiana State University, signed a statement advocating "justice, decency, and humility" in race relations. Though his wife was denied a job by the local school board and Evans himself ultimately resigned, he received "strong support from his congregation"; a federal grand jury later indicted three men, including a state senator, for tapping phones of religious leaders who had signed the statement. In the second incident, a Sunday school teacher in Lebanon Junction, Ky., who taught that God was no respecter of racial lines, gave up the position because of "isolation and abuse" in 1953. Southard, "Are Southern Churches Silent?," *Christian Century*, November 20, 1963, 1429–32.

18 Segregationism seemed to have the upper hand in the Central Mississippi Presbytery of the PCUS, the Alabama Diocese of the Episcopal Church, and dozens (perhaps more) of individual Baptist churches. See n. 34, below, and Gardiner H. Shattuck, *Episcopalians and Race: Civil War to Civil Rights* (Lexington: University Press of Kentucky, 2000). See also Chapter 6, n. 28, above, and Ernest Q. Campbell and Thomas F. Pettigrew, *Christians in Racial Crisis: A Study of Little Rock's Ministry* (Washington, D.C.: Public Affairs Press, 1959).

19 Few of these resolutions made any biblical references, and those that did were fleeting. Several came from small churches in South Carolina, reproducing almost identical boilerplate that seems to have originated with the Santee Baptist Association, which refers to Acts 17. Most were defensive, taking umbrage at the SBC's joining the chorus that labeled segregationists un-Christian. The most interesting argument came from the First Baptist Church of Farmerville, La.: If segregation is wrong, "why has the God of both races so wonderfully blessed the area of the Southern Baptist Convention and made it the Bible belt of the world, yet it is the only area where segregation has been practiced[?]" The Farmerville Resolution carried shortly after President Dwight Eisenhower sent troops to enforce desegregation at Little Rock. Bayonets would only destroy "brotherhood and goodwill," the resolution said. Farmerville Resolution, November 6, 1957, CLC Papers, SBC Archives, box 11.

20 *Time* magazine, reporting on the issue in 1965, concluded: "More often than not . . . ministers have found that a strong stand on [in favor of] civil rights pays off in the collection plate. A common experience is that attempts to silence the church through financial pressure inspire more sympathetic laymen to make up for any lost pledges." Interestingly, many of the cases *Time* covered were in the North. The biggest withdrawal of a contribution occurred in Chicago: "When Episcopal Father James Jones of Chicago, the director

of diocesan charities, was jailed last June for taking part in a civil rights demonstration, one layman rescinded a $750,000 pledge to the church's chari-
table agencies." The second biggest was in New York: The "new passion for
selective giving reached a peak last month when New York's Episcopal Bishop
Horace Donegan . . . announced that a parishioner had stricken from his will
a pledge of $600,000 toward completion of the Cathedral of St. John the
Divine. . . . The purpose of withholding the money, said Donegan, was to
show disapproval of [Donegan's] stand on civil rights—including speeches,
sending priests to Selma, installing a Negro canon at the cathedral, and integrating parishes." "The Price of Conviction," *Time*, November 19, 1965.

21 For resolutions, see SBC Archives: CLC Papers, box 11; Executive Committee Papers, boxes 1, 54, 66, 76, 73, 82, 88, 100; Hays Papers, box 2; and Allen
Papers, no box number. One might credit the claim of one of these—Mt. Olive
Association, Oakdale, La.—to represent 38 churches, though the language of
the resolution is unclear: there may have been a single representative from
each of the 38 churches, with varying degrees of authority, if any, to speak for
each respective congregation, or some churches may not have sent a representative but were included in the count simply because there were that many
in the association.

22 These are 1957 figures from the (annual) *Southern Baptist Handbook* (Nashville: Convention Press, 1958), 9. Subtracting the SBC-affiliated churches in
nonsouthern states and Mexico from the total, there were 28,321 SBC-affiliated churches in the South. The number of SBC churches in each of the
eleven former states of the Confederacy in 1957 was as follows: Alabama,
2,737; Arkansas, 1,147; Florida, 1,145; Georgia, 2,633; Louisiana, 1,216; Mississippi, 1,770; North Carolina, 3,237; South Carolina, 1,438; Tennessee, 2,583;
Texas, 3,759; and Virginia, 1,316. Of other former slave states, Kentucky had
3,286 SBC churches in 1957, Maryland had 141, and Missouri had 1,723. The
District of Columbia had 51. All of these and Oklahoma (1,231 SBC churches)
were considered southern for purposes of the 28,321 tally.

23 Miller to Harry E. Dawkins, December 12, 1957, CLC Papers, SBC Archives,
box 11.

24 The 34:1 claim is in "Letters from Southern Baptists on the Work of the
Christian Life Commission," ibid. By my count, however, there are 31 clearly
negative letters from individuals (14 identifiable as pastors) in the CLC files.
(Although there are more than 31 letters in the "negative" CLC file, many are
simply requests for information or pleas that the SBC remain or become neutral on segregation.) I did not count the letters in the "favorable" file, but it
is much thinner. The weight of the mail appears even more negative if petitions of protest are included: not counting duplicates in separate sets of files,
there are 32 such petitions in the CLC files, an additional 20 in the Executive
Committee Papers, and 1 more in the Allen Papers.

25 Miller advised one segregationist church, "During this year we have received
a total of 20 of these resolutions, 12 of which have come from South Carolina." A. C. Miller to Summerton Baptist Church, Summerton, S.C., Decem-

ber 10, 1957, CLC Papers, SBC Archives, box 11, f. 9. The SBC had received 31 resolutions that year, by my count, 19 from South Carolina.

26 Avant to Routh, October 22, 1963, Executive Committee Papers, SBC Archives, box 82. See a similar letter from the Rev. Fred Laughon to A. C. Miller, June 25, 1957, and related correspondence, CLC Papers, ibid., box 11.

27 Ritchey to Miller, October 17, 1957, CLC Papers, ibid., box 11. Avery Lee, a pastor in Rushton, La., and a state representative of the CLC, wrote independently to the commission about the same problem and to the state Baptist magazine (which had run an editorial calling for the abolition of the CLC): "I must 'protest the protest of the Mansfield deacons.'" If the SBC eliminated the CLC, it would eliminate the agency that did all the work of value relating to "alcohol . . . gambling, narcotics, delinquency, pornographic literature, [and] malpractices of both business and labor." The segregationists "might be surprised to find" that the position of the CLC represented more Southern Baptists than they thought. Lee offered to defend the CLC in the state Baptist paper, the *Message*. Lee to Dr. [Finley] Tinnin, cc. Miller, July 7, 1957, ibid.

28 Searcy Garrison to Porter Routh, n.d. [ca. 1959], Executive Committee Papers, SBC Archives, box 54.

29 William Lancaster to A. C. Miller, November 18, 1957, CLC Papers, ibid., box 11. Lancaster warned that segregationist sentiment was nonetheless high, hinting that the vote might not go so well for the SBC in future years.

30 Williams to Brooks Hays, November 11, 1957, with attachments, Hays Papers, ibid., box 2. The Newberry boilerplate was also adopted by Mt. Zion Baptist Church, Camden, S.C.

31 Religious News Service press release, October 10, 1957, copy in Executive Committee Papers, ibid., box 82.

32 Avery Lee to George Ritchey, July 7, 1957, cc. to A. C. Miller, CLC Resource Files, ibid., box 11, f. 9. It was customary for SBC presidents to serve two terms, and Hays was reelected in May 1958. I am indebted to Bill Sumners and his expert staff at the SBC Library and Archives in Nashville for sharing their knowledge of Hays, the CLC, SBC procedures, and related matters. It was unusual for a sitting member of Congress to be head of the SBC. In 1956, while leading the CLC, Hays, like most southern members of Congress, signed the Southern Manifesto defying the *Brown* decision. Still, segregationists saw him as soft on the issue and pointed to his association with the CLC as evidence of his treachery. See Kyle Day, "The Fall of Southern Moderation: The Defeat of Brooks Hays in the 1958 Congressional Election for the Fifth District of Arkansas" (M.A. thesis, University of Arkansas, 1999).

33 Miller to Santee Baptist Association, November 5, 1957, CLC Resource Files, SBC Archives, box 11, f. 9. If Mark Newman's figures are correct, Miller understated his case with "100 to 1": the ratio was actually about 180 to 1. Newman, *Getting Right with God: Southern Baptists and Desegregation, 1945–1995* (Tuscaloosa: University of Alabama Press, 2001), 24.

34 Statement of the Session of First Presbyterian Church of Jackson (protest-

ing the Report of the Council on Christian Relations, which was adopted by the PCUS, mainly on grounds of the Westminster Confession's injunctions against politics) and Letter from Ruling Elders of Trinity Presbyterian Church, Montgomery, in *SPJ*, June 19, 1957, 6–10; Petition to the Central Mississippi Presbytery by the Session of Central Presbyterian Church, Jackson, in *SPJ*, November 13, 1957, 14–15. In the last case, the presbytery accepted the petition. Central Mississippi Presbytery Records, October 17, 1957, PCUS Archives. (A copy of the Montgomery letter made its way into the CLC Resource Files, SBC Archives, box 11; it was first printed in the *Messenger*, June 7, 1957.)

35 Birmingham Presbytery Records, 1964, 29, 36–37, PCUS Archives.

36 *SPJ*, April 9, 1958, 7–9. The "Ban" was a subtitle of the printed speech (paragraphing altered from original).

37 See "Billy Graham Makes Plea for an End to Intolerance," *Life*, October 1956, 138–51. Graham attended all-white colleges in the South, but also Wheaton College (now the center of his publishing and broadcasting empire), which was founded by abolitionists. There he met and, according to biographer William Martin, befriended a few black students. In his early crusades, he followed the practice of Billy Sunday, segregating crowds except in nonsouthern cities. But during his Washington crusade in 1952, he announced that there would be no discrimination in seating, stating that at conversion "you become obedient to spiritual laws. You begin to love persons of all races, regardless of the color of their skin." He accepted segregation later that year in Jackson, Mississippi, but denounced it—and then backtracked under pressure, saying he did not wish to get involved in "local issues." At a revival that year at Rice University, though he accepted the local committee's segregation policy, he insisted that the black section be moved out of an inconvenient spot in the sun. Also in 1952 he declared at the SBC that it was the Christian duty of all Baptist colleges to admit Negro students. Then in 1953, he told the committee of sponsors for his upcoming crusade in Chattanooga that he could not accept segregated seating, as was the custom there. "When the committee balked, [Graham] went to the crusade tabernacle and personally removed the ropes marking the section reserved for blacks." Few black attendees changed sections, and "many people may not have realized what Graham had done—the incident passed without comment in the local papers." (An authorized biographical work, Russ Busby's *Billy Graham: God's Ambassador* [Minneapolis: Billy Graham Evangelistic Association, 1999], 212, adds: "Disappointingly, the attendance of blacks was sparse" in Chattanooga.) A few months later Graham accepted a Dallas committee's segregated seating, but, Martin writes, "ushers made no attempt to hinder the small number of blacks who chose to sit in areas reserved for whites." When a black Detroit newspaper criticized Graham for going along with the officially segregated seating, Graham's crusade director replied that Dallas law required segregation and Graham would not break the law. Martin writes that "some black churchmen in Detroit continued to doubt Graham's commitment, but others participated

actively on various committees and were quite visible on the platform and in the choir and usher corps." Graham complained that sports and business were ahead of the church in "getting together racially. And church people should be the first to step forward and practice what Christ taught—that there is no difference in the sight of God." He also warned that discrimination hurt U.S. foreign policy and missionary work abroad. Martin, *A Prophet with Honor: The Billy Graham Story* (New York: Morrow, 1991), 168–72. In 1956 the *Chicago Daily News* reported, "Evangelist Billy Graham called on America's churches Wednesday night to 'set an example' in the battle for racial integration. . . . 'Northern churches should take the lead.'" He added: "'There is a need to go slow, however, particularly in the Southern states.'" Graham, who had just returned from a tour of the Far East, continued, "'The racial situation in the United States—especially the recent expulsion of a Negro woman student from the University of Alabama—has caused a loss of American prestige abroad.'" "Integration Plea Made by Graham," *Chicago Daily News*, March 15, 1956. See also "No Color Line in Heaven: Billy Graham," *Ebony*, September 1957, 99–104.

38 While the historic struggle was going on in Little Rock in 1957, segregationists distributed pamphlets denouncing Graham. "Billy Graham Leads Massive Campaign to Integrate Churches of Little Rock," copy in Bates Papers, SHSW, box 5. A segregationist leaflet, entitled "The Gospel Truth about Segregation" (ca. 1963), led off by saying, "There is not one word of truth in Billy Graham's statements." Copy in Hodges Papers, North Carolina Division of Archives and History, box 227. The only person who has been allowed into Graham's personal papers apparently found significant evidence of his denunciation by segregationists. Martin, *Prophet*, 234–35, 249.

39 Mrs. Willard Steele to Bell, June 2, 1958, Bell Papers, BGC, f. 47-8. Bell replied: "Your criticism of Billy Graham seems to me most unjust. I *know* how he feels and I fully agree with him. He feels that so far as the preaching of the Gospel is concerned, he must preach to all on an unsegregated basis. With his world-wide ministry, any other policy would destroy his opportunity to reach three-fourths of the millions of the world. Your suggestion that he might approve racial intermarriage is shocking. Preaching the Gospel to peoples of all races has nothing to do with such folly." Bell to Steele, June 10, 1958, ibid.

40 Bell to Wm. McIntire of Charlotte, N.C., January 14, 1959, responding to handwritten note from McIntire, January 12, 1959, ibid., f. 15-15.

41 Bell to Edward Jones of Decatur, Ga., October 21, 1958, ibid. Bell wrote: "Billy does not believe in integration any more than you and I do. The point is that he feels, along with me, that *legal* or forced segregation is unchristian and that segregation should be on a voluntary basis." Bell made a similar disavowal of Graham's intention to lead integration efforts—"not substantiated by the actual quotations from Billy, himself," etc. Bell to Mrs. Peake of Norfolk, Va., August 7, 1956, ibid., f. 41-11.

42 Bell wrote A. C. Miller that the issue was beclouded by "extremists on both sides." As for Governor Timmerman, "Someone has misinformed him about

Billy's policies." The issue does not come up, he said: people of both races sit where they like without fanfare. Bell seemed to be offering Timmerman assurances when he pointed out that the newspapers did not report on the seating. Bell suspected that "Dr. Bob Jones, who has been fighting Billy so constantly," might have planted this idea with Timmerman—"giving him a very inaccurate picture of Billy's position. I know that Dr. Jones said that if he came to preach in Greenville, South Carolina, he would raise the issue there." Bell to Miller, October 13, 1958, ibid., f. 43-12.

43 Paul J. Mason to George Wallace, April 24, 1965; Rev. Marvin Deitz to Wallace, May 5, 1965; Mrs. L. P. Munger to Wallace, June 16, 1965; G. F. Young to Wallace, June 16, 1965; Mrs. Guy Vining to Wallace, June 16, 1965—all in Wallace Papers, ADAH, box RC2 G312. In Wallace's file is a photograph and news clipping from the *Mobile Press Register* showing Wallace meeting with Graham at the state capitol. Wallace also received a clipping from *Grit*, May 2, 1965, headlined, "Billy Graham Will Preach Civil Rights," which stated that Graham had "embarked on a personal civil rights crusade that will take him during the next few months into key states in the South." The article continued:

> "I am a southerner," [Graham] said, "and I have a voice in the South, so I will try to provide the leadership I can." . . . His mission, he said, will be to "bring the healing message of the gospel to bear on racial barriers and social and political injustice." He added that he feels the churches of the South are not providing the leadership they should in the campaign for civil rights.
>
> Dr. Graham has preached previously in places of racial tension: in 1957 in Little Rock, Ark.; in 1958 in Clinton, Tenn., and last year in Birmingham, Ala. He has consistently refused to preach before segregated gatherings in the South.

D. G. Hendrix sent Wallace pamphlets criticizing Graham, noting the huge amounts of money Graham made and his friendly relations with the Catholic Church. Hendrix to Wallace, September 28, 1965, ibid.

44 Some anti-Graham examples include W. J. Simmons to Waring, November 21, 1958; carbon of Frank Haile of Knoxville to Graham, December 15, 1958; Harold Edwards to Waring, April 1, 1960; and L. L. Ferebee to Waring, May 17, 1961—all in Waring Papers, SCHS, box 401. On the pro-Graham side are an undated petition from Johns Island, "We the undersigned request the News and Couriers to restore the column 'Billy Graham's Answers,'" with twenty signatures; Mrs. G. E. Nicholson to Waring, May 30, June 6, 1961; Mrs. R. P. Gillespie to Waring, June 12, 15, 1961; Willard L. Hardin Jr. to Editor, [n.d.]; Mrs. P. G. Parker to Waring, July 24, 1961; and five postcards, dated May 30, June 2, 3, 5, 9, 1961—all in ibid.

45 The article, subheadlined "Southern-Born Evangelist Declares War on Bigotry," quoted Graham: "There are a lot of segregationists who are going to be sadly disillusioned when they get to Heaven—if they get there. . . . 'I'll tell you, [Graham] warns whites, 'we are going to have a revival that will wipe

away racial discrimination. . . . I tell you there is no superior race in God's sight.'" He was "underscoring the old warning that there is no color line in Heaven. From that fact, he draws a corollary: there should be no color line on earth." *Ebony*, September 1957, 99–104.

46 See Graham's scrapbooks, BGC. The quotation is from Nelson Bell to Mrs. W. E. Kibler of Kingsport, Tenn., November 1, 1958, Bell Papers, BGC, f. 15-15. Bell made the same point to the executive secretary of the CLC, maintaining that the papers' silent treatment was the reason that "there has been no trouble." Bell to A. C. Miller, October 13, 1958, ibid., f. 43-12.

47 *Alabama Baptist*, July 8, 1965, dateline Miami Beach. Graham also warned that churches should keep quiet about politics and sound off more on their own areas of responsibility such as soul winning and moral problems. "He praised government leaders, especially President Johnson."

48 Historians have not done much with this either, so far as I am aware. The only treatment I know of is in Lee Porter's fine dissertation, which (citing the *Baptist Message*, March 1, 1956, 1) quotes Graham's response, from Tokyo in 1956, to Criswell's remarks to the South Carolina legislature: "My pastor and I have never seen eye to eye on the race question. My views have been expressed many times and are well known." Porter, "Southern Baptists and Race Relations, 1948–1963" (Th.D. diss., SBTS, Fort Worth, Tex., 1965), 98.

49 King's sermon was apolitical. For a full recording of it, see BGC, Tape T-495.

50 King quoted in David J. Garrow, *Bearing the Cross: Martin Luther King, Jr., and the Christian Leadership Conference* (New York: Morrow, 1986), 104. For a broader treatment of the entertainment industry's economic motive to smudge racial lines, see David L. Chappell, "Hip Like Me: Racial Cross-Dressing in Popular Music before Elvis," in Brian Ward, ed., *Media, Culture, and the Modern African American Freedom Struggle* (Gainesville: University Press of Florida, 2001).

51 See Carter Woodson, *The History of the Negro Church* (Washington, D.C.: Associated Publishers, 1921); James Melvin Washington, *Frustrated Fellowship: The Black Baptist Quest for Social Power* (Macon, Ga.: Mercer University Press, 1985); William E. Montgomery, *Under Their Own Vine and Fig Tree* (Baton Rouge: LSU Press, 1993); Evelyn Brooks Higginbotham, *Righteous Discontent: The Women's Movement in the Black Baptist Church, 1880–1920* (Cambridge: Harvard University Press, 1993), esp. chap. 3; William H. Becker, "The Black Church: Manhood and Mission," in Timothy E. Fulop and Albert J. Raboteau, eds., *African American Religion: Interpretive Essays in History and Culture* (New York: Routledge, 1997), 179–99; Christopher Beckham, "The Paradox of Religious Segregation: White and Black Baptists in Western Kentucky, 1855–1900," *Regional Kentucky Historical Society* 97 (Summer 2000): 305–22.

52 Freundt said that his church had no members who were active in the Citizens' Councils. His members would have "looked down upon" the councils. But in his congregation was Ross Barnet's campaign manager, who became head of the Mississippi State Sovereignty Commission. "I grew up thinking segregation was the will of god," Freundt stated. (He could go fishing with a black

church janitor but never thought of him as being "in church.") Freundt, interview transcript, PCUS Archives. It is useful to consider the context of the desegregation of a major Charleston church, as reported by the local newspaper, under the headline, "First Presbyterian Church to Accept Negro as Member. . . . Its first Negro in more than 100 years." The paper reported that the church's elders were now implementing "a policy first established by the denomination in 1865 that stated there was 'no place for segregation in the church.' This policy has been reiterated through General Assembly action at least six times since." The pastor explained that his church was not "'breaking the bonds of segregation' since the long established church principles 'do not recognize color as a test of membership.'. . . When the church was first organized here in 1819, there were both white and Negro families among its charter members." The church had never barred attendance or membership to Negroes by any formal order, the pastor said. The admittance of a black member was not unusual but, in the paper's paraphrase, was consistent with "the principles of church policy as endorsed by the General Assembly and subscribed by the representative presbyteries and local churches." The pastor quoted Scripture—"'Mine house shall be called a house of prayer for all people'"—and noted that new members were admitted by an assembly of the membership, not by the pastor. *Charleston Daily Mail*, September 9, 1960, copy attached to Dickinson to Bell, Bell Papers, BGC, f. 23-7.

In 1962 the head of the PCUS, J. McDowell Richards, thought it was "common knowledge that Columbia Theological Seminary had adopted" a policy of desegregation "many years ago, . . . far ant[e]-dating the decision of the Supreme Court in 1954." He believed that the seminary admitted Negro students when it was still located in Columbia, S.C. (prior to 1927). The "first negro to be admitted to classes in Decatur was enrolled in the Spring of 1947. Of course this was a much simpler step for us to take than for most other institutions, since it is hard for anyone to argue that white and negro ministers should not study together." Richards to Mrs. Paschall, July 19, August 30, 1962, Richards Papers, PCUS Archives, box 62. Bell noted, "Here in Montreat, we always accept Negroes who come to our church (last Sunday there was a Negro girl in my Sunday school class and at church, and many of us made a point of welcoming her), and, if indicated, we would accept them into the membership of the church." This was in contrast to the "forced" intermingling and "crusading" for desegregation, which Bell denounced, since it diverted one from bringing sinners to Christ and robbed one's preaching of spiritual depth. Bell to the Rev. Zan White, CTS, June 9, 1965, Bell Papers, BGC, f. 54-18. This sort of thing seems to have been less common— or at least less frequently acknowledged—among midcentury southern Baptists than among southern Presbyterians. But see Mark Newman (*Getting Right*, 135) on a rural Deep South Baptist church—Oak Grove Baptist Church, Greene City, near Paragould, Ark.—that admitted ten black members in 1954 because there was no black church in the vicinity for them to attend.

53 See Azza Layton, *International Politics and Civil Rights Policies in the United*

States, 1941–1960 (Cambridge: Cambridge University Press, 2000), and Mary Dudziak, *Cold War, Civil Rights: Race and the Image of American Democracy* (Princeton, N.J.: University of Princeton Press, 2000).

54 Victor Glass and A. C. Miller, "Southern Baptists and the Negro," Committee Report to SBC, 1958, Race Relations Collection, SBC Archives, box 1.

55 Miller to Dr. C. C. Warren, November 19, 1957, CLC Resource Files, ibid., box 11. Miller had prepared a report "on the racial question," but 21 of 30 members of the CLC met before the convention and unanimously agreed not to submit it. Nonetheless, a speaker in the convention discussed his report and put the CLC "in the wrong light. There is nothing I can do or say about this except to wait out the storm that it has helped to raise. . . . Since that time we have been trying to make a strategic withdrawal and concern ourselves with other fields. . . . But such a withdrawal is not easy in the midst of conflict." It would have been "easier—much easier—to have ignored entirely the situation at Little Rock. But when the politicians had made such a mess of it, and were continuing to oppress some of the people who are our brothers in Christ as well as free American citizens, should we have had nothing to say?"

56 Porter Routh, address to South Carolina Baptist Convention, November 15, 1961, p. 3, Executive Committee Papers, SBC Archives, box 88.

57 Resolution adopted by synod, Virginia Synod Records, 1960, p. 31, PCUS Archives.

58 Glass and Miller, "Southern Baptists and the Negro," Committee report to SBC, 1958, p. 8, Race Relations Collection, SBC Archives, box 1. Similar expressions of concern about Catholic competition are in the report on Christian relations, adopted by the Alabama Synod of the PCUS, 1950, copy in ibid., box 4. See also "Are Southern Baptists Doing Enough?," *Helping Hand* (published by the SBC), 2d quarter, 1950, p. 1, copy in Wooley Papers, SBC Archives, box 14.

59 The missionary complained, "What good can the Peace Corps do as they say in effect, 'I (Americans) hate Negroes at home, but love them in Africa'?" SBC press release, May 24, 1961, Race Relations Collection, SBC Archives, box 1. A similar complaint from a missionary in Buenos Aires, with a supporting editorial, was published in the *Arkansas Baptist*, October 10, 1957, 4–5. A dozen similar voices are quoted in the leaflet, "Your Missionaries Speak" [ca. February 1965], copy in Race Relations Collection, SBC Archives, box 1. The Sherwood Baptist Church of Albany, Ga., reprinted some of these in its program of February 10, 1965, copy in Race Relations Collection, SBC Archives, box 1. Segregationist defenses against missionary pressures can be found in John B. Hayes to Luther Copeland, July 11, 1957, copy in Allen Papers, SBC Archives, no box number, and in a press release quoting the Louisiana Baptist Convention, which "regretted 'that certain of our missionaries have difficulties arising out of publicity given to racial problems.'" The convention recommended a campaign of counter publicity, emphasizing "the good that is being done" and that Louisiana's Negroes mainly "prefer to have schools and

churches of their own." Press release from the Baptist Press, November 23, 1957, Race Relations Collection, SBC Archives, box 1.

60 *SBC Annual*, 1961, 84.

61 Samuel Southard, "Are Southern Churches Silent?," *Christian Century*, November 20, 1963, 1429–32. Southard also observed that it was "hard to silence missionaries from one's home state." He reported that after a Mississippi Baptist journal printed a missionary's letter in 1962, which asked Christians to adopt Christian views on race at home in order to support missions abroad, "protests flooded in on the editor." The editor replied: "But she is a native of our state and a missionary! It is our conviction that she has a right to be heard." He gave other examples. For more on this, see Porter, "Southern Baptists," 23, 130–32, and Newman, *Getting Right*, 135–45.

62 Blake Smith, Pastor of University (Southern) Baptist Church, Austin, Tex., quoted in press release from *Christianity and Crisis*, March 3, 1958, p. 3, in Race Relations Collection, SBC Archives, box 1. This was for a series pointing out "discrepancies between denominational utterances on a national level and practices in local levels." Similarly, in 1961 the Permanent Committee on World Missions of the Mississippi Synod of the PCUS reported, "Because of the widely publicized political and social upheavals that have troubled several of these continents and hindered the progress of our missionary efforts, the program of World Missions now appears to be on trial in many congregations." Many were asking, "Have we come to the end of the missionary era?" The committee reminded the synod: "As we have recognized from the very beginning, Christ has said, 'Go ye into all the world and preach the Gospel to every creature.' Therefore, we have no other course than to obey." The synod adopted the recommendation. Synod of Mississippi Records, 1961, p. 42, PCUS Archives.

63 Bell quoted in *Life*, October 1956, 159.

64 King, Steele, Shuttlesworth, call for conference, Montgomery Improvement Association News Release, January 7, 1957, Rustin Papers, microfilm, reel 4.

65 E. Butler Abington to A. C. Miller, November 8, 22, 1957, CLC Papers, SBC Archives, box 11.

66 McLin to A. C. Miller, n.d. [early 1957], ibid.

67 G. W. and M. H. Simmons to Porter Routh, Executive Committee Papers, ibid., box 82. The letter, apparently from two members of the same family, is written in the first-person singular. Extremist laymen in Alabama had already organized, the writer said, and would push for withdrawal from the SBC unless something was done to change its "left-wing trend." His church had been contacted about forming a laymen's group in Mississippi, and members of the church planned to participate in it.

68 Brady, *Black Monday* (Jackson, Miss.: Citizens' Councils of America, 1955), 48.

69 King to Bayard Rustin, September 20, 1956, Rustin Papers, microfilm, reel 4.

70 Smiley to J. Swomley, dated [by a different hand] March [2?], 1956, ibid.

1 See Numan V. Bartley, *The Rise of Massive Resistance: Race and Politics in the South during the 1950s* (Baton Rouge: LSU Press, 1969), and Neil R. McMillen, *The Citizens' Council: Organized Resistance to the Second Reconstruction, 1954–1964* (Urbana: University of Illinois Press, 1971). See also I. A. Newby, *Challenge to the Court: Social Scientists and the Defense of Segregation, 1954–1966* (Baton Rouge: LSU Press, 1967); Jeff Roche, *Restructured Resistance: The Sibley Commission and the Politics of Desegregation in Georgia* (Athens: University of Georgia Press, 1998); and Matthew D. Lassiter and Andrew B. Lewis, eds., *The Moderates' Dilemma: Massive Resistance to School Desegregation in Virginia* (Charlottesville: University Press of Virginia, 1998).

2 At midcentury there were many self-corroding elements in the southern white mind: strong memories of the Civil War (segregationists never seriously considered secession: James J. Kilpatrick wrote, "We may in the end have to comply; we offer no vain threats of civil war"—"The Right to Interpose," *Human Events*, December 24, 1955); recognition that the regional labor market had been integrated into national and international labor markets; the declining respectability of racism among scientific and other intellectual authorities, and the related integration of the regional information market into a national stream of mass communications; the experience of individual soldiers in World War II who saw the devastation caused by Nazi policies of racism and who sometimes saw black soldiers serving as well as white ones; the irresistible appeal of white musicians like Benny Goodman and Frank Sinatra who proudly paid homage to black musicians and often performed with them; defeatism and a sense of futility about the struggle to maintain "tradition" in a changing world; and perhaps—who can say?—a suspicion that maybe some of these Negroes really did deserve a little more respect and opportunity. On the last point, see Tom P. Brady, *Black Monday* (Jackson, Miss.: Citizens' Councils of America, 1955).

3 H. H. Hyman and P. B. Sheatesly examine the opinion polls in "Attitudes toward Desegregation," *Scientific American* 195 (December 1956): 35–39. Earl Black covers single-issue campaigns in his indispensable *Southern Governors and Civil Rights: Racial Segregation as a Campaign Issue in the Second Reconstruction* (Cambridge: Harvard University Press, 1976).

4 Byrnes speech, quoted at length in Grace Graham, "Negro Education Progresses in South Carolina," *Social Forces* 30 (October 1951–May 1952): 429–38 (quotations, p. 429). In the event, Byrnes succeeded in levying a 3 percent sales tax and issued bonds to create a school building fund. He claimed that two-thirds of the fund went to black schools, though only 40 percent of the state's schools were black. For data and background I have relied on James F. Byrnes, *All in One Lifetime* (New York: Harper, 1958); David Robertson, *Sly and Able: A Political Biography of James F. Byrnes* (New York: Norton, 1994); George McMillan, "Integration with Dignity" (1963), reprinted in *Perspectives in South Carolina History: The First Three Hundred Years*, ed. Ernest M.

Lander Jr. and Robert K. Ackerman (Columbia: University of South Carolina Press, 1973), 381–91; and Kari Fredrickson, "'The Slowest State' and 'Most Backward Community': Racial Violence in South Carolina and Federal Civil-Rights Legislation," *South Carolina Historical Magazine* 98 (April 1997): 177–202.

5 This might have been easier in Byrnes's state than elsewhere: Virginius Dabney pointed out that South Carolina, though it had "next to the highest percentage of Negroes in its population, had one of the best lynching records of all the Southern states during the decade which ended January 1, 1941." Dabney attributed this to a state law (on the books since 1896) holding counties responsible for the practice within their borders. Under the law, the state collected a $2,000 fine from each of seven counties that had lynchings between 1913 and 1931. Dabney, *Below the Potomac: A Book about the New South* (New York: Appleton-Century, 1942), 185.

6 John T. Kneebone, *Southern Liberal Journalists and the Issue of Race, 1920–1944* (Chapel Hill: University of North Carolina Press, 1985), 211–12. Kneebone notes that readers did not respond negatively to the desegregation proposal: to Dabney's amazement, 87 of 114 of the published letters endorsed it. As Kneebone states, Graves misrepresented the public's attitude in his "Chance-Taking South," *Virginia Quarterly Review* 21 (Spring 1945): 161–73.

7 Dabney to Graves, April 26, 1949. Dabney, who defended states' rights as a crucial component of his liberalism in his epochal *Liberalism in the South* (Chapel Hill: University of North Carolina Press, 1932), abandoned states' rights for a time in support of the New Deal, but by 1948 he had returned to a pro–states' rights position. Dabney to Graves, February 14, 1948. Both letters in Graves Papers, BPL, 830.1.6.1.6. Dabney (*Below the Potomac*, 124, 185) counseled against federal anti–poll tax and antilynching legislation, saying that state action was more effective. Though he remained liberal on many issues, he showed the deepest contempt for the integrationism of Sarah Patton Boyle. See Dabney to Thomas Waring, February 21, 1955, Waring Papers, SCHS, box 432. By 1950, Kneebone notes, Dabney was calling himself a "conservative." Other southern liberals, from Ellis Arnall to Mark Ethridge and Hodding Carter, all supported states' rights and defended segregation. See Arnall in *Atlanta Journal*, January 23, 1945; Carter to Graves, February 6, 1950, and Ethridge to Graves, August 2, 1948, both in Graves Papers, BPL, 830.1.6.1.6.

8 Putnam, *Race and Reason: A Yankee View* (Washington, D.C.: Public Affairs Press, 1961), 113. See nn. 36–39 below.

9 Graham, "Negro Education Progresses," 429. To Jack Bass and Walter De Vries, in *The Transformation of Southern Politics: Social Change and Political Consequence since 1945* (New York: Basic Books, 1976), 254, Byrnes "was perhaps the one man of sufficient stature in the South who might have been able to offer regional leadership toward acceptance rather than defiance" of the Supreme Court's desegregation order. Congressman Frank Boykin of Alabama was a member of perhaps four different chapters of the "White Citizens

Council"—he was not sure how many, because he had too little time to follow through with the organizations. But, he told Byrnes, "if we could get somebody that could put their time in for just a little while and properly organize it, . . . it would be the greatest thing that ever happened to our country." Boykin believed that the councils lacked effective leadership, "but with your great brain, your great ability and your understanding heart," you "can do more on this problem than anybody I know. . . . You, Jimmy, can save not only the South, but the Nation." Boykin to Byrnes (eight pages), May 21, 1956, Byrnes Papers, CU, box 839 (1).

10 Graves to Landrum, April 15, 1951, Graves Papers, BPL, 830.1.7.1.7. In his *The Fighting South* (New York: Putnam, 1943), Graves devoted a chapter (pp. 49–64) to the "centripetal force." There he admitted: "The poll tax in the South is an abomination and ought to be abolished, but if the national rather than the state government is permitted to do the abolishing there is opened a field of federal interfering which is sure to ignore . . . the delicate and special set-up involved" (p. 63). So, too, would federal action against lynching—which was "almost extinct in the South until the wartime racial agitators provoked it again"—be counterproductive.

11 Graves, "Tuskegee Solution," *Birmingham News Herald*, ca. July 10, 1957 (paragraphing altered from original), copy in Martin Papers, LC, box 158, f. 8.

12 Ibid.

13 Graves, quoting Waring and Kilpatrick, in ibid. Graves found Martin's use of "Nigra" in quotations particularly irksome: "Mr. Martin continues to have Southern whites say 'Nigra,' not understanding that they think they are saying 'Negro' and are as near it as Northerners who say 'Knee-grow.' The right pronunciation is somewhere between this too-long 'e' and the South's pin-for-pen pronunciation." Martin's series ran in the *Saturday Evening Post*, June 15–July 13, 1957; his book—*The Deep South Says Never* (New York: Ballantine, 1957)—had additional content. A reader in Summerton, S.C., wrote, "Most of us who live in this section believe that the NAACP is the master of the art of perverting the truth; but . . . John Bartlow Martin has outclassed them in this art." J. T. Touchenberry to Editor, *Saturday Evening Post*, July 27, 1957, 4.

14 Another example is in the newsletter of the Montgomery County Citizens' Council, which aimed at upper-class white women who were spotted by the Negro press "chauffe[u]ring their nursemaids and cooks" to work. These women were lending de facto aid to the bus boycott. The Negro press was delighted: "You white women can now read what the negro thinks of you. Are you too lazy to do your own work? . . . It is indeed time for you to organize with white people. Yes, as strong as the negroes have solidified." *States' Rights Advocate*, July 28, 1956, 3, copy in NAACP Papers, LC, ser. III.A, box 282. In 1958 the investigator of the Mississippi Sovereignty Commission reported on efforts to organize an anti-NAACP among black Mississippians, which his top black informant, Percy Greene, advised him would cost $10,000 to start: "Greene said the NAACP in Mississippi and also in the entire south

is strong because it is well organized and not because the majority of negroes support it." Zack Van Landingham to File, December 4, 1958, Sovereignty Commission Records, MDAH, item 2-5-1-56. According to Edward P. Lawton, *The South and the Nation* (Fort Myers Beach, Fla.: Island Press, 1963): "In the struggle since 1954 over the High Court's decision on segregation, the South has managed its campaign very badly. Having no counterpart to the National Association for the Advancement of Colored People, with its widespread organization, its funds and its political influence, if the South were really determined to win, it should have created a non-partisan body to make its true case known in the North and abroad, and even in the South itself" (p. 13). Carleton Putnam (*Race and Reason*, 49, 88) went to great lengths to demonstrate that the NAACP was really run by white people. His pronounced nativism shows up here in his attributing NAACP organization (and egalitarianism generally) to non–Anglo Saxon immigrants.

15 The quotations in this and the previous two paragraphs are from Wall to Kilpatrick, June 14, 1954, and Kilpatrick to Wall, June 15, September 29, 1954, Kilpatrick Papers, UVA, 6626-b, box 2. Wall was one of the leaders of the school-closing movement in Prince Edward County. For more on the need to organize, see W. J. Simmons, "Organization: The Key to Victory," *Citizen*, February 1962, 7, and the notice of the "Citizens' Council Conference in Jackson on October 25-26," whose theme was "Organization Is the Key to Victory!," *Citizen*, September 1963, 9.

16 Byrnes to Graves, September 8, 1949, Byrnes Papers, CU, f. 1333.

17 Kilpatrick to J. B. Wall, June 14, 1954 (spelling corrected), Kilpatrick Papers, UVA, 6626-b, box 2. Though a racist, Kilpatrick, like many white southerners, could not make his racism override other things that he valued. He was always repulsed by southerners who chose racism over everything else. When a student at the University of Virginia invited Kilpatrick to be on a public debate team with the anti-Semitic propagandist John Kasper (an Ezra Pound protégé who became a kind of folk hero to the Ku Klux Klan, though he never joined it) and Floyd Flemming, the leader of what Kilpatrick called "the notorious Seaboard White Citizens' Council," Kilpatrick replied, "I emphatically would not appear on the same journalistic platform with these creatures." The presence of such leaders at such a prominent place would "do incalculable harm to the university and to the South as a whole." He urged Governor Lindsay Almond of Virginia not to accept the invitation that would be extended to him. Kilpatrick to J. L. Almond, April 9, 1957, Kilpatrick Papers, UVA, 6626-b, box 7.

18 *Richmond Times-Dispatch*, July 29, 1957.

19 *Shreveport Times*, August 21, 1957, copy in NAACP Papers, LC, ser. III.A, box 282.

20 Workman, *The Case for the South* (N.Y.: Devin-Adair, 1960), vii. On the decision of Byrnes and Talmadge to turn against the Klan, see David M. Chalmers, *Hooded Americanism: The First Century of the Ku Klux Klan, 1865–1965* (1965; reprint, Chicago: Quadrangle, 1968), 337. John Temple Graves lauded

Byrnes for opposing the Klan. Graves column, *Columbia Record*, January 19, 1955, Byrnes Papers, CU, box 51.

21 James Haskins with Kathleen Benson, *Nat King Cole: A Personal and Professional Biography* (Chelsea, Mich.: Scarborough House, 1984), 138–43; Graves, draft of *American Mercury* article, "The South to Power," 7 (the finished article ran in the July 1956 issue), and Dabney to Graves, July 30, 1956, both in Graves Papers, BPL, 830.1.8.1.8. Dabney added that he had made other efforts, in his own recent article in *The American*, to set "forth the low reputation of the North Alabama Citizens Councils, and the fact that they are widely looked down on by other Councils."

22 Graves to James F. Byrnes, July 6, 1955, and Byrnes to Graves, July 15, 1955 (Byrnes declined the invitation), Byrnes Papers, CU, f. 816 (2). For background on Horton, see Glenn T. Eskew, *But for Birmingham: The Local and National Movements in the Civil Rights Struggle* (Chapel Hill: University of North Carolina Press, 1997), 107.

23 Waring to Graves, February 8, 1960, Graves Papers, BPL, 830.1.9.1.9.

24 Harris quoted in *Time*, April 7, 1961.

25 By this time, the only sure way to defy desegregation orders was to close public schools, as Governor Orval Faubus had done in Little Rock in 1958–59. It worked well for Faubus, in the sense that he became popular with segregationists—he had been known as a moderate or worse before then—and enjoyed their esteem over a remarkably long career afterward. But it was a disaster for lower-level segregationists, who ultimately turned the capital city's chamber of commerce—and, perhaps more significantly, a group of influential upper-class clubwomen—against them. This allowed moderate segregationists (those willing to alleviate pressure with tokenism) to take control of the school board in a recall election that drove extremists off the board. Faubus himself had moderated his position by then. See Roy Reed, *Faubus: Life and Times of an American Prodigal* (Fayetteville: University of Arkansas Press, 1997), 177–79. When Virginia took a similar course, the effect was devastating, since Virginia had led the doctrinal battle and lent a respectability to massive resistance that Faubus lacked. Governor Ernest Vandiver "capitulated" in Georgia, too.

26 Sass to William D. Workman, February 12, 1960, with attached memo, "Let's Stop Running Away from the Battlefield! A Segregationist View of the Policy of State-Ordered Closing of Schools," Workman Papers, USC, box 1.

27 Waring and Graves exchange, February 8, 10, 16, 1960, Waring Papers, SCHS, box 401, and Graves Papers, BPL, 830.1.9.1.9. By this time massive resistance in Virginia had crumbled, and Waring was urging his readers to "endure" but not "accept" token desegregation. Referring to the Georgia Tech protest, Waring wrote, "Such signs, and the capitulation in Virginia, persuaded me to take my current tack rather than continue to demand total resistance." The next year Waring agreed with Graves's disapproval of "vehement rightists," such as the John Birchers: "Robert Welch has done our cause harm, in my judgment." Waring to Graves, April 15, 1961, Waring Papers, SCHS, box 401.

28 Kilpatrick to J. L. Frank, January 2, 1956, Kilpatrick Papers, UVA, 6626-b, box 61. He had anticipated the difficulty three years before: "Frankly I see no immediate answer to the dilemma in which conservative Southerners find themselves. . . . If you know of any rational way out, I'd like to hear it." Kilpatrick to Frank, January 9, 1953, ibid., box 2. One of the few prominent religious segregationists, Finley Tinnin of the Louisiana Baptist Association, had a similar view. See Chapter 6, n. 28, above.

29 Walter J. Suthon Jr., "The Dubious Origin of the 14th Amendment," *U.S. News & World Report*, July 20, 1956. Other attacks on the Fourteenth Amendment include Brady, *Black Monday*, 15-16 (Brady stuck to his interpretation, if somewhat obliquely, in his interview with the University of Southern Mississippi: Brady, interview transcript, USM, 46); Lawton, *The South and the Nation*, 16, 121-23, 207-8; and Richard W. Edmonds, "Scandalous Origin of the 14th Amendment" and "Validity of the 14th Amendment Never Tested," chaps. 5 and 6 of *Foundation for Segregation* (Columbus, Ga.: Richard W. Edmonds, 1957), 39-58. David Lawrence, editor of *U.S. News & World Report*, believed "that the fourteenth Amendment was never legally ratified." Lawrence, quoted in Carleton Putnam to Lawrence, August 11, 1959, copy in Waring Papers, SCHS, box 430. (Lawton also relies on Lawrence.) William J. Simmons gave mild, fleeting expression to this view in "Why Segregation Is Right," speech at Notre Dame University, March 7, 1963, in Association of Citizens' Councils of Mississippi Files, MDAH, box 3, p. 6.

30 Byrnes, "The Supreme Court Must Be Curbed," *U.S. News & World Report*, May 18, 1956; Kilpatrick, "The Right to Interpose," *Human Events*, December 24, 1955; Satterfield, "The Growth of Federal Power," *Louisiana Bar Journal* 9 (May 1961): 19-28; "Law and Lawyers in a Changing World," presidential address, *Reports of the American Bar Association* 87 (1962): 516-42; "President's Page," *ABA Journal* 48 (July 1962): 565, 611-12. A retired judge from Missouri asked Byrnes why he did not "attack the Constitutionality of this [the Fourteenth] amendment," but apparently Byrnes did not reply. Hoy to Byrnes, October 8, 1956, Byrnes Papers, CU, 780 (1). R. Carter Pittman, the prominent (Dalton) Georgia lawyer and white supremacist, embraced the Fourteenth Amendment's equal protection clause—subsuming it under a tradition of narrow legal equality and equal opportunity, in opposition to spurious, foreign doctrines of equal condition. Pittman, "Equality versus Liberty: The Eternal Conflict," *ABA Journal* 46 (August 1960): 873-80, esp. 874, 877. Pittman also accepted the Fourteenth Amendment because its last clause reserved the power to carry out equal protection to *Congress* (not the courts). Pittman, "The Supreme Court, the Broken Constitution, and the Shattered Bill of Rights" (pamphlet based on four speeches, 1954-56, distributed by the States' Rights Council of Georgia, Atlanta), copy in Martin Papers, LC, box 232, f. 8.

31 Putnam, *Race and Reason*, 20.

32 David J. Mays gave a state-by-state summary of all the segregation practices of the northern and southern states at the time of ratification of the Four-

teenth Amendment in "A Question of Intent," Statement before the U.S. Senate, Judiciary Committee, Subcommittee on Constitutional Amendments (reprinted as a pamphlet distributed by the Virginia Commission on Constitutional Government, 1959, 1967). The insistence that the amendment did not apply to schools made compromise legislation at the national level difficult to imagine. When Senator A. Willis Robertson of Virginia introduced a bill in 1956 to allow states to operate segregated or nonsegregated schools, a Raleigh lawyer, I. Beverly Lake, wrote to Sam Ervin, "There is a great deal of danger in Senator Robertson's proposal. It seems to be inconsistent with the interposition resolutions being adopted by Virginia and other States. Does it not concede that the Supreme Court was correct in saying that the Fourteenth Amendment applies [properly to that issue]?" Congress had no authority to pass such a bill unless the amendment indeed applied to school desegregation. To concede that point was to concede the whole game. "The possibility which disturbs me is that, having proposed the Robertson bill, Southern Senators may find it difficult to raise constitutional objections" to civil rights bills. Congress would implicitly sanction the Supreme Court's new interpretation of the Fourteenth Amendment. Ervin shared "your misgivings in respect to the Robertson resolution." Lake to Ervin, February 10, 1956, and Ervin to Lake, February 14, 1956, Ervin Papers, UNC-CH, box 15.

33 Wills offers a spirited and witty dismissal of the states' rights tradition in American constitutional thought in *A Necessary Evil: A History of American Distrust of Government* (New York: Simon and Schuster, 1999). Other recent contributors to the debate suggest that Wills's conclusions are not as self-evident as he seems to believe. See Lance Banning, *The Sacred Fire of Liberty: James Madison and the Founding of the Federal Republic* (Ithaca, N.Y.: Cornell University Press, 1995); Akhil Reed Amar, *The Bill of Rights: Construction and Reconstruction* (New Haven: Yale University Press, 2000); and Forrest McDonald, *States' Rights and the Union: Imperium in Imperio, 1776–1876* (Lawrence: University Press of Kansas, 2000).

34 Kilpatrick borrowed to a lesser extent from Thomas Jefferson's related Kentucky Resolutions of February 1799, which claimed more extreme state powers than interposition.

35 The Georgia, Louisiana, Mississippi, and Virginia legislatures adopted interposition laws. Georgia went further—against Kilpatrick's wishes—and declared the Supreme Court's decision "null, void, and of no effect." Kilpatrick opposed these words as too inflammatory, indeed treasonous. He was joined in that view by such segregationists as John P. Coleman, governor of Mississippi. In that state the moderate segregationists managed to keep "nullification" out of the state's resolution, but had to swallow similar words saying that *Brown* was "invalid and of no lawful effect." The Mississippi resolution did restrict its resistance to "lawful, peaceful, and constitutional means," however. (This was the sort of language that segregationist leaders in Congress had used to defang the Southern Manifesto so that moderates would sign it.) Kilpatrick insisted on sticking with James Madison's example and avoiding

John C. Calhoun's. He knew that the bluff of Georgia's hotheaded segregationists could all too easily be called. For they were hinting at secession, which Kilpatrick knew the white South would never risk over segregation. South Carolina took an even less confrontational stance in its resolution of protest against *Brown*, avoiding Kilpatrick's word "interposition" as well as "nullification." The legislative developments are ably covered in *Southern School News*, January 1956, March 1956, April 1956, and June 1956.

36 Putnam's book was also promoted by Thomas R. Waring (who wrote the foreword), John Temple Graves, and James J. Kilpatrick. See Graves to Waring, April 13, 1961 (box 401), Kilpatrick to Waring, April 1, 1959 (box 430), and Waring to Putnam, March 20, 1959 (box 430), all in Waring Papers, SCHS. Later, a "Putnam Letters Committee" promoted Putnam's ideas. On Putnam and other segregationists who emphasized biological arguments, see John P. Jackson Jr., "In Ways Unacademical: The Reception of Carleton S. Coon's *The Origin of Races,*" *Journal of the History of Biology* 34 (2001): 247–85. A longer attack on egalitarianism appears in Putnam's *Race and Reality: A Search for Solutions* (Washington, D.C.: Public Affairs Press, 1967).

37 The quotations in this and the previous two paragraphs are from Putnam to Waring, December 4, 1959, Waring Papers, SCHS, box 430.

38 Waring to Putnam, December 7, 1959, ibid. Waring also expressed resignation about the moral argument, a resignation that often appears in segregationist correspondence: "I doubt whether the public will accept a moral justification. I think people will go on bootlegging segregation, while paying lip-service to integration, until they get a bellyful as they did with the hypocrisy of prohibiting alcohol."

39 Copies of Putnam to Byrnes and Putnam to Lawrence, both dated August 11, 1959, and Waring to Putnam, August 13, 1959, in ibid.

40 Byrnes, Memo of remarks at Abbeville, S.C., attached to Byrnes to T. F. Wannamaker, June 13, 1950, Byrnes Papers, CU, f. 778.

41 See John Egerton, *Speak Now against the Day: The Generation before the Civil Rights Movement in the South* (New York: Knopf, 1994), 116–18; Robertson, *Sly and Able*, 86–94, 190–200; and Bryant Simon, *A Fabric of Defeat: The Politics of South Carolina Millhands, 1910–1948* (Chapel Hill: University of North Carolina Press, 1998), 38–39, 211–12.

42 Dan T. Carter, *The Politics of Rage: George Wallace, the Origins of the New Conservatism, and the Transformation of American Politics* (New York: Simon and Schuster, 1995), 297, 342, 356–60.

43 See David L. Chappell, "Religious Ideas of the Segregationists," *Journal of American Studies* 32 (1998): 248, n. 16.

44 Reprints of Hurston's essay appeared under various titles in southern newspapers—e.g., *Asheville Times* (N.C.), n.d., copy in Ervin Papers, UNC-CH, box 340), and *Richmond Times-Dispatch*, August 22, 1955, *Montgomery Advertiser*, January 7, 1956, and *Arkansas Faith*, May 1956, 14, copies in Bates Papers, SHSW, box 4.

45 Byrnes, address at Bennettsville, S.C., September 26, 1957, 1–2, Byrnes Papers,

CU, f. 879 (1). For other examples of segregationists' trumpeting of black support, see "Negro Business Men Opposing Extremists," *Citizens' Council* 2 (November 1956) and reprint from the black newspaper, *Newark Telegram*, "You Can't Eat Integration," in *Citizens' Council* 2 (January 1957). See also letters to the black self-proclaimed "Prophet," W. D. Willett, "National Evangelist, Spiritual Counselor, Divine Healer, formerly of Little Rock," from Governor Herman Talmadge (Ga.), November 22, 1954, and from Senator John D. McClellan (Ark.), October 7, 1957, and the pamphlet and Sunday school lesson plan from Frank Garrett Sr., "Christianity Review Segregation or Integration"—all in Bates Papers, SHSW, box 5, f. 13. And see "A Negro Takes a Look at NAACP's 'Northern Big Shots'" (on Webster McClary), *Richmond Times-Dispatch*, September 21, 1955; "Negro Archbishop Blasts NAACP Aims," *County Record* (of Williamsburg County, S.C.), February 16, 1956, and the leaflet "A Negro Attacks Integration" (apparently reprinted from the *Richmond Times-Dispatch*, August 22, 1955)—all in Waring Papers, SCHS, box 432. A Chattanooga segregationist, expressing surprise that "so many true loyal Southerners supported" a pro-integration report from the PCUS Christian Relations Council, wrote: "My negro cook says—'God made me black and He made you white—HE made us different—if he had wanted us the same HE would have made us the same." Mrs. Willard Steele to Nelson Bell, June 2, 1958, Bell Papers, BGC, f. 47-8.

46 Four of the ten issues of the *Councilor* in the NAACP papers carried "But the Negro Himself"; an additional two carried major news stories making the same point ("Color Communism and Common Sense," about former black Communist Party leader Manning Johnson's confessions, January 1959, and "Negro Editor Says His Race 'Being Used' in Rights Fight," September 1957), NAACP Papers, LC, ser. III.A, box 282.

47 Payne, *I've Got the Light of Freedom: The Organizing Tradition and the Mississippi Freedom Struggle* (Berkeley: University of California Press, 1995), 42. Payne emphasizes the coercion involved in getting the signatures.

48 November 1955 Gallup Poll, cited in Abigail Thernstrom and Stephan Thernstrom, *America in Black and White: One Nation, Indivisible* (New York: Simon and Schuster, 1997), 318, 616 n. 13. The Thernstroms' gloss on the 53 percent is instructive:

> It is tempting to dismiss this evidence on the grounds that blacks in the South in those days were probably unwilling to state their true opinions to pollsters, most of whom were white. Although this hypothesis is plausible, it cannot be squared with the results of another Gallup poll just a few weeks later, which showed that 82 percent of southern blacks approved of a recent Interstate Commerce Commission ruling against segregation in transportation. . . . If so many southern blacks were willing to admit to holding views about segregated transportation that were contrary to those of most southern whites, it is hard to see why they would dissemble when questioned about segregation in education. The roughly fifty-fifty split in opinion among southern blacks is probably as accurate as most polling results.

49   One cannot help wondering whether segregationists who enlisted black sup-
     port, such as Mississippi's Sovereignty Commission, got their money's worth
     from black supporters and informants. The frequently absurd triviality of
     black informants' reports suggests an audacious version of "puttin' on ol'
     massa." Also significant is the commission's failure to get white editors to
     go along with its efforts to control information. See, e.g., Van Landingham
     to Director, September 23, 1959, Sovereignty Commission Records, MDAH,
     items 1-15-0-9 (cf. 1-15-0-8) and 2-79-1-17. The investigator worried over "the
     fact that there are many negroes working over Mississippi and other South-
     ern States using the segregation issue as a racket in attempting to solicit funds
     from white people." The commission was investigating the matter, and mean-
     while he was "advising people over the state not to contribute funds to any
     of these negroes until we have investigated them." Van Landingham to D. H.
     Coleman, August 11, 1959, ibid., item 2-88-0-19.
50   See, e.g., Nelson Bell's correspondence in March 1958 with Darby Fulton,
     Tyler Payton, and Clennon King—the last described by Payton as "an emi-
     nent Negro professor of history at Alcorn College in Mississippi," who wrote
     for the right-wing *American Mercury* and proposed a small-scale coloniza-
     tion program for American Negroes in Africa. Bell Papers, BGC, f. 41-10.
     See also Clennon King, "I Speak as a Southern Negro," *American Mercury*
     (January 1958), and the Rev. James Dees to "a Negro clergyman," Septem-
     ber 4, 1957, Bell Papers, BGC, f. 43-12; The Rev. J. W. Jones, Editor of the
     Community Citizen "(A Negro Newspaper), New Albany, Mississippi," re-
     printed in the right-wing *Militant Truth* (Greenville, S.C.) 16, no. 2 (Janu-
     ary 1960): front page; and "Confidential Memo" and "Supplemental Note"
     from John H. McCray to News Editors and Broadcasters, attached to McCray
     to William Workman, January 24, 1955, in Workman Papers, USC, box 20.
     The Sovereignty Commission Records show the most extensive effort to gar-
     ner and fabricate black support. See, e.g., the well-stuffed files on Davis Lee,
     Clennon King, and editor Percy Greene, esp. items 1-4-0-26, 1-17-0-11, 1-23-
     0-65, 1-28-0-5, 1-56-0-2, 1-56-0-4, 2-52-0-10, 2-72-1-50, 2-72-1-61, 2-88-0-
     19, 2-111-2-62, 2-126-1-38, 3-41-0-2, and 5-4-0-56.
51   Moore to Byrnes, n.d., and Moore to Byrnes (from the Furman University
     campus), December 1, 1955, Byrnes Papers, CU, f. 824 (4). Revealing in a dif-
     ferent way is the entirely straight memo from Sovereignty Commission in-
     vestigator Zack Van Landingham, who had been informed that actor Stepin
     Fetchit "felt the same way about segregation as we do. . . . It was decided that
     if this Negro felt the way about segregation as had been stated it would be a
     good idea to express his views to newspaper reporters and to have photogra-
     phers present also." The actor accepted an invitation to appear with several
     reporters, including Bill Minor of the *New Orleans Times-Picayune*. Fetchit
     stated that he was not an NAACP member; he had toured the country in
     1927 raising funds for it, but the organization had changed since then. "He
     expressed the opinion that the Communist party had infiltrated to a certain
     extent the NAACP. He said he was against forced integration and was of the

opinion that the NAACP was over zealous and had gone too far. . . . He also said, however, that he did not want to be held up and called an Uncle Tom by members of his own race, and for that reason did not want to appear to be against the NAACP in every respect. He admitted that the NAACP had severely criticized him in the past because of some of the roles he had played in motion pictures." He did not give "a definite answer to a number of questions but tried to talk around the questions. About the only thing definite that could be gained was the fact that he was for God and against Communism." Van Landingham to Director, May 4, 1959, Sovereignty Commission Records, MDAH, item 2-79-1-17.

52 Harry McKinley Williams's forthcoming work on Schuyler will show a strong opposition to protest and litigation akin to the apolitical economic "uplift" strategy of Booker T. Washington. Unlike Hurston, however, Schuyler believed in racial integration—indeed, in cultural assimilation and interbreeding—as an ultimate goal. See Williams, "George Schuyler's Berlin Speech of 1950," paper presented at the Organization of American Historians Conference, St. Louis, April 2, 2000. See also Henry Louis Gates, "A Fragmented Man: George Schuyler and the Claims of Race," *New York Times Book Review*, September 20, 1992, 31, 42–43, and Schuyler, *Black and Conservative* (New Rochelle: Arlington House, 1966).

53 The *State* (Columbia, S.C.) reprinted an editorial by Lee, entitled "Negro Editor Says Integration Is Not Best for His Race," on March 9, 1959. Waring wanted to play the Lee story big but apparently backed off after looking into his background. Lee, Waring learned, published scandal sheets aimed at black audiences (*Newark Telegram*, *Jacksonville Mirror*, and *Savannah Daily Journal*), and his own career was plagued by scandal. On December 27, 1958, the *Baltimore Afro-American* reported that Lee had confessed to murder in 1927 and was sentenced to eighteen years in prison. He had been married four times. He had been charged with libel. NAACP president Roy Wilkins condemned him in print: "We do not know what motivates Mr. Lee, whether it is the revenue he receives from white advertisers and contributors or some other factor. We do know that he faithfully follows the line laid down by the White Citizens' Councils and other like race-hate organizations." Waring was able to learn from various sources that Lee had a reputation among fellow black journalists as "a 'newspaper tramp' always looking for an easy way to turn a dollar. The general opinion in the Negro press is that he is prostituting himself in his editorials and in the kind of scandal sheet he is putting out" and that he "has had some sort of dealings with Senator Russell and that one or more of his editorials have been inserted in the Congressional Record." One of Waring's contacts claimed: "I believe he prostitutes his writing of editorials and have personally seen checks which he had from such southerners as Sen. George of Ga., Sen. Eastland of Mississippi and Rep. Rankin of Mississippi. . . . I don't know what representations he made to get such checks, but I have a good idea." Materials on Lee in Waring Papers, SCHS, box 412.

The Sovereignty Commission also promoted Lee for a time, but by March 1959 it had obtained information from a black source it considered more reliable—Percy Greene—that Lee was "the greatest fraud being perpetrated on the Southern people. . . . Greene states that Lee is an ex-convict and a forger and is merely trying to practice a fraud on the white people by collecting money whenever he can get a newspaper to publish some article he has written." Van Landingham to Director, March 19, 1959, Sovereignty Commission Records, MDAH, item 2-111-1-4. Apparently the commission had similar troubles with Clennon King. See, e.g., Robert Welch to commission, August 6, 1968, ibid., item 1-28-0-93, and clippings that trace King's convictions, releases, and ultimate expatriation, items 1-28-0-68 to 1-28-0-91.

Carleton Putnam, in *Race and Reason*, 89, 35, 57-58, also cites Davis Lee and elsewhere mentions that he had gotten "word from many colored people agreeing with my position." Nelson Bell's *SPJ* carried Lee's defense of the South: There was "more to the Negro and white relationship in the South than Jim Crowism" on one side and integration efforts on the other, which had dominated the news. Lee, "True Picture of the South Missed by Writers," *SPJ*, August 21, 1957, 6. The Rev. W. R. Farley of Dallas, Tex., made a similar argument, adding that the Negro race was "being misled by many agitators." Farley, "From a Southern Negro," *Methodist Challenge*, June 1955, 3-4.

54 Quoting freely from a Citizens' Council report, Bayard Rustin complained that "in the Delta the Negro church is bought and paid for by the Council, with very few exceptions. Many ministers are in debt to the members of the Citizens Council. These clergymen denounce the NAACP as radical and misguided." According to the report, Rustin noted, the council had "given backing to the conservative class of Negro in the area and has given them courage to speak out in opposition to the radical NAACP element." "Fear in the Delta," *Liberation*, October 8, 1956, reprinted in *Down the Line: The Collected Writings of Bayard Rustin* (Chicago: Quadrangle, 1971), 65-66.

55 White segregationists frequently accused integrationists of hypocritical or unconscious disdain for the Negro, professing their own true love: T. Robert Ingram wrote of integrationists' "fastidious hatred of the black race": the integrationists "imply that he [the Negro] is not worthy to company this earth in your presence." Since integrationists sought to *change* the black race (deliberately by improving its condition or inadvertently by interbreeding) they denied God's wisdom in creating it: "To pant after an integration of the races— a new race—is to say that God made a mistake when he made them!" Ingram, "The Spirit of Anti-Christ," in Ingram, ed., *Essays on Segregation* (Houston, Tex.: St. Thomas Press, 1960), 94. Similarly, Judge Tom Brady (of Brookhaven, Miss.), in the first popular anti-*Brown* manifesto, blamed the "High Priests of Washington" for "blow[ing] again and stronger upon the dying embers of racial hate, distrust and envy." Brady argued that white southerners understood the Negro better than the Supreme Court, which based its decision on the "theory" and "a few uncorrelated facts" of "Gunner" Myrdal. Brady challenged any of his white opponents to match his experience:

If you had a negro mammy to take care of you and keep you from eating dirt; if you played with negro boys when a boy; if you have worked with and among them, laughed at their ribald humor; if you have been stunned by their abysmal vulgarity and profanity; if you can find it in your heart to overlook their obscenity and depravity; if you can respect and love their deep religious fervor; if you can cherish their loyalty and devotion to you, then you are beginning to understand the negro.

   If you have had a negro man and his wife and children live and work with you on your place . . . and you . . . have fed and clothed all of them and protected them from anyone who would harm them; if you have bought the school books for their children . . .

Brady, *Black Monday* 44, 47. Brady also proudly quoted W. E. B. Du Bois's famous article, "Does the Negro Need Separate Schools?," 34–35.

56 Workman, "Truth Is Negroes Do Want Racial Integration," *Citizens' Council* 1 (December 1955): 3. Fannie Lou Hamer had a similar perspective: "When the white man made his greatest mistake is when he put us behind. If he'd put us in front we wouldn't've had a chance to watch him. So he put us behind, we watched every move he made. We know him. He doesn't know us, but we know him." Hamer, interview transcript, Project South, Stanford University, MFDP, chap. 55, 0491–8.

57 Maass, "The Secrets of Mississippi: Post-Authoritarian Shock in the South," *New Republic*, December 21, 1998, 21. A similar pattern is detectable in Van Landingham to Director, September 18, 1959, Sovereignty Commission Records, MDAH, item 1-15-0-7. For background, see Yasuhiro Katagiri, *The Mississippi State Sovereignty Commission: Civil Rights and States' Rights* (Jackson: University Press of Mississippi, 2001).

58 See, e.g., Jonathan Daniels, *A Southerner Discovers the South* (New York: Macmillan, 1938); W. J. Cash, *The Mind of the South* (New York: Knopf, 1941); and Harry S. Ashmore, *An Epitaph for Dixie* (New York: Norton, 1958). See also Morton Sosna, *In Search of the Silent South: Southern Liberals and the Race Issue* (New York: Columbia University Press, 1977), and Richard King, *A Southern Renaissance: The Cultural Awakening of the American South, 1930–1955* (New York: Oxford University Press, 1980).

CONCLUSIONS

1 Among studies that find abiding contradictions at the heart of American values, see Edmund Morgan, *The Puritan Dilemma* (Boston: Little, Borwn, 1958); Karen Halttunen, *Confidence Men and Painted Women: A Study of Middle-Class Culture in America* (New Haven: Yale University Press, 1986); Richard Bushman, *The Refinement of America: Persons, Houses, Cities* (New York: Knopf, 1992); and Daniel Walker Howe, *Making the American Self: Jonathan Edwards to Abraham Lincoln* (Cambridge: Harvard University Press, 1997).

Archival and
Manuscript Sources

Alabama Department of Archives and History, Montgomery
  Alabama State Sovereignty Commission Papers
  John Patterson Papers, Gubernatorial and Private
  George Wallace Papers

Amistad Research Center, Tulane University, New Orleans
  Anti-Defamation League Papers
  John Field Papers
  Fannie Lou Hamer Papers
  James Lawson materials (in various collections)
  National Association for the Advancement of Colored People,
    Louisiana Field Office Director's Records
  National Association of Intergroup Relations Papers
  Race Relations Information Center Papers
  Charles Sherrod Papers
  United Church Board Ministries, Race Relations Papers
  Daniel Webster Wynn Papers

Anti-Defamation League Office, New York
  Clipping Files

Billy Graham Center, Wheaton College, Wheaton, Illinois
  L. Nelson Bell Papers
  Christianity Today Papers
  Billy Graham Evangelistic Association, Media Office Files
  Billy Graham Scrapbooks and Clipping Files
  Billy Graham Sermons and Radio Addresses (on tape)
  Interview Transcripts
  Vernon Patterson Papers
  Press Conference Transcripts

Birmingham Public Library, Birmingham, Alabama
  Birmingham Police Department, Surveillance Files
  Asa Carter Papers
  Bull Connor Papers
  John Temple Graves Papers
  Arthur Hanes Papers
  National Association of States' Rights Papers

Boston University, Boston, Massachusetts
  Martin Luther King Papers

Clemson University, Clemson, South Carolina
  James F. Byrnes Papers
  Strom Thurmond Papers

Federal Bureau of Investigation Headquarters, Freedom of Information Act
    Reading Room, Washington, D.C.
  COINTELPRO White Hate Files

Florida State University Archives, Tallahassee
  Transcripts of Interviews by Jackson Lee Ice

Howard University, Founders' Library, Washington, D.C.
  Civil Rights Documentation Project, Interview Transcripts
  J. Waites Waring Papers

Library of Congress, Washington, D.C.
  Leadership Council on Civil Rights Papers
  John Bartlow Martin Papers
  National Association for the Advancement of Colored People Papers

Lyndon B. Johnson Library, Oral History Collection, University of Texas,
    Austin

Macon Public Library, Macon, Georgia
  Charles Bloch Papers

Martin Luther King Library and Archives, Martin Luther King Center, Atlanta
  Septima Clark Interview Transcript
  Martin Luther King Papers
  Slater King Papers
  Rufus Lewis Interview Transcript
  Montgomery Bus Boycott Papers
  R. D. Nesbitt Interview Transcript
  S. S. Seay Interview Transcript
  Fred Shuttlesworth Papers
  Southern Christian Leadership Conference Papers

Microfilm Sources
  Bayard Rustin Papers
  Student Nonviolent Coordinating Committee Papers

Mississippi Department of Archives and History, Jackson
   Association of Citizens' Councils of Mississippi Files
   Mississippi Sovereignty Commission Records
   John Bell Williams Papers

North Carolina Division of Archives and History, Raleigh
   Luther Hodges Papers

Presbyterian Church in the United States Archives, Montreat, North Carolina
   Marion Boggs Papers
   Wade Boggs Papers
   Albert Freundt Interview Transcript
   Arnette Gamble Papers
   Local History Collection
   J. McDowell Richards Papers
   Donald Shriver Papers
   Various bound Presbytery and Synod Records

South Carolina Historical Society, Charleston
   Herbert Ravenal Sass Papers
   Thomas Waring Papers

Southern Baptist Convention Archives, Nashville, Tennessee
   Clifton Allen Papers
   Baptist History File — Racc Relations
   Christian Life Commission Papers
   Christian Life Commission Resource Files
   Executive Committee Papers
   Brooks Hays Papers
   Race Relations Collection
   D. C. Wooley Papers

Stanford University, Stanford, California
   Project South Interviews

State Historical Society of Wisconsin, Madison
   Americans for Democratic Action Papers
   Daisy Bates Papers

University of Arkansas, Fayetteville
   Citizens' Councils of America Literature Collection

University of Georgia, Athens
   Clifford Brewton Papers
   Roy Harris Papers
   Richard Russell Papers
   Herman Talmadge Papers
   Ernest Vandiver Papers

University of Memphis, Mississippi Valley Collection
   James Lawson Interview Transcripts

University of Mississippi, Oxford
  James Eastland Papers (sanitized, incomplete)
  Race Relations Collection
  William Whittington Papers

University of North Carolina, Chapel Hill
  Sam Ervin Papers
  Wesly Critz George Papers
  Erwin Holt Papers
  Southern Oral History Program, Interview Transcripts

University of South Carolina, Modern Political Collections, Columbia
  Solomon Blatt Papers
  William Jennings Bryan Dorn Papers
  Marion Gressette Papers
  Modjeska Simkins Papers
  William D. Workman Papers

University of Southern Mississippi, Hattiesburg
  Unita Blackwell Interview Transcript
  Tom P. Brady Interview Transcript
  Larry Guyot Interview Transcript
  Fannie Lou Hamer Interview Transcript
  Sammy Rash Interview Transcript
  Fred Winyard Interview Transcript

University of Virginia, Charlottesville
  Harry F. Byrd Papers
  Virginius Dabney Papers
  Leon Dure Papers
  James J. Kilpatrick Papers
  Mosby Perrow Papers
  Howard Smith Papers

Vanderbilt University, Nashville, Tennessee
  Divinity School Archives — "Students" File
  Kelly Miller Smith Papers
  James Stahlman Papers

Bibliographical Essay

Many specific bibliographical matters—the religiosity of Franklin Roosevelt, the measurement of lynching, etc.—are handled in the notes. What follows is a guide to the sources and secondary works that inspired or restrained the general ideas in each chapter.

LIBERALS

The phrase "American liberalism" has sounded fishy since the publication of books like J. G. A. Pocock, *The Machiavellian Moment: Florentine Political Thought and the Atlantic Republican Tradition* (Princeton, N.J.: Princeton University Press, 1975); Alasdair C. MacIntyre, *After Virtue: A Study in Moral Theory* (Notre Dame, Ind.: University of Notre Dame Press, 1981); and Michael J. Sandel, *Liberalism and the Limits of Justice* (New York: Cambridge University Press, 1982)—not to mention historical studies of American political culture by Caroline Robbins, *The Eighteenth-Century Commonwealthman* (Cambridge: Harvard University Press, 1959); Marvin Meyers, *The Jacksonian Persuasion: Politics and Belief* (rev. ed., New York: Vintage, 1960); Bernard Bailyn, *Ideological Origins of the American Revolution* (Cambridge: Harvard University Press, 1967); Gordon S. Wood, *Creation of the American Republic, 1776–1787* (Chapel Hill: University of North Carolina Press, 1969); Eric Foner, *Free Soil, Free Labor, Free Men: The Ideology of the Republican Party before the Civil War* (New York: Oxford University Press, 1970); Daniel Walker Howe, *The Political Culture of the American Whigs* (Chicago: University of Chicago Press, 1979); Jean H. Baker, *Affairs of Party: The Political Culture of Northern Democrats in the Mid-Nineteenth Century* (Ithaca, N.Y.: Cornell University Press, 1983); and others. Liberalism can no longer be considered the central theme of American history, at least not in the sense that Louis Hartz believed it was in *The Liberal Tradition in America: An Interpretation of American Political Thought since the Revolution* (New York: Harcourt, 1955)—a consensus on formal equality, private property, opportunity, etc. Still, the world of the 1930s–60s looks like a heyday of liberalism, a period when liberals appeared (to their enemies at least) to be in the driver's seat, when a perceptive man like Hartz could be forgiven for seeing liberalism all over the American past.

For my conception—perhaps too general—of liberalism through World War II, I have relied on L. T. Hobhouse, *Liberalism* (1911; reprint, New York: Oxford University Press, 1964); J. B. Bury, *A History of Freedom of Thought* (New York: Holt, 1913); Guido de Ruggiero, *The History of European Liberalism*, trans. R. G. Collingwood (1927; reprint, Boston: Beacon Press, 1959); Ernst Cassirer, *The Philosophy of the Enlightenment* (1932; trans. Fritz C. A. Koelln and J. P. Pettegrove, Princeton, N.J.: Princeton University Press, 1951); Harold J. Laski, *The Rise of European Liberalism: An Essay in Interpretation* (London: Allen and Unwin, 1936); Christopher Dawson, *The Judgment of the Nations* (New York: Sheed and Ward, 1942); and William Aylott Orton, *The Liberal Tradition: A Study of the Social and Spiritual Conditions of Freedom* (New Haven: Yale University Press, 1945). Hobhouse, Bury, Cassirer, and Laski view the origins of liberalism as essentially anti-Christian (opposed to Christianity as it actually existed, especially in France); Ruggiero does not exactly put it that way but sees liberalism dying wherever there is no conflict between church and state. Dawson and Orton, however, regard liberalism as deriving from a specific kind of Christianity; they also note that liberals denied or were unaware of their Christian roots.

There are other ways to see liberalism. Peter Berkowitz, in *Virtue and the Making of Modern Liberalism* (Princeton, N.J.: Princeton University Press, 1999), for example, attempts to defend liberalism against post-Rawls critics, who claim that liberalism enervates the sense of social responsibility on which a humane (let alone liberal) public life depends. But Berkowitz's is an odd rescue attempt. He establishes that what he calls "extraliberal" virtues were, in fact, on the minds of the great liberal thinkers. Far from effectively defending liberalism, Berkowitz proves that the best liberal thinkers were smart enough to understand that they had to look outside liberalism for whatever they needed to redeem liberal societies. Scholars like J. G. A. Pocock partake of a similar project. They show that the thinkers who constitute the great liberal tradition, who were once disdained for their alleged lack of depth, responsibility, or historical grounding, actually had those things in abundance. But those are the things that made them great, not the things that made them liberal. In this light, the most durable complaint about liberals is not that they were dangerously shallow or naive, but that they took the religious or classical virtues of their societies for granted. They were so busy trying to construct a liberal superstructure on the base of these foundational virtues that they did not see the need to reproduce or defend the virtues. They did not realize how vulnerable their foundations were to decay or destruction.

Writers who see liberalism as living on "borrowed time"—taking for granted the spiritual and cultural resources that liberals depend on but do nothing to replenish—draw on both traditions of interpretation of liberalism. H. Richard Niebuhr, who sketches out a countervailing "prophetic" tradition, advances a borrowed-time argument in *The Kingdom of God in America* (New York: Harper,

1937), 194–95; so does Mircea Eliade in *The Sacred and the Profane: The Nature of Religion* (1957; trans. Willard R. Trask, New York: Harper, 1959), 203–13. On borrowed time, see also Glenn E. Tinder, *The Political Meaning of Christianity: The Prophetic Stance: An Interpretation* (New York: Harper, 1991), and Pierre Manent, *An Intellectual History of Liberalism*, trans. Rebecca Balinski (Princeton, N.J.: Princeton University Press, 1994).

LIBERAL FEARS OF SELF-INSUFFICIENCY

Expressions of the post-Christian need to generate solidarity and commitment include Auguste Comte, *Système de politique positive, ou Traité de sociologie instituant la religion de l'humanité*, 4 vols. (Paris, 1851–54); George Eliot, *The Mill on the Floss* (1860) and *Daniel Deronda* (1872); John Stuart Mill, *Autobiography* (London: Longmans, 1873) and *Nature, the Utility of Religion, Theism* (posthum. pub., 1874; reprint, New York: Library of Liberal Arts, 1958); Josiah Royce, *The Religious Aspect of Philosophy* (Boston: Houghton-Mifflin, 1885), bk. I, chaps. 1, 6, 7, and *The Philosophy of Loyalty* (1908); Oliver Wendell Holmes Jr., "Memorial Day" (1884), "A Soldier's Faith" (1895), and other speeches in the section, "A Fighting Faith," in *The Mind and Faith of Justice Holmes*, ed. Max Lerner (Boston: Little, Brown, 1943), 3–27, also in *Collected Works of Justice Holmes*, ed. Sheldon Novick, 5 vols. (Chicago: University of Chicago Press, 1995), 3:462–67, 486–92; Henry Demarest Lloyd, *Wealth against Commonwealth* (New York: Harper, 1894), chaps. 22, 34, 35; William James's essays and his *Varieties of Religious Experience: A Study in Human Nature* (New York: Longmans, 1902); Jane Addams, who ends with a Christlike resignation simply to live among the poor and to adopt their concerns, in *Twenty Years at Hull House* (1910; reprint, New York: Signet, 1960), chaps. 2–6; Herbert Croly, *The Promise of American Life* (1909; reprint, Indianapolis: Bobbs-Merrill, 1965), 69–71, 281–87; and Emile Durkheim, *Moral Education* (1925; trans. Everett Wilson and Herman Schnurer, Glencoe, Ill.: Free Press, 1956). T. R. Wright explores this theme in *The Religion of Humanity: The Impact of Comtean Positivism on Victorian Britain* (Cambridge: Cambridge University Press, 1986). David W. Levy explores the Comtean roots of twentieth-century American liberalism in *Herbert Croly of the New Republic: The Life and Thought of an American Progressive* (Princeton, N.J.: Princeton University Press, 1985).

Variations on the theme appear in Fyodor Dostoyevsky, *The Brothers Karamazov* (1880); Wallace Stevens, "Sunday Morning" (1915); George Orwell, *A Clergyman's Daughter* (1935); and Walter Lippmann, *A Preface to Morals* (New York: Macmillan, 1929), which finds inspiration in a "humanist" religion.

The best book on the key figure in my first chapter is Robert B. Westbrook's *John Dewey and American Democracy* (Ithaca, N.Y.: Cornell University Press, 1991). Alan Ryan, in *John Dewey and the High Tide of American Liberalism* (New York: Norton, 1995), is more critical than Westbrook of Dewey's attempts to reconstruct "religion" without faith. Anthony Cook, in *The Least of These: Race,*

Law, and Religion in American Culture (New York: Routledge, 1997), 48, 116, 141–42, is less critical than Westbrook, expressing hope for an expansion of Dewey's notion of religion, believing that some of the "dimensions of the traditional religion [that were] lambasted by Dewey" can be grafted onto it: specifically, a recognition of "human depravity and evil," "a real awareness" of the limits of individual power, and a recognition of human interdependence. Robert N. Bellah attempted a similar divorce of modern "religion" from faith in *Beyond Belief: Essays on Religion in a Post-Traditional World* (New York: Harper and Row, 1970). Steven Rockefeller highlights the vestiges of Dewey's parents' Protestantism in his sensible and thorough *John Dewey: Religious Faith and Democratic Humanism* (New York: Columbia University Press, 1991).

Samuel H. Beer, who later became head of Americans for Democratic Action (ADA), also attempted, in *The City of Reason* (Cambridge: Harvard University Press, 1949), to revive a sense of purpose and a belief in man's ability to control the future—despite abundant evidence of the past failures of human reason and inadjudicable disagreements as to what was true and good. It is significant that Beer thought that belief in a transcendent God was necessary for such a restoration of human confidence. He was confident (more confident than Dewey, on whom he drew) that one could find this "God" through reason. Beer granted that earth could never be like heaven but showed his great optimism in his explanation of the "problem" of evil, as posed in the Book of Job. According to Beer, Job suffered mercilessly because all laws, including the covenant by which God had promised Israel prosperity in return for keeping His law, were only pragmatic approximations, not absolute certainties. There was no reason to doubt the general statistical pattern that God favored those who kept His law (pp. 126–30).

Joseph Wood Krutch, in *The Modern Temper: A Study and a Confession* (1929; reprint, New York: Harcourt, Brace, 1956), thought the whole effort to fill the vacuum left by Christianity to be futile. Krutch more readily accepted that art and science—and the humanism that his contemporary Walter Lippmann, among others, attempted to revive—were as impotent as Christianity in the face of modern knowledge and disenchantment. George Steiner echoed and elaborated on Krutch's thesis in *The Death of Tragedy* (New York: Knopf, 1961).

Skepticism that modern religion could inspire solidarity, sacrifice, and commitment any better than liberalism is also expressed by H. Richard Niebuhr, who, in *The Social Sources of Denominationalism* (1929; reprint, New York: Holt, 1957), complained that Christianity reproduced the divisions of society. Thus Christianity failed to save civilization from social conflict, as it had promised; instead, it worsened civilization's most destructive conflicts. Robert and Helen Lynd, in their classic *Middletown: A Study in Contemporary American Culture* (New York: Harcourt, Brace 1929), saw the "secular interests" and loyalties of industrialization destroying religion along with other social bonds, although they thought religion was yielding more slowly (especially among the working class and among women) than family, neighborhood, friendship, and the common school. Later Robert Handy, in "The American Religious Depression, 1925–

1935," *Church History* 29 (March 1960): 3-16, suggested that American churches were in a "religious depression" long before the economic depression of the 1930s. John Dewey, incidentally, used a similar phrase, "the present depression in religion," in *A Common Faith* (1934), reprinted in his *Later Works*, 17 vols. (Carbondale: Southern Illinois University Press, 1986), 9:8.

The idea that modern man's loss of faith was dangerous may have entered liberal discourse in the 1930s via the Lynds' book, surely one of the great jeremiads of American social thought. Richard H. Pells, in *Radical Visions and American Dreams: Culture and Social Thought in the Depression Years* (New York: Harper and Row, 1973), 27, takes the Lynds as a starting point for his observation that "the recurring desire for some sort of group ethos, the insistence on new forms of cultural adjustment, the assumption that social change in America had to mean more than political reform would all become major themes in [the 1930s] as well." Richard Fox's "Epitaph for Middletown," in *The Culture of Consumption: Critical Essays in American History, 1880-1980*, ed. Richard Wightman Fox and T. J. Jackson Lears (New York: Pantheon, 1983), interprets the Lynds' work as part of the tradition of the American jeremiad. See also R. Alan Lawson, "The Cultural Legacy of the New Deal," in *Fifty Years Later: The New Deal Evaluated*, ed. Harvard Sitkoff (Philadelphia: Temple University Press, 1985), 155-86.

James A. Wechsler, in *Reflections of an Angry Middle-Aged Editor* (New York: Random House, 1960), 114-15, not only voiced the typical liberal yearning for some religious or postreligious form of inspiration but also suggested that the civil rights movement played a great role in supplying what was missing from liberalism:

> Civil rights has become to the politics of the present what the drive for union organization was to the politics of the 1930's. The issue is both deeply moral and economic; it involves the conscience and sense of justice of many who do not happen to be black just as the emergence of unionism in the mass-production industries evoked the sentimental allegiance of many who did not happen to be industrial workers. And, like any great issue, it brings new, irritating complexities to the lives of simple political men, most of whom tell themselves that everything could be quietly worked out if "agitators" did not muddle matters by refusing to play the game and wait for the long run.

Wechsler also emphasized that pressure from abroad drove American politicians to act.

LIBERAL RELATIONS WITH RACISM

Excellent discussions of the general problem of Jim Crow's origins in a modern, liberal program include Virginius Dabney, *Liberalism in the South* (Chapel Hill: University of North Carolina Press, 1932); Howard N. Rabinowitz, *Race Relations in the Urban South, 1865-1890* (New York: Oxford University Press, 1978); John W. Cell, *The Highest Stage of White Supremacy: The Origins of Segre-*

gation in South Africa and the American South (New York: Cambridge University Press, 1982); and Dewey W. Grantham, *Southern Progressivism: The Reconciliation of Progress and Tradition* (Knoxville: University of Tennessee Press, 1983). Scholars of American liberalism and the midcentury civil rights struggle have not sufficiently considered the implications of these studies for their own topics.

On the context of civil rights and racial politics in the first part of the American liberal heyday, in the New Deal years, vital works include Jervis Anderson, *A. Philip Randolph: A Biographical Portrait* (New York: Harcourt Brace Jovanovich, 1973); John B. Kirby, *Black Americans in the Roosevelt Era: Liberalism and Race* (Knoxville: University of Tennessee Press, 1980); Nancy J. Weiss, *Farewell to the Party of Lincoln: Black Politics in the Age of FDR* (Princeton, N.J.: Princeton University Press, 1983); and Harold Cruse's old warhorse, *The Crisis of the Negro Intellectual* (New York: Morrow, 1967). These all highlight black leaders' and intellectuals' disappointments and conflicts of interest with liberals and white leftists. They are useful correctives to more recent treatments of the Roosevelt years by John Egerton and Patricia Sullivan, who seem to me to view the New Deal years Whiggishly, as a period of advance *toward* a true confrontation with racism. Egerton's *Speak Now against the Day: The Generation before the Civil Rights Movement in the South* (Knopf, 1994) and Sullivan's *Days of Hope: Race and Democracy in the New Deal Era* (Chapel Hill: University of North Carolina Press, 1996) follow the tradition of liberals like Gunnar Myrdal, who assume a general pressure for equality in the progress of economic development and the spread of education; they see racial equality as "rooted in the ethos" (to use Sullivan's phrase) of liberal reform in the New Deal (p. 220; cf. pp. 163–64, 167–68). My reviews of Egerton and Sullivan in the *African American Review* (Spring 1997 and Spring 1999, respectively) spell out my objections. Allen Kifer, "The Negro under the New Deal" (Ph.D. diss., University of Wisconsin, 1961), and Harvard Sitkoff, *A New Deal for Blacks* (New York: Oxford University Press, 1978), provide more balanced overviews. Eric Arnesen's thorough and perceptive *Brotherhoods of Color: Black Railroad Workers and the Struggle for Equality* (Cambridge: Harvard University Press, 2001) puts a key figure, A. Philip Randolph, in historical context.

On the small number of New Dealers who aided the cause of civil rights, see, in addition to works cited in the notes, Walter White, *A Man Called White* (New York: Viking, 1948); Virginia Durr, *Outside the Magic Circle: Autobiography of Virginia Foster Durr*, ed. Hollinger F. Barnard (1985; reprint, New York: Simon and Schuster, 1987); Blanche Wiesen-Cook, *Eleanor Roosevelt*, 2 vols. to date (New York: Viking, 1992–), 2:153–89, 509–37; Wilma Dykeman and James Stokely, *Seeds of Southern Change: The Life of Will Alexander* (1962; reprint, New York: Norton, 1976); John Salmond, *Southern Rebel: The Life and Times of Aubrey Willis Williams* (Chapel Hill: University of North Carolina Press, 1983); John Salmond, *Conscience of a Lawyer: Clifford Durr and American Civil Liberties* (Tuscaloosa: University of Alabama Press, 1990); Thomas Kreuger, *And Promises to Keep: The Southern Conference for Human Welfare, 1938–1948* (Nashville, Tenn.: Vanderbilt University Press, 1967); Linda Reed, *Simple Decency and Common*

Sense: The Southern Conference Movement, 1938–1963 (Bloomington: Indiana University Press, 1991); J. Joseph Huthmacher, *Senator Robert Wagner and the Rise of Urban Liberalism* (New York: Athenaeum, 1968); Graham White and John Maze, *Harold Ickes of the New Deal: His Private Life and Public Career* (Cambridge: Harvard University Press, 1985); and H. A. Watkins, *Righteous Pilgrim: The Life and Times of Harold Ickes* (New York: Holt, 1990), 199–201.

Historians have not done much with Glenn Frank. In the 1920s Frank was one of the founders of the Citizens National Committee for Sacco and Vanzetti. Earlier, he had championed active, participatory democracy, as a way to discipline intellectuals as well as to raise the level of public knowledge, in the Forum movement of the Progressive Era. See Daniel Aaron, *Writers on the Left: Episodes in American Literary Communism* (New York: Harcourt, Brace and World, 1961), 419; Ellis W. Hawley, *The Great War and the Search for a Modern Order: A History of the American People and Their Institutions, 1917–1933* (New York: St. Martin's Press, 1979), 54; Kevin Mattson, *Creating a Democratic Public: The Struggle for Urban Participatory Democracy during the Progressive Era* (University Park: Pennsylvania State University Press, 1998), 45. On Frank's ideas, see Glenn Frank, "Christianity and Racialism: Has the Ku Klux Klan the Right to Celebrate Christmas?," *Century* 109 (1924–25): 277–84; his farewell series of articles in *Century* 110 (1925): 370 ff., 502 ff., 626 ff.; and his contribution to the "If I Were a Dictator" series in *Nation* 133 (December 23, 1931): 688–91.

POST–WORLD WAR II LIBERALS AND THEIR ALLEGED BREAK FROM THE LIBERAL PAST

American liberals' sail trimming, beginning in the recession of 1937, is one of Alan Brinkley's major points in *The End of Reform: New Deal Liberalism in Recession and War* (New York: Knopf, 1995). Brinkley portrays the liberals as having more freedom to choose their destiny than does Ellis W. Hawley, whose *New Deal and the Problem of Monopoly: A Study in Economic Ambivalence* (Princeton, N.J.: Princeton University Press, 1966) sees the liberals abandoning structural reform earlier (e.g., pp. 142, 146, 359). David L. Stebenne, in *Arthur J. Goldberg: New Deal Liberal* (New York: Oxford, 1996), 76–77, 99–100, 418, sees a pragmatic postwar motivation for some of the sail trimming: many liberals lowered their expectations only after they, like Arthur Goldberg, "became convinced of the futility of more confrontational strategies for bettering workers' lives" (p. 99).

On the alleged chastening of post–World War II American liberals, see the studies of Arthur M. Schlesinger Jr. cited above in Chapter 1, n. 54, and John Patrick Diggins, *The Rise and Fall of the American Left* (New York: Norton, 1992), 192–93, 206, and *Up from Communism* (New York: Harper, 1975), 274–76; William O'Neill, *A Better World: The Great Schism: Stalinism and the American Intellectuals* (New York: Simon and Schuster, 1982), chaps. 5, 7, 10, 11; Thomas Bender, *New York Intellect: A History of Intellectual Life in New York City, from 1750 to the*

Beginnings of Our Time (Baltimore: Johns Hopkins University Press, 1987), 316–18; Neil Jumonville, *Critical Crossings: New York Intellectuals in Postwar America* (Berkeley: University of California Press, 1991), 124–26; and Stebenne, *Goldberg*, 42–43, 61. Jumonville, in *Henry Steele Commager: Midcentury Liberalism and the History of the Present* (Chapel Hill: University of North Carolina Press, 1999), 117, 161, 187, 293, regards another influential liberal historian as a notable contrast to the "tragic and ironic sense" that so many see at work in Schlesinger. My point is not to deny that Schlesinger and others "felt the impact" (p. 117) of Reinhold Niebuhr's dark perspective, as Jumonville says, but only to dispute that they felt it as deeply and transformatively as Jumonville and most historians imply.

Other indispensable works on twentieth-century American liberalism include, in addition to Hartz's *Liberal Tradition in America*, Richard Hofstadter, *The American Political Tradition and the Men Who Made It* (New York: Knopf, 1948) and *Anti-intellectualism in American Life* (New York: Knopf, 1963); Christopher Lasch, *The New Radicalism in America: The Intellectual as a Social Type* (New York: Knopf, 1963); Martin Luther King Jr., *Where Do We Go from Here: Chaos or Community?* (New York: Harper and Row, 1967); Daniel Patrick Moynihan, *Maximum Feasible Misunderstanding: Community Action in the War on Poverty* (New York: Free Press, 1969); R. Alan Lawson, *The Failure of Independent Liberalism, 1930–1941* (New York: Putnam, 1971); John Rawls, *A Theory of Justice* (Cambridge: Harvard University Press, 1971); Christopher Jencks, *Inequality: A Reassessment of the Effect of Family and Schooling in America* (New York: Basic Books, 1972); William Julius Wilson, *The Declining Significance of Race: Blacks and Changing American Institutions* (Chicago: University of Chicago Press, 1978); Jennifer L. Hochschild, *The New American Dilemma: Liberal Democracy and School Desegregation* (New Haven: Yale University Press, 1984); Jonathan Rieder, *Canarsie: The Jews and Italians of Brooklyn against Liberalism* (Cambridge: Harvard University Press, 1985); James T. Kloppenberg, *Uncertain Victory: Social Democracy and Progressivism in European and American Thought, 1870–1920* (New York: Oxford University Press, 1986); Stephen Gillon, *Politics and Vision: The ADA and American Liberalism* (New York: Oxford University Press, 1987); Lizabeth Cohen, *Making a New Deal: Industrial Workers in Chicago* (New York: Cambridge University Press, 1990); Jim Sleeper, *The Closest of Strangers: Liberalism and the Politics of Race in New York* (New York: Norton, 1990); Alan Brinkley, *Liberalism and Its Discontents* (Cambridge: Harvard University Press, 1998); Elizabeth Sanders, *Roots of Reform: Farmers, Workers, and the American State, 1877–1917* (Chicago: University of Chicago Press, 1999); and George Packer, *The Blood of the Liberals* (New York: Farrar, Straus, and Giroux, 2000).

Of the many available biographies of key liberal figures, I have found the following particularly useful: Nelson Lichtenstein, *The Most Dangerous Man in Detroit: Walter Reuther and the Fate of American Labor* (New York: Basic Books, 1995); Stebenne, *Goldberg*; and Carl Solberg, *Hubert Humphrey: A Biography* (New York: Norton, 1984).

On the ranking of civil rights among American liberals' priorities, W. E. B. Du Bois's journal *Phylon* closely monitored white coverage of the issue in a "Race in Periodicals" index at the end of every year. The first year's index noted, "In the periodicals of 1939 the matter of race has not been widely discussed." *Phylon* 1 (1939): 100. The coverage grew, according to *Phylon*, over the war and post-war years, especially in liberal organs. But it was not until the mid-1950s that civil rights began to rival what had seemed to liberal editors and activists more important issues. Peter J. Kellog, in "Northern Liberals and Black America: A History of White Attitudes, 1936–1952" (Ph.D. diss., Northwestern University, 1971), concludes that when the major liberal organs—*New Republic* and *Nation*—wrote about race before the mid-1950s, they tended to confine themselves to stories on atrocities. That practice conformed with liberals' aberration theory—that racism was a peripheral rather than a systemic problem, not something that threatened or characterized liberal society at its core. In *Contempt and Pity: Social Policy and the Image of the Damaged Black Psyche, 1880–1996* (Chapel Hill: University of North Carolina Press, 1997), Daryl Michael Scott's analysis of scholarly work on racial issues over most of the twentieth century adds an important insight: liberal and conservative social scientists share common racist assumptions of black people's incapacity to deal with their own plight.

Two books on Myrdal aided my understanding of his vast research project, its reception, and its ramifications: David W. Southern, *Gunnar Myrdal and Black-White Relations: The Use and Abuse of "An American Dilemma," 1944–1969* (Baton Rouge: LSU Press, 1987), and Walter A. Jackson, *Gunnar Myrdal and America's Conscience: Social Engineering and Racial Liberalism, 1938–1987* (Chapel Hill: University of North Carolina Press, 1990). Southern focuses more on the reception, influence, and historical position of the Myrdal report. Jackson focuses more on the production and publication of Myrdal's research and the way Myrdal's own life intertwined with the subsequent history of his report. The two overlap somewhat, with Jackson offering a more nuanced and plausible (not at all unsympathetic) view of Myrdal's motives and preconceptions. But Southern is indispensable for the way Americans received the study. I relied heavily on both.

The Myrdal report has had a great influence in American intellectual life, more honored by dissents and refutations than by confirmations. Among the most interesting works that take Myrdal as their point of departure, see Hochschild, *New American Dilemma*, and C. Eric Lincoln, *Race, Religion, and the Continuing American Dilemma* (New York: Hill and Wang, 1984). The Myrdal thesis has recently been revived but carefully modified by the most ambitious work in the social science of race in America since 1944, Abigail and Stephan Thernstrom's *America in Black and White: One Nation, Indivisible* (New York: Simon and Schuster, 1997).

How wrong was Myrdal in projecting his optimism onto the black population? The distribution of pessimism and optimism about human nature in the black intellectual journals *Phylon, Midwest Quarterly, Negro Quarterly,* and *Journal of Negro Education* in the 1940s appears roughly even, though with respect to domestic policy, these journals lean in a slightly pessimistic direction. The NAACP organ, *Crisis,* on the other hand, is more optimistic. (Du Bois had left *Crisis* in 1934 and started *Phylon* in 1939.) Although I have not read black newspapers as comprehensively as I have the periodicals, my sampling of the editorial, op-ed, and letters columns of the *Amsterdam News, Baltimore Afro-American, Chicago Defender, Kansas City Call, Los Angeles Sentinel, Michigan Chronicle,* and *Pittsburgh Courier* suggests the same rough balance. The standard (nonscientific) overviews and compendia of Negro opinion in those days also reflect a diversity of views on human nature: Roi Ottley, *New World A-Coming* (1943; reprint, New York: Arno, 1969); Rayford W. Logan, ed., *What the Negro Wants* (Chapel Hill: University of North Carolina Press, 1944); and Bucklin Moon, ed., *Primer for White Folks* (Garden City, N.Y.: Doubleday, Doran, 1945). Contrary to Myrdal's gradualist optimism, Ottley observed that the most popular black leader, A. Philip Randolph, believed "that only in periods of great social upheaval can Negroes make fundamental gains" (p. 251). Myrdal's view of black culture cannot account for the pronounced pessimism of the two black literary best-sellers of the period, Richard Wright's *Native Son* (1941) and Ralph Ellison's *Invisible Man* (1952). Nor is there any Myrdalian optimism in two celebrated efforts to reconstruct the minds of admittedly unusual representatives of uneducated southern black folk: Theodore Rosengarten, *All God's Dangers: The Life of Nate Shaw* (New York: Knopf, 1974), and Nell Painter, ed., *Narrative of Hosea Hudson: His Life as a Negro Communist in the South* (Cambridge: Harvard University Press, 1979). In two recent compendia of interview transcripts that tap memories of the Jim Crow era from the perspective of the 1990s—Michael Honey, ed., *Black Workers Remember: An Oral History of Segregation, Unionism, and the Freedom Struggle* (Berkeley: University of California Press, 1999), and William Chafe et al., eds., *Remembering Jim Crow: African Americans Tell about Life in the Segregated South* (New York: New Press, 2001)—I can detect no consistent recollection of Myrdalian optimism.

Mass opinion analyses of the late twentieth century seem to be more precise than anything Myrdal attempted. Jennifer L. Hochschild, in *Facing Up to the American Dream: Race, Class, and the Soul of the Nation* (Princeton, N.J.: Princeton University Press, 1995), has done the sort of detailed analysis of recent mass African American opinion that Myrdal would have had to do to establish the truth of his 1944 assumption of general black optimism. Hochschild finds poor African Americans to be more optimistic (often tragically so) than either affluent African Americans or white Americans generally. A less precise survey in 1964 found black respondents overwhelmingly optimistic on broad questions. (Are things getting better for Negroes? Will the day come when whites accept

Negroes? etc.) But it also found majorities believing that the federal government was moving too slowly and that civil rights demonstrations had been very useful in forcing such change as there had been. The 1964 survey did not find a clear majority among black urban southerners as to whether things were better, or getting better faster, in the North. See Gary T. Marx, *Protest and Prejudice: A Study of Belief in the Black Community* (New York: Harper and Row, 1967). Looking back to antebellum times, Donald G. Mathews, in *Religion in the Old South* (University of Chicago, 1977), 215, identified a difference between black and white evangelical southerners: black Christians lacked white Christians' sense of personal complicity in original sin; but unlike liberals, black Christians "did not lapse" into "optimistic sentimentalism." Like white evangelicals, black Christians "prayed to be released from sins, but unlike their masters, they were locked into a form of bondage which could be objectified, cast outside the self in a manner unavailable to whites." The slaves "did not dwell on the taint of their bondage; they celebrated their release from it." White Christian converts said that they had "broken down" under preaching; black converts said that they had been "lifted up."

THE INTELLECTUAL HISTORY OF MODERN BLACK PROPHETS

If they did not think like Myrdal, what were the ideas of midcentury civil rights leaders? The frustrating tendency of scholars to reduce Martin Luther King's intellect to what he learned as a child in "the" black church seems to date from Joseph R. Washington, who wrote in 1964 — *Black Religion: The Negro and Christianity in the United States* (Boston: Beacon Press, 1964), 3 — that King was "a remarkable product of the South; barely tainted by his academic exposure in the North." To view King this way is to exclude all of his attempts to justify, codify, transform, and apply his thoughts as a literate adult—not to mention the entire record he left behind for historians. Even the otherwise scrupulous August Meier brushes aside the intellectual content of King's speeches and writings as a "superficial" and "eclectic" amalgam of undigested and irreconcilable elements. (Despite his dismissive stance, Meier—"The Conservative Militant," in *Martin Luther King, Jr.: A Profile*, ed. C. Eric Lincoln [New York: Hill and Wang, 1970], 144–56—manages to capture much of the essence of King's intellectual character.) The arrested-development thesis has been elaborated by others who follow the lead of the black nationalist scholar James Cone (see Chapter 3, n. 31). This seems related to a broader anti-intellectualism in studies of civil rights (see below).

Among those who take King's ideas seriously, Ralph E. Luker, focusing on King's doctrine of the Kingdom of God, moves him more wholeheartedly into the Social Gospel tradition than I, emphasizing King's doctrine of man, would do. But, like the Niebuhr scholars cited in Chapter 2, n. 5, Luker—"Kingdom of God and Beloved Community in the Thought of Martin Luther King, Jr.," in *The Role of Ideas in the Civil Rights South*, ed. Ted Ownby (Jackson: University Press of Mississippi, 2002), 42, n. 15—is careful to reduce the distance that Niebuhr exaggeratedly put between himself and the Social Gospel. I do not know whether Luker would agree with me that King's doctrine of man is far more decisive in explaining his public career as a civil rights leader than his somewhat sentimental (and to my mind muddled) notions of the Kingdom of God and of the "beloved community." Luker's knowledge of King's thought is second to none, and his historical work on the social gospel and race—*The Social Gospel in Black and White: American Racial Reform, 1885–1912* (Chapel Hill: University of North Carolina Press, 1991)—is illuminating. The difference between me and Luker, apart from our judgments of the relative importance of the doctrines of man and of the Kingdom, apparently has to do with my inability to see anything terribly profound or original in "Personalism." I fail to see how the term could distinguish, let alone inspire, anything important in modern Protestant thought or practice. James J. Farrell, in *Spirit of the Sixties: The Making of Postwar Radicalism* (New York: Routledge, 1997), and Eugene McCarraher, in *Christian Critics: Religion and the Impasse in Modern American Social Thought* (Ithaca, N.Y.: Cornell University Press, 2000), find Personalism pervasive among left-leaning social critics after World War II. McCarraher names the *Catholic Worker* disciple Robert Ludlow as "the most trenchant and comprehensive theorist of Christian personalism." Yet, he observes, Ludlow admitted that Personalism was a "hodge-podge . . . a plank here and there from the various radicalisms" (p. 118). Again, my point is that no one seems to have articulated what Personalism is in such a way as to differentiate it from other influences. My own reading of the Boston Personalists suggests that King may have found them attractive not only because of their emphasis on human personality, but also because they could accommodate a decidedly illiberal (by King and Bayard Rustin's lights, "fundamentalist") emphasis on a personal *God*. Scholars who stress King's Personalism tend to overlook that part.

King's 1948 essay on Jeremiah, the "rebel prophet," gets considerable play in Chapter 3. This essay culminates in a justification of Personalism that King admittedly used sometimes as a catch-all for his various theological preferences. I believe, however, that Personalism does not distinguish King from run-of-the-mill divinity students of midcentury America. Nor does it isolate the elements of his intellectual predispositions and training that figure decisively in his later social activism and leadership. His Personalist associations, in short, have little to do with what makes him memorable; they do little to explain his historical significance. Most scholars have accepted King's professions of Personalism at face value and have not inquired further into what that doctrine could have done to set him off from thousands of charlatans and dilettantes who also professed Personalism and obviously took it to different conclusions. How can so eclectic and indecisive a patchwork of doctrines explain anything?

In this book, I do not attempt to summarize or to simplify the complicated, changing, and often inconsistent elements of King's thinking under a single label. To do so would be to mirror the oversimplification, or the evasiveness, of those who stress his Personalism. Rather, I try to isolate two things that turn out to be the same thing: which elements of his intellectual life helped him justify or explain his self-sacrificial commitment to a struggle for earthly equality and which elements gave him some common ground with others similarly motivated?

I use the term "prophetic" to characterize these elements. I do not claim that these elements characterize the whole man (as if any label could), but simply that they work well to place the public, adult King in a historical tradition. See King, "The Significant Contributions of Jeremiah to Religious Thought," written for James Bennett Pritchard's Old Testament course at Crozer Theological Seminary, November 1948, *Papers of Martin Luther King, Jr.*, ed. Clayborne Carson et al., 4 vols. to date (Berkeley: University of California Press, 1992–), 1:181–95. King developed his prophetic streak in his essay, "Jacques Maritain," 1951, *PMLK* 1:436–39, and other works cited in the notes to Chapter 3 above.

The emphasis on Personalism is in Kenneth L. Smith and Ira G. Zepp, *Search for the Beloved Community: The Thinking of Martin Luther King, Jr.* (Lanham, Md.: University Press of America, 1986). Though I argue that Smith and Zepp exaggerate King's Personalism, their book is nevertheless useful and insightful. The other major attempt at an intellectual biography of King, John Ansbro's *Martin Luther King, Jr.: The Making of a Mind* (Maryknoll, N.Y.: Orbis, 1982), also overplays the Personalism, but it, too, is sober, intelligent, and thorough. These books remain the best introductions to King's thought other than King's own works. See also Warren E. Steinkraus, "Martin Luther King's Personalism and Non-violence," *Journal of the History of Ideas* 34 (January–March 1973): 97–110.

Robert Franklin, Lewis Baldwin, and Albert J. Raboteau use the word "prophetic" to characterize King's thought, emphasizing that he stood apart from the mainstream. See Franklin, "Religious Belief and Political Activism in Black America," *Journal of Religious Thought* 43 (Fall–Winter 1986–87); Baldwin, *There Is a Balm in Gilead: The Cultural Roots of Martin Luther King, Jr.* (Minneapolis: Fortress Press, 1991) and *To Make the Wounded Whole: The Cultural Legacy of Martin Luther King, Jr.* (Minneapolis: Fortress Press, 1992); and Raboteau, *A Fire in the Bones: Reflections on African-American Religious History* (Boston: Beacon Press, 1995). Raboteau also, without explicit reference to Myrdal, finds in black religion a general departure, beginning as far back as the eighteenth century, from the notion that white Americans were simply not living up to their "national creed." As racism proved intransigent, Raboteau writes, black religion began to perceive the creed itself as wrong. By the end of the nineteenth century, many black clergymen came to see discrimination as more than a mere anomaly "in the overall progress of national destiny"; they concluded that the centrality and durability of racism made the whole national experiment a failure. They thought that theirs was a messianic mission of moral leadership, a mission that "contradicted the national myth" (pp. 59–63, 71–72, 169, 187). Richard Lischer, in *The Preacher King: Martin Luther King, Jr. and the Word That Moved America* (New York: Oxford University Press, 1995), 221, sees King carrying "a modified version" of his "Ebenezer Gospel" (the one he preached at his father's Ebenezer Baptist Church) "into world history." Lischer sums up the elements of this gospel as a "quest for justice, yearning for redemption, insistence on nonviolence, embrace of suffering, prophetic rage." Anthony E. Cook, in *The Least of These: Race, Law, and Religion in American Culture* (New York: Routledge, 1997), 48, 102–4, 110, 115–17, finds at the heart of the civil rights movement a "prophetic" Christianity that synthesizes traditional, conservative, and neo-orthodox with modern pragmatic and liberal tenets.

What I call "prophetic Christianity" is not necessarily divorced from the social concerns that, in the twentieth century, came to be associated (wrongly, I think) with liberal theology. In particular, the great theologian of the Social Gospel, Walter Rauschenbusch, stressed the prophetic tradition as his great source. His *Christianity and the Social Crisis* (New York: Macmillan, 1907) begins with the Hebrew Prophets (pp. 1–44), and his *Theology for the Social Gospel* (1917; reprint, Nashville, Tenn.: Abingdon, 1945), especially the core chapter, "The Kingdom of God," is a jeremiad on how the community of Christians has fallen away from the original idea of the Kingdom of God. The prophetic core of the Social Gospel at its best may explain the attraction it held for Martin Luther King Jr.

On Reinhold Niebuhr, in addition to his own *Moral Man and Immoral Society* (New York: Scribner's, 1932), the indispensable works are the widely read contemporary collection by Charles Kegley and Robert Brettall, *Reinhold Niebuhr: His Religious, Social, and Political Thought* (New York: Macmillan, 1956); Donald B. Meyer, *The Protestant Search for Political Realism, 1919–1941* (1960; reprint, Middletown, Conn.: Wesleyan University Press, 1988); Richard Fox, *Reinhold Niebuhr: A Biography* (New York: Pantheon, 1985); and Christopher Lasch, *The True and Only Heaven: Progress and Its Critics* (New York: Norton, 1991).

Though Niebuhr spent a good deal of time denouncing the Social Gospel, much of his "prophetic" alternative can be traced back to the leading theologian of the Social Gospel, Rauschenbusch. Like most great thinkers, Rauschenbusch often transcended the limitations and oversimplifications of the school he headed, a point Niebuhr did not acknowledge. His brother was more careful:

> Washington Gladden and Walter Rauschenbusch . . . distinguished themselves from their liberal contemporaries by keeping relatively close to evangelical notions of the sovereignty of God, of the reign of Christ and of the coming kingdom. In Rauschenbusch especially the revolutionary element remained pronounced; the reign of Christ required conversion and the coming kingdom was crisis, judgment as well as promise. Though his theory of the relations of God and man often seemed liberal he continued to speak the language of the prophets and St. Paul. (H. Richard Niebuhr, *Kingdom of God*, 194)

This work of the younger Niebuhr is a helpful and evocative treatment of the prophetic tradition. Another is Norman Cohn, *The Pursuit of the Millennium* (London: Secker and Warburg, 1957).

Prophetic rantings about corruption and society's fall from first principles are also the stock-in-trade of the "civic Republican" tradition that has recently been identified as a major theme in American political culture. See, e.g., Pocock's *Machiavellian Moment* and Wood's *Creation of the American Republic*. There seem to be as many different versions of this Republicanism as there are books on the subject. The intertwining of prophetic and Classical Pagan ideas of corruption and revitalization through modern history might be worth investigating.

Bayard Rustin's own writings represent him well. See especially *Down the Line: The Collected Writings of Bayard Rustin* (Chicago: Quadrangle, 1971) and *Strategies of Freedom: Changing Contours of Black Protest* (New York: Columbia, 1976). Jervis Anderson's pioneering biography—*Bayard Rustin: Troubles I've Seen* (New York: HarperCollins, 1997)—is thorough and perceptive.

Modjeska Simkins and James Lawson have gotten surprisingly scant treatment by historians. I relied on their writings and the long interviews with Simkins (by Jacquelyn Hall) and Lawson (by Joan Beifus and David Yellin); see the notes in Chapters 3 and 4. Most of the secondary work on Simkins is by Barbara Aba-Mecha, aka Barbara Woods. See Aba-Mecha, "Black Woman Activist in Twentieth-Century South Carolina: Modjeska Monteith Simkins" (Ph.D. diss., Emory University, 1978); Aba-Mecha, "South Carolina Conference of the NAACP: Origins and Major Accomplishments, 1939-1954," *Proceedings of the South Carolina Historical Society* (1981): 1-27; and Woods, "Modjeska Simkins and the South Carolina Conference of the NAACP, 1939-1957," in *Women in the Civil Rights Movement* (Brooklyn: Carlson, 1990), 99-120. On Lawson, the following were helpful: Byron Plumley Jr., "Searching for a Place to Stand: Reflections of Spiritually-Rooted Social Activists" (Ph.D. diss., Union Institute, 1993); David Halberstam, *The Children* (New York: Random House, 1998); and Peter Ackerman and Jack DuVall, *A Force More Powerful: A Century of Nonviolent Conflict* (New York: St. Martin's Press, 2000).

Material on Fannie Lou Hamer is vast but scattered. See Hamer, *To Praise Our Bridges: An Autobiography* (Jackson, Miss.: KIPCO, 1967), copy in Labadie Pamphlets Collection, University of Michigan, and reprinted in Dorothy Abbott, ed., *Mississippi Writers* (Jackson: University Press of Mississippi, 1986), 321-30; Hamer, interview with J. H. O'Dell, transcript in *Freedomways* (2d Quarter 1965): 231-42, and speech to NAACP Legal Defense Fund Institute, May 7, 1971, in Gerda Lerner, ed., *Black Women in White America: A Documentary History* (New York: Vintage, 1992); Kay Mills, *This Little Light of Mine: The Life of Fannie Lou Hamer* (New York: Dutton, 1993); Chana Kai Lee, *For Freedom's Sake: The Life of Fannie Lou Hamer* (Urbana: University of Illinois Press, 1999); John Dittmer, *Local People: The Struggle for Civil Rights in Mississippi* (Urbana: University of Illinois Press, 1994), 125-26, 408; and Charles Payne, who captures the way Christian faith sometimes reinforced the pragmatic skill and intelligence that Hamer and others showed, in *I've Got the Light of Freedom: The Organizing Tradition and the Mississippi Freedom Struggle* (Berkeley: University of California Press, 1995), 154-55, 194, 242, 309, 425. The Mississippi Sovereignty Commission did not have much on Hamer, but see Sovereignty Commission Records,

Mississippi Department of Archives and History, Jackson (MDAH), no. 1-104-0-24. The Hamer Papers at the Amistad Research Center, Tulane University, contain little material that would shed light on her ideas. Also rather thin on ideas are Hamer's interview transcripts in the Howard University Library's Civil Rights Documentation Project (CRDP); in the University of Southern Mississippi Collection; in Pat Watters and Reese Cleghorn, *Climbing Jacob's Ladder* (New York: Harcourt, 1967), 363–75; and in Emily Stoper, *The Student Nonviolent Coordinating Committee: The Growth of Radicalism in a Civil Rights Organization* (1968; reprint, Brooklyn, N.Y.: Carlson, 1989).

During interviews, those who worked with Hamer spoke of her intellectual leadership. Larry Guyot (interview transcript, University of Southern Mississippi) called her "the Biblical expert" in the Mississippi movement, the one who drew the connections between "the Biblical exaltations for liberation and what we were talking about now." Hamer "could wrap" biblical discourse around the struggle "any time that she wanted to and move in and out to any frames of reference." Guyot stressed that she was a local resource, however—somewhat contrary to Hamer's own emphasis on the imported character of the movement in her state. Guyot insisted that the students of the 1960s "didn't *produce* Fannie Lou Hamer; we simply found her." According to the Rev. Sammy Rash (interview transcript, University of Southern Mississippi), Hamer was "just an inspiration" and "just a born genius." Rash and many others testified to the depth of her religious commitments. Other interesting meditations on Hamer's role include Ed King, "Go Tell It on the Mountain: A Prophet from the Delta," and other pieces by Danny Cullom, Charles McLaurin, and June Johnson, in *Sojourners*, December 1982, and Stephen L. Carter, "The Religious Resistance of Fannie Lou Hamer," *God's Name in Vain: The Wrongs and Rights of Religion in Politics* (New York: Basic Books, 2000).

John Lewis is so far his own best interpreter. See Lewis, with Michael D'Orso, *Walking with the Wind: A Memoir of the Movement* (New York: Simon and Schuster, 1998). Clayborne Carson is insightful and thorough in his treatment of Lewis, as he is with so many others, in *In Struggle: SNCC and the Black Awakening in the 1960s* (Cambridge: Harvard University Press, 1981).

Perhaps the most perceptive and sympathetic account of Robert Moses, including his mysterious name change, abandonment of the movement, and expatriation, is Lewis's *Walking with the Wind*. Like others, Lewis recalls Moses emphasizing that the struggle would be long, that there would be, in Lewis's paraphrase, "frustration and setbacks and often a feeling of more loss than success." Yet from Lewis's telling, it seems that Moses became brittle, unable to live the lesson he had taught to so many others, partly because they seemed to depend on him so absolutely for this lesson (pp. 187, 242, 250, 283, 293, 295–96, 351). As comprehensive a study as we are likely to get of this elusive and enigmatic character is Eric Burner's *And Gently He Shall Lead Them: Robert Parris Moses and Civil Rights in Mississippi* (New York: New York University Press, 1994).

THE INTELLECTUAL HISTORY OF THE CIVIL RIGHTS MOVEMENT
AND POLITICAL NONVIOLENCE

In their assessment of the intellectual substance of the civil rights movement, most scholars seem to have followed the lead of a pioneering historian of SNCC, Emily Stoper (*SNCC*), who minifies the ideology SNCC began with: most black members "were not intellectuals and were admirers above all of the non-intellectual virtues of courage and charisma." To Stoper, there was no significant "intellectual" activity in SNCC, which had merely a simple "set of ideas . . . centered around nonviolence as a way of life." Following the unfortunate lead of some prominent SNCC veterans, Stoper and most writers draw a false dichotomy between this and nonviolence "as a tactic," which Stoper claims came to dominate SNCC (pp. 9, 25–30, 106). The SNCC Papers, on microfilm, are so fragmentary and disorganized that such claims are difficult to verify. On the other hand, it is clear that the SCLC (and FOR and CORE, to say nothing of Gandhi and his disciples) developed and promoted the use of nonviolence as a tactic. Though Martin Luther King sometimes spoke hopefully of a distant future when all might be pacifists, he did not say that his followers had to adopt nonviolence as a way of life—to renounce self-defense if their home was attacked, for example. See King, *Why We Can't Wait* (New York: Harper and Row, 1964), 152; King, *Where Do We Go from Here?* (New York: Harper, 1967), 27; and Andrew Young, *An Easy Burden: The Civil Rights Movement and the Transformation of America* (New York: HarperCollins, 1996), 120. What King and other tacticians insisted on was that, as long as people gathered together to force concessions from an oppressive system, they had to maintain nonviolent discipline: it was suicidal to indulge in violence when they were so obviously outgunned. (This was not the case in South Africa, for instance, where once-nonviolent leaders like Nelson Mandela renounced nonviolence and were able to win: they had a black majority, external sources of weaponry, and refuge in neighboring states.) There was, to be sure, a long, generally sterile debate within SNCC over nonviolence as a tactic versus nonviolence as a way of life, but many other philosophical and theological ideas were discussed in SNCC meetings and publications, too. Stoper (*SNCC*, 105 ff.) claims that, although Bob Moses was the only black intellectual in the original SNCC group, he "seems to have had little ideological influence on the black members of SNCC." For reasons laid out in Chapters 3–5 of this book, and perhaps because I define intellectual somewhat more broadly than Stoper, I find this—and scholars' general assumption that the movement had no significant intellectual history—hard to swallow.

The intellectual history of the civil rights struggle has nonetheless been illuminated by the works already cited by Clayborne Carson, Peter Kellog, David Southern, Walter Jackson, Ted Ownby, and also by a handful of other works that take the ideas in the movement seriously, though those draw mostly on sources outside the movement proper: among them, see especially Richard King, *Civil Rights and the Idea of Freedom* (Athens: University of Georgia Press, 1996);

Timothy B. Tyson, *Radio Free Dixie: Robert F. Williams and the Roots of Black Power* (Chapel Hill: University of North Carolina Press, 1999); and Carol Polsgrove, *Divided Minds: Intellectuals and the Civil Rights Movement* (New York: Norton, 2001).

AFRICAN AMERICAN RELIGION AND POLITICS

A major theme from the earliest historiography of African American religion to the present has been the tension between accommodation and protest. Carter Woodson, in *The Negro Church* (1921; reprint, New York: Arno, 1972), found the black clergy drawn into politics (which he often thought a diversion from more effective work) after Emancipation, with the "Conservatives" in control after Reconstruction, though they were constantly challenged by "Progressives." Woodson then saw development of the social mission to the point where, by 1921, the church was the most important force for the uplift of the race. Benjamin Mays and Joseph Nicholson, though they tended to emphasize an apolitical otherworldliness, also perceived a conflicting social activism in *The Negro's Church* (New York: Institute of Social and Religious Research, 1933). Hart and Anne Nelsen, in *The Black Church in the Sixties* (Lexington: University Press of Kentucky, 1967), almost inverting Ernst Troeltsch, distinguished between "churchlike" black churches, which could inspire militancy as part of a posture of service to the community, and "sectlike" black churches, which tended to dampen militancy with emotional otherworldliness. (The church-sect typology dates back to Troeltsch, who in *The Social Teachings of the Christian Churches* [1911; trans. Olive Wyon, 2 vols., New York: Macmillan, 1931] saw churches joining the state to enforce upper-class domination and sects working from the bottom up on behalf of the lower classes.) The Nelsens aimed to refute Gary Marx, who, in *Protest and Prejudice*, claimed to find an inverse relationship between intense religiosity and civil rights militancy. More recently, C. Eric Lincoln and Lawrence Mamiya, in *The Black Church in the African American Experience* (Durham, N.C.: Duke University Press, 1990), 221–23, 234–35, see a "dialectic" between conservative "survival" and radical "liberation" strategies. Peter Paris, in *The Social Teaching of the Black Churches* (Philadelphia: Fortress Press, 1985), finds an almost constant resistance to racism, which tends to be reformist rather than revolutionary. In *Righteous Discontent: the Women's Movement in the Black Baptist Church* (Cambridge: Harvard University Press, 1993), Evelyn Brooks Higginbotham, drawing on Eugene Genovese, argues that the "prophetic" role, which resists oppression, is in constant tension with the "priestly," which tends to accommodate it (pp. 15–16).

John Dittmer, Charles Payne, and other experts on Mississippi provocatively posit a far more secular movement there than scholars have found elsewhere in the South. Dittmer (*Local People*) notes that the sight in the 1960s of a Delta church packed with protesters was anomalous, unprecedented: "In Mississippi the institutional church did not stand in the forefront of civil rights activity, and black ministers were conspicuously absent from the front ranks of movement leadership." Medgar Evers, among others, was frustrated "over the clergy's lack of support, complaining that 'some ministers are . . . in that class of people who won't be hurt by belonging to the [NAACP], but who won't give us 50 cents for fear of losing face with the white man.'" Many activists believed that white leaders used "reliable" Negro ministers like Percy Greene to gain control. Dittmer cites with approval the view of Mays and Nicholson, John Dollard, and others that the black church functioned as an opiate. He also notes that the SCLC never established a base in Mississippi "in part because of NAACP opposition." Dittmer also observes, however: "If the institutional church was not a positive force in the fifties, faith in God certainly was. . . . Prayer, the singing of hymns and spirituals, and the lessons of the biblical teachings were a staple of mass meetings, and the belief that God was on their side sustained Mississippi blacks during the worst of the white reign of terror" (pp. 74, 77–79). Payne (*I've Got the Light of Freedom*) sees protest growing out of a rich culture of civic participation in the era of World War II. That culture generated a sense of efficacy among influential black Mississippians. Men generally gained this sense of efficacy through ownership of property. Women, on the other hand, tended to gain it from participation in church activity. Payne's is a more secular view of protest and a more functional view of religion than I think plausible for the whole southern movement. But Payne (along with Dittmer) makes it irresistible for at least a significant part of Mississippi. Stephen G. N. Tuck echoes Dittmer's and Payne's effort to de-emphasize religion in his fine state study, *Beyond Atlanta: The Struggle for Racial Equality in Georgia, 1940–1980* (Athens: University of Georgia Press, 2001). With such intelligent work focusing on apparently nonreligious aspects of the civil rights struggle, one might expect a historiographical debate to emerge on the civic versus religious sources of the struggle, though so far that has not happened. Given the exceptions these scholars grant—and the anti-institutional religion propounded by King, Modjeska Simkins, Fannie Lou Hamer, and other activists—one wonders whether such debate might yield closer agreement on the role of "religion." The apparent disagreements often appear to be a matter of overly institutional, and sometimes overly functional, definitions.

ON THE SOCIAL EFFECTS OF REVIVALS

For historical treatments of the social effects of religious revivals, see, e.g., Alice Felt Tyler's classic, *Freedom's Ferment: Phases of American Social History to 1860* (Minneapolis: University of Minnesota Press, 1944); Whitney R. Cross, *The Burned-over District: The Social and Intellectual History of Enthusiastic Religion in Western New York, 1800–1850* (Ithaca, N.Y.: Cornell University Press, 1950); David Brion Davis, ed., *Ante-bellum Reform* (Baltimore: Johns Hopkins University Press, 1967); Paul E. Johnson, *A Shopkeeper's Millennium: Society and Revivals in Rochester, New York, 1815–1837* (New York: Hill and Wang, 1978); Rhys Isaac, *The Transformation of Virginia, 1740–1790* (Chapel Hill: University of North Carolina Press, 1982); Allen Tullos, *Habits of Industry: White Culture and the Transformation of the Carolina Piedmont* (Chapel Hill: University of North Carolina Press, 1989); and Robert H. Abzug's ambitious attempt to capture the religious essence that held the Second Great Awakening and the various reform movements together, *Cosmos Crumbling: American Reform and the Religious Imagination* (New York: Oxford University Press, 1995). Richard J. Carwardine sees revivalism fostering political agitation on both sides of the Mason-Dixon line in his subtle and engaging *Evangelicals and Politics in Antebellum America* (Knoxville: University of Tennessee Press, 1997). Years ago Cheryl Shanks, a gifted scholar of international migration and theories of sovereignty, prophetically told me, "One day you will read Karen Fields's book on the Jehovah's Witnesses in what is now Malawi and Zambia, and it will change your life." At the time, both predictions sounded implausible to the point of absurdity. But I did and it did. I can think of no better work to illuminate the unpredictable force of religious enthusiasm in the modern world—or to show how much an esoteric-sounding study of obscure and distant folk can tell us about our own world—than this brilliant book by Karen E. Fields with its misleadingly modest title: *Revival and Rebellion in Colonial Central Africa* (Princeton, N.J.: Princeton University Press, 1981).

On the enumeration of "Awakenings," William McLoughlin saw a third "Great Awakening" between 1890 and 1920, and, more tentatively, a fourth (under way as he wrote) from roughly 1960 to 1990 or so, but his notion and periodization have not caught on among historians. It remains the convention (despite Jon Butler's brilliant iconoclasm, about which see below) to refer only to the First (roughly 1740s) and Second (roughly 1800–1840) Great Awakenings. Few historians ever think of there having been a Third or a Fourth, or at any rate not with the transformation of politics and society that they grant to the First and Second. Tom Wolfe, in his famous essay on the "Me Decade," suggested tongue-in-cheekily that various drug-related cults of the 1960s and 1970s constituted a "Third Great Awakening," roughly equivalent in years to what McLoughlin thought might be a Fourth. Wolfe, *Mauve Gloves and Madmen, Clutter and Vine, and Other Essays* (New York: Bantam, 1977), 111–47. Wolfe saw the first two Great Awakenings as nothing but destructive of tradition. Jon Butler, in "Enthusiasm Described and Decried: The Great Awakening as Interpretive Fiction," *Journal of American History* 69 (September 1982): 305–25, and *Awash in a Sea of Faith: Christianizing the American People* (Cambridge: Harvard University Press, 1990), throws cold water on the whole business of distinguishing and numbering "awakenings." Like many of Butler's fans, I find myself somewhat sheepishly incapable of getting along without certain interpretive fictions.

The point of C. C. Goen's volume, *Broken Churches, Broken Nation: Denominational Schisms and the Coming of the American Civil War* (Macon, Ga.: Mercer University Press, 1985), was all but commonplace to previous historians. It has been explored in a number of excellent books since Goen, notably Mitchell Snay's *Gospel of Disunion: Religion and Separatism in the Antebellum South* (Cambridge: Cambridge University Press, 1993), and Carwardine's *Evangelicals in American Politics*. It is also commonplace—and has been at least since the appearance of Alan Heimert, *Religion and the American Mind: From the Great Awakening to the Revolution* (Cambridge: Harvard University Press, 1966), despite controversy over some of Heimert's specifics—that a religious split, still sometimes referred to as the First Great Awakening, presaged the American Revolution. That notion, too, has remained alive in more recent scholarship, notably in Isaac, *Transformation of Virginia*, and in Patricia Bonomi, *Under the Cope of Heaven; Religion, Society, and Politics in Colonial America* (New York: Oxford University Press, 1986).

A great mystery in scholarship on the civil rights struggle is why no one has asked what would seem to be the obvious question: whether great upheavals in the churches might have shaped *that* struggle and the response of the general population to it. Why not ask whether the largely voluntary separation of black parishioners into denominations of their own, following and in some cases preceding the Civil War, was the formative historical precedent? Why not ask whether the Billy Graham revival had something to do with the culmination of the struggle in the 1950s and early 1960s? Historians are beginning to overcome their blindness to religion in modern history—their once blithe assumption that modernity entails secularization. Many have duly noted that religion must have had something to do, at least in a crude functional sense, with black protest in the 1950s–60s. (It has always been easier for modern historians to think of poor, undereducated peoples as being driven by religious motives or leaders than for them to see the effect of religion on the luckier classes.) They need to go deeper.

SEGREGATIONISTS' PUBLIC RELIGION

My conclusion that segregationists generally avoided religious topics is based on a reading of the full run of the segregationist organs *The Citizen* and *Citizens' Council*, numerous copies of the *Augusta Courier* (Georgia), and the *Councilor* (Louisiana); the relevant collections in the Library of Congress (the segregationist literature collected by the NAACP, the Leadership Council on Civil Rights, and reporter John Bartlow Martin, author of "The Deep South Says Never"); the files of local civil rights leaders who monitored the opposition, such as Little Rock's Daisy Bates, whose papers are in the State Historical Society of Wisconsin, Madison; the collection of segregationist propaganda (Citizens'

Councils of America Literature) in the University of Arkansas Library; the office files of the New Orleans branch of the Anti-Defamation League of B'nai B'rith (which monitored and infiltrated racist groups), now at the Amistad Research Center, Tulane University (related collections in the ADL's files in New York have not been opened to researchers, though I have combed through the ADL's vast collection of newspaper clippings, available on microfilm in its New York office); the FBI's "COINTELPRO White Hate" Files, FBI Headquarters, Washington, D.C.; the papers of the Association of Citizens' Councils of Mississippi, MDAH; a significant portion of the files of the Mississippi Sovereignty Commission, also at the MDAH, but scheduled to go "on line" shortly after this book goes to press; and the office files of such leading segregationists as Solomon Blatt, Charles Bloch, Harry Byrd, James F. Byrnes, Eugene "Bull" Connor, William Jennings Bryan Dorn, Sam Ervin, Wesley Critz George, John Temple Graves, Marion Gressette, Roy Harris, James J. Kilpatrick, Lester Maddox's press secretary (John Brewton), John Patterson, Richard Russell, Howard Smith, Strom Thurmond, George Wallace, Thomas Waring, John Bell Williams, and William D. Workman. All of these files contain healthy samples of segregationist propaganda. The same items recur enough to give the impression that, together, they constitute a representative sample of what was available in the 1950s and early 1960s.

In my interpretation of these sources, I differ with scholars like Bill Leonard, "A Theology for Racism: Southern Fundamentalists and the Civil Rights Movement," in Tony Badger et al., eds., *Southern Landscapes* (Tübingen: Stauffenberg Verlag, 1996), 165–81. The heart of the disagreement, it seems to me, is that I do not consider racism to be the central issue. To be sure, there is, as Leonard shows, an overwhelming racism in southern white culture. The black activists of the 1950s–60s certainly would have liked to eliminate racism from the hearts and minds of their enemies. But they did not succeed in doing that, and for most of them, hearts and minds were not the primary targets. Their primary targets were the historically and geographically specific institutional expressions of racism: legal segregation and disfranchisement. They largely succeeded in destroying those targets, and that, it seems to me, is what historians most need to explain.

The racism expressed by southern ministers is not the issue: ample racism was articulated by the allies of the movement as well as its enemies (as the younger activists of the 1960s frequently pointed out). What is significant are two things: (1) the evidence that southern white ministers did not contribute much, and showed little enthusiasm for, the defense of legal segregation (let alone disfranchisement); and (2) the frequent condemnation of the southern white church in general by segregationist advocates. These things, which previous scholars have overlooked, are what I emphasize.

I have a different disagreement with Charles Marsh, whose *God's Long Summer: Stories of Faith and Civil Rights* (Princeton, N.J.: Princeton University Press, 1997) provides a useful analysis of the "theology" of Klansman Sam Bowers. (Marsh's sources of Bowers's political thought do not strike me as centering or depending on their religious references, most of which seem incidental, but that is not my main objection.) Marsh's implication that Bowers was a representative segregationist clashes with the findings of my research. My research indicates that Bowers and his ilk were atypical, indeed were shunned by most prominent segregationist leaders. Marsh has another chapter on the Rev. Douglas Hudgins, a leading white minister in Jackson. Hudgins fits the pattern I found of conservative southern clergymen who insisted on depoliticizing the church. Though unquestionably a segregationist, Hudgins ultimately failed to contribute creatively to the cause; rather, he was typical of the churchmen about whom Roy Harris, Carleton Putnam, and other segregationist leaders complained. I find Hudgins far more typical of segregationist clergymen than Bowers. I also think that the conflict between the public positions of Hudgins and Bowers has great significance — not because it reveals any moral difference in the private condition of their souls, but because it represents a profound, indeed fatal, division over political strategy. Marsh sees Hudgins and Bowers as two peas in a pod. Perhaps they were in their innermost hearts. But surely historical understanding of the public phenomenon we call the civil rights struggle depends on a frank reckoning with public positions. The positions that people rallied around in public — whatever their various dark and unseemly individual motivations — constituted the common ground on which their social movement was based. The public positions have the added advantage of being accessible. (There is, by contrast, no basis for adjudicating scholars' conflicting assumptions about the unrecorded motives of different individuals.) It seems to me there is a prima facie difference between the public Hudgins and the public Bowers, one that takes on great significance when placed in the context of the rest of the available material on segregationist propaganda and strategy, which Marsh does not consider. For these reasons, I see Marsh's work as somewhat misleading.

Andrew Michael Manis, *Southern Civil Religions in Conflict: Black and White Baptists and Civil Rights, 1947–1957* (Athens: University Press of Georgia, 1987), rightly paints the white southern Baptists who grappled with race as a confused and conflicted lot. Yet he overdramatizes the "holy war" between black and white Baptists. The religious conflict appears to be a lot more lopsided than Manis — or Marsh — seems willing to admit: the few active black churches had all the confidence and solidarity; the white churches were hesitant and factious. The white side of the cultural war had few "holy" overtones, while the black side was holier than just about any modern cause before or since. Despite Manis's thesis, his evidence vindicates the complaint of segregationist leaders that I stress: that southern white churches did not contribute sufficiently to the cause and were not consistent or enthusiastic in their support.

Perhaps the most thoughtful scholar of recent southern Baptist history, J. Wayne Flynt, occasionally treats the segregation controversy with uncharacteristic haste. For instance, in *Alabama Baptists: Southern Baptists in the Heart of Dixie* (Tuscaloosa: University of Alabama Press, 1998), 460–61, Flynt observes that "conservatives" won a debate in the 1959 convention to "delete" a resolution commending Brooks Hays for his stand on integration, because a majority of delegates feared that the resolution would enrage the laity in their churches.

This may have been an example of clerical cowardice, but it did not mean that the Southern Baptist Convention was repudiating its integrationism, as Flynt comes close to suggesting. Rather, the SBC delegates were seeking to dampen the uproar, or to take the convention out of politics—whether in the hope that segregation would be strengthened or weakened or unaffected we cannot say. As noted in Chapter 8 of this study, the leading southern white group that worked *for* desegregation, the Southern Regional Council, sought as eagerly as the SBC to remove the issue from the realm of public controversy. The SRC believed that publicity hindered desegregation: Publicity forced political candidates to agitate the issue and polarize opinion, when many of them preferred to avoid it. At any rate, segregationists wanted more than silence and neutrality from their leaders, as I argue in Chapters 6–8. Flynt seems closer to the truth about biblical arguments for segregation when he writes, "There was no exact correlation between fundamentalist theology and resistance to integration," than when he later writes, "Like white Baptist defenders of slavery a century earlier, southern racism fed off biblical literalism" (p. 458). Though careful and consistent on other points, Flynt seems to have strayed from his evidence with the latter statement, which he never develops or substantiates. It is hard to reconcile this slip with the judgment of another careful Baptist historian, Edward L. Queen: "Opposition to integration, with perhaps one exception [Criswell], was never formulated on the basis of religion. Opposition to segregation was almost inevitably so formed." Queen, *In the South the Baptists Are the Center of Gravity: Southern Baptists and Social Change, 1930–1980* (Brooklyn, N.Y.: Carlson, 1991), 92–93.

Mark Newman's thorough studies of southern Baptists reinforce my view of deep division over segregation in that denomination. He adds evidence of a general momentum toward acceptance of desegregation. See, e.g., Newman, "The Arkansas Baptist State Convention and Desegregation, 1954–1968," *Arkansas Historical Quarterly* 56 (Autumn 1997): 294–313, "The Baptist State Convention of North Carolina and Desegregation, 1945–1980," *North Carolina Historical Review* 85 (January 1998): 1–28, and *Getting Right with God: Southern Baptists and Desegregation, 1945–1995* (Tuscaloosa: University of Alabama Press, 2001). Randy J. Sparks's equally thorough work on Mississippi—"'A Search for Life's Meanings': Mississippi's White Sunday Schools, White Churches, and the Race Question, 1900–1967" (paper presented at 1997 meeting of the Organization of American Historians, in author's possession) and "'A Search for Life's Meanings': Religion and Civil Rights," chapter 10 of his *Religion in Mississippi* (Jackson: Mississippi Historical Society, 2001)—also depicts conflict among Baptists, and in other denominations, and a movement toward acceptance of desegregation. Like Flynt—and like the early pioneer in the field, Lee Porter—Newman and Sparks see a three-stage chronological progression; they differ on characterizing and delimiting the first two stages but view the third as acceptance of desegregation (for Newman, somewhat ahead of the general white population, though not far, and for Flynt, somewhat behind).

Though much of the data seem to fit that three-stage progression—which does not, strictly speaking, conflict with my reading—I find it a bit too neat to be plausible and have chosen not to emphasize it in my account. I have greatly benefited from the work of Flynt, Newman, and Sparks, three careful and intelligent scholars, and from discussions with them about the evidence. See also Lee Porter, "Southern Baptists and Race Relations, 1948–1963" (Th.D. diss., Southwestern Baptist Theological Seminary, Fort Worth, Tex., 1965). Also illuminating on the southern Baptists were Foy Valentine, "A Historical Study of Southern Baptists and Race Relations, 1917–1947" (Th.D. diss., Southwestern Baptist Theological Seminary, Fort Worth, Tex., 1949); John Lee Eighmy, *Churches in Cultural Captivity: A History of the Social Attitudes of Southern Baptists* (Knoxville: University of Tennessee Press, 1972); and Queen, *Baptists Are the Center of Gravity*. Paul Harvey's soon-to-be published work on a Baptist "folk theology" of segregation may provide a breakthrough in understanding the lay side of the apparent divide between clergy and laity over segregation. See Harvey, "Religion, Race, and the Right in the Baptist South, 1945–1990," in *Religion and Politics in the South*, ed. Glenn Feldman (forthcoming, Tuscaloosa: University of Alabama Press, 2004). I have also benefited greatly from long, searching discussions of the evidence with Harvey.

Other large southern white denominations are well covered in Joel L. Alvis Jr., *Religion and Race: Southern Presbyterians, 1946–1983* (Tuscaloosa: University of Alabama Press, 1994); Donald E. Collins (despite his misleading title), *When the Church Bell Rang Racist: The Methodist Church and the Civil Rights Movement in Alabama* (Macon, Ga.: Mercer University Press, 1998); Gardiner H. Shattuck, *Episcopalians and Race: Civil War to Civil Rights* (Lexington: University Press of Kentucky, 2000); and Robert Christy Douglas, "Power . . . in the Church of Christ, . . . a Case Study of Black Civil Rights" (Ph.D. diss., University of Southern California, 1980).

The present study also owes a great debt to pioneering work on southern white churches in cultural captivity (in addition to the works already cited on antebellum southern religion's support for pro-slavery ideology) by Liston Pope, *Millhands and Preachers: A Study of Gastonia* (New Haven: Yale University Press, 1942); Kenneth K. Bailey, *Southern White Protestantism in the Twentieth Century* (New York: Harper and Row, 1964); Samuel S. Hill, *Southern Churches in Crisis* (1966) and *Southern Churches in Crisis Revisited* (1999), both published in Tuscaloosa by the University of Alabama Press; Eighmy, *Churches in Cultural Captivity*; and David Edwin Harrell Jr., ed., *Varieties of Southern Evangelicalism* (Macon, Ga.: Mercer University Press, 1981).

SEGREGATIONISM MORE GENERALLY

Of published segregationist sources, Edward P. Lawton, *The South and the Nation* (Fort Myers Beach, Fla.: Island Press, 1963), is perhaps the most eloquent and readable tract. Lawton claims, "I do not favor segregation per se, nor do I approve of the methods used in some parts of the South to deprive Negroes of equal justice and civil rights. I am, however, a supporter of states' rights." Lawton's is probably the only segregationist book that stands the test of time—that can be read today for more than historical interest. But two others from the period are written with an intelligence and an honesty that make them especially valuable to students of history (they may have had correspondingly less propaganda value at the time): James J. Kilpatrick, *The Southern Case for School Segregation* (New York: Crowell-Collier Press, 1962), and William D. Workman, *The Case for the South* (New York: Devin-Adair, 1960). More notorious, and perhaps more widely read than all of these, was Tom P. Brady's *Black Monday* (Jackson, Miss.: Citizens' Councils of America, 1955), which is unblushingly racist. Brady's book has the merit of showing how unpredictable southern conservative opinion was in the 1950s—an odd amalgam of evangelical fervor and rigid Darwinianism. It embraces the Christian and the Darwinian cases for monogenesis yet claims to find "three species of man" (not merely "races") in natural history. (Species are conventionally defined as incapable of interbreeding.) Brady disavows a belief in white supremacy, insisting only on strict racial *differences*; he slips, however, into many expressions of white—and, interestingly, "Mongoloid"—superiority to the "Negroid race." But his belief in "white" and "Oriental" superiority is mild compared to his strong philo-Semitism, which he seems to think necessary to maintaining a biblical line of "white" supremacy. Carleton Putnam was, it seems, the most widely quoted and distributed segregationist author—and an avowed Yankee. He was also frank in his racism, though he made more of an effort to gather the trappings of scientific respectability around his claims and tended to embarrass educated segregationists less than Brady did. See Putnam, *Race and Reason: A Yankee View* (1961) and *Race and Reality: A Search for Solutions* (1967), both published in Washington, D.C., by Public Affairs Press.

Since the pioneering studies of the late 1960s-early 1970s—I. A. Newby, *Challenge to the Court: Social Scientists and the Defense of Segregation, 1954–1966* (Baton Rouge: LSU Press, 1967); Numan V. Bartley, *The Rise of Massive Resistance: Race and Politics in the South during the 1950s* (Baton Rouge: LSU Press, 1969); Neil R. McMillen, *The Citizens' Council: Organized Resistance to the Second Reconstruction, 1954–1964)* (Urbana: University of Illinois Press, 1971); Francis M. Wilhoit, *The Politics of Massive Resistance* (New York: Brazilier, 1973); and Earl Black, *Southern Governors and Civil Rights: Racial Segregation as a Campaign Issue in the Second Reconstruction* (Cambridge: Harvard University Press, 1976)—scholarly work on segregationism has been thin. This is surprising, given how much attention historians have lavished on the black side of the struggle. Most scholars simply cite Bartley or McMillen, if they consider the segregationists at all, and leave it at that. Essential earlier work on the subject includes Guion Griffis Johnson, "The Ideology of White Supremacy, 1876-1910," in *Essays in Southern History*, ed. Fletcher M. Green (Chapel Hill: University of North Carolina Press, 1949): 124–56; James W. Vander Zanden, "The Ideology of White Supremacy," *Journal of the History of Ideas* 20 (June–September 1959): 385–402; John Bartlow Martin, *The Deep South Says "Never"* (New York: Ballantine, 1957); Dan Wakefield, *Revolt in the South* (New York: Grove, 1960); and James Graham Cook, *The Segrega-tionists* (New York: Appleton-Century-Crofts, 1962).

A local study, Jeff Roche's *Restructured Resistance: The Sibley Commission and the Politics of Desegregation in Georgia* (Athens: University of Georgia Press, 1998), presents a fine-grained analysis of the subtleties and ambiguities of genteel seg-regationism. Roche's work, like Bartley's and McMillen's, is indispensable. But, as also happens in the earlier books, Roche's evidence of segregationist disorga-nization and infighting gets somewhat obscured by his devotion to exposing the "tyranny" that intimidated moderate voices into silence and by his zeal to prove the "success" of segregationism (in his case, one particular strand of segrega-tionism) in delaying desegregation. Other scholars who emphasize the variety of segregationist strategies, and tend to see them as examples of segregationist resiliency rather than weakness, include Karl Campbell, "Last of the Founding Fathers: Senator Sam Ervin and the Road to Watergate" (Ph.D. diss., University of North Carolina, 1995), and Charles Bolton, "Mississippi's School Equaliza-tion Program, 1945–1954: A Last Gasp to Try to Maintain a Segregated Educa-tional System," *Journal of Southern History* 66 (November 2000): 781–814. I made a partial response to this line in "Religious Ideas of the Segregationists," *Journal of American Studies* 32 (1998): 237–62. My view is this: These studies provide ex-amples of resiliency if and only if one considers the aim behind segregationism to be something other than the preservation of segregation.

It should not surprise us that segregationists were often opportunists who had goals other than their stated aim of segregation, or that many were simply buy-ing time or diverting attention from other concerns. The trouble with consid-ering them victors is that they were not a "they" without the collective cover of segregationism: some individuals or factions among them prospered to varying degrees, some did not. To say that segregationists lost the battle does not re-quire us to establish that all segregationists were dispossessed or disfranchised— or that all structures of power and all economic opportunities were opened up to all black people. My point is simply that the segregationists failed in their stated, collective, and public aim of preserving the legal institution of forced segrega-tion. To be sure, all people involved in the civil rights struggle—on both sides— had interests other than the preservation or destruction of the movement's direct targets. Those who ended up maintaining their position and power—including a number of segregationist editors and politicians—can certainly be seen as sur-vivors, even in some sense as wily and devious individual victors in a multifaceted social and political struggle over issues other than civil rights. (So some slave-owners or some Nazi collaborators managed to survive and even to prosper after the wars that destroyed their regimes.) Nearly all social and military struggles in history have had similar complexities. But the surviving or prospering segrega-tionists are not victors *as segregationists*, since segregation was destroyed (along with disfranchisement).

Matthew D. Lassiter and Andrew B. Lewis, eds., *The Moderates' Dilemma: Massive Resistance to School Desegregation in Virginia* (Charlottesville: University

Press of Virginia, 1998), bring together some essays that break away from the emphases of other scholars, though their prepublication title, "The Fragility of Massive Resistance," reflected that break more faithfully than the bland, misleading title under which the collection was finally published. Clive Webb's insightful *Fight against Fear: Southern Jews and Black Civil Rights* (Athens: University of Georgia Press, 2001) suggests the breadth of segregationism—and of disinclination to take public exception to it—in southern culture. It also throws cold water on romantic nostalgia for a golden age of solidarity among outcast groups. John P. Jackson Jr.'s work on the biological arguments for segregation, and the continuity of these arguments with earlier and later forms of organized racism, is indispensable. See, e.g., Jackson's "In Ways Unacademical: The Reception of Carleton S. Coon's *The Origin of Races*," *Journal of the History of Biology* 34 (2001): 247–85. Kari Fredrickson provides useful historical background in *The Dixiecrat Revolt and the End of the Solid South, 1932–1968* (Chapel Hill: University of North Carolina Press, 2001).

Historical work on individual segregationists has been illuminating, especially Glen Jeansonne, *Leander Perez: Boss of the Delta* (Baton Rouge: LSU Press, 1977); Nadine Cohodas, *Strom Thurmond and the Politics of Southern Change* (Macon, Ga.: Mercer University Press, 1994); Gilbert C. Fite, *Richard B. Russell, Jr., Senator from Georgia* (Chapel Hill: University of North Carolina Press, 1991); Dan T. Carter, *Politics of Rage: George Wallace, the Origins of the New Conservatism, and the Transformation of American Politics* (New York: Simon and Schuster, 1995); Campbell, "Last of the Founding Fathers"; Ronald L. Heinemann, *Harry Byrd of Virginia* (Charlottesville: University Press of Virginia, 1996); Roy Reed, *Faubus: Life and Times of an American Prodigal* (Fayetteville: University of Arkansas Press, 1997); and Elizabeth Jacoway, "Jim Johnson of Arkansas," in Ownby, *Role of Ideas.*

In addition to the works on Niebuhr, southern religion, and African American religion, I found the following necessary to get a handle on religion in modern America generally: Will Herberg, *Protestant, Catholic, Jew* (Garden City: Doubleday, 1955); William G. McLoughlin, *Modern Revivalism: Charles Grandison Finney to Billy Graham* (New York: Ronald Press, 1959); Philip Rieff, *The Triumph of the Therapeutic: Uses of Faith after Freud* (1966; reprint, Chicago: University of Chicago Press, 1987); George M. Marsden, *Fundamentalism and American Culture: The Shaping of Twentieth-Century Evangelicalism* (New York: Oxford University Press, 1980); Mark A. Noll, *The Scandal of the Evangelical Mind* (Grand Rapids, Mich.: W. B. Eerdmans, 1984); Robert A. Orsi, *The Madonna of 115th Street: Faith and Community in Italian Harlem, 1180–1950* (New Haven: Yale University Press, 1985); Nancy Tatom Ammerman, *Bible Believers: Fundamentalists in the Modern World* (New Brunswick, N.J.: Rutgers University Press, 1987); Robert Wuthnow, *Restructuring of American Religion: Society and Faith since World War II* (Princeton, N.J.: Princeton University Press, 1988); William C. Martin, *A Prophet with Honor: The Billy Graham Story* (New York: Morrow, 1991); Paul S.

Boyer, *When Time Shall Be No More: Prophecy Belief in Modern American Culture* (Cambridge: Harvard University Press, 1992); R. Laurence Moore, *Selling God: American Religion in the Marketplace of Culture* (New York: Oxford University Press, 1994); John T. McGreevy, *Parish Boundaries: The Catholic Encounter with Race in the Twentieth-Century Urban North* (Chicago: University of Chicago Press, 1996); Joel A. Carpenter, *Revive Us Again: The Reawakening of American Fundamentalism* (New York: Oxford University Press, 1997); and Eugene McCarraher, *Christian Critics: Religion and the Impasse in Modern American Social Thought* (Ithaca, N.Y.: Cornell University Press, 2000).

There is no room to cover the vast historiography on the civil rights movement, but a few studies bear mentioning, particularly the justifiably celebrated works by David J. Garrow, *Bearing the Cross: Martin Luther King, Jr., and the Christian Leadership Conference* (New York: Morrow, 1986); Taylor Branch, *Parting the Waters: America in the King Years, 1954–1963* (New York: Simon and Schuster, 1988); and those already mentioned by Carson and Payne. The emphasis in scholarship over the last quarter century has been on local, grassroots activists, especially female ones (Payne's work is an invigoratingly original variation on the main theme of the genre). Apart from Payne and others cited above by Dittmer and Tuck, I have benefited from fine local studies by William Chafe, *Civilities and Civil Rights: Greensboro, North Carolina, and the Black Struggle for Freedom* (New York: Oxford University Press, 1980); Robert J. Norrell, *Reaping the Whirlwind: The Civil Rights Movement in Tuskegee* (New York: Knopf, 1985); Adam Fairclough, *Race and Democracy: The Civil Rights Struggle in Louisiana, 1915–1972* (Athens: University of Georgia Press, 1995); Glenn T. Eskew, *But for Birmingham: The Local and National Movements in the Civil Rights Struggle* (Chapel Hill: University of North Carolina Press, 1997); Jonathan S. Bass, *Blessed Are the Peacemakers: Martin Luther King, Jr., Eight White Religious Leaders, and the "Letter from Birmingham Jail"* (Baton Rouge: LSU Press, 2001); and John A. Kirk, *Redefining the Color Line: Black Activism in Little Rock, Arkansas, 1940–1970* (Gainesville: University Press of Florida, 2002). My thinking on the civil rights struggle has also been shaped by nonlocal works: Leslie W. Dunbar, *A Republic of Equals* (Ann Arbor: University of Michigan Press, 1966); Pat Watters, *Down to Now: Reflections on the Southern Civil Rights Movement* (New York: Pantheon Books, 1971); Jack Bass and Walter De Vries, *The Transformation of Southern Politics: Social Change and Political Consequence since 1945* (New York: Basic Books, 1976); Frances Fox Piven and Richard A. Cloward, *Poor People's Movements: Why They Succeed, How They Fail* (New York: Pantheon Books, 1977); Doug McAdam, *Political Process and the Development of Black Insurgency* (Chicago: University of Chicago Press, 1982); Aldon D. Morris, *Origins of the Civil Rights Movement: Black Communities Organizing for Change* (New York: Free Press, 1984); Jennifer Hochschild, *New American Dilemma*; Adam Fairclough, *To Redeem the Soul of America: The Southern Christian Leadership Conference and Martin Luther King, Jr.* (Athens: University of Georgia Press, 1987); David R. Goldfield, *Black, White, and Southern: Race Relations and Southern Culture, 1940 to the Present* (Baton Rouge: LSU Press, 1990); Hugh Davis Graham, *The Civil Rights Era: Origins and Development of National Policy, 1960–1972* (New York: Oxford University Press, 1990); Michael K. Honey, *Southern Labor and Black Civil Rights: Organizing Memphis Workers* (Urbana: University of Illinois Press, 1993); and John Higham, ed., *Civil Rights and Social Wrongs: Black-White Relations since World War II* (State College: Pennsylvania State University, 1999).

Acknowledgments

One name fits on the cover, enough to carry the blame for all mistakes and short-comings within. For any virtues that may accompany these, however, credit cannot honestly be monopolized.

Money was usually my most urgent need. I am commensurately grateful to those who sent me some. This book began during a postdoctoral *Wanderjahr* in the former Soviet Union, which gave me time to read through the rich southern U.S. and African American collections in the Lenin Library, the M. I. Rudomino All Russia State Library for Foreign Literature, and the American Studies "kabinet" at Moscow State University. The trip was financed by a Fulbright Lectureship at Moscow State. I thank Sasha Kormilets, Evgeny and Marina Yaskov, Viktor Tirikhov, my students from all over the former Soviet empire, Elizabeth Moore, and the Council on International Exchange of Scholars for making that experience possible. The National Endowment for the Humanities paid for: eight weeks in Mississippi in Charles Reagan Wilson's enlightening Summer Seminar on Southern Religion, where I broke ground on what became Chapter 5 and got invaluable feedback; a summer institute at the W. E. B. Du Bois Institute at Harvard, where I worked on the first four chapters; and a summer stipend, which allowed me to do much of the research that went into Chapter 8 and some that went into Chapter 4. I thank the endowment and its underpaid, overtalented staff for their support. The Harry Frank Guggenheim Foundation gave me a year's worth of living and travel expenses, which enabled me to finish the research for Chapters 6–8 and to get a good chunk of the writing done. I heartily thank the foundation, and especially Karen Colvard and Joel Wallman, who in addition to providing much-needed lunch and encouragement when I faced some trying research obstacles, headed off bureaucratic plots to siphon "overhead" off of my grant. I would have had to abandon this project if not for their help. The University of North Carolina Press invested more than an advance and a photo grant in this book, but I thank Chuck Grench, David Perry, and others there for that kind of support, which made it possible to savor the other kinds.

Closer to home, I am grateful to the University of Arkansas for easing my teaching burdens. It would be blasphemous to call the leave I was granted in 1999 a "sabbatical"; it was in fact half of that. But the dean of Arts and Sciences, Randall Woods, and his Faculty Development Committee made me an honest man by filling out that leave with what they call a "full-time research assignment." The resulting year away from the ringing phone and the grade book enabled me to get most of the writing done and to fill in the research gaps that opened up as I wrote. The university had earlier allowed me to concentrate on research, including some that drew me far from home for long periods, with three "research incentive grants" and one "research stipend." I thank Dean Woods, the College of Arts and Sciences, the university, and their various donors—especially the hard-pressed taxpayers of Arkansas—for all that support, witting and unwitting. Without it, this book (and the outside grants) would not have been possible.

Librarians control resources that ought to be more valuable than money. In my experience, however, they are more generous with what they have than those who control the money. My gratitude to them borders on the obsessional, and my great fear is that I neglected to record (or lost my record of) the name of one or more who helped me. With apologies to any I might omit, my hearty thanks go to the following for their extravagant knowledge and helpfulness: at the Alabama Department of Archives and History, Rickie Brunner, Norwood Kerr, Mark Palmer, Daniel Richardson, and Ken Tilley; at the Amistad Research Center at Tulane University, Brenda Square; at the New York office of the Anti-Defamation League of B'nai B'rith, Allan Schwartz and Barbara Erlich are not librarians, but they rose up to help me navigate my way into the ADL's clipping files; at the University of Arkansas, Steve Chism, Ellen Compton, Michael Dabrishus, Misha Gardner, Angela Hand, Beth Juhl, Mikey King, Georgia Kunze, Elizabeth McKee, Necia Parker-Gibson, Anne Prichard, Ethel Simpson, Kristine Jo Shrauger, and Denise Stramel; at the Billy Graham Center in Wheaton, Illinois, Robert Shuster and especially Paul Ericksen; at the Birmingham Public Library, Jim Baggett; at Clemson University, Alan Burns, Michael Ferry, and Linda Kohl; at Emory University, Randall Burkett; at the University of Georgia, Laura Cline, Pam Dean, Stephen Mielke, and Sheryl Vogt; at Howard University, Esmé Bahn; at the Library of Congress, Fred Bauman, Katie McDonough, Elizabeth Money, and Joe Sullivan; at the Middle Georgia Archives, Washington Memorial Public Library in Macon, Muriel McDowell-Jackson; at the Mississippi Department of Archives and History, the great shepherd of resources who is himself a great resource, Clinton Bagley; at the University of North Carolina, Richard Shrader and John White; at the Presbyterian Historical Society, Bill Brock, Diana Sanderson, and especially Bill Bynum; at the University of South Carolina, Susan Dick, Herb Hartsook, and Kate Moore; at the South Carolina Historical Society in Charleston, I was fortunate to benefit from Steve Hoffius's presence, before he left a great vacuum there by moving on; at the Southern Baptist Convention's Library and Archives, Jean Forbis and especially Bill Sumners; at Vanderbilt University, Cathy Smith and also Strawberry Luck (who really couldn't help me much, I just love saying her name); at the University of Virginia, Christina Deane, Margaret Hrabe, and Michael Plunkett; and at the State Historical Society of Wisconsin, Karen Lamoree.

For their help in getting me over, under, or around the new universe of obstacles I encountered while tracking down photos, I am indebted to the amazing Angela Hand of the University of Arkansas Library; to Robert Shuster of the Billy Graham Center; to Russ Busby of the Billy Graham Evangelistic Association, who went above and beyond the call of duty; to Susan Hiott and Laurie Varenhorst of Clemson University; to Don Veasey of the Birmingham Public Library; to Clay Carson of the Martin Luther King Papers Project at Stanford; to Ed King; to James Lawson; to Barbara Cooper of the First Baptist Church, Dallas; to Evelyn Tackett and Gretchen Cook of Bellhaven College; to Walton Harrison Reeves Sr. and Walton Harrison Reeves Jr. of Atlanta; and especially to Monica Taylor, whose efficiency and resourcefulness as an underpaid research assistant regularly astonished me.

Once I started trying to make sense of my research, several people managed to read portions of the manuscript, though they all looked busier than the people who didn't manage. Their criticisms and suggestions made the book better and its author humbler: Tony Badger (first by virtue of many things besides the alphabet), Paul Boyer, Alan Brinkley, Richard Brodhead, Bob Brugger, Vernon Burton, Karl Campbell, Dan Carter, James Cobb, Joe Crespino, Bill Dusinberre, Adam Fairclough, Karen Fields, J. Wayne Flynt, Richard Fox, Jane Garrett, Elizabeth Fox-Genovese, Willard Gatewood, Eugene Genovese, Allison Graham, Adam Green, Paul Greenberg, Paul Harvey, Walter Jackson, James H. Jones, J. Wayne Jones, Charles Joyner, Richard King, John "Captain" Kirk, Don Lamm, George Lewis, Sean Lucas, Ralph Luker, Don Mathews, Steven Niven, Ted Ownby, James Patterson, Steve Prothero, John Shelton Reed, Roy Reed, Heather Cox Richardson, Barbara Savage, Beth Schweiger, Jim Sleeper, Mitchell Snay, Jenny Walker, Brian Ward, Clive Webb, Elliott West, Harry McKinley Williams, Patrick Williams, Charles Reagan Wilson, and Dan Woods. Words are not adequate to convey my thanks to these people, but I intend to buy them an adequate number of drinks in the years to come. Some went further and read nearly the entire manuscript, which was fatter and rougher than it became after they pulled my coat about its excesses: Martha Bayles, Jane Dailey, Chuck Grench, Darryl Hart, Carol Mann, Mark Noll, Michael O'Brien, Monica Taylor, Robb Westbrook, Suzanne Wolk. I doubt there are drinks enough left in the world, or time, to repay them, but I aim to make some progress in that direction. It does not diminish my debt to these people to suggest that any reader who has gotten this far owes them something, too.

Guest lecturing opportunities opened chapter drafts to helpful questions and comments that I would otherwise have missed. There are audience members about whom I remember everything to this day but their names. The hosts will have to accept thanks for them: at Yale, John Mack Farragher and Robin Winks; at Emory, Elizabeth Fox-Genovese; at the University of Memphis, Joseph Hawes; at Cambridge, Tony Badger; at the University of Nottingham,

Richard King; at the University of Rochester, Ted Brown and Mary Young. I also thank the hosts of a number of special conferences whose audiences helped refine my arguments: at the European Association of American Studies at the University of Vienna, Waldemar Zacharasiewicz; at the Martin Luther King Memorial Conference at the University of Newcastle upon Tyne, Brian Ward; at the Porter Fortune Symposium at the University of Mississippi, Ted Ownby; at the Massive Resistance Colloquium at the University of Sussex, Clive Webb; at the Southern Intellectual History Circle at Edgefield, South Carolina, Vernon Burton and Michael O'Brien. O'Brien deserves additional thanks for restoring my faith in conferences. The yearly SIHC that he set in motion has spun off so many stimulating ideas and friendships that such things no longer seem accidental by-products of academic life.

Colleagues and students at the University of Arkansas shaped my life and work in ways I could not have imagined, let alone planned. Many of the following also read or listened to some version of some portion of what evolved into this book, then improved it: Tammy Abdel-Fatah, Chuck Adams, Brent Aucoin, Jim Bird, the late Diane Blair, Lori Bogle, Bob Brinkmeyer, Alessandro Brogi, Evan Bukey, Joe Carruth, Jim Chase, Robert Childers, Debra Cohen, Pat Conge, Lynda Coon, Julie Courtwright, Mike Davis, Kyle Day, David Edwards, Don Engels, Willard Gatewood, Jill Geer, Diane Gleason, Joel Gordon, Lauren Green, Allison Hogge, James H. Jones, Jimmy Wayne Jones, Donald Judges, Matthew Katz, Tom Kennedy, Ken Kinnamon, Kyle Labor, Bob Laurence, Jeff Littlejohn, the late Patrick McCune, Larry Malley, Michael Martin, William Maxwell, Erin McKelvey, Ed Minar, Beth Motherwell, Gwenn Okruhlik, Cyndi Nance, Matt Pallister, Janine Parry, Maha Penny, Mike Raley, Brent Riffel, Carl Riley, Charles Robinson, Rebecca Robinson, the late Adolph Reed Sr., Roy Reed, Linda Schilcher, Bill Schreckhise, Tom Senor, Steve Sheppard, David Sloan, Gerald Sloan, Steve and Lindsley Smith, Steve Striffler, Dan Sutherland, Monica Taylor (again), Henry Tsai, Gene and Kurt Tweraser, Borislava Vasileva, Gene Vinzant, Dargan Ware, Jeannie Whayne, Elliott West, Patsy Watkins, Nudie Williams, Patrick Williams, Randall Woods.

The world is going to hell on a sled, but the black humor and comradeship of friends far and near have made the ride more enjoyable and believable than any heaven could be. Many named above already fit in this category, but the following bear special mention: Bill Arkin, Evan and Anita Bukey, Allison Burnett, Jim Chase, Mark Headley, Joe Horwitz, Jeremy Hyman and Lynn Jacobs, Chris Lehmann, Mikey King and Jim Bruner, Lisa Leech, Jason Martinez, Jim Mott, Bryan McCann and Mary Hunter, Cyndi Nance, Doug Noble, Mike Pierce and Tricia Starks, Karon Reese and Steve Striffler, Ken and Regina Serbin, Cheryl Shanks, Jim Sleeper, Richard Stein, Cathy Tumber, Lisa Valkenier, Jessica Vandervoort, Karin Weaver and Russ Colton, Suzanne Wolk. None of the above would cut much ice had I not been prepared by the support and forgiveness of siblings (Jennifer, Jon, Clay, Jake, Bogie, Misa, Addison), parents and step-parents (Sally, Sheryl, Vere, Walter), in-laws (Joe and Gail), and, miraculously, wife and child (Heather and Antonio). I am not done thanking them.

Index

Page numbers in italics refer to photographs.

Aba-Mecha, Barbara (a.k.a., Barbara Woods), 311
Abernathy, Ralph, 90
Abzug, Robert, 316
Acts 17:26 ("nations of men" and "the bounds of their habitation"), 73, 112, 113, 251 (nn. 20, 21, 22, 23), 252 (n. 24), 254 (n. 30), 257 (n. 35), 264 (n. 69), 270 (n. 19)
Adams, Henry, 57
Addams, Jane, 299
Albany movement, 90, 92, 98–99
Allen, Clifton, 117, 255 (n. 33), 261 (n. 53)
Allport, Gordon, 214 (n. 49)
An American Dilemma (Myrdal), 37, 42–44, 48, 55, 58–62
American Friends Service Committee, 57
Americans for Democratic Action (ADA), 26, 29, 32–37, 198 (n. 11), 199 (n. 14), 204 (n. 53), 206 (n. 6), 209 (n. 21), 210 (nn. 22, 27), 211 (n. 30), 213 (n. 44), 224 (n. 44), 300
American States' Rights Association, 163, 263 (n. 61), 266 (n. 79)
Anderson, Jervis, 224 (n. 42), 225 (n. 45), 302
Ansbro, John, 309
Anti-Catholicism, 148–49, 162, 278 (n. 58)

Anticlericalism, 125–35, 139–41, 263 (n. 61), 264 (n. 68), 265–67. *See also* Expulsion of ministers; Resolutions of segregationist protest from churches
Anti-intellectualism, 229 (n. 1), 234 (n. 31), 313
Anti-Semitism, 119, 162, 252 (n. 23), 259 (n. 42), 260 (n. 48), 264 (n. 67)
Anti-southern stereotypes, 29–30, 82–83, 103, 187–88, 192, 244 (n. 53)
Apathy, 101, 109–10, 112, 123, 154–55, 161, 170, 182–83, 249 (n. 48), 263 (n. 61), 283 (n. 14), 287 (n. 38)
Arnesen, Eric, 302
Arnold, Thurman, 19–20, 202 (n. 42)
Arrested-development thesis, on Martin Luther King Jr., 48, 54, 219 (n. 17), 222 (nn. 31, 32), 223 (n. 35), 307
Avant, W. Ray, 136

Badger, Tony, 245 (n. 2)
Bailey, Josiah, 9–10
Baker, Ella, 67, 78, 230–31 (n. 5)
Baldwin, Lewis, 47, 309
Barry, Marion, 69
Barth, Karl, 3, 27, 50, 53, 205–6, 221 (n. 24)
Bartley, Numan, 154, 322
Bass, Jonathan S., 222 (n. 33)

Bates, Daisy, 108, 317
Beats, the, 82
Beck, E. M., 212 (n. 33)
Beckett, Henry, 206 (n. 6)
Beer, Samuel H., 205 (n. 1), 300
Bell, Daniel, 25
Bell, Derrick, 214 (n. 49)
Bell, L. Nelson, 117–21, *118*, 124, 128,
    132, 133, 140–43, 150, 258–60, 268
    (n. 10), 274 (n. 39), 277 (n. 52), 291
    (n. 53)
Bellah, Robert, 244 (n. 52), 300
Bellfrage, Sally, 80, 239 (n. 12)
Bellhaven College, 113, 249 (n. 14). *See
    also* Gillespie, G. T.; Smith, Morton
"Beloved community," 69, 307–8
Benham, Charles O., 251 (n. 23), 266
    (n. 80)
Bercovitch, Sacvan, 217 (n. 10)
Berkowitz, Peter, 298
Bevel, Diane. *See* Nash, Diane
Bevel, James, 69
Biblical justifications of segregation.
    See Segregation
Birmingham, Ala., 60, 88, 95, 138, 155–
    56, 163, 189, 275 (n. 42). *See also*
    "Letter from the Birmingham City
    Jail"
Black, Earl, 322
Black nationalism and separatism, 54,
    75, 145, 219 (n. 17), 222 (nn. 31, 32),
    226 (n. 50), 227 (n. 51), 234 (n. 29),
    307
Black segregationists, 173–76, 282
    (n. 41), 288 (nn. 46, 47, 48), 289
    (nn. 49, 50, 51), 290 (nn. 52, 53),
    291 (n. 54, 55), 292 (n. 56). *See also*
    Greene, Percy; King, Clennon
Blackwell, Unita, 238 (n. 4), 240
    (nn. 23, 24), 241 (n. 30), 242 (n. 31)
Blatt, Solomon, 318
Blease, Cole, 172
Bloch, Charles, 165, *166*, 259 (n. 42),
    318
Bodenhammer, William, 249 (n. 11)
Boggs, Wade, 129
Bolton, Charles, 323
Bonomi, Patricia, 317
Bork, Robert, 168

"Borrowed time": liberalism on, 298–
    99
Bowers, Sam, 318–19
Bowles, Chester, 11
Boykin, Frank, 281 (n. 9)
Brady, Tom P., 151, 184, 280 (n. 2), 285
    (n. 29), 291 (n. 55), 322
Branch, Taylor, 225 (n. 45), 325
Branscomb, Harvie, 127, 265 (n. 74)
Brightman, Edgar Sheffield, 50, 53, 54,
    220 (n. 19), 221 (n. 27), 222 (n. 32)
Brinkley, Alan, 199 (n. 14), 303
Broderick, Francis, 68
Brodhead, Richard, 217 (n. 10)
Brotherhood of Sleeping Car Porters.
    See McLaurin, B. F.; Randolph, A.
    Philip
Brown, Henry Billings, 145
Brown v. Board of Education decision, 1,
    36, 42, 105, 107–8, 109, 125, 126, 131–
    32, 138, 151, 160, 169, 174, 211 (n. 29),
    247 (n. 6), 256 (n. 33), 261 (n. 54),
    267 (n. 3), 272 (n. 32), 277 (n. 52),
    281 (n. 9), 286 (n. 35)
Brundage, W. Fitzhugh, 212 (n. 33)
Bryce, Lord, 38
Buber, Martin, 85
Buchanan, George, 63–64
Buckley, William F., 139, 250 (n. 20)
Burckhardt, Jacob, 57
Burner, Eric, 235 (n. 35), 239 (nn. 9,
    10, 11), 312
Burns, Leon, 109, 113, 123, 128, 251
    (n. 23), 252 (n. 24), 264 (n. 68)
Busby, Russ, 273 (n. 37)
Bushman, Richard, 292 (n. 1)
Butler, Jon, 202 (n. 37), 316
Byrd, Harry F., 33, 318
Byrnes, James F., 11, 126, 145, 155–56,
    157, 158, 161, 162, 163, 165, 167, 171,
    172, 173–74, 198 (n. 9), 280 (n. 4),
    281 (nn. 5, 9), 283 (n. 20), 318

"Caesar, appeal unto," 184. *See also*
    State: role of
"Caesar, render unto," 99–102, 109,
    122–23, 139–40, 178. *See also* Separa-
    tion of religion and politics
Calhoun, John C., 158, 286 (n. 35)

Campbell, Ernest, 254 (n. 29)
Campbell, Karl, 323
Campbell, Will D., 231 (n. 6), 267 (n. 3)
Camus, Albert, 78, 80–83, 182, 185
Carmichael, Stokely (later known as
    Kwame Toure), 85, 88
Carpenter, Charles, 265 (n. 72)
Carr, Johnnie, 87
Carson, Clayborne, 231 (n. 7), 309, 312,
    313, 325
Carter, Asa, 163
Carter, Dan, 172–73
Carter, Stephen L., 244 (n. 52)
Carwardine, Richard, 316, 317
Chafe, William, 306, 325
Chandler, A. P. "Happy," 173
Children of Light, Children of Darkness
    (Niebuhr), 26, 68, 207 (nn. 7, 9), 213
    (n. 41)
Childs, Marquis, 10
Christianity Today, 139, 143, 150, 253
    (n. 25), 260 (n. 45)
Christian Layman, 125, 126, 263 (n. 66)
Christian Life Commission (SBC),
    134, 137–38, 147, 150–51, 249 (n. 9),
    271 (n. 24), 272 (nn. 27, 32), 277
    (n. 55)
Church-state separation. *See* Separa-
    tion of religion and politics
Citizens' Councils, 109, 112, 115, 122,
    125, 128, 137, 150, 151, 159, 162–63,
    173–74, 248 (nn. 8, 9), 250 (n. 20),
    281 (n. 9), 283 (nn. 15, 17), 284
    (n. 21), 290 (n. 53), 291 (n. 54),
    317–18
City of Reason (Beer), 205 (n. 1)
Civil rights movement: success of, 8,
    154, 179–86, 188, 323
Civil rights plank: in 1948 Democratic
    convention, 33–35, 207 (n. 10), 209
    (n. 21), 211 (n. 30)
Civil War, 5, 6, 8, 153, 188–89, 280
    (n. 2), 287 (n. 35)
Clark, Septima, 95–96
Class division and conflict, 26–27, 28,
    30, 72, 82, 176–78, 187, 188–89, 206
    (n. 5), 226 (n. 50), 232 (n. 20), 235
    (n. 38), 260 (n. 49), 282 (n. 14)
Clifford, Clark, 198 (n. 9)

Coercion, 27, 28, 32, 51–52, 55, 57, 58,
    59–62, 63, 66, 68, 74–75, 76, 80, 84–
    85, 103, 117–18, 140, 153, 162, 174–75,
    186, 206 (nn. 5, 7), 207 (n. 9), 216
    (n. 5), 225 (n. 46), 225 (n. 48), 227
    (nn. 51, 53), 227 (n. 54), 231 (n. 11),
    232 (nn. 15, 16), 237 (n. 50), 238
    (n. 52), 256 (n. 33), 257 (n. 34), 258
    (nn. 38, 39), 261 (n. 53), 268 (n. 10),
    274 (n. 41), 277 (n. 52), 289 (n. 51).
    See also Nonviolence
Cohen, Lizabeth, 203 (n. 50)
Cohn, Norman, 310
Cold War, 103, 147, 148–49, 186, 208
    (n. 10), 244 (n. 54), 274 (n. 37)
Cole, Nat "King," 163
Coleman, John P., 286 (n. 35)
Commager, Henry Steele, 304
A Common Faith (Dewey), 14, 200
    (nn. 22, 23), 201 (nn. 32, 33)
Communists, communism, and anti-
    communism, 15, 24–25, 26–28, 30,
    32–34, 51, 55, 57, 80, 103, 124, 128,
    140, 148–49, 160, 193, 197 (n. 2), 204
    (n. 53), 206 (n. 6), 207 (n. 10), 208
    (n. 16), 209 (nn. 18, 19), 211 (n. 30),
    213 (nn. 40, 42, 44), 219 (n. 18), 263
    (n. 61), 264 (n. 69), 266 (n. 80), 267
    (n. 83), 289 (n. 51)
Complacency. *See* Apathy
Comte, Auguste, 15, 299
Cone, James, 219 (n. 17), 222 (n. 31),
    307
Congress of Racial Equality (CORE),
    56, 84
Connor, Eugene "Bull," 95, 318
Conservatism, 5, 12–14, 24–25, 99,
    108, 117–21, 139–40, 143, 161, 177–78,
    179–80, 193, 209 (n. 19), 216 (n. 7),
    259 (n. 44), 260 (n. 45), 281 (n. 7),
    285 (n. 28), 314
Constitution, U.S.: fourteenth
    amendment, 166–67, 285 (nn. 29,
    30); proslavery provisions, 168;
    supremacy clause (Art. 6), 167;
    tenth amendment, 167–68. *See also*
    Interposition; State rights
Constitutionalism, 100, 165–71, 261
    (n. 54)

Consumerism, 4
Conversion experiences, 3-4, 68, 73, 91-95, 187, 240 (n. 23), 243 (n. 51), 273 (n. 37)
Cook, Anthony, 310
Corruption. *See* Power
Counts, John, 255 (n. 33)
Cowling, Dale, 116-17, 257 (n. 34)
Cox, Oliver C., 213 (nn. 39, 42)
Criswell, W. A., 114-15, *115*, 123-24, 142, 143, 148, 253 (nn. 27, 28), 255 (n. 31), 262 (n. 58), 276 (n. 48), 320
Cruse, Harold, 302

Dabney, Virginius, 156-58, 162, 163, 197 (n. 5), 267 (n. 6), 281 (nn. 5, 6, 7), 284 (n. 21)
Dahl, Robert, 41
Dalton, Ted, 131
Daniel, Carey, 108-9, 113-14, 116, 128, 248 (n. 9), 252 (n. 24), 255 (n. 32)
Davies, John, 256 (n. 33)
Davis, David Brion, 253 (n. 25)
Death of a Yale Man (Ross), 19
Dees, James, 111, 121, 133, 146, 250 (n. 19), 260 (n. 50)
Delbanco, Andrew, 217 (n. 10), 218 (n. 13)
Demagoguery, 150, 155-56, 170, 172-73, 189, 258 (n. 40)
Democratic ideals, 15, 31, 52, 172, 184-85, 207 (n. 9), 226 (n. 51), 265 (n. 77). *See also* Equality
Democratic Party, 1, 2, 9-12, 32-36, 90, 103, 143, 147, 148-49, 158, 161, 192, 197 (n. 2), 198 (n. 9), 201 (n. 35), 209 (n. 21), 211 (n. 30)
Dewey, John, 3, 13-18, *16*, 19, 20, 21, 24, 42, 52, 161, 199 (nn. 16, 17, 19), 200 (nn. 20, 22, 23), 201 (nn. 32, 33, 36), 203 (n. 51), 204 (nn. 55, 59), 224 (n. 40), 299-300, 301
DeWolf, Harold, 222 (n. 32)
"Disenchantment of the world, the," 22, 73, 95
Disestablishment. *See* Separation of religion and politics
Disraeli, Benjamin, 177

Dittmer, John, 235 (n. 35), 239 (n. 5), 241 (n. 26), 314-15
Dollard, John, 315
Donnegan, Horace, 271 (n. 20)
Dorn, William Jennings Bryan, 125, 318
Douglas, Ann, 212 (n. 40)
Douglas, Robert Christy, 321
Douglass, Frederick, 45, 47, 76, 94, 238 (n. 57)
DuBois, W. E. B., 39, 44, 213 (n. 42), 292 (n. 55), 305
Dudziak, Mary, 244 (n. 54)
Duke, David, 178
Dunbar, Les, 82
DuPont, Jesse Ball, 127, 264 (n. 70)
DuPont, King Solomon, 96
Durkheim, Emile, 15, 200 (n. 25), 201 (n. 32), 299

Eastland, James, 129, 290 (n. 53)
Ebony, 141, 144, 274 (n. 37), 275 (n. 45)
Edmonds, Richard W., 285 (n. 29)
Edwards, Jonathan, 97, 217 (n. 10)
Egerton, John, 302
Eighmy, John Lee, 321
Eisenhower, Dwight D., 1, 33, 147, 168, 170, 209-10, 248 (n. 8), 270 (n. 19)
Election: Calvinist doctrine of, 200 (n. 23)
Eliot, George, 299
Ellison, Ralph, 39, 44, 306
"Emotionally potent oversimplifications," 62, 98, 169-70, 202 (n. 38), 208 (n. 16)
End of Ideology (Daniel Bell), 25
Ends and means, political: relationship between, 100, 155, 170, 187
Epps, Jesse, 91
Equality, 8, 72, 78, 83, 101, 102-3, 109, 112, 146-47, 179, 184-85. *See also* Democratic ideals
Ervin, Sam, 145, 165, 286 (n. 32), 318
Eskew, Glenn, 239 (n. 8), 325
Evangelicalism, evangelicals, and evangelism, 71, 90, 98, 112, 119-20, 140-41, 143, 147-49, 180, 184, 259 (n. 44), 262 (n. 58). *See also* Missionaries and missions

Evans, Bruce, 270 (n. 17)
Evans, Medford, 112, 114, 125, 250 (n. 20)
Evers, Medgar, 315
Existentialism, 82, 214 (n. 48)
Expulsion of ministers, 132–35, 139, 267 (n. 3), 268 (n. 12), 269 (nn. 16, 17), 270 (n. 20). *See also* Anticlericalism; Resolutions of segregationist protest from churches

Fairclough, Adam, 216 (n. 1), 228 (n. 55), 325
Farley, W. R., 291 (n. 53)
Farmer, James, 56, 68
Farrell, James J., 308
"Fascism," 15, 24–25, 38
Faubus, Orval E., 284 (n. 25)
Faulkner, William, 60
Fellowship of Reconciliation, 55, 68, 231 (n. 10)
Ferber, Michael, 244 (n. 52)
Fetchit, Stepin, 289 (n. 51)
Fields, Karen, 102, 316
Finlay, James, 241 (n. 26)
Finney, Charles Grandison, 97
Flemming, Floyd, 283 (n. 17)
Flynt, J. Wayne, 246 (n. 5), 319–20, 321
Football, 164, 258 (n. 40), 284 (n. 27)
Force. *See* Coercion
Forman, James, 80, 85, 90, 230 (n. 5), 235 (n. 38)
Foster, W. G., 131
Fox, Richard, 41, 205–6 (n. 5), 208 (n. 16), 213 (n. 41), 301, 310
Francisco, Clyde T., 253 (n. 25)
Frank, Ed, 231 (n. 6)
Frank, Glenn, 22–23, 202 (nn. 45, 47), 303
Franklin, Robert, 47, 309
Frazier, E. Franklin, 234 (n. 31)
Fredrickson, George, 253 (n. 25)
Fredrickson, Kari, 324
Freedman, Paul, 253 (n. 25)
Freedom Rides, 56, 75, 149
Freundt, Albert, 115, 122, 124, 146, 276 (n. 52)
Fulop, Timothy, 238 (n. 57)
Fulton, J. Wayne, 131

Fundamentalism, 45, 47, 97, 118, 119, 259 (nn. 43, 44), 261 (n. 54). *See also* Evangelicalism, evangelicals, and evangelism; Jones, Bob; McIntire, Carl

Galbraith, John Kenneth, 41
Gallimore, T. F., 119, 259 (n. 42)
Gamaliel, 183–84
Gamble, W. Arnette, 117–18, 124, 258 (n. 40), 262 (n. 59)
Gambrell, C. B., 267 (n. 83)
Gandhi, Mohandas K., 28, 50, 55, 57, 58, 68, 74, 76, 84–85, 206 (n. 7), 221 (n. 22), 224 (n. 45), 227 (n. 52), 231 (n. 10)
Garrett, Frank, Sr., 253 (n. 25)
Garrow, David, 225 (nn. 45, 47), 234 (n. 33), 238 (n. 52), 325
Gates, Henry Louis, 290 (n. 52)
Genesis 9:18–29. *See* Ham, curse of
Genovese, Eugene D., 314
George, Walter, 36, 197 (n. 6), 210 (n. 27), 290 (n. 53)
Gillespie, G. T., 110, 112–13, 114, 122, 124, 249 (n. 14), 250 (nn. 15, 16), 266 (n. 82)
Gilmore, Thomas, 94
Goen, C. C., 317
Goldberg, Arthur, 204 (n. 53), 211 (n. 29), 303
Goldwater, Barry, 139, 250 (n. 42)
Goodman, Benny, 280 (n. 2)
Gordon, Clyde, 116, 257 (n. 35)
Grady, Henry, 145, 158, 197 (n. 5)
Graetz, Robert, 263 (n. 66)
Graham, Allison, 244 (n. 53)
Graham, Billy, 6, 96–97, 138, 140–44, *142*, 242 (nn. 34, 35), 247 (n. 6), 273 (n. 37), 276 (n. 49), 317
Grant, Joanne, 230 (n. 5)
Grassroots. *See* Great-man theories; Ordinariness: of activists
Graves, John Temple, 156–60, *159*, 161, 163–64, 282 (nn. 10, 13), 283 (n. 20), 284 (n. 27), 287 (n. 36), 318
Gray Amendment, 131
Great Awakenings, 87, 97, 101–2, 316. *See also* Revivals and revivalism

Great-man theories, 20, 45, 87, 186.
  See also Ordinariness: of activists
Greene, Percy, 282 (n. 14), 289 (n. 50),
  291 (n. 53), 315
Greensboro (N.C.) sit-ins, 69
Gregg, Richard, 84
Gressette, Marion, 125, 263 (n. 63), 318
Griffin, Marvin, 164
Guerry, Edward, 110, 261 (n. 54)
Guilt-fear continuum, 233 (n. 25)
Guyot, Larry, 96, 312
Gwaltney, L. L., 248 (n. 6)

Halberstam, David, 230 (n. 3)
Halttunen, Karen, 292 (n. 1)
Ham, curse of, 113, 116–17, 126, 252
  (nn. 24, 25), 254 (n. 30)
Hamby, Alonzo, 210 (nn. 21, 29)
Hamer, Fannie Lou, 71–75, 74, 78, 99,
  112, 145, 182, 185, 187, 191, 232–34,
  239 (n. 12), 243 (n. 45), 292 (n. 56),
  311–12, 315
Hargis, Billy James, 251 (n. 23)
Harris, Roy, *129*, 163, 171, 177, 249
  (n. 13), 318, 319
Hartz, Louis: and his critics, 297–98,
  304
Harvey, Paul, 254 (n. 29), 321
Hatch, Nathan, 102 (n. 37)
Hawley, Ellis, 303
Hawthorne, Nathaniel, 31, 208 (n. 14)
Hays, Brooks, 108, 116, 137, 138, 245
  (n. 3), 246 (n. 5), 248 (nn. 8, 9),
  319
Hearst, William Randolph, 141, 143–
  44
"Hearts and minds," 62, 102–3, 158,
  183, 184, 318. *See also* Legitimacy;
  Respectability
Hegel: Martin Luther King Jr.'s al-
  leged debt to, 46
Heimert, Alan, 102, 317
Higginbotham, Evelyn Brooks, 314
Higgs, Bill, 90
Hochschild, Jennifer, 44, 303, 304,
  305, 306, 325
Hofstadter, Richard, 12, 23, 202
  (n. 42), 204 (n. 56), 205 (n. 2), 304
Holland, Ida, 95–96

Holly, Buddy, 144
Holmes, Thomas J., 269 (n. 12)
Holt, Len, 237 (n. 46)
Honey, Michael, 306
Hook, Sidney, 15
Hope vs. optimism, 1, 48, 53, 56, 60–
  62, 68, 72, 86, 154, 178, 227 (n. 52),
  231 (n. 11), 232 (nn. 14, 16), 238
  (nn. 56, 57)
Horsley, J. Shelton, 267 (nn. 5, 6)
Horton, Olin, 163, 249 (n. 13), 263
  (n. 61), 284 (n. 22)
Howe, Daniel Walker, 292 (n. 1)
Hudgins, Douglas, 319
Humanism, 4, 51, 53, 69, 299, 300
Human nature, 4, 13, 19, 25–28, 30, 37–
  42, 44–86, 181–82, 185, 199 (n. 16),
  204 (nn. 57, 59), 206 (nn. 5, 6, 7,
  8, 9), 208 (n. 16), 220 (n. 21), 221
  (n. 28), 222 (n. 30). *See also* Hope vs.
  optimism
Humphrey, Hubert, 34–36, 42, 199
  (n. 14), 210 (n. 27), 211 (n. 30)
Hurston, Zora Neale, 173–74, 287
  (n. 44), 290 (n. 52)
Hutchison, William, 205 (n. 5)
Hyde, Homer H., 267 (n. 83)

Ickes, Harold, 9–10, 197 (nn. 3, 4)
Idealism. *See* Materialist explanations
Ideology, 24–25
Individualism, 21–22, 39–41, 117, 139,
  160–61, 165, 207 (n. 9)
Individualism, Old and New (Dewey),
  200 (n. 20), 201 (n. 36)
Inerrantism, biblical, 115, 250 (n. 15),
  255 (n. 31)
Ingram, T. Robert, 110–11, 122, 261
  (n. 54), 291 (n. 55)
Institutions: faith in and defense of,
  3, 17, 20, 39–41, 72, 149, 213 (n. 44),
  214 (n. 48), 237 (n. 47), 315
Intellectuals, 6–7, 44–45, 53, 78, 80,
  165, 170, 187, 191, 312–14
Interposition, 168–71, 245 (n. 2), 249
  (n. 9), 285 (n. 30), 28 (nn. 32, 35)
Interpretation of Christian Ethics
  (Niebuhr), 214 (n. 46), 218 (n. 13)
Isaac, Rhys, 102, 317

Isaiah, 47, 217–18, 220 (n. 20)
Ivey, G. L., 163

Jackson, John P., 287 (n. 36), 324
Jackson, Walter, 38, 42, 213 (nn. 38, 41), 215 (n. 52), 305, 313
Jacobs, J. I., 248 (n. 7)
James, William, 13, 14, 199 (n. 16), 299
Jefferson, Thomas, 168–69, 286 (n. 34)
Jeremiah, 46–48, 50–51, 65, 217–18, 220 (n. 20), 300, 308–10
Jesus, 31, 50, 56, 63, 74
Job, 50, 63, 66, 220 (n. 20), 229 (n. 60), 300
John Birch Society, 173, 250 (n. 20), 284 (n. 27)
Johnson, Lyndon B., 36, 144
Johnson, Paul, 102
Jones, Bayard, 264 (n. 72)
Jones, Bob, 275 (n. 42)
Jones, Edward, 254 (n. 30)
Jones, James, 270 (n. 20)
Juhan, Bishop Frank, 127
Jumonville, Neil, 304

Kasper, John, 162, 283 (n. 17)
Katagiri, Yasuhiro, 292 (n. 57)
Kean, Melissa Fitzsimmons, 265 (n. 74)
Kellog, Peter, 209 (n. 20), 210 (n. 29), 305, 313
Kelly, J. Forrest, 254 (n. 30)
Kennan, George, 41, 58, 224 (n. 44)
Kennedy, David, 37–38
Kennedy, John, 33, 147, 148–49, 156
Kierkegaard, Soren, 203 (n. 49)
Kifer, Allen, 302
Kilpatrick, James J., 140, 159–60, 161, 164, 167, *169*, 170–72, 177, 283 (n. 17), 285 (n. 28), 286 (nn. 34, 35), 287 (n. 36), 318, 322
King, Clennon, 289 (n. 50), 291 (n. 53)
King, Coretta Scott, 91
King, Ed, 234 (n. 29)
King, Frank, 133–34
King, Lonnie, 80
King, Martin Luther, Jr., 1, 6, *44*, 45–55, 58–59, 63, 66, 67, 68, 69, 74–75,

78, 80–81, 84, 87–88, 89, 90–95, 96–97, 98, *99*, 107, 119, 124, 144, 145, 150, 151, 154, 163, 185, 216 (n. 6), 217–23, 262 (n. 60), 276 (nn. 49, 50), 307–10, 313, 315
King, Martin Luther, Sr., 218 (n. 11)
King, Mary, 82–83, 239 (n. 9)
King, Richard, 42–43, 241 (n. 26), 313–14
King, Slater, 98
Kingdom of God, doctrine of, 69, 307–8, 310
Kirksey, Henry, 176
Kneebone, John, 156, 281 (nn. 6, 7)
Knight, Albion, 265 (n. 72)
Kolb, William, 35, 210 (n. 25)
Krutch, Joseph Wood, 300
Ku Klux Klan, 156, 162–63, 173, 283 (nn. 17, 20), 318–19
Kuryla, Peter, 231 (n. 6)

Lake, I. Beverly, 286 (n. 32)
Lancaster, William, 272 (n. 29)
Landrum, Lynn, 158
Lasch, Christopher, 205 (n. 2), 206 (n. 5), 213 (n. 41), 236 (n. 41), 304, 310
Lassiter, Matthew, 323–24
Laughon, Fred, 134–35, 248 (n. 7)
Lawrence, David, 171, 259 (n. 42), 282 (n. 29)
Lawson, James, 67–71, *70*, 75, 76, 107, 127, 230 (nn. 3, 4), 231–32, 265 (n. 74), 311
Lawton, Edward P., 165, 283 (n. 14), 285 (n. 29), 321–22
Layton, Azza, 244 (n. 54)
Leadership, 12, 23, 53, 64–66, 68, 78–81, 96, 105, 132, 144, 160–61, 165, 176–78, 180, 214 (n. 49), 232 (n. 20), 234 (n. 31), 235 (n. 38), 240 (n. 24), 275 (n. 43), 281 (n. 9), 312
Lee, Avery, 272 (nn. 27, 32)
Lee, Chana Kai, 73, 233 (n. 23)
Lee, Davis, 175, 289 (n. 50), 290 (n. 53)
Lee, Taeku, 244 (n. 53)
Leech, Ken, 244 (n. 52)
Legitimacy, 6, 150–51, 177. *See also* Respectability

Leloudis, James, 216 (n. 1)
LeMay, Curtis, 173
Leonard, Bill, 318
"Letter from the Birmingham City
  Jail" (Martin Luther King, Jr.), 6,
  54, 124, 151
Levison, Stanley, 54–55
Levy, David W., 299
Lewis, Andrew B., 323–24
Lewis, David L., 213 (n. 42)
Lewis, John, 69, 75–78, 77, 88–90,
  92, 230 (n. 3), 234, 236 (n. 38), 239
  (n. 10), 312
Lewis, Rufus, 87
Lewis, Sinclair, 19, 98
The Liberal Imagination (Trilling),
  24–26, 204 (nn. 54, 58)
Liberalism, 2–5, 8, 9–46, 47, 50–
  52, 54, 60–62, 63–64, 69, 71, 73,
  83, 85–86, 103, 110, 119, 161, 172,
  178, 179–80, 187–88, 189, 193, 197
  (nn. 5, 6), 198 (n. 9), 199 (n. 19),
  201 (nn. 35, 36), 202 (nn. 42, 46),
  203 (nn. 51, 52), 204 (nn. 53, 55,
  56, 57), 205 (nn. 1, 2), 206–7, 208
  (nn. 13, 14), 209 (n. 20), 210 (nn. 25,
  28), 211 (n. 30), 213 (nn. 40, 44), 214
  (n. 48), 217 (n. 11), 218 (n. 13), 220
  (n. 21), 226 (nn. 50, 51), 228 (n. 57),
  235 (n. 38), 237 (n. 47), 281 (nn. 6,
  7), 297–314. *See also* Equality; Individualism
Liberalism and Social Action (Dewey),
  15, 199 (n. 17), 204 (n. 59)
Liberals: alleged chastening of, 4, 24,
  26, 37, 41–42, 57, 204 (nn. 53, 56),
  205 (n. 2), 303–4; sincerity of, 3, 36,
  42–43, 227 (n. 51)
Lichtenstein, Nelson, 210 (n. 28)
Life, 117
Lin, Maya, 2
Lincoln, Abraham, 217 (n. 10)
Lincoln, C. Eric, 305, 314
Lippmann, Walter, 21–22, 24, 199
  (n. 19), 202 (nn. 43, 44), 204 (n. 55),
  299
Lischer, Richard, 218 (n. 16), 238
  (n. 56), 309–10
Literalism. *See* Inerrantism, biblical

Little Rock crisis, 105, 108, 116, 138,
  168, 173–74, 189, 270 (n. 19), 274
  (n. 38), 278 (n. 55), 284 (n. 25)
Loeb, Jim, 33–34, 35, 204 (n. 53), 210
  (n. 25)
Lost cause, 161, 177–78
Lott, Trent, 178
Lowitt, Richard, 201 (n. 35)
Luker, Ralph, 216 (n. 7), 307–8
Lynching and capital punishment, 36,
  158, 212 (nn. 32, 33), 281 (nn. 5, 7),
  282 (n. 10), 297. *See also* Ku Klux
  Klan
Lynd, Robert and Helen, 14, 38, 300,
  301
Lyon, Henry, 249 (n. 11)
Lyttle, Emma Knowlton Humphreys,
  258 (n. 38)

Maas, Peter, 176
Macdonald, Dwight, 58
Macon, Leon, 246 (n. 5), 247 (n. 6)
Maddox, Lester, 177, 318
Madison, James, 168–69, 286 (n. 35)
Malcolm X, 3, 62, 74, 97, 243 (n. 51)
Mamiya, Lawrence, 314
Manent, Pierre, 299
Man in Revolt (a.k.a., *The Rebel*,
  Camus), 81
Manis, Andrew, 239 (n. 8), 319
March on Washington Movement, 56,
  84, 302, 306. *See also* Randolph, A.
  Philip
Marsh, Charles, 262 (n. 56), 318–19
Martin, John Bartlow, 159–60, 282
  (n. 13), 317
Martin, William, 273 (n. 37)
Marx, Gary, 306–7, 314
Marx and Engels, 15, 30, 185, 191–92,
  193. *See also* Communists, commu-
  nism, and anti-communism
Mass media: role of, 69, 95, 103, 126,
  141–44, 154, 257 (n. 35), 262 (n. 60),
  281 (n. 6), 282 (nn. 13, 14)
Materialist explanations: of historical
  change, 191–93, 226 (nn. 50, 51).
  See also Class division and conflict;
  Marx and Engels
Mathews, Don, 307

Mays, Benjamin, 54, 215 (n. 51), 223 (n. 34), 241 (n. 28), 314, 315
Mays, David J., 285 (n. 32)
McCain, James Ross, 267 (n. 3)
McCarraher, Eugene, 244 (n. 52), 308, 325
McCoy, Donald, 209 (n. 21)
McCrady, Edward, 265 (n. 72)
McDonough, Julia Anne, 215 (n. 51)
McElvaine, Robert S., 203 (n. 50)
McGreevy, John, 210 (n. 28), 325
McIntire, Carl, 118, 259 (n. 44), 260 (n. 48)
McLaurin, B. F., 211 (n. 36)
McLin, William, 151
McLoughlin, William, 101, 316
McMillen, Neil, 154, 322
McNeill, Robert, 133–34, 268 (n. 10), 268 (n. 12)
Means. See Ends and means
Media. See Mass media
Meier, August, 68, 217 (n. 7), 307
Mencken, H. L., 19
Merton, Thomas, 223 (n. 35)
Methodists, 269 (n. 16)
Migration, rural to urban: as progress, 82–83, 225 (nn. 48, 50)
Mill, John Stuart, 13, 48, 199 (n. 17), 224 (n. 40)
Millennialism, 96, 102. See also Premillennialism
Miller, A. C., 134, 136–38, 147, 246 (n. 3), 269 (n. 13), 278 (n. 55)
Miller, Donald G., 129, 266 (n. 82)
Miller, Keith, 54, 222 (nn. 31, 32)
Miller, Perry, 217 (n. 10)
Miller, T. R., 120–21, 128, 132, 260 (nn. 47, 49)
Miller, William Robert, 218 (n. 15)
Mills, C. Wright, 39
Miracles, 91–96, 186–87
Missionaries and missions: foreign and domestic, 147–50, 274 (nn. 37, 39), 278 (n. 59), 279 (nn. 61, 62)
Mississippi Freedom Labor Union, 74
Mississippi State Sovereignty Commission, 176, 276 (n. 52), 282 (n. 14), 289 (nn. 49, 50, 51), 291 (n. 53), 292 (n. 57), 311–12

Montgomery, William, 145
Montgomery boycott, 58, 68, 76, 87, 90, 91, 151–52, 154, 207 (n. 9), 282 (n. 14)
Montgomery Improvement Association, 84, 92
Moore, Amzie, 90, 239 (n. 12)
Moore, Marshall, 174
Moral Education (Durkheim), 200 (n. 25), 201 (n. 32)
Moral Man and Immoral Soceity (Niebuhr), 26–27, 39–41, 76, 85, 206 (n. 7), 208 (n. 16), 214 (n. 46), 218 (n. 13), 220 (n. 19), 242 (n. 40), 310
Morgan, Edmund S., 292 (n. 1)
Morgenthau, Hans, 41, 58
Morris, Aldon, 84, 92, 234 (n. 33)
Moses, Bob, 78–83, 79, 88–90, 92, 100, 180, 182, 185, 187, 234–37, 239 (nn. 9, 10), 239 (n. 12), 243 (n. 51), 312, 313
Mumford, Lewis, 58
Murphy, Edgar Gardner, 197 (n. 5)
Muste, A. J., 56, 57, 68
Myrdal, Gunnar, and Myrdaleries, 3, 37–45, 40, 48, 50, 55, 58–62, 63, 72, 84, 103, 184, 208 (n. 10), 213 (nn. 38, 44), 214 (n. 48), 216 (nn. 1, 2), 219 (n. 18), 226 (n. 48), 227 (n. 52), 237 (n. 47), 245 (n. 2), 268 (n. 12), 302, 305–6, 309

Nash, Diane (a.k.a. Diane Nash Bevel), 69, 85
National Association for the Advancement of Colored People (NAACP), 10–11, 63, 65, 68, 72, 83, 109, 125–26, 156, 160, 170–71, 174–75, 209 (n. 21), 211 (n. 30), 237 (nn. 47, 49), 282 (nn. 13, 14), 289 (n. 51), 290 (n. 53), 291 (n. 54), 317; Legal Defense Fund, 146, 165
Nationalism, 15–17, 22. See also Black nationalism and separatism
Nelsen, Anne and Hart, 314
Neo-orthodoxy, 3, 27, 45–46, 47, 50–51, 119, 218 (n. 13), 220 (n. 21), 221 (n. 24)
Nesbitt, R. D., 87
Nevins, William Manlius, 249 (n. 11)

Newby, I. A., 228 (n. 56), 322
New Deal, 9–12, 21–22, 192, 205 (n. 2), 208 (nn. 13, 14), 302–3
Newman, Mark, 135, 246 (n. 6), 269 (n. 17), 277 (n. 52), 279 (n. 61), 320
News media. *See* Mass media
Nicholson, Joseph, 215 (n. 51), 223 (n. 34), 314, 315. *See also* Mays, Benjamin
Niebuhr, H. Richard, 14, 206 (n. 5), 218 (n. 13), 298, 300, 310
Niebuhr, Reinhold, 3, 26–28, 37, 38, 39–41, 45, 46, 47–48, 50–54, 58, 68, 69, 76, 80–81, 82, 85, 98, 100, 202 (n. 38), 205 (n. 2), 206–7, 208 (nn. 14, 16), 213 (nn. 41, 42), 214 (nn. 46, 48), 216 (n. 5), 219 (n. 17), 220 (nn. 19, 21), 221 (nn. 24, 26, 28), 222 (nn. 29, 30, 32), 224 (n. 44), 227 (n. 52), 236 (n. 38), 304, 307–8, 310
Niven, Steven, 251 (n. 23)
Noll, Mark, 265, 324
Nonviolence, 2, 28, 55, 57–58, 60, 63, 68, 74–75, 84–85, 96, 103, 186, 206–7, 216 (n. 5), 225 (nn. 46, 48), 232 (n. 16), 238 (n. 4), 242 (n. 31), 260 (n. 45), 310. *See also* Pacifism (Tolstoyan)
Norris, George, 18, 201 (n. 35)

Ole Miss. *See* University of Mississippi
Opiate: black churches as, 54, 72, 94, 98–99, 102, 174–76, 193, 232 (n. 20), 234 (n. 33), 237 (n. 47), 241 (nn. 26, 28), 291 (n. 54), 314–16
Optimism and pessimism, 38, 42, 44–45, 46, 48, 50–51, 53–54, 55, 61–62, 65, 181, 215 (nn. 49, 51), 216 (n. 2), 221 (n. 28), 237 (n. 47), 245 (n. 2), 306–7. *See also* Hope vs. optimism; Human nature
Ordinariness: of activists, 63, 65, 71–74, 100–101, 153–54, 186, 189–90
Original Sin. *See* Human nature
Orwell, George, 63, 299
Outlaw, Almarene, 257 (n. 34)
Outside agitator, myth of, 174–76
Ownby, Ted, 308, 313

Pacifism (Tolstoyan), 28, 56–58, 62, 82, 85, 207 (n. 9)
Packer, George, 205 (n. 2), 214 (n. 45), 304
Panek, Nathalie, 204 (n. 53)
Patriotism, 100
Payne, Charles, 174, 233 (n. 23), 241 (n. 30), 288 (n. 47), 311, 314–15, 325
Payton, Tyler, 289 (n. 50)
Pells, Richard, 301
Perez, Leander, 171
Perfectionism, 119–20, 207 (n. 9)
Perkins, Carl, 144
Perkins, Frances, 203 (n. 49)
Personalism, 52–54, 221 (n. 27), 222 (n. 32), 308–9. *See also* Brightman, Edgar Sheffield
Pettigrew, Thomas, 254 (n. 29)
Pew, J. Howard, 139–40, 143
Pittman, R. Carter, 285 (n. 30)
Plagiarism: by Martin Luther King Jr., 51, 52–53
The Plague (Camus), 82
Pluralism, interest-group, 41
Pocock, J. G. A., 297, 298, 311
Polhill, Lucius, 245 (n. 3)
Pollard, Ramsey, 246 (n. 5)
Poll tax, 10, 12, 282 (n. 10)
Polsgrove, Carol, 314
Pope, Liston, 102, 321
Populism and populists, 154, 198 (n. 9)
Porter, Lee, 247 (n. 6), 276 (n. 48), 279 (n. 61), 320–21
Powell, Adam Clayton, 224 (n. 45)
Power: corrupting effects of, 27, 31–36, 72, 81, 235 (n. 38)
The Power of Nonviolence (Gregg), 84
Premillennialism, 86, 238 (n. 57). *See also* Millennialism
Presbyterian Church: in U.S. (southern Presbyterians), 5–6, 105, 107–8, 117, 121, 125, 128, 131, 138, 139, 143, 144–45, 147–50, 253 (n. 24), 258 (n. 36), 261 (n. 52), 270 (n. 18), 272 (n. 34), 277 (n. 52), 279 (n. 62)
Presley, Elvis, 144
Press. *See* Mass media
Progress: belief in, 3, 5, 26–27, 28, 29–30, 31, 37–45, 57, 59, 71, 72, 73, 76,

81, 82–84, 179, 181, 182, 225 (n. 48), 226 (n. 50)

Prophetic tradition, the, 3–4, 45–54, 56–57, 62–63, 65–66, 72–73, 83–84, 85–86, 133–34, 149, 179–86, 187, 217–19, 223 (n. 35), 232 (nn. 16, 18), 233 (n. 22), 236 (n. 38), 308–11, 314

Proslavery ideology and theology, 5, 105, 112, 121–22, 149–50, 154, 165, 167–68, 188, 196 (n. 1). *See also* Slavery

Pruden, Wesley Frank, 116

The Public and its Problems (Dewey), 199 (n. 19)

"Pulpit envy," 3, 6, 11, 13–25, 37, 42, 69, 86, 179, 189, 199 (nn. 16, 18, 19), 200 (n. 20, 25), 202 (n. 40), 203 (nn. 51, 52), 204 (n. 53)

Putnam, Carleton, 129–30, 158, 167, 170–71, 287 (n. 36), 291 (n. 53), 319, 322

Queen, Edward, 247 (n. 6), 320, 321

Quest for Certainty (Dewey), 14

Raboteau, Albert, 219 (n. 16), 223 (n. 35), 238 (n. 57), 241 (n. 26), 309

Race and Reason (Putnam), 170

Racism, 7, 11, 22, 28–30, 35, 37, 42, 43, 50, 58–59, 62, 64, 81, 86, 97, 101, 107, 109, 111, 112, 114, 120, 121, 140–41, 143, 145–46, 149, 155, 167, 170–72, 175–78, 180–82, 183, 185, 206 (n. 7), 207 (nn. 8, 9, 10), 208 (nn. 11, 12), 210 (n. 28), 214 (n. 49), 215 (n. 54), 280 (n. 2), 281 (n. 6), 283 (n. 17), 309, 318, 321–22

Ramsey, Brooks, 269 (n. 17)

Randolph, A. Philip, 56, 197 (n. 6), 227 (n. 52), 302, 306

Rankin, Robert, 290 (n. 53)

Rash, Sammy, 312

Rauschenbusch, Walter, 53, 206 (n. 5), 310

Rawls, John: and his critics, 297–98, 304

"Realism" (in foreign policy), 41

Rebel, The (Camus). See *Man in Revolt*

Reed, Ralph, 178

Religion: definitions of, 201 (n. 32), 315. *See also* Separation of religion and politics; Social and political preaching

Republican ideals (classical civic virtue, etc.), 47, 76–78, 83, 94, 311

Republican Party, 22, 103, 149, 192, 197 (n. 2), 201 (n. 35), 202 (n. 45)

"Resistance," 154, 186

Resolutions of segregationist protest from churches, 135–39, 270 (n. 19, 20), 271 (nn. 21, 24, 25), 272 (nn. 26, 30). *See also* Anticlericalism; Expulsion of ministers

Respectability, 155, 156–60, 161, 162–63, 169–71, 172–73, 176–78

Revivals and revivalism, 4–5, 87–104, 179, 187, 240 (n. 13), 241 (n. 26), 242 (n. 44), 243 (nn. 47, 51), 314, 315–16

Revolution and revolutionaries, 47, 57, 59–60, 76, 84, 102, 144, 177, 185, 226 (n. 51), 234 (n. 32), 237 (n. 49)

Rice University, 265 (n. 74), 273 (n. 37)

Richards, J. McDowell, 267 (nn. 2, 3), 277 (n. 52)

Richberg, Donald, 24

Ritchey, George, 136–37

Robertson, A. Willis, 286 (n. 32)

Robertson, Pat, 178

Roche, Jeff, 323

Roosevelt, Eleanor, 9–10, 197 (n. 3)

Roosevelt, Franklin, 9–12, 20, 22, 23–24, 197 (n. 6), 201 (n. 35), 203 (nn. 49, 51), 297

Rose, Arnold, 214 (n. 49)

Ross, Malcolm, 19

Ruetten, Richard, 209 (n. 21)

Russell, Richard, 164, 172, 290 (n. 53), 318

Rustin, Bayard, 54–63, 61, 66, 67, 68, 74, 78, 80, 84–85, 97, 151, 187, 219 (n. 18), 223–27, 230 (n. 5), 231 (n. 10), 235 (nn. 35, 38), 236 (n. 39), 291 (n. 54), 308, 311

Sacrifice, 1, 6, 7, 8, 13, 14, 17–18, 37, 41, 42, 48–49, 56, 57–58, 62–63, 66, 69, 72, 74, 76, 80, 81, 86, 95–96, 107, 110, 150, 153, 156, 163–64, 180, 189, 224 (n. 40), 300

Sass, Marion Hutson, 164
Satterfield, John, 165, 167
Schlesinger, Arthur, 26–32, 29, 35, 37, 38, 46, 50, 62, 86, 156, 204 (n. 56), 205 (n. 2), 207–8, 209 (nn. 18, 19), 214 (n. 49), 236 (n. 38), 303, 304
School-closing, 164, 284 (n. 25)
Schuyler, George, 175, 290 (n. 52)
Scott, Daryl, 305
Seay, S. S., 92
Secularization: theory of, 202 (n. 37), 179–80, 182, 298–301, 317, 324
To Secure These Rights (presidential commission report, 1947), 34, 42, 64, 207 (n. 10), 214 (n. 49)
Segregation: biblical justifications of, 109–10, 112–17, 126, 128, 136, 140, 165, 168, 250–57 (nn. 20, 35), 261 (n. 54), 264 (n. 69), 270 (n. 19)
Sellers, Cleveland, 85, 230 (n. 5), 236 (n. 38)
Separation of religion and politics, 99–100, 101, 138, 139, 243 (n. 45), 244 (n. 52), 246 (nn. 5, 6), 256 (n. 33), 257 (n. 35), 261 (n. 55), 267 (n. 3), 276 (n. 47), 277 (n. 52), 278 (n. 55), 320. See also Social and political preaching
Sewanee. See University of the South
Shanks, Cheryl, 316
Sharpeville Massacre, 2
Shattuck, Gardiner, 264 (nn. 70, 73), 321
Shuttlesworth, Fred, 88, 89, 97, 99–100, 150, 239 (nn. 6, 8)
Simkins, Modjeska, 63–66, 64, 74, 75, 181–82, 187, 227–29, 311, 315
Simmons, William J., 125, 248 (n. 8), 285 (n. 29)
Simon, Bryant, 196 (n. 2), 203 (n. 50)
Sims, Charles, 262 (n. 58)
Sinatra, Frank, 280 (n. 2)
Sitkoff, Harvard, 302
Slavery, 250 (n. 20), 307. See also Pro-slavery ideology and theology
Smiley, Glenn, 68, 15–52, 224 (n. 45), 232 (n. 12)
Smith, Adam, 41

Smith, E. D. "Cotton Ed," 172, 197 (n. 6)
Smith, Gerald L. K., 161
Smith, Kelly Miller, 231 (n. 11)
Smith, Kenneth, 217 (n. 8), 309
Smith, Lillian, 58
Smith, Morton, 113, 122, 252 (n. 24)
Snay, Mitchell, 317
Social and political preaching: opposition to, 122–30, 246 (n. 5), 247 (n. 6). See also Anticlericalism; Separation of religion and politics
Social gospel, 45, 119, 206 (n. 5), 216 (n. 7), 307–8, 310
Socialism, 101. See also Communists, communism, and anti-communism
Solidarity, 87, 90, 104, 105, 107–8, 110, 123, 134–35, 150–52, 154–55, 159–61, 163–65, 168, 170, 176, 178, 180, 181–82, 187–89, 231 (n. 11), 245 (n. 2), 249 (nn. 9, 13), 258 (n. 38), 260 (n. 45), 261 (n. 53), 279 (nn. 61, 62, 67), 280 (n. 2), 281 (n. 6), 281 (n. 9), 282 (nn. 14, 15), 284 (n. 25), 299, 300, 319
South Africa, 2, 97, 148
The South and the Nation (Lawton), 165, 321–22
Southard, Samuel, 149, 262 (n. 60), 269 (n. 17), 279 (n. 61)
Southern, David, 38, 213 (nn. 38, 41), 305, 313
Southern Baptist Convention (SBC), 5–6, 105, 107–8, 116, 117, 122–23, 128, 134–35, 136–38, 139, 143, 144–45, 147–51, 245–49, 255–58, 261 (n. 53), 261 (n. 55), 262 (n. 58), 270 (n. 19), 271 (nn. 21, 24), 279 (n. 67), 319–21
Southern Baptist Theological Seminary, 262 (n. 60)
Southern Christian Leadership Conference (SCLC), 67, 68, 84
Southern Conference for Human Welfare (SCHW), 10
Southern Manifesto, 105, 245 (n. 2), 272 (n. 32), 286 (n. 35)
Southern Presbyterian Journal, 117, 138, 251 (n. 23), 252 (n. 24), 258 (n. 36), 261 (n. 52), 291 (n. 53)

Southern Presbyterians. *See* Presbyterian Church: in U.S.
Southern Regional Council, 133, 172, 215 (n. 51), 262 (n. 60), 267 (n. 6), 320
Sparks, Randy, 266 (n. 80), 320–21
Speak Truth to Power (1955 pamphlet), 56–58, 224 (nn. 42, 44)
Speed, Dan, 92
"Spiritual discipline against resentment," 68, 73–74, 80–81
Stafford, G. Jackson, 256 (n. 33)
Stahlman, James, 127–28, 265 (n. 74)
Stakelessness, 234 (n. 33)
State: role of, 2, 35–37, 46, 52, 57, 66, 100, 101, 147, 148, 153, 155, 163, 184, 188, 189, 197–98 (n. 6). *See also* "Caesar, appeal unto"; "Caesar, render unto"
State rights, 155–58, 161, 167–71, 258 (n. 38), 282 (n. 10), 285 (nn. 29, 30), 286 (n. 33), 286–87, 322. *See also* Constitution, U.S.; Constitutionalism; Interposition
Stebenne, David, 204 (n. 53), 209 (n. 20), 210 (n. 29), 303
Steele, C. K., 92, 150
Steele, Mrs. Willard, 263 (n. 61), 274 (n. 39), 288 (n. 45)
Stembridge, Jane, 78
Stoper, Emily, 229 (n. 1), 313
Student Non-violent Coordinating Committee (SNCC), 66–67, 69, 72, 75–80, 84–85, 99, 229 (n. 1)
Sugrue, Thomas, 210 (n. 28)
Sullivan, H. T., 248 (n. 6)
Sullivan, Pat, 302
Sumners, Bill, 246 (n. 5), 272 (n. 32)
Sunday, Billy, 19, 273 (n. 37)
Suthon, Walter J., 285 (n. 29)

Taft, Robert, 31, 208 (n. 13)
Taft-Hartley Act, 12
Television. *See* Mass media
Talmadge, Eugene, 172
Talmadge, Herman, 158, 162, 163
Thernstrom, Abigail and Stephan, 288 (n. 48), 305

Thomas, Albert S., 261 (n. 54), 265 (n. 72)
Thoreau, Henry David, 75
Thurmond, Strom, 33, 35, 125–26, 156, 207 (n. 10), 264 (n. 67), 318
Tiananmen Square, 2, 8
Tillich, Paul, 78, 205–6 (n. 5)
Timmerman, George Bell, 141, 252 (n. 33), 274 (n. 42)
Tinder, Glenn, 244 (n. 52), 299
Tinnin, Finley, 248 (n. 6), 253 (n. 28), 285 (n. 28)
Tolnay, Stewart, 212 (n. 33)
Tompkins, Jane, 208 (n. 14)
"Totalitarianism," 38
Toure, Kwame. *See* Carmichael, Stokely
Townsend, Kathleen Kennedy, 244 (n. 52)
Trammell, Seymore, 173
Trilling, Lionel, 3, 24–26, 38, 204 (nn. 54, 58)
Troeltsch, Ernst, 314
True and Only Heaven (Lasch), 206 (n. 5), 213 (n. 41), 236 (n. 41), 238 (n. 56)
Truman, Harry, 12, 33, 42, 64, 138, 144, 147, 172, 207 (n. 10), 209 (n. 21)
Tuck, Stephen, 315
Tucker, Donald, 95–96, 241 (n. 30)
Tugwell, Rexford, 9, 23–24, 203 (n. 49)
Tullos, Allen, 102
Turnipseed, Andrew "Doc," 269 (n. 16)
Tyson, Tim, 314

Uncertainty, 17–18
"Unearned suffering is redemptive," 50, 220 (n. 20), 309–10
Union for Democratic Action. *See* Americans for Democratic Action
U.S. News and World Report, 171
Unity. *See* Solidarity
University of Mississippi, 105, 267 (n. 3)
University of the South, 127, 264 (nn. 70, 72)

Vanderbilt University, 69, 127–28, 265
(n. 74)
Vandiver, Ernest, 284 (n. 25)
The Varieties of Religious Experience
(James), 199 (n. 16)
Vial, Dan, 126
The Vital Center (Schlesinger), 26–28,
30–32, 50, 161, 205 (nn. 1, 2), 207–8,
209 (nn. 18, 19)

Wade, Robert A., 264 (n. 67)
Wagner, Robert, 9, 12
Waldrep, Chris, 212 (nn. 32, 33)
Walker, Wyatt Tee, 78, 96–97
Wall, J. Barrye, 160, 283 (n. 15)
Wallace, George, 88, 141, 172–73, 275
(n. 43), 318
Wallace, Henry, 33–34, 35, 36, 197 (n. 1)
Wallis, Jim, 244 (n. 52)
Waring, Thomas R., 111, 141, 143–
44, 159, 163, 164, 170–72, 175, 260
(n. 48), 284 (n. 27), 287 (nn. 36, 38),
290 (n. 53), 318
Warren, Robert Penn, 78–82, 235
(n. 36)
Washington, Booker T., 173
Washington, Joseph R., 219 (n. 17),
307
Watson, Tom, 158
"Weapons of the weak." *See* "Resis-
tance"
Webb, Clive, 324
Weber, Max, 22, 191–92
Weber, Timothy P., 238 (n. 57)
Wechsler, James, 34, 203 (n. 52), 301
Weiss, Nancy, 197 (n. 2), 302

Welch, Robert, 291 (n. 53)
Westbrook, Robert, 18, 200 (n. 24),
299–300
Westminster Confession (1647), 122,
139, 261 (n. 52), 272 (n. 34)
White, Walter, 36, 198 (n. 8)
White Citizens' Councils. *See* Citi-
zens' Councils
Wilkerson, Doxey, 213 (n. 42)
Wilkins, Roy, 42, 213 (nn. 44), 290
(n. 53)
Willkie, Wendell, 22
Williams, Dan, 137
Williams, Harry McKinley, 290
(n. 52)
Williams, John Bell, 125, 318
Williams, Paul, 215 (n. 51)
Wills, Garry, 168, 286 (n. 33)
Wilmore, Gayraud, 94
Witherspoon, John, 139
Wolfe, Tom, 316
Wood, Gordon, 297, 311
Woods, Barbara. *See* Aba-Mecha,
Barbara
Woodson, Carter, 314
Workman, William D., 128, 162, 175–
76, 246 (n. 4), 265 (n. 77), 318,
322
World War II, 11–12, 24–25, 30, 57, 153
Wright, Richard, 44, 306
Wright, T. R., 299

Yance, Norman Alexander, 135
Young, Andrew, 82, 99

Zepp, Ira, 217 (n. 8), 309